OCEANIA AND BEYOND

F. P. KING, EDITOR

OC

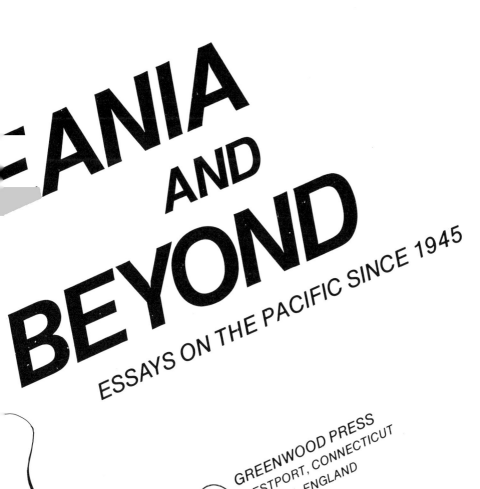

EANIA
AND
BEYOND

ESSAYS ON THE PACIFIC SINCE 1945

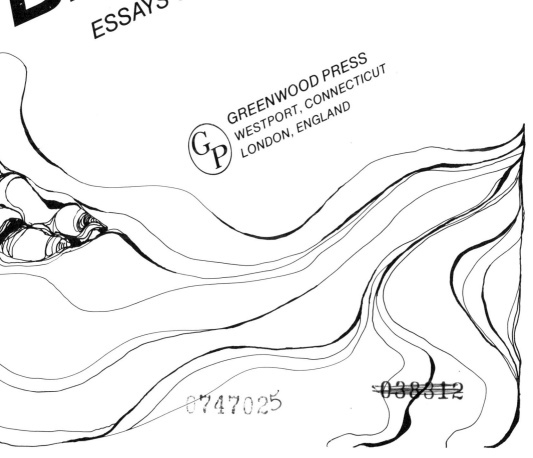

GREENWOOD PRESS
WESTPORT, CONNECTICUT
LONDON, ENGLAND

Library of Congress Cataloging in Publication Data

Main entry under title:

Oceania and beyond.

   Includes bibliographical references and index.
   1. Oceania—Politics and government—Addresses, essays, lectures. 2. Oceanica—Economic conditions—Addresses, essays, lectures. I. King, F. P.
DU 29.025   309.1'9   76-5261
ISBN 0-8371-8904-7

Library of Congress Catalog Card Number: 76-5261
ISBN: 0-8371-8904-7

First published in 1976

Greenwood Press, a division of Williamhouse-Regency Inc.
51 Riverside Avenue, Westport, Connecticut 06880

Manufactured in the United States of America

Dedicated to
C. Hartley Grattan

Contents

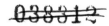

List of Maps

List of Tables

Foreword

Few of us who have been involved in the vast region of the Pacific Basin can have a detailed knowledge of any but a small part of that region. The present collection of essays is welcome because it makes an important contribution to the reservoir of information on what has been happening over the past three decades and provides material for comparative study of the problems faced by the island nations in the Pacific.

As one whose experience has been confined to the Southwest Pacific, I have found the essays on Micronesia of particular interest–if only because the themes are not unfamiliar. One sentence by Lazarus E. Salii, particularly, suggests the nature of our responsibilities in Oceania both past and future: "We were witnessing the birth of an economy which would soon be–and today now is– thoroughly dependent on imported goods, contracted skills, and annual outside aid." When I say "our" responsibilities, I refer to us, the Americans, Australians, British, French, and New Zealanders who have been cast in the role of colonizers of these island nations.

We must also agree with Noel Grogan that our success in facing our responsibilities must be judged in relation to three themes: questions relating to land tenure, the pace and style of development and political institutions, and the pace and orientation of economic development programs. It has not been possible to give within this one anthology a detailed account of the way in which these themes have been dealt with in each of the island groups for which Australia, Britain, France, and New Zealand have been responsible; but there is enough to put us on inquiry. And I am chauvanist enough to suggest that such an inquiry begin with Angus Ross, editor, *New Zealand's Record in the Pacific Islands in the Twentieth Century* (Auckland, 1969).

Another theme explored in this anthology is that of regional cooperation. Richard Herr's description of some of the tribulations of the South Pacific Commission and John Thomson's account of the work of the South Pacific

Forum—particularly of the South Pacific Bureau for Economic Cooperation (SPEC)—remind us of the need for, and the difficulties involved in, achieving such functional cooperation. This surely is the only way in which the island groups of Oceania can expect to overcome the disabilities of small size, limited resources, and vast distances.

The problems of the island groups of Oceania are not those of Australia and New Zealand, if only because these are countries of European settlement. The period since World War II has seen both Australia and New Zealand seeking to establish their places as Pacific powers. The story is well told in this anthology by Hartley Grattan and is supplemented by Theo Roy's paper on the development of New Zealand's defense policy.

Papua New Guinea is still another story. This recently independent state has affiliations with the islands of Oceania, but size, resources and geography give it the status of an emerging Pacific power. The choices before Papua New Guinea are analyzed in the essay by Ralph Premdas.

We shall all be grateful that Frank King has brought together these scholarly contributions.

C. C. Aikman
High Commissioner for New Zealand in India
5 December 1975

Acknowledgments

B. K. Macdonald wishes to acknowledge the financial assistance given to him by the Australian National University, the University Grants Committee of New Zealand, the Nuffield Foundation, and Massey University, which enabled him to research his article thoroughly. Both the editor and Donald McTaggart would like to give special thanks to Duane Stormont for preparing the maps used in this book. The editor received encouragement and help during the early stages of this work from several former colleagues at the University of Guam: George Boughton, Mary Muna, Paul Richardson, Arthur Auten, and the late W. Scott Wilson. He would also like to thank Dirk Ballendorf and all of the other contributors for their exceptional cooperation throughout the preparation of this manuscript.

Introduction

This anthology of sixteen new essays and one set of maps should be of interest to both students and general readers. The authors come from a number of different professions and have divergent backgrounds and interests. Generally one could call this work a mosaic of recent Oceania (the islands of the Pacific) by people who share a common viewpoint starting with the Pacific Basin and not the Pacific Rim. The authors see both inside and outside of the region; and this is fitting, for one should not write in an historical sense about Oceania alone. One should always be aware of those industrialized metropolitan nations on the borders of the Pacific Ocean and in Europe that, in modern times, have had inordinate influence on the island continent of Australia, the large islands of New Zealand and Papua New Guinea, the Solomons, the Carolines, the Marianas, the Marshalls, the New Hebrides, Fiji, the Society, Samoan, and Hawaiian Islands, and all the important and little known islands and atolls between.

The justification for the bifocalism that the authors share is their conviction that most of the islanders of the Pacific, including the Aborigines of Australia, have lost a large measure of the autonomy that was theirs before the arrival of European explorers, traders, and settlers. As is true of North America and many other parts of the globe, the region's past "is at once an integral portion of the history of the expansion of Europe and also of the variegated history of nation-building in 'new' lands."[1] These influences still operate today, hence the title of this book. The major topic being examined here is not colonialism or imperialism or neo-colonialism as such, but bilateral isolation of the sort that has separated colony from colony by focusing the attention of the Pacific peoples on a number of different foreign homelands. This peculiar isolation has been, until recently, Oceania's most conspicuous common characteristic.

Although it is difficult for an anthology of this sort to have a logical development, hopefully it does have a coherent design. Part I deals with Micronesia and the securing of America's position as Oceania's pre-eminent power following World War II. The United States certainly had acquired permanent interests in the Pacific during the nineteenth century, when it annexed the Midway Islands, Hawaii, and the Philippines, and purchased title—one way or another— to Eastern Samoa and Guam;[2] but there were dramatic extensions of those interests after 1945, at the very time the United States was acquiescing in the decolonization of the Philippines, which made the United States' Pacific empire come alive. First, the Hawaiian Islands became a state of the Union. Second, after decades of nearly total neglect of the sort that American Samoa still suffers, Guam, and, in a different way, Okinawa, quickly became Oceania's foremost bastion of modern warfare: an anchorage for atomic submarines, a major strategic bombing base, a complex center for military communications, a nuclear storehouse, and an advance ship repair facility. Although political and economic development lagged until the 1960s, eventually Guam emerged as one of the most bustling, tawdry, affluent distribution and tourist centers in the Pacific. Third, the United States became the administering authority, on behalf of the United Nations, of the Trust Territory of the Pacific Islands (Micronesia).

It is difficult to find defenders, or even apologists, for the American administration of Micronesia. Possibly it is because there have been so few effective critics. Perhaps the first part of this book will help to remedy this situation. Even though the Trust Territory is America's last frontier, it has rarely been understood, acknowledged, or publicized as such. As was true during earlier times, the Americans found themselves masters of a sovereignty which was diffuse, economically underdeveloped, and truly foreign. It is disturbing to note, after reading the essays in this first section, how many blunders have been made, especially considering America's prior experiences in the Caribbean, Panama, its own South, Southwest, West, Hawaii, and Alaska. It is one of the great ironies in modern American history that the American government and its civil servants have thus far consistently administered Micronesia without any apparent understanding of the past. Unwilling to use force—as had been used on the earlier frontiers and in the Philippines—and restrained by the United Nations and world opinion, the United States has been baffled by problems requiring thoughtful political solutions. Lacking true colonial will or skills, deficient in planning and organization, unwilling to commit the money and expertise needed for the development of Micronesia's natural resources, and saddled with a military establishment that knows and understands only its own narrow tactical objectives, it is not surprising that this trusteeship has been unsuccessful.

The essays in Part II deal with the regional problems Oceanic nations currently are facing and with the relations of Oceania with nations outside the Pacific Basin. Historically, as one of the contributors puts it, the Southwest Pacific, and especially Australia, has been viewed by the metropolitan powers as only a shadow region "under the overhang of Asia." Given this, Australia, as Oceania's leading power, albeit a secondary one by world standards, is "required to maneuver to effectuate its purposes within the constrictions of Big Power policies." While this may be a perfectly accurate description of how things look from the State Department, Whitehall, the *Quai d'Orsay,* the Pentagon, Canberra, and various other vantage points, there are numerous signs that Oceanic nations are no longer willing to accept this as a realistic appraisal. Part of this has to do with the disappointment that the two Old Dominions—Australia and New Zealand—feel now that Britain has joined the Common Market. Part of it results from the success that Fiji, Western Samoa, and other islands have had with their independence. Part of it has to do with the lessening of tension in the world brought about by détente, which in the Pacific means that Japan and China are no longer regarded as inherently hostile toward Oceania. And part of it surfaces as an uneasy suspicion that the United States may not be a suitable or reliable replacement for British power in the Southwest Pacific. All of these changes have, of course, important implications, because they suggest conditions in the region may now be ripe for greater solidarity than has ever been known in the past.

The essays in Part III deal with the attitudes and policies of France, the United States, and the United Kingdom toward their own possessions in Oceania and toward the region in general. These vary widely, as one would expect, from intransigence, incapacity, and indifference to the imperialist notion that possesssions are merely useful economic and strategic appendages. One should not suppose, however, that the authors have limited themselves to studying and writing about anachronistic political and economic behavior in the modern world, for they are more than mere antiquarians dealing with contemporary anomalies. The real importance of the essays in the last section is their analyses of the sociopolitical reactions of Oceania's inhabitants to these policies and of the alternatives that are implied, if not stated. Rather than being studies of the "old Pacific," these articles suggest where part of the future lies.

Without attempting to foreclose other conclusions that the readers of this book may reach, it may be appropriate at this point for the editor to offer some of his own.

The years since World War II will be remembered in the Pacific as the time when Oceania emerged not only as a semantic concept but also as a useful designation for a new region that was no longer antipodal, appendant, or auxiliary. The dramatic change—which was most notable in the South Pacific where it was abetted by Australia, New Zealand, and the United Kingdom—was perhaps more unheralded, orderly, and peaceful than that experienced elsewhere in the world; but it was no less timely and significant for the people concerned.

Seemingly the postwar settlement restored the *status quo ante bellum.* But this quiet restoration of imperial power was quick with the seeds of important political changes that rapidly revealed the basic illness of the colonial system. The Americans, in fact, won the war in the Pacific, with important but limited support from the British, Australians, and New Zealanders, while the traditional powers in the region were conspicuously absent from either the defense or liberation of their subjects. Unquestionably, the wartime performance of these powers, such as Britain and the Netherlands, was symptomatic of their long-term incapacities, their waning influence during the depressed 1930s, and their reordering of priorities after 1945 back toward their own internal concerns. As was true of Australia and New Zealand, they also passed into an era of political maturity in which restraint was foremost in their minds. It is difficult to say which came first—recognition of their incapacity and vulnerability as world powers, or their awareness of the futility of attempting to hold nonessential territories in the face of changed metropolitan attitudes.[3] The effect was the same.

The exceptions were France and the United States, the former because its conservative attitudes and colonial elites had weathered the anti-colonial radicalism of the difficult postwar period and because France desperately needed the wealth of New Caledonia and found a new strategic justification for its Pacific role with the advent of the nuclear age.

Postwar administrations in the United States, in contradistinction to the other powers, temporarily, were unchallenged and untroubled by their voters. Nevertheless, there was an atmosphere during the postwar period in which a conservative government, while triumphant militarily and economically, was worried by visibly weakening allies and beset on all sides by turmoil and uncertainty. As a result, it was not surprising that the Secretary of the Navy, James V. Forrestal, who was the leading architect of American policy in the Pacific, should have thought about the region in grandiose terms:

> I take it as a premise about all discussions of world peace that the
> United States is to have the major responsibility for the Pacific Ocean
> security, and if this premise is accepted there flows from it the accep-
> tance of the fact that the United States must have the means with which
> to implement its responsibilities.[4]

It was also not surprising that the United States' successful wartime experiences, coupled with a concern for national security, influenced postwar policies to an inordinant extent.

> ... we must maintain strong Pacific bases. Single island positions cannot
> be considered strong bases. Selected islands can, however, together with
> Guam, form a far-reaching mutually supporting base network, although
> each alone would fall far short of being an impregnable bastion.
> Large-scale offensives cannot be mounted from a small island base.
> An appropriate base network, however, permits full exploitation of
> mobility of forces, which was such a vital factor in victory in the
> Pacific.[5]

Clearly, it was no accident that Micronesia and Guam were virtually placed in a position of strategic bondage.

Lord Hailey has observed that "the dynamic which determines the shape given by an administration to its institutions is really supplied by its conception of the total picture which the territory is likely ultimately to present."[6] It is clear that since World War II, Britain, in contrast to France and the United States (and one might add Chile and Ecuador, which hold, respectively, Easter Island and the Galapagos Islands), conceived of Oceania as a region composed of sovereign nations living in a spirit of commonwealth. While Britain's direct influence will likely come to an end within the foreseeable future, a more durable union can be expected to remain in the form of the Commonwealth. The same might be said of New Zealand and Australia where colonial failure has now freed them to pursue more positive and constructive policies.[7]

The anachronistic positions of France and the United States in the long run are less certain. France continues to use its Pacific colonies for narrow economic and military purposes. There has been resistance to such policies within and without these colonies, and there seems no reason to suppose such resistance will not continue and intensify. The United States' dynamic is equally unimaginative and predictable. While the statuses of American Samoa and Guam have been fixed by Washington, consent has never been forthcoming from the peoples of these territories and pressures for adjustments are surfacing. In Micronesia, the United States already has lost the initiative and has substituted reaction for planning. While the impact of the United States as purveyor of Western culture has been both profound and superficial, it seems unlikely that any specifically American influence will remain for long unless there are unforeseen, atypical, and radical changes of attitude in Washington. The problem all along has been that in a postcolonial world, the United States has only reluctantly and niggardly fulfilled its mandatory obligations in the Pacific, which humanitarian concerns should have brought forward freely.[8]

Since 1945, more than eighty percent of the peoples of the Pacific (including those of Papua New Guinea, but excluding from these figures those of New Zealand, Australia, and the Hawaiian Islands) have ceased to be colonial subjects. If we added the peoples of New Zealand and Australia to these calculations, it would become even more patent that only a fraction of Oceania resembles the prewar world of metropolitan powers and island dependencies.[9] The era when the Pacific basin was a great crossroad of colonial power has waned. The most important result of this is the region's recent political and economic emergence. With the conjoining of the general weakening of metropolitan ties and a number of pressures working toward integration at many levels and in many ways, Oceania today has greater promise for development than ever before.

NOTES

1. C. Hartley Grattan, *The Southwest Pacific to 1900: A Modern History* (Ann Arbor, Mich., 1963), preface.

2. See Paul M. Kennedy's superb *The Samoan Tangle: A Study in Anglo-German-American Relations, 1878-1900* (New York, 1974). The standard text is Paul Carano and Pedro C. Sanchez, *A Complete History of Guam* (Tokyo and Rutland, Vt., 1964).

3. F. H. Hinsley, *Power and the Pursuit of Peace: Theory and Practice in the History of Relations Between States* (Cambridge, 1967), p. 359.

4. Forrestal's diary entry of April 17, 1945, *The Forrestal Diaries,* ed. Walter Millis (New York, 1951), p. 45.

5. Letter from Forrestal to *The New York Times,* September 24, 1946, p. 28. For confirmation that this line of thinking remained official thinking and had the enthusiastic approval of John Foster Dulles and Dean Rusk in 1950, see Sir Percy Spender, *Exercises in Diplomacy: The ANZUS Treaty and the Colombo Plan* (New York, 1969), pp. 85-9. For powerful denunciations of Naval rule in the Pacific see editorials and letters in *The New York Times:* September, 3, 1946, p. 18; October 3, 1946, p. 26; October 21, 1946, p. 30.

6. Lord Hailey, "Native Administration in Africa," *International Affairs* 23 (July 1947), 338.

7. See Editor's Introduction, *New Zealand's Record in the Pacific Islands in the Twentieth Century,* ed. Angus Ross (Auckland, 1969), p. 8.

8. See Eugene J. McCarthy, *The Limits of Power: America's Role in the World* (New York, 1967), p. 183. E. J. Kahn, Jr. has aptly commented that, "Nowhere, and at no time, has America had a comparable opportunity to demonstrate how its resources, skills, and techniques can be used to make an underdeveloped region become, in a contemporary phrase, emergent." *A Reporter in Micronesia* (New York, 1965), p. 9.

9. These figures are derived from population figures given in *Pacific Islands Year Book,* ed. Judy Tudor (11th ed.; Sydney, 1972).

MAPS OF OCEANIA

THE ISLAND WORLD OF THE PACIFIC

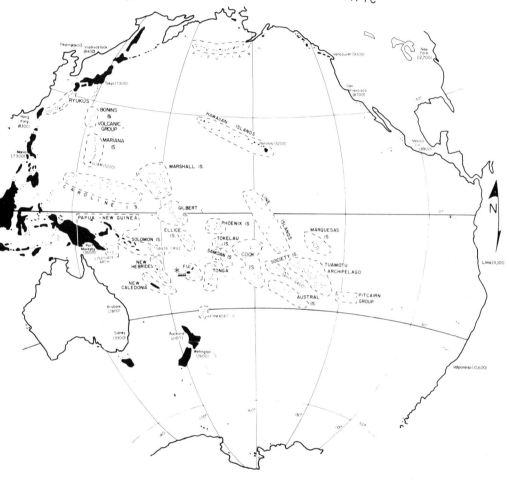

DUANE STORMONT

DISTANCES (0,0 0 0) are in kilometers
from Suva, FIJI ✳

PROJECTION: Lambert's Zenithal Equal-Are

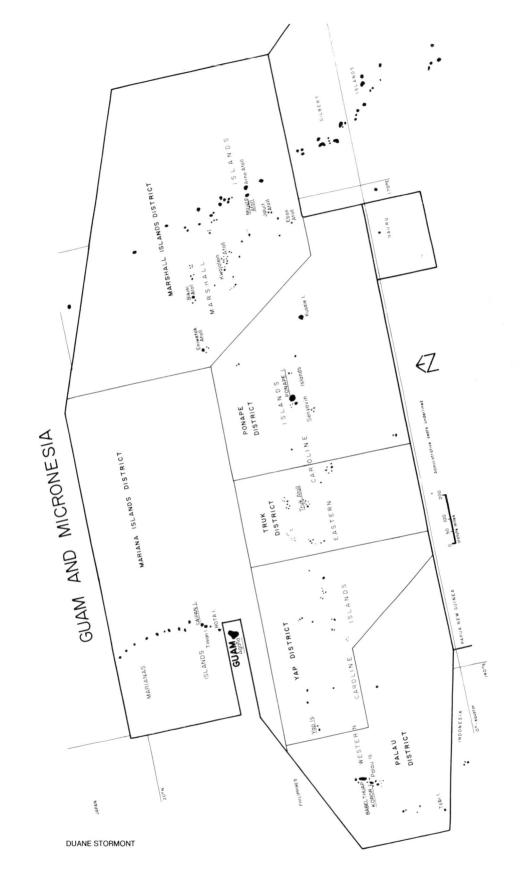

GUAM AND MICRONESIA

MARIANA ISLANDS DISTRICT

MARIANAS

ISLANDS

SAIPAN I.
Tinian I.
ROTA I.

GUAM ♥
Agana

MARSHALL ISLANDS DISTRICT

MARSHALL

ISLANDS

Enwetok
Atoll

Bikini
Atoll

Kwajalein
Atoll

Majuro Arno Atoll
ATOLL

Jaluit
Atoll

Ebon
Atoll

GILBERT

ISLANDS

NAURU

170°E

Kusaie I.

PONAPE
DISTRICT

CAROLINE

ISLANDS

PONAPE I.

Senyavin
Islands

TRUK
DISTRICT

EASTERN

Truk Atoll

YAP DISTRICT

CAROLINE

ISLANDS

WESTERN

Yap Is.

PALAU
DISTRICT

BABELTHUAP
KOROR
Palau Is.

Tobi I.

PHILIPPINES

INDONESIA

0° equator

140°E

PAPUA NEW GUINEA

Administrative seats underlined

0 50 100   200
statute miles

N

JAPAN

20°N

DUANE STORMONT

REGIONAL SPHERES OF INTEREST
of Australia and New Zealand

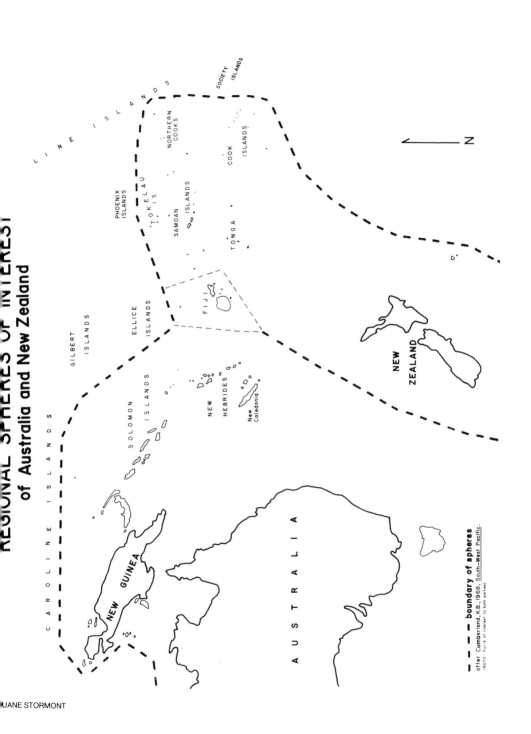

LINE ISLANDS

SOCIETY ISLANDS

NORTHERN COOKS

COOK ISLANDS

PHOENIX ISLANDS

TOKELAU IS.

SAMOAN ISLANDS

TONGA

GILBERT ISLANDS

ELLICE ISLANDS

FIJI

CAROLINE ISLANDS

SOLOMON ISLANDS

NEW GUINEA

NEW HEBRIDES

New Caledonia

NEW ZEALAND

AUSTRALIA

N

— — — boundary of spheres

after Cumberland, K.B., 1968, South—West Pacific.
(NOTE: Fiji is of interest to both parties)

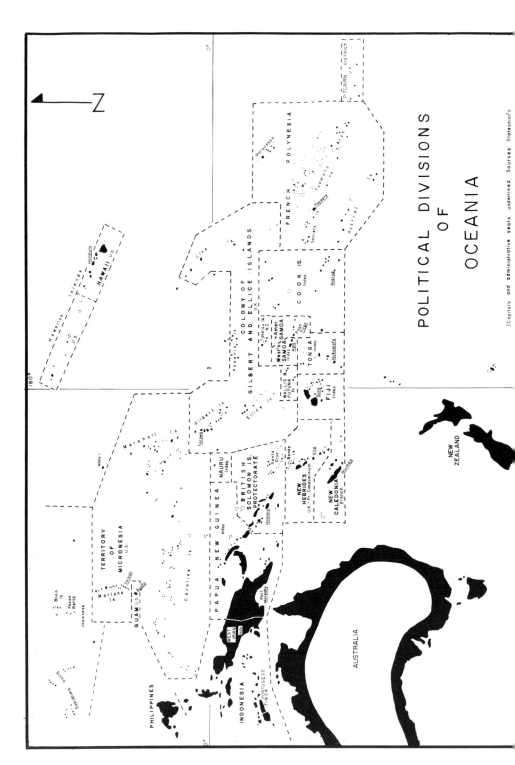

POLITICAL DIVISIONS
OF
OCEANIA

(Capitals and administrative seats underlined. Sources Statesman's

DUANE STORMONT

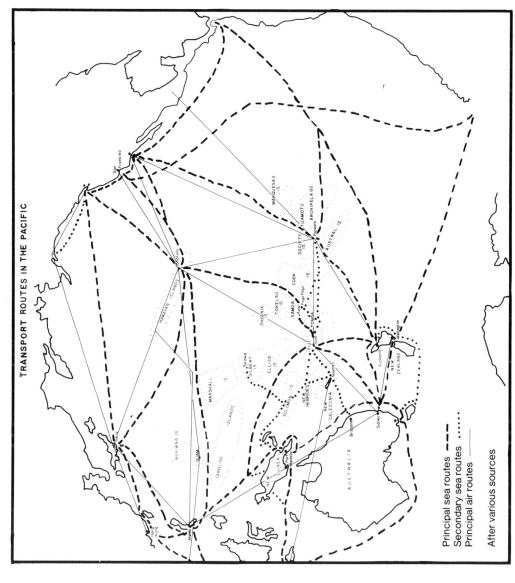

TRANSPORT ROUTES IN THE PACIFIC

Principal sea routes ▬ ▬ ▬
Secondary sea routes • • • • • •
Principal air routes ————

After various sources

DUANE STORMONT

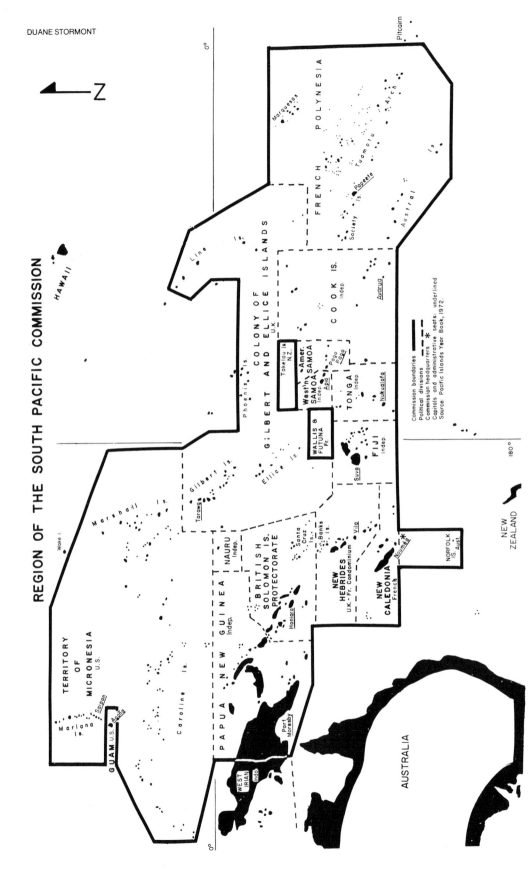

PART I

MICRONESIA AND THE UNITED STATES OF AMERICA

LAZARUS E. SALII

1

Liberation and Conquest in Micronesia

During the past few years, the United States' administration of the Trust Territory of the Pacific Islands has entered its final stages. Meetings between United States and Micronesia representatives, though beset by numerous problems, have established the basis on which to end the United Nations Trusteeship Agreement, to establish a new Micronesian government, and to negotiate a new definition of the American role in our part of the Pacific. My purpose, in what follows, is to discuss the nature and impact of the United States administration, which was brought to our islands nearly three decades ago. I will discuss the relationship of restraint, antagonism, and mutual need that arose between America and Micronesia; and I will close with an indication of some of the ironies and paradoxes that will continue to confront America and Micronesia in years to come.[1]

When American military forces swept ashore in Micronesia, near or at the end of World War II, they came as both liberators and conquerors. They ended a Japanese dominion that, had it been permitted to continue its complete control of almost all aspects of Micronesian life, would have all but obliterated Micronesian races and cultures within one more generation.

During the past twenty-five years of American control in Micronesia, many Micronesians have fashioned nostalgic histories of the Japanese rule: colonial cities it built, the roads it cut through jungles, its initiatives in fishing, mining, and agriculture. They remember Japan for its discipline, its industry, its sense of purpose—qualities that frequently have been lacking in the American trusteeship.

Whatever its usefulness for rhetorical purposes, this is not a nostalgia in which I, or most other Micronesian leaders, choose to participate. Japan's assimilation of Micronesia would have resulted in the permanent loss of our cultures, and our ethnic identities. Since our whole purpose in recently negotiating with the Americans has been to resist such an assimilation, I will not pretend that we would have welcomed—or would welcome it today—at the hands of the Japanese. Whatever criticisms are registered against America, I will not fault it for having broken, if only by accident, the "Japanization, or Okinawaization," of Micronesia.[2]

If the Americans came as liberators, they were surely also conquerors. As numerous administrators, visiting congressmen, task forces from Washington have rarely failed to remind us, control of Micronesia was "purchased" at a high cost in American blood. Of course, this argument overlooks certain crucial Micronesian claims: that the basic ownership of Micronesia's islands is a right of the Micronesian people; that the islands were not and are not for sale for blood or for money; that the blood spilled "coming over the reef"—another favorite phrase—was not spilled at the request, or for the benefit of the Micronesian people. Still, we realize that the conquest of Micronesia and the control that resulted from that conquest remain paramount factors in America's thinking about Micronesia.

Americans came as liberators and conquerors and, as such, they have remained. Both these roles figured importantly in the United Nations Trusteeship Agreement, which has provided the basic terms of America's control of Micronesia since 1947. The role of liberator was reflected in the economic and social goals of the Agreement particularly in its provisions for the education and well-being of the people of Micronesia and, most importantly, in its specification that Micronesia be brought to the point where our people would themselves determine an appropriate new political status of "self-government or independence." The role of conqueror, however, was reflected in the designation of Micronesia as a strategic trusteeship, with a proviso enabling the United States to alienate and to fortify our islands and to veto any change in our political status that challenged the control they won during the war.

These broad terms of the American trusteeship are perhaps familiar to you. So, too, is the fact that America's roles as a conqueror and liberator have often clashed and that, when this has happened—at Kwajalein, at Eniwetok and Bikini, in the year-to-year freedom of the Trusteeship Agreement, and even in our recent status negotiations with American representatives—the role of conqueror has always prevailed. Whether America will ever be able to sort out and reconcile such a diversity of interests and cross-purposes remains to be seen, although I am sure they have my best wishes and the best wishes of Micronesia in this undertaking. Meanwhile, we Micronesians who have lived under the Trusteeship and who now are witnesses to its finale have our own diversity of interests and our own cross-purposes to sort out and to reconcile.

Like most Micronesian legislators who now find themselves across a negotiating table from United States representatives, I am a product of the American period in Micronesia. In my generation and in myself I can find evidence of the various aspects of the United States Trusteeship and of the tension and turmoil that result from the conflict between the best and the worst America has accomplished in our islands and in ourselves.

I suspect that the best aspect of the American period was the administering authority's willingness to educate Micronesians. To be sure, the educational system they brought to our islands was often ill-suited to Micronesia. Many early textbooks, programs, and teachers came no closer than California to the reality of Pacific life. But there was never any question about America's basic willingness to fully educate Micronesians. Unlike the Japanese, who generally offered nothing more than a grade school education and some highly circum-scribed vocational training, the United States was determined to educate at least some Micronesians as far as it was possible for them to go. They sent us to regional high schools, to colleges abroad, and kept us there. And there—not on the playing fields of Eton but in the Trust Territory dormitories in Guam and Hawaii—Micronesia's battle for a new political status was begun. It was there that we learned the familiar lessons of unity, democracy, sovereignty, and self-government, the lessons that generations of American students have absorbed and taken for granted, the lessons, which upon our return to our home islands, to the crowded district centers, to the equally crowded government offices, we found could not be satisfied in Micronesia. Our expectations could not be ful-filled; not in a strategic trusteeship, not in a United States territory, not by an administrator who uneasily alternated between his role as conqueror and his role as liberator.

Now I come, as all of us who returned home came, to the worst aspects of the American trusteeship. We quickly found that the options we had believed were open to us actually were foreclosed. They were foreclosed not only by the terms of the Trusteeship, but by the economy that was then developing in Micronesia—an economy already racing away from the self-sufficient, subsis-tence economy of our fathers to a system in which imported goods (some of them necessary, many of them trivial) were making inroads on Micronesian life. We were witnessing the birth of an economy which would soon be—and today now is—thoroughly dependent on imported goods, contracted skills, and annual out-side aid. It was not a pleasant process to contemplate; and most troublesome was the fact that we were its products, we were its educated imports. In Micro-nesia, the life of our fathers was being lost and the ideals of their sons could not be realized.

There may be a way out of the predicament I have just described, and I believe that we are beginning to discover it. I am not sure that I would have believed at first that the Congress of Micronesia was to be the instrument of our escape. When it began in 1965, the Congress was more an advisory coun-cil than a true legislature; its laws were subject to vetoes that could not be overridden, it had almost no power of the purse, and practically all of its members (myself included) were also middle-level and white-collar employees of the executive branch of the Trust Territory Government. We were a Congress of amphibious creatures—half government executive and half elected Congress-man—and we were almost equally powerless in both our chosen elements. All that we had in our Congress was a forum and we made the most of it—freely, naively, sometimes irresponsibly. There was a gadfly's delight in calling one's immediate superior to a Congressional hearing and closely interrogating him on the administrative mishaps we had witnessed and, in some cases I am sure, been a parfy to. In a general way, I suppose the Congress stood for more and better government without really considering its effect on the political future of the Territory. One thing of true value did result from the Congress, however; this was the slow and definite growth of unity among the various Micronesian leaders who met in the Congressional chambers on Saipan. It was a untiy that any previous foreign administration in Micronesia would have taken pains to discourage, an unprecedented unity with incalculable implications for the future of the Islands. There are two other points to remember about the Micronesian unity that developed in our Congress. First, it was a unity sponsored and financed by our administration. Secondly and paradoxically, it was a unity that derived, in large part, from our common opposition to that administration.

In the late 1960s, three developments occurred that transformed the Congress, altered completely the form of political life in Micronesia, and began the process that will end with the termination of our American Trusteeship. The first came in 1969, when members of Congress were obliged to choose between their administrative and legislative roles. Those who remained with the Congress became full-time Congressmen who were more serious and committed than ever before. The second event was the Congress's determined and deeply-felt effort to pass a major piece of legislation which in itself would have transferred the ultimate power over Micronesia's lands from an American-controlled executive branch to a Micronesian Congress. Twice the bill was passed; twice the bill was vetoed by the High Commissioner. The third major development, which was partially a result of our failure to capture eminent domain in Congress, was the initiative Congress took in seeking to end the United Nations Trusteeship, to end the intolerable power that the Trusteeship vested in our liberator-conqueror, and to begin a new political status in Micronc

Since 1969, we have endeavored to persuade the United States that Micronesia ought to become a self-governing state in free association with the United States. This relationship of free association involves four basic principles and legal rights. These are Micronesia's right to self-determination, to make its own laws, to control its land, and to end unilaterally any future relationship with the United States. We particularly insisted on the right of unilateral termination as an indispensable safeguard for a small island state in a relationship with a global superpower. Unilateral termination is a final insurance not only against our being abused or ignored but also against our being embraced to death. After some initially discouraging responses, the United States has acceded, or substantially acceded, on all four of these crucial matters.

The United States, in turn, has demanded sweeping powers over Micronesian foreign affairs and defense and already has requested certain continuing military base rights and options in Micronesia. These are troublesome requests, but we are now more confident than ever that there exists a basis for self-government in Micronesia and for an honorable future partnership with the United States. And there is some hope that, with Micronesian control of government, we may find our way out of the economic as well as political difficulties that confront us, also that we might yet strike a decent, stable non-exploitative balance between the freedom and expectations of twentieth-century life and the Micronesian values that are still full of meaning for the islands we were born on and the Micronesian people who will always remain there.

There remains one great, nagging footnote to this story, however, and I would be giving a false report if I did not record it. We all have heard how scattered are

the islands of Micronesia, a mere seven hundred square miles of land in three
million miles of sea; how its peoples are divided by distance, by religion, by their
six major ethnic groups, by nine mutually unintelligible languages. This, all of
this, is true. Under American administration, however, we have been unified; our
support from our liberator and opposition to our conqueror united us. We were
united first by his very presence here; we were united by the Trusteeship that
bound us together; we were united in the schools to which we were sent and in
our reaction to the society to which we returned; we were united in the Congress
our administrator sponsored, and we were united in our congressional criticism
of the programs our administrator proposed. We were united in seeking a change
of status, and now—as we approach agreement on status—we are beginning to
lose our unity. The America we loved and we fought now is on the edge of withdrawal from the government of Micronesia, and we Micronesians find ourselves
looking at each other in a new light.

Separatist tendencies are flaring up again in Micronesia. Already one district
long-oriented towards close membership to the American territorial system
has sought its own negotiations with the United States, and others consider
separate negotiations for their own purposes.[3] Already debate begins about the
division of government revenues among districts, about the apportionment of
executive powers between districts, about the necessary strength or the necessary
weakness of a future central government. Ironically, this is occurring just as
Micronesia approaches the unique political status that will give its people greater
control of the issues affecting their lives than they have ever had. Just at this
crucial moment, Micronesia begins to divide and fragment. The unity we developed under our liberator-conqueror begins to desert us. This does not speak well
for the future of Micronesia.

We must concede that thus far in our history, it has always been the threatening presence of foreigners, of conqueror-liberators, that has united us. Fear of
what others might do to our islands has united us. And yet, perhaps Micronesians
would do well to remember that no matter what status we achieve, our islands
will always be small, our numbers will always be limited. Micronesia will always
be threatened, and for this reason, we must always remain united. The interests
of the great powers swing back and forth like a pendulum over our islands; the
pendulum swings from one side to another, moving away and returning, but
never ceasing to hang above us, never forgetting our presence down below. In the
days and years to come there will be ample reason for our islands to remain together, and there is hope, only hope, that in time we may find something more
than fear to unite us.

NOTES

1. The original version of this paper was given at the sixth Waigani Seminar in
Papua New Guinea on May 1, 1972.

2. See Carl Heine's discussion of this in *Micronesia at the Crossroads: A Reappraisal of the Micronesian Political Dilemma* (Honolulu, 1974), pp. 14-5, 20.

3. *Editor's note.* The Mariana Islands District began separate negotiations with the United States in December, 1973, to become an American commonwealth. The Marshall Islands District and the Palau District have also established their own political status commissions, but thus far these two districts have not asked for separate negotiations with the United States. On June 17, 1975, the voters of the Marianas approved a covenant to establish a Commonwealth of the Northern Marianas by a vote of 3,939 to 1,060. Subsequently, President Gerald Ford has encouraged the U.S. Congress to approve this covenant. On July 12, 1975, elected representatives from all six districts of the Trust Territory met on Saipan to begin a ninety-day Constitutional Convention. See *Highlights* (Office of the High Commissioner [Saipan, July, 1975]).

SHERWOOD LINGENFELTER
DANIEL T. HUGHES

2

The Democratization of the United States Trust Territory of the Pacific Islands

Although the exact nature of the future political status of the United States Trust Territory in Micronesia is still uncertain, it is clear that within the next few years there will be drastic alterations in the political ties of Micronesia with the United States and in the Micronesian political system itself. At this time it is most appropriate that we review the American administration of this area and see what lessons might be learned from past experience. In this review we shall examine the following topics: (1) the nature of the pre-American administrations; (2) the approach of the American administration; and (3) the responses of the indigenous Micronesian systems.

PRE-AMERICAN ADMINISTRATIONS

In 1494, according to the Treaty of Tordesillas, Spain assumed responsibility for all the islands of the Pacific. Actually Spain concentrated her attention on the Marianas, particularly on Guam, which served as a station in the lucrative galleon trade between Mexico and the Philippines. The rest of Micronesia was largely neglected by the Spanish administration.

During the latter part of the nineteenth century, Germany moved into the power vacuum in Micronesia. In 1885 she declared a protectorate over the Marshalls, took possession of Yap, and laid claim to Truk, Ponape, and Kusaie. Leo XIII arbitrated the dispute between the two powers, confirmed Spain's claim to the Carolines as well as to the Marianas, but awarded the Marshalls to Germany. Despite the edict of Leo XIII, Germany's economic interest in the Carolines and the Marianas remained strong and her trading companies continued to operate in these areas. When the United States defeated the Spanish in 1898, Germany purchased the Carolines and the Marianas except for Guam, which became a United States possession at that time.

Spain never made very serious efforts at economic development in the Carolines and the Marianas. Even in the Marianas, aside from the use of Guam as a station in the galleon trade, her only concerns were to Christianize the indigenous population and to maintain her own administration of the area with a minimum of effort and expense to herself.

The German administration of Micronesia was quite a different affair. It continued the pattern of indirect rule established by the Spanish, but it gave much stronger and more detailed directions to the indigenous leaders than the Spanish had given. Health measures were instituted and public schools erected on most of the inhabited islands. On the larger, more populated islands, roads were constructed or extended. In a drive to establish a monetary economy and an economic stability in its colony, the German administration instituted individual land ownership in many parts of Micronesia and required the new land owners to plant large numbers of coconut trees on the land. This move marked the beginning of the large-scale copra industry throughout Micronesia.

During World War I, the Japanese took possession of Germany's Micronesian colony. They remained in control of the area until they were displaced by the Americans in 1945 after World War II. The Japanese administered the islands under the auspices of the League of Nations just as the United States later administered them under the auspices of the United Nations. From the beginning, the Japanese followed a policy of economic development and of rapid colonialization. Great numbers of Japanese migrated to Micronesia, particularly to the larger district centers. Japanese colonial government exercised much more direct rule than either the Spanish or the Germans had. It continued to use indigenous leaders as its spokesmen with the Micronesians, but it was quick to replace those who were not compliant enough with its directives.

AMERICAN ADMINISTRATION

Change from Policy of Previous Colonial Administrations

In 1945 the latest colonial power entered Micronesia. The United States military occupied the former Japanese possessions, and with United Nations sanction the United States initiated the Trust Territory of the Pacific Islands. The United States Navy administered this territory until the President assigned these responsibilities to the United States Department of the Interior in 1951.

According to the terms of the United Nations Trusteeship Agreement, the United States and the Trust Territory administration are committed to fostering political development toward self-government in the territory. In 1948 the Naval administration stated that its official policy was that the Micronesians should be granted the highest degree of self-government they could assimilate, and that the administration would assist them to conduct their government and manage their affairs within the framework of their own socio-political institutions and traditions. Commenting on this policy statement, Dorothy Richard says that the Naval administration never considered the term "self-government" to imply democracy specifically, and she quotes Admiral Fiske, the Deputy High Commissioner, as saying, "We advocate self-government—not necessarily democracy."[1] However, in a short time this policy was revised to one of actively inculcating American-style democratic processes and institutions on every level of government. Self-government became equated with American-style democracy.

With this policy of Americanization of Micronesia, the American posture in Micronesia became as fundamentally colonial as that of the Japanese. According to H. C. Brookfield, colonialism is "a thoroughgoing, comprehensive and deliberate penetration of a local or 'residentiary' system by the agents of an external system, who aim to restructure the patterns of organization, resource use, circulation and outlook so as to bring these into linked relationship with their own system."[2] Because of the policy of introducing an American-style democracy, the penetration and restructuring of traditional Micronesian systems that took place under the American administration far out-distanced those of the previous foreign regimes.

Establishing an American-Style Political Structure

A major step in "democratizing" Micronesia was the formation of 118 municipalities throughout the territory in 1948. These municipalities were to be the basic political units of the territorial government. Ordinarily, they corresponded to the traditional Micronesian socio-political units. Each municipality has a chief executive official called the Municipal Magistrate. At first these officials could either be chosen by popular election or they could be appointed by the American administrator of the district. Although elections ideally were preferred by the American administration, in many cases the District Administrator followed the simpler course of appointing traditional chiefs as Magistrates. Later the administration instituted a program of chartering the municipalities, and the election of Magistrates was specified in each charter. The charters also established a Legislative Council of elected members in each municipality. Thus the executive and legislative powers were split between the Magistrate and the Council. The American-style division of political power was completed by establishing municipal judges as a third branch of local government.

On the district level, advisory groups of Micronesian leaders were established to assist the District Administrator. These gradually evolved into District Legislatures, which are elected bodies with lawmaking authority over each of the six districts in Micronesia. They are the legislative bodies that parallel the District Administrator's position. Finally, in 1965, the Congress of Micronesia was formed with elected representatives from all six districts and with legislative jurisdiction over the entire territory. Thus the Congress of Micronesia is the legislative counterpart to the High Commissioner. Table 1 shows the executive and the legislative officials in the introduced political system on all three levels of government in Micronesia.

TABLE 1

Levels of Government in Micronesia

	Executive Official	Legislative Official
Territorial Level	High Commissioner	*Micronesian Congressman
District Level	District Administrator	*District Legislator
Municipal Level	*Magistrate	*Municipal Councilman

*Official elected by Micronesians.

According to the official description of the political structure in the Trust Territory, the ultimate authority rests with the U.S. Secretary of the Interior. The United States Government exerts its authority in the Trust Territory through this office. However, if one examines the distribution of power and influence within this system of organization, a slightly different picture emerges. Groups such as the United Nations and the U.S. Department of State and Department of Defense are not found in the official descriptions of the power structure, but in practice they often exert power and influence at the highest level of this structure. The Trusteeship Council of the United Nations reviews the status of the territory each year, and the reports of these inspections have provoked new policy and action on several occasions. The Departments of State and Defense are also very much interested in the status of the territory. The Department of State attempts to influence policies that affect the international relations of the United States. The Department of Defense seeks greater security and permanent strategic rights in the area. Each of these interest groups has direct access to the President of the United States, who has the final word on territorial policy; and they have used this access to influence the directions of territorial administration.

Another factor in the division of power enters the scene on the territorial level. In the American counterpart to the Trust Territory political organization, there is a professed equality between the legislative and the executive branches of government. In the Trust Territory the power of the executive branch far outweighs that of the legislative branch. The decisions of the legislative branch are always subject to the veto of the executive branch. The Congress and the legislatures may override executive veto, but the decision is made by the next higher executive in the hierarchy, with the Secretary of the Interior being the final authority. It would be false to say that the legislative bodies are not influential, but their powers are definitely circumscribed by the administration.

Another approach in examining the political organization in the Trust Territory is to break down the structure according to the degree of distance existing between the various levels and the indigenous system. From this view we find that the elected legislative branches are most closely in touch with the local population. The members of these groups are respected members of their communities, although most have been educated to some degree to the outlook of the administration.

Parallel to the district legislatures are the American executive officials appointed by the High Commissioner. These officials do not, however, have the same degree of contact and interaction with the people. In most districts the officials of the administration enjoy special quarters set apart from the local people and have restricted facilities for their own relaxation and entertainment. Therefore, while officials and legislators reside in the same district, their customary life styles create a cultural and social distance between them.

The significance of distance in looking at a governmental structure lies in its relevance for communication and feedback between governors and the governed. When dealing with the processes of planned political change, communication distance becomes a very important variable. In Micronesia, the territorial level of government is of necessity confined to one location, earlier in Guam and currently in Saipan in the Marianas. In the government, the administrative officials live, work, and relax apart from the local inhabitants, except for those Micronesians who are employed on the staff. While there is regular contact in the administrative center, the officials do not encounter personally the problems of the territory much more than if they lived in Hawaii or even California.

Perhaps most significant for understanding the directions that development took in Micronesia is the location of final policy determination in Washington, D.C. The President, the Congress, and the Office of Territories frame the major policies for the Trust Territory, yet have no accountability to the subjects affected by these policies. This, of course, stems from the very nature of colonial rule.

Process of Restructuring the Political System

Demands for change in the political systems of Micronesia originated with the United Nations, the United States Congress, and the U.S. Departments of State and Defense. The framing of policies to satisfy these demands occurred in the Office of Territories at a time when Micronesians had no influence. The planners formulated a model for government borrowed directly from the structure of the U.S. Federal Government and adapted slightly to the administrative hierarchy already established in the territory. This model was then transmitted to the territorial government with the charge of interpreting and implementing it among the local Micronesian populations.

The implementation of these goals and plans for change was passed through two levels of administrative officials, or "brokers." The Office of the High Commissioner served as the voice of the U.S. government, transmitting decisions made in Washington to lower level officials in Micronesia. District officials transmitted directives from the High Commissioner to their subjects and feedback from their subjects to the High Commissioner. Since the High Commissioner's task was to execute policy rather than to define it, the feedback was used primarily to aid in implementation rather than in definition of policy. The chartering of the Congress of Micronesia in September 1964 furnished an organized legislative structure that could demand reconsideration of policy decisions by the Secretary of the Interior; but by this time the major program for political change had been largely accomplished across the territory. The previous Council of Micronesia, which had met as early as 1956, was no more successful than District Administrators in interjecting Micronesian designs into the program for change.

The significance of the interrelationship among these four levels of decision-making and policy should not be underestimated. The ultimate plan and policy for each local area was determined outside of that area in a distant and impenetrable locus of power, and it was buffered by two levels of brokers. The execution of plans and the implementation of policy, however, occurred on the local level between protagonists who had to work together, yet who lacked the authority to determine precisely what form of organization or what rules for allocating power would serve to expedite their mutual desires or mediate their conflicting interests. To understand the implications of this administrative system for directed change, it is useful to look at the nature of the models for change employed at both levels of the system.

In the 1950s the general model for political development in Micronesia, defined in the Office of Territories, but emerging from a broader climate of opinion among government leaders and political scientists of that period, was evolutionary in perspective and proceeded in a direct line from "primitive" types of organization to democracy. Democracy, however, was very narrowly defined. Since political power in the United States was split among administrative, legislative, and judicial branches of government, it was taken for granted that the same division could be made in the territorial government. The new leaders required to effect the new system were assigned single function roles, assuring that no overlap would occur between separate areas of authority. The organization designed to flesh out the model included unicameral district legislatures and local municipal governments. The executive and judicial structures of the territorial government completed the requirements of the trichotomy. At the local levels of each district, the municipality system followed a generalized model of small town American government. A magistrate was chief executive officer and sometimes judge. The municipal council formed his legislative counterpart. The role assignments of magistrate, legislator, councilman, and even traditional chief were set in the general policy for development emerging from the territorial government.

In each of the separate districts, then, a rigid plan for change had to be translated, interpreted, and applied by an American official to an indigenous people and leadership. The products of this task were a series of trial organizations in which administrators and local leaders maneuvered to accomplish their own objectives and at the same time to accomodate the demands or wishes of the higher echelons of the hierarchy. Various organizational alternatives were introduced to achieve the broad general goal. A unicameral legislature including traditional chiefs was chartered in Palau. A unicameral legislature excluding chiefs was chartered in Yap, and a bicameral legislature was formed in Ponape. None of these structures satisfied the general goal, and they were periodically revised to force the direction of change toward the general model. Part of the variation was due to the separate administrators whose definitions and methods of implementation differed; and part was created by the need for strategic compromise to overcome perceived resistance to administrative plans. After each compromise a new stage of negotiations was initiated to meet the territorial government's demand to push on.

The ultimate consequences of this program were a series of district legislatures and municipal governments, the forms of which satisfied the demands from Washington and the United Nations, but which left much to be desired by the Micronesian people. Along with the sometimes disfunctional legislatures, the changes perpetuated confusion between traditional and elected leaders over the rules for decision-making and allocation of power. In most cases administrative officials carefully manipulated changes to push traditional leaders farther and farther into the background.

Problem of Restructuring the Political System

Perhaps the most serious fault involved in the process of restructuring the political organization of Micronesia was the failure of the Trust Territory planners to recognize the existence of fully operative traditional political systems. A number of assumptions made by the planners appear consistently in the history of political change in Micronesia. Among these are: (1) traditional governments are unrepresentative and therefore bad; (2) the traditional political structures are unable to cope with the present demands or needs of the current administration; (3) traditional leaders oppose planned change and create a stumbling block to development; and (4) the superior knowledge and political skills of the administering government must necessarily be transferred to the colonized for them to adapt effectively to the modern world. Such a transfer requires extensive political education and new indigenous leadership.

The tragedy of these assumptions is that they precluded a serious study of existing political structures, which might have supplied alternative models for a viable plan of development and change. Robert McKnight particularly has decried the insistence upon development without careful consideration of possible in-cultural modernization. From his own study of Palau he has shown how this approach forced change at the expense of the traditional system and leaders who in many ways were more responsive to and representative of the people than those introduced.[3]

One disastrous result of the failure to recognize the validity of existing political structures has been the lack of effective communication between the Trust Territory Administration and the Micronesian people. The blame for much of the non-communication falls on the administration. All too often the channels were, and continue to be, open only one way, from top to bottom. Without feedback, the administration fails to recognize that it has educated Micronesians in forms and symbols, without supplying their essential function and content. It has failed to recognize that the only effective change is that in which the elite and the people are taught the content, power, and functions of the new political institutions.

RESPONSE OF INDIGENOUS SOCIETIES

Nature of Indigenous Systems

The traditional political systems of Micronesia are so varied that very few generalizations are valid for all of the societies there. Three elements that do seem important in all systems are lineage membership, the control of land, and the traditional perspective. The very name "Micronesia" (the small islands) indicates the limited quantity, and therefore the valuable nature, of land in these societies. Ordinarily land is owned by an extended kinship group, frequently a lineage. Birth into a particular lineage determines an individual's social, economic, and political position within his society; or more precisely, an individual's lineage defines the general limits, often quite broad, within which he can maneuver for power. Thus there is a good deal of flexibility and competition within most Micronesian societies despite the ascriptive nature of leadership.

A traditional society is one in which the primary meanings of life and the standards and motivations for behavior are defined in an authoritative past. Members of such societies conceive of the past as the source of truth, and also as the source of rules and examples for right conduct. The ancestors are frequently guardians of these precepts and lend to the past its aura of sacredness and its power to sanction those who deviate from the right path.

Micronesian societies are traditional in perspective. Their primary organizations are unilineal kinship groups that trace descent from common ancestors. Authority in these societies is most often assigned to the founding clans or lineages of the community, which enjoy superior rank and provide the organization through which the community functions. The elders of these kin groups supply the leadership for the community. The rules for making decisions and distributing power are defined in tradition, and they include codes of strict respect, public humility and restraint, and a consensus agreement for decision-making.

The assignment of leadership to royal clans and lineages creates a dynastic image of the Micronesian polity. The nature of political responsiveness within this framework, however, denies the possibility of a royal hierarchy with unrestrained power. Selection of leaders is rarely so rigidly defined that competition and conflict are excluded. In fact, myriad cases in the ethnographic literature show the opposite is true. Heirs apparent face intense competition for the throne and in past history often lost. Such rivalry forces leaders to win the support of the people and to maintain this support through continual attention to their needs and wishes. While Micronesian leaders receive great deference and respect, they are not able to remain aloof from the will of their constituents. They rarely make any decision without first discussing the issues in a council of chiefs and elders and obtaining consensus agreement. Leaders usually maintain face-to-face contact with their people.

Goals of Indigenous Societies

Whenever a colonial power envelopes traditional societies with vast military and economic power, its administration induces changes to draw these small social systems into their network of dependency relationships. The ultimate goal of the colonial government is to serve its own ends, whether economical or political, and the traditional society is then faced with a struggle for survival. Because of its limited power the traditional society cannot resist by force, but is dependent upon wit and flexibility to assure its continued identity. This is precisely how many traditional leaders responded to the new "democratic" political structure in the Trust Territory. The traditional leaders fought hardest to retain or to regain control over policy formation and the distribution of power in their traditional spheres of influence. This goal stands above all others in importance; it is certainly motivated by personal desires to retain power and influence, but it is rooted much deeper in the system of beliefs that defines their people. Without such commitment to their own political ethos, they would have succumbed quickly to the pressures of the colonial government. Instead, these beliefs have supplied the resilience to survive and the currents that ultimately erupt into independence and disentanglement from colonial dependency. Traditional leaders, however, are also quite willing and eager to tap the new sources of wealth, power, and prestige. The requirements for successful manipulation of new sources of power are accomodation and absorption. James Nason has shown that the traditional chiefs on Etal purposefully conceded to colonial demands what they considered advantageous and managed to absorb or ignore demands to their disadvantage. Throughout their history of subservience, they have never relinquished command of their own interests.[4]

Fischer and Dahlquist have illustrated similar efforts by some traditional leaders on Ponape to retain control and to tap new sources of power. In this case the paramount chiefs used traditional obligations incurred with the bestowing of titles to draw new economic and political leaders into their sphere of obligation. The chiefs then distributed the economic gains acquired to broaden their base of support.[5] This action reflects the ultimate objective of traditional leadership: to enjoy the approval, respect, and support of the people.

Adjustment and Adaptation

The American-style democratic system has induced different structural changes in Micronesian societies than did the indirect rule policy of the earlier colonial administrations. In their policies the German and Japanese governments decreed a new mediating status at the top of Micronesian political systems, but no structural change below. Frequently, the individual appointed to this position was a paramount chief; but if not, he did not interfere with the jurisdiction of that chief. In most cases the position was accepted, redefined to fit into the traditional framework, and business followed as usual. For example, the position of magistrate, introduced on Etal in the Mortlocks, was defined as "messenger," and the paramount chief and lineage chiefs continued to make decisions.[6] Micronesians capitalized on administrative ignorance of their languages and conducted affairs as much as possible in their own way.

The American government introduced the most far-reaching organizational changes, including completely new forms of local and district government. Micronesian responses to such drastic innovations varied widely. Lingenfelter found that in the case of the Yap Council even a new form of government may be filled with traditional content and adapted to create a very effective organization.[7] Nason has described an entirely different case on Etal. There the traditional organization decided to adopt a new system, and it established an elected municipal council to serve as a check on the power of the magistrate. Membership on the council included mostly younger, educated men who were thought to be knowledgeable in dealing with the alien administration.[8]

Change in the organizational structure itself then does not appear as a critical variable in explaining Micronesian adaptation. The government introduced similar structures across Micronesia, producing widely varying responses. Perhaps more basic than changes in organization are changes in what some anthropologists and political scientists call *regime;* i.e., the rules for decision-making and allocations of power.

Regime lies at the very core of political process. Changes in regime may reshape completely the alignment of power, while continuity in regime may withstand any number of organizational alterations without significant change in power. The cases described by Lingenfelter and Nason illustrate this point clearly. The Yap Islands Legislature was an inept organization dependent upon the Yap Council for guidance until Peace Corps lawyers instructed them in the procedures for utilizing their power. Within a very short time, legislators manipulating these new rules assumed the central role for making policy on Yap. The situation on Etal was entirely different. There the people established a new organization with an accompanying set of new leaders, but retained the same set of responsibilities, obligations, and procedures for reaching decisions. The relationship of new leaders to the people was defined essentially in the same way, and Nason concludes that in goals, regime on Etal has changed little, if at all.[9]

The implications for change in regime extend one step further to the rules for recruiting and legitimizing political leadership. When traditional methods for recruitment are ignored or revised according to new rules and procedures, the new leaders may be illegitimate in the eyes of the community. The consequences of such illegitimacy are: the refusal of the people to support the leader, insecurity and ineffectual leadership from the elite, and general breakdown in the political process. As an example of this, the American administration intervened in the question of succession on Arno, but the solution proved more painful than the problem. The winner was unable to mobilize support from his constituents and his community lapsed into a directionless political vacuum.[10]

In marked contrast, the criteria for recruiting leaders on Etal were changed drastically by the people themselves. Working through the traditional procedures of public discussions and consensus, the Etalese decided that their leaders should be younger, educated men who were experienced in the ways of the alien administration. They were to be elected to form a council of six and to exercise the authority once held by the chiefs. They were given complete control over island affairs, and they led the people. First and foremost, they were legitimate. They enjoyed the complete support of the people, and they were responsible and responsive in the same manner as the old traditional chiefs.

CONCLUSION

Generalizing from our review of the colonial administrations in the Trust Territory, we would say that any program of political modernization (whether it involves the introduction of a particular type of democratic structure or not) should include the following elements:

1. *Indigenous participation.* Genuine political modernization will not occur without effective participation of the indigenous people in defining both the goals and the directions that development will take.

2. *Flexible planning.* In colonial systems political development is most often changed to forms native to the colonial officials rather than to forms most compatible with modernization of existing structures. In order to modernize existing structures rather than to destroy them, it is necessary to identify multiple alternatives from among western, eastern, and traditional societies. Artificially maintained foreign institutions should be abandoned and a new formal government constructed, founded as far as possible upon tradition and designed to meet the needs of contemporary society.

3. *Flexible implementation.* First, models selected for implementation should be flexible, adjusting to the conditions present. The more rigid a system, the more rapidly it becomes disfunctional. Uniformity. created by rigidity, is in itself of little value. Secondly, indigenous leaders should be educated in the skills of political process as well as in the formal attributes of the new system. Forms, like buildings, may be pleasing to observers, but without significant functions they are worthless. Thirdly, new roles should be defined explicitly and their importance conveyed to the people. Successful innovation must be based upon local support, which is impossible to obtain without clear definitions of both position and function.

4. *Two-way communication.* Successful continuation of political innovations requires consistent, open channels of communication between leaders and the people. Planning and education should include definition of such channels and instruction in their use.

5. *Economic support.* To survive, any political system must have a strong economic base. Economic development is therefore fundamental to successful political development. Without it, the new governmental forms will collapse soon after colonial supports are withdrawn.

One final conclusion can be drawn from our review. Successful adaptation to change for traditional societies consists of the retention of control over regime, or the rules and procedures for making decisions and allocating power. Changes in regime, however, destroy the canons of legitimacy and undermine the mechanisms of support essential to a dynamic political system.

NOTES

1. Dorothy Richard, *United States Naval Administration of the Pacific Islands* (Washington, D.C.: Office of Naval Operations, 1957), III, 385.
2. H. C. Brookfield, *Colonialism, Development and Independence: The Case of the Melanesian Islands in the South Pacific* (Cambridge, 1972), pp. 1-2.
3. Robert McKnight, "Rigid Models and Ridiculous Boundaries: Political Development and Practice in Palau, Circa 1955-64," in *Political Development in Micronesia,* Daniel T. Hughes and Sherwood Lingenfelter, eds. (Columbus, 1974), pp. 37-53.
4. James Nason, "Political Change: An Outer Island Perspective," in Hughes and Lingenfelter, op. cit., pp. 117-42.
5. John Fischer, "The Role of the Traditional Chiefs on Ponape in the American Period." and Paul Dahlquist, "Political Development at the Municipal Level: Kiti, Ponape," in Hughes and Lingenfelter, op. cit., pp. 166-77, 178-91.
6. Nason, op. cit., p. 131.
7. Sherwood Lingenfelter, "The Process of Elite Formation in a Changing Micronesian Society," in Hughes and Lingenfelter, op. cit., pp. 54-71.
8. Nason, op. cit., p. 138.
9. See Nason, op. cit., p. 139, and Lingenfelter, op. cit., pp. 64-5.
10. Michael Rynkiewich, "Some Problems of Succession Among Arno Marshallese," Hughes and Lingenfelter, op. cit., 163-5.

BIBLIOGRAPHY

Brookfield, H. C. *Colonialism, Development and Independence: The Case of the Melanesian Islands in the South Pacific.* Cambridge: Cambridge University Press, 1972.

Dahlquist, Paul. "Political Development at the Municipal Level: Kiti, Ponape," in Daniel T. Hughes and Sherwood Lingenfelter (eds.), *Political Development in Micronesia.* Columbus: Ohio State University Press, 1974.

Fischer, John. "The Role of the Traditional Chiefs on Ponape in the American Period," in Hughes and Lingenfelter, op. cit.

Lingenfelter, Sherwood. "The Process of Elite Formation in a Changing Micronesian Society," in Hughes and Lingenfelter, op. cit.

McKnight, Robert. "Rigid Models and Ridiculous Boundaries: Political Development and Practice in Palau, circa 1955-64," in Hughes and Lingenfelter, op. cit.

Nason, James. "Political Change: An Outer Island Perspective," in Hughes and Lingenfelter, op. cit.

Richard, Dorothy. *United States Naval Administration of the Trust Territory of the Pacific Islands.* 3 vols. Washington, D.C.: Office of Naval Operations, 1957.

Rynkiewich, Michael. "Some Problems of Succession Among Arno Marshallese," in Hughes and Lingenfelter, op. cit.

DIRK A. BALLENDORF
HOWARD SEAY

3

Catalysts or Barnacles in Micronesia: The First Five Years of the Peace Corps

When the history of Micronesia is written a hundred years hence, historians and sociologists may well make reference to the 1960s and 1970s as the "Volunteer Period" of development. In the five years from 1966 to 1971, some 1500 Peace Corps Volunteers (PCVs) from the United States served in Micronesia in nearly every major activity area. At one point in 1968, there were about 800 Peace Corps people, including trainees, in the Trust Territory (TT). At the time this represented about one Peace Corps worker for every 93 Micronesians, and their numbers outran those of the administering Trust Territory personnel by almost three to one. Certainly this group—by numbers if by nothing else—must have had a significant effect on the area's development. Or did they? It is an interesting question and one that may wait for answers, in the final analysis, for many more years. But even without the perspective of history, some have said that the volunteers have made "outstanding and valuable" contributions. Others have contended that they created nothing but "headaches for all concerned, including themselves." Although these statements are views in the extreme, debate over the worth of PCVs in the islands has been constant since their arrival.[1] Former Peace Corps Director Joseph Blatchford is on record as having said: "The Peace Corps should never have gone to the Trust Territory in the first place." On the other hand, another former Director, Jack Vaughn, said that the volunteers were doing "a magnificent job" in Micronesia. Such differing opinions prompt a closer look at the presence of the Peace Corps in the islands and what its contributions have been there.

Methodologies employed to assess the impact of the Peace Corps on a country or population have been generally more descriptive than empirical. Anecdotal evidence is frequently offered in efforts to assess the effects of the volunteers' work on a community's socio-economic character. In order to be comprehensive, it is necessary to make assertions derived from unstructured observations rather than from a firm empirical data base. Therefore, those commenting upon Peace Corps impacts must understand that they must accept vulnerability in making statements that are only partially supported by hard data. It must also be understood that such assertions can be open to more than one set of conclusions.

The PCVs' story begins appropriately with a consideration of how they came to Micronesia in the first place. The Trust Territory is, after all, an "American place" and apparently not an area where the Peace Corps, whose mandate for service is confined to foreign developing countries, would be utilized. In 1960 the Trust Territory administration, under the leadership of the High Commissioner and with the strong backing of the Secretary of the Interior, appealed to the U.S. Congress for a ceiling increase in order to better meet the American commitment to the Micronesians under the United Nations Trusteeship Agreement. Justification for this appeal was based upon a series of reports and surveys done in Micronesia which indicated that progress in the islands was not being made as rapidly and effectively as the administration desired. As a result of this concerted effort, the Congress passed a law in July 1962 (PL87-541) which raised the Trust Territory ceiling from $7.5 million to $17.5 million, and by so doing ushered in a new era in the development of Micronesia. Education, particularly elementary education, was designated as the first area for major improvement. It was a large task. Not only were many new school buildings required, but many more teachers were needed as well to implement a new and accelerated program. In 1962 the High Commissioner's annual report stated that "more than 500 new classrooms would be needed" together with "more than 275 U.S. elementary teachers."

It was at about the same time, in 1962, that the Peace Corps was getting underway as a new government agency, and it seemed that its resources—particularly in providing elementary school teachers—would be ideal for helping to implement the program in the Trust Territory. But there was an immediate legal problem. The Peace Corps was an agency limited to providing assistance to foreign countries only. Since Micronesia was administered by the United States, was it really a "foreign" country? There were two aspects to the problem. One had to do with the question of Micronesia's status; the other with funding authority. The Peace Corps felt that it had the legal authority to send volunteers because Section 5A of the Peace Corps Act said that the President may enroll Volunteers for service "abroad." Further, Sections 25A and B defined "abroad" as any area outside of "the several states and the District of Columbia." But the year before, in the development of the legislation that became the Peace Corps Act of 1962, the executive branch submitted a position paper to the Senate Foreign Relations Committee in which they were careful to point out that "the word territories is included in the definition of 'United States' " and that the proviso was included precisely in order to "avoid the implication that Peace Corps Volunteers might be assigned to the territories of the United States." It seemed to be an impasse; the Peace Corps could not serve in the United States or in any territory thereof. But the problem was solved with the stroke of a pen. The Trust Territory of the Pacific Islands was declared not a "territory of the United States." The matter of funding arose in connection with a proviso in the Interior Department's Appropriations Act of 1954, which specifically stated that: "No funds appropriated by any act and no funds which are available or which may become available from any source whatever, shall be used for administration of the Trust Territory of the Pacific Islands, except as may be especially authorized by law."[2] That seemed clear enough. But the conflict was once again resolved with the stroke of a pen. It was declared that the assignment of PCVs to the Trust Territory would not violate the law because they would not be used for the "administration" of that area.

With the legal questions resolved, the Peace Corps planned a program for the islands. Their congressional presentation for 1963 contained a description of a Trust Territory program consisting of sixty-three volunteers working in the fields of education and community development with training to begin in the summer of 1963. But it aroused the opposition of Representative Otto Passman whose concern was fiscal rather than legal. In a letter to Peace Corps Director Sargent Shriver, he said in part:

> In view of the fact that the U.S. financial assistance to the Trust
> Territory is very near the maximum specified by law, and the further
> question as to whether the Peace Corps should be diverting its re-
> sources to an area already being provided for by another agency of
> the federal government, I am of the firm opinion that this particu-
> lar project should not proceed on any basis until the Committee has
> had an opportunity to review it.[3]

The Peace Corps then postponed its proposals for Micronesia. It is probable, but not provable, that the decision was political, i.e., that the Peace Corps was unwilling to tangle with Congressional opposition, and it recognized there were abundant opportunities elsewhere in the developing world. And so the Peace Corps placed Micronesia on the shelf.

But problems in Micronesia continued. In 1963, President John F. Kennedy appointed a commission to study conditions there and make recommendations. This group, headed by Anthony Solomon, was distressed by what it found and specifically suggested that PCVs be dispatched to assist in teaching and in other development programs. Armed with the Solomon report, the Peace Corps felt that it could and should operate in Micronesia.

Then another legal problem arose. It was the Economic Opportunity Act (OEO) of 1964. This act also provided for volunteers to help meet communities' needs for economic and social assistance; and it specifically included the Trust Territory as a "domestic place."[4] The issue was whether its specific conferral of authority on the OEO Director to provide volunteers for the Trust Territory in effect repealed the Peace Corps' more general authority to do so. Once again the lawyers were summoned, and it was decided that the provisions of both the Peace Corps and OEO Acts relating to volunteers were *in pari materia*; that is, they related to the same matter of providing volunteers to assist people in de-velopment. There was, in this view, no real conflict between them. But that brought up the further legal question of which of the two acts would apply.

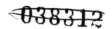

Did the Congress in enacting the OEO legislation intend to repeal the Peace Corps Act as it applied to the Trust Territory?[5] The purposes of the two acts were carefully studied. Although both agencies were in the business of providing volunteers to offer assistance, their purposes were not found to be the same, and in fact it was quite conceivable that the Congress could have intended that both the OEO and the Peace Corps should be able to operate in the Trust Territory. The OEO Act had its stated purpose "to mobilize the human and financial resources of the nation to combat poverty in the United States." The purposes of the Peace Corps Act were "to promote world peace and friendship" through providing volunteers "to help the peoples of other countries and areas in meeting their needs for trained manpower and to help promote a better understanding of the American people on the part of the peoples served, and a better understanding of other peoples on the part of the American people." Since the purposes of these acts were judged to be different, no conflict was seen in the authority of the Peace Corps to send volunteers to Micronesia, and in addition, there was no reason why the OEO could not have programs also, although they expressed no intent of doing so in the case of the Trust Territory.[6]

But it was still two years before the Peace Corps really got serious about mounting a program in Micronesia. In the meantime, reports critical of the American administration in the islands continued to be generated. These included reports from the World Health Organization, a special report by the U.S. Ambassador to the Trusteeship Council, and also a "petition of grievances" about health conditions submitted by the fledgling Congress of Micronesia. In January 1966, the Peace Corps initiated discussions with Department of Interior officials, the High Commissioner, and Micronesian leaders. Subsequently, the idea of a program was brought up with the newly-formed Congress of Micronesia as well as with the various District Legislatures in the islands. The result was an overwhelming endorsement of a Peace Corps program to begin as soon as practicable.

Once the Peace Corps had clear authority for sending volunteers and official requests in hand, the next question was: What will the Peace Corps do in Micronesia? It could easily take its cues from the many critical reports that had been written about the performance of the U.S. administration over the years. And it did. The initial programming teams followed the criticisms almost point by point and used them to justify Peace Corps assistance and then to delineate what that assistance might be in the large social service areas of education and health, as well as in public works and administration. But more than just help to meet needs, the Peace Corps intended to provide an exemplary pace-setting service as well. Ross Pritchard, the Peace Corps Regional Director for the Far East, put the intentions quite succinctly:

> The Peace Corps intends to alter substantially in a relatively short period of time, say three to five years, the twenty year record of neglect and dismal achievement. [Also] given the wide variety of programming opportunities, we seek in the TT to develop comprehensive programs in health, education, and development that will provide guidelines for use elsewhere in the developing world.[7]

This statement conveys the impression that the Peace Corps was a well organized technical/developmental assistance agency capable of mustering large numbers of professional people and specialized resources that could be effectively focused upon very complex problems. But was a mistaken impression, which unfortunately many people held even in the face of evidence and experience to the contrary. Warren Wiggins, Peace Corps Deputy Director at the time the program planning began in Micronesia, said of the organization:

> We don't have a tough task like economic development or political change. Our charge is relatively simple; the charge we received from the Congress. The first purpose is to provide skills to interested countries when desired. Our second purpose is to increase the understanding of Americans by other peoples. And the third purpose is to increase the understanding of other peoples by Americans. These are rather simple notions and they don't give too much of a guide to programming.[8]

The Peace Corps, as an agency, had never been charged with economic development *per se,* and the truth is that it never had the capacity to attempt the execution of such a charge. Its staff members, with very few exceptions, were not professional development specialists. They were talented generalists who came to help and serve. Their amateurishness in the economic development areas was considered a strength, not a weakness. And in all cases their service was temporary and not career-directed. But still the Peace Corps went into Micronesia intent upon a development miracle it was manifestly unable to perform.

The PCVs were not unlike the staff in the above respects. They were a collection of individuals who interpreted their own roles within the loosely knit structure of a "program." A PCV has a unique status as a person working for the U.S. government. He is not actually a federal employee, but rather is sponsored, as it were, by the government and serves at no one's behest but his own.[9] He has a peculiar kind of open-ended contract, and his only commitment to it is a highly personalized, moral one. A PCV goes into a situation more than into a job and he can quit, be fired, or even rehired at the end of his tour. More importantly, his activities in that assignment are prescribed more than proscribed. The general articulation and acceptance of this view of the Peace Corps was more of an ideology than a bureaucracy. While most Trust Territory officials acquiesced to such descriptions, they did not really ponder carefully what it would all mean, operationally, in Micronesia. Even the Peace Corps staff apparently did not ponder and did not know. What in fact it meant was that PCVs would not be bound to the politics of any Trust Territory program or to the underlying administrative assumptions of any policy or point of view. They were free to call a spade a spade—and frequently did. In a bureaucracy as structured as the Trust Territory administration, such outspokenness was virtually intolerable. If anyone ever thought seriously about all of this, they failed to act on it beforehand. The Peace Corps staff cannot be blamed too much for this failure. They sought always to harmonize two disparate points of view: the ideology of the agency with the way Americans perceive organizations and development. This is always a thankless—and perhaps impossible—

task. Nevertheless, the Peace Corps leadership took themselves very seriously in casting these articulate and passionate amateurs as super-developers. Certainly the Americans in the Territory needed help. It was very clear that the Micronesians wanted big changes, and the PCVs were abundantly available.

In order to get moving quickly with an idea that was already five years old, the request for volunteers was taken to the White House, and, on May 5, 1966, President Lyndon B. Johnson in a letter to Peace Corps Director Jack Vaughn said that he hoped to see "the greatest possible involvement of the Peace Corps" in Micronesia, and that he was "confident that the Peace Corps can make a major contribution in this area." A massive recruiting campaign was instituted, and program staff were appointed. The response was tremendous. In the first month of recruitment, over 2500 applications came in specifically for Micronesia; many PCVs serving in other countries requested transfers to Micronesia; and others, near termination, wanted to re-enlist for a second tour in Micronesia.

Some 395 volunteers arrived, much-heralded, in Micronesia in late October 1966, to work in the areas of education, health, public works, and administration. Their arrival was indeed the culmination of a long train of events, which involved the most curious and controversial programmatic justification for the Peace Corps.

Uneasiness characterized the beginning of the Trust Territory/Peace Corps relationship. Many administration people suffered from an inferiority complex as developers, which led to defensiveness and even paranoia. Some volunteers, and unfortunately some staff, tried to capitalize on this by emphasizing their impossible roles as super-developers. The Micronesians often played one against the other. During the first two years, the Peace Corps staff and the Trust Territory administrators made the grievous error of becoming adversaries, which was heady but certainly not in the best developmental interests of the people. The TT people, many of whom were outstanding professional developers and administrators in spite of popular reputations to the contrary, had learned from their experience that it was usually better to think before acting in the islands. The Peace Corps, on the other hand, generally assumed that action of any kind was the paramount developmental catalyst. The desideratum was to help people develop themselves. Both agencies had different approaches and resources, and these were brought together quickly and inadequately in a climate of confusion and uncertainty. In serious matters it is always better to plan before implementing; the trouble was that the TT administration was high on planning and low on performance. When the opportunity for action presented itself in the form of PCVs, no one in Micronesia was able to move ahead decisively on a clear course and utilize volunteers effectively. Volunteer architects, civil engineers, and urban planners plunged themselves into designing housing developments, roads, bridges and town plans—assisted by PCV surveyors. Government grant-in-aid proposals were written and submitted by PCVs to build municipal water systems, catchments, and small docking facilities. Activities such as these were described by someone as "social brick-and-mortar" projects. Others encouraged the formation of small fishing and farming cooperatives; some helped small business entrepreneurs to establish and keep books. There were even efforts to start local newspapers. By the end of the first year or two, more activity had been generated in education and health—in fact in all areas—than had been generated in the more than twenty years of American administration. But the results of that year or two of tumultuous activity were lamentable. The Peace Corps, a victim of its own rhetoric, set about to transform Micronesia; and the Micronesians waited expectantly. They wanted roads and electricity and jobs and money—all the things that the TT administration, for good reasons, had never been able to create. The Peace Corps' efforts in economic development did not work because they could not work. And the failure was costly: exasperated animosity between TT officials and the Peace Corps, high termination rates for disillusioned PCVs, and, most pernicious of all, the aborted expectations of the Micronesians.

The failure of the Peace Corps to effect real improvement in the area of economic development (a judgement now freely held by all concerned) tends to mask the evidenced success of the Peace Corps in other areas, such as education, legal aid, and, to a lesser extent, public health. To be sure there were severe attending problems, but these latter programs worked reasonably well.

With the arrival of the Peace Corps in strength, there were suddenly more non-Micronesian teachers in the islands than ever before. The PCVs, together with the U.S. contract teachers already there, totaled nearly three hundred. Most all worked on the primary level. As the volunteers got to their field assignments, particularly on the outer islands, school enrollments rose dramatically and unexpectedly. The Micronesians saw the opportunity for their youngsters to learn English from native speakers, and most jumped at the chance. Not since the enforced attendance of "Japanese times" had there been so many school-age children actually in the classrooms.

The sudden increase in pupils, however, brought some unanticipated problems. One was in the area of logistics and supply. Outer island teachers needed food and basic essentials including mail delivery, for which boats had to be purchased or built, supply officers had to be designated or hired, and schedules had to be devised and followed. Professional supervision and support was another problem area. There were simply not enough supervisors to backstop the efforts of the PCVs, in most cases young and inexperienced, who needed more support than did the professional contract teachers. The supply of textbooks and institutional materials was suddenly strained, and often new materials waited for months in district center warehouses before they could be distributed to the field teachers.

Similar things happened in the health area. The PCV health aides, of which there were eighty to begin with, were stationed in the outer islands and the district centers. They were in no sense medical practitioners. Mostly, they were liberal arts graduates trained to help Micronesian health aides implement preventive public health measures. Specifically, they were trained to take a health census and to assist with the administering of tuberculin tests. But their presence represented that of trained foreigners who had greater medical skills than those possessed by the Micronesian health workers. Many were called upon to perform medical tasks: diagnose disease, prescribe medicines and treatments, cauterize wounds, and even deliver babies. Aside from administering some first aid, they could do none of these. But on the outer islands they frequently did help diagnose by calling the district center on their two-way radios and describing symptoms to the medical doctors there. Cases of appendicitis were diagnosed over the radio merely because there was a PCV on a remote island with communications. Particularly in the case of children, there was little choice once the diagnosis was made but to send a plane to evacuate the patient. As incidents like this increased, tremendous bills were run up in med-evacs, much to the embarrassment of Trust Territory Officials with short emergency budgets.

The fourteen volunteer lawyers in the first groups were perhaps the most visible of all. Most of them had more than one assignment; they worked variously for the District Legislatures, the land offices, municipal government officials, the Congress of Micronesia, and the public defenders' offices. Never before had there been so many lawyers in the islands. In some districts they found that Micronesians were being represented in the public defenders' offices by civil service public safety officers, who were preparing cases because no one else even vaguely familiar with legal terms was available. As the PCV lawyers moved in, many cases were held up because they wanted to prepare them properly, thus creating a backlog that upset numerous court schedules. Some PCV lawyers helped draft legislation on both the national and district levels. This entailed, at times, actually suggesting what legislation might be appropriate. Untrained Micronesian legislators relied heavily on the PCV lawyers' advice and legal skills.[10] In a short time, the volunteer lawyers found themselves in positions of responsibility and influence far exceeding what their age and experience would prescribe.

A singular situation with PCV lawyers arose in 1967 when Judge Robert Clifton, of the California Superior Court, and his wife arrived as volunteers. Because Judge Clifton was a retired judge of long years' experience, TT people and Micronesians alike wanted to use his abilities on the bench. (Judge Clifton himself suggested that he would be contented as a farm worker, but finally said he would be willing to serve in whatever capacity was requested.) In due course he was appointed to the Supreme Court of Micronesia. Oddly enough, it was later determined that in such a position he was ultimately responsible to the U.S. Secretary of the Interior who in fact had a higher government rank than did the Director of the Peace Corps.

The results of all these activities are largely matters of opinion and speculation. No quantitative studies were ever made at the time, and none have been made since. There is no way of telling, for example, how much English reading scores were boosted among pupils because of the presence of PCV teachers. Nor is it known by how much the incidence of certain diseases was reduced, and so on. Nevertheless, there was an impact. It was something that could be felt more than measured. The volunteers helped promote a political and social awareness that had not been present before. The Peace Corps cannot take all the credit for this, but they can take some, and incidents can be found as examples of their contribution. A PCV couple living on Kili Island in the Marshalls—the place where Bikini refugees were placed at the time of the thermonuclear testing of the 1950s—wrote an appeal to the United Nations in the name of the people to help get them returned to their home island. This rather bold effort, which some considered improper, set an example of intelligent and direct confrontation for many Micronesians. Quite a number of PCVs wrote to their Congressmen in the United States complaining about, or merely describing, conditions in the islands. This encouraged a certain awareness of Micronesia among the members of the Congress which was, and has been, healthy. In some instances members of the TT administration were outraged by PCV complaints and reports; nevertheless, as citizens in a United States trusteeship, this was their right—perhaps even their duty—as citizens.

Some Trust Territory people accused PCVs of politically manipulating Micronesians in ways that were antithetical to "U.S. interests" in the area. This naturally came about because volunteers reacted not to geopolitical realities and concerns (which, of course, the administration had to) but rather to black and white moral issues, which were more obvious to their minds and which in fact were the basis of their motivation for coming to the islands in the first place. It was an exhilarating role for them as reformers, and, again, an operational instance of the distinction between Peace Corps Volunteers and government employees. After the establishment in 1968 of the Congress of Micronesia's Future Political Status Committee, discussion about political options became rampant throughout the Territory. The volunteers' discussions were unfettered by official hypotheses and represented the widest possible range of political alternatives. Most PCVs felt that independence was the only way Micronesians (or any supposedly national group) should go, and many said so. There was no "Hatch Act" that applied to volunteers. The Peace Corps staff always instructed PCVs to "stay out of politics." In other countries it was quite clear what staying out of politics meant, but in Micronesia the line was finer and often broken. It was not unusual for Micronesian chiefs and elected magistrates to ask help from PCVs in writing letters to government officials. Such correspondence was sometimes informational, but there were also complaints and grievances. The volunteers never saw such activity as antithetical to their roles. An American official from the State Department's UN Liaison Office even reported once that after the arrival of the volunteers in the Trust Territory there was "an increased quantity and improved quality of petitions from Micronesians."[11]

The large numbers of volunteers in Micronesia opened the United States to outside criticism, seldom from Micronesians themselves, that they were neo-colonialists. But, more substantively, their availability in large numbers made it easy for TT officials, and even some of the Micronesian leaders, to request volunteers for many positions that should have been filled by locals. Some departments requested PCVs because they were cheaper (the Peace Corps paid most of their expenses), and also because they did not require the training and continuous supervision that a Micronesian in a newly-localized position might need. The Peace Corps staff, while keenly aware of this trend, did little to stop it. And here was an example of the Peace Corps substituting action for thought: It is always easier to do than to teach another how to do. This approach to programming, which the Peace Corps too often embraced, was convenient and expedient but not very developmental. It had the effect of depriving many Micronesians of jobs that they should have held. It is curious, but those most embittered by this development were the volunteers themselves, particularly those in the district centers where they could witness the phenomenon most clearly. They described the inconsistencies and paradoxes of this approach eloquently and frequently. "We're nothing more than 'cheap labor' for the TT," one PCV said before leaving disillusioned. Such utterances were common and typical. An example of how widespread and serious this feeling became can be noted in the case of Palau, where Peace Corps operations there closed down altogether in 1969. The Peace Corps District Director, after thoroughly discussing the matter with those concerned, reported that "there is no further need for volunteers. The Palauans have decided that they can handle things for themselves."[1] The truth was that the Peace Corps Director in Palau, sick of providing volunteers as cheap labor for the TT, made that decision in behalf of the Palauans: he refused to oversee the continuance of doing things for the Palauans that they were capable of doing for themselves. It was the beginning of wisdom.

But the Palau example did not inspire such actions in other districts. The Peace Corps continued to send volunteers elsewhere in the Territory although their numbers steadily decreased. In 1971, the Palau program was quietly reinstituted and another district director eventually appointed. At about this time, either through insight or weariness, the Peace Corps decided to assume the role of providing manpower for the Trust Territory; the original flamboyant spirit decayed or matured. In any event the PCVs gradually became, in effect, "junior TT people" and thereby sacrificed some credibility among Micronesians. To be sure, the volunteers continued, and still continue, to serve very useful purposes, and they are appreciated by Micronesians and TT officials alike. But their function changed after 1971, and the merits of their new posture will have to be assessed differently.

Let us return now to our earlier question of the Peace Corps' contribution during, roughly, their first five years in Micronesia. What has it been? Clearly those volunteers who worked to provide infrastructure and promote economic development largely failed as a group. The cooperatives they helped start, the brick-and-mortar projects they helped design, the businessmen's books they kept in order; these achievements more often than not faded after they left. But history will no doubt reveal that such Peace Corps ventures were minor contributions anyway. The lasting ones will probably be revealed in education; here were the things that PCVs did well—teaching, exploring, and promoting new awarenesses in young people. The effects of these efforts are yet to be seen. Today they are only glimmers, as expressed perhaps in a comment made recently by a freshly arrived Micronesian student to the United States: "Ah, yes, the PCVs, I had one once as a teacher. It was she who first taught me that science is real, and encouraged me to come to the university."

NOTES

Peace Corps material relating to operations in Micronesia was taken from official files at Peace Corps Headquarters, Washington, D.C., office of the General Counsel.

1. As of this writing there are about 170 Peace Corps volunteers in Micronesia.

2. U.S. House of Representatives. Department of the Interior *Appropriations Act*, 1954.

3. Letter from Representative Otto Passman to R. Sargent Shriver, March 8, 1962, *Peace Corps Files* (Washington, D.C.).

4. The Act authorized the OEO Director to recruit, select, train, and "in cooperation with other federal, state and local agencies involved, assign volunteers to work in meeting the health, education, welfare, or related needs of Indians living on reservations, migratory workers and their families, residents of the District of Columbia, Puerto Rico, Guam, American Samoa, the Virgin Islands, or the Trust Territory of the Pacific Islands." *Economic Opportunity Act of 1964*, Section 603 (a) (2), as amended. U.S. House of Representatives (Washington, D.C.).

5. The U.S. Attorney General had made procedures in such cases quite clear: "Even where two acts are not, in express terms, repugnant, yet, if the latter act covers the whole subject of the first, and embraces new provisions, plainly showing that it was intended as a substitute for the first act, it will operate as a repeal of that act." U.S. Attorney General, Opinion 28, 70, 74 (1909).

6. In late 1968, however, the OEO did begin Community Action Programs in each Micronesian district.

7. Far East Regional Director to Peace Corps Congressional Liaison, Peace Corps Memorandum, May 22, 1967.

8. Warren Wiggins, "The Decision-Making Process in the Peace Corps" (Paper delivered at the State Department, March 4, 1963).

9. An official agency historian, Robert G. Carey, describes this peculiar status very well in his book, *The Peace Corps* (New York: Praeger, 1970), p. 68: "The PCV is not an employee of the US government. He has volunteered his services [and] travels on [a private passport and visa] and is subject to the laws of the country in which he serves. He has fewer priviledges [and] more freedom than. . . other federal employees. He lives and works closely with his hosts, he can criticize US policies, and he can travel with few restrictions."

10. Since the High Commissioner had the absolute veto power, there was never a real danger of any US policies being indirectly undermined by Peace Corps Volunteers.

11. Memorandum of a conversation. CDO with UN Liaison Officer at State Department; Country Desk Officer/Micronesia to Acting Peace Corps Director, March 6, 1968. *Peace Corps Files* (Washington, D.C.).

12. Peace Corps Memorandum. Palau District Director to PC/Micronesia Director, September, 1969.

BIBLIOGRAPHY

Various *Briefing Papers, 1966-1973,* Peace Corps/Micronesia, NANEAP Regional Officer, Washington, D.C.

Peace Corps Act, U.S. House of Representatives, 1962.

Trust Territory Annual Reports, 1960-1973, Department of the Interior, Washington, D.C.

MONIKA KEHOE

4

Language and Politics in Guam and Micronesia

Although few mainlanders, either American, Australian, or Asian, know or care much about Guam or Micronesia, those working and living in the West or Southwest Pacific are aware of the social, economic, and political disquiet in the area as Micronesia (the U.S. Trust Territory of the Pacific) attempts to work out its future political status. Many Micronesians express sharp dissatisfaction with the United states administration, accusing it of cultural imperialism. They point to Guam, with its high crime rate, its polluted beaches, its clogged roads, and its arsenal of munitions, as an example of what is in store for their own islands under continued American influence. On the other hand, Guam, with all its defects, exhibits a strong pro-American sentiment in spite of a small "Brown Power" movement, which persist as an undercurrent flowing against the overwelming tide of patriotism and intercultural affability. The nearby Marianas, which are tied culturally to Guam and destined, according to "reliable sources," to house the redeployment of military forces from forward positions in Asia, reflect the same cooperative spirit; they comprise the only part of Micronesia opting for United States Commonwealth status. In return, the U.S. government, more specifically the Department of Defense, has a strategic in terest in all the islands and wants to retain them as a safeguard against possible deter ioration in relations with what has been known as the Far East but has now become the Near West.

How much of the cooperative attitude on Guam, itself, can be attributed to the seduction of the prevailing American way of life and how much is the result of the Organic Act of 1950, which conferred citizenship on all Guamanians, is a point of considerable socio-political interest. However, the history of colonialism suggests that, whatever the reason for any developing region's choice of a national model or affiliation, one of the most important vehicles for persuasion is language. Without a common tongue, communication of ideology is impossible All the imperial powers have been intent on promoting their national languages in the areas under their jurisdiction, recognizing it as a uniquely unifying force in social and political life.[1] Through learning the language of the ruling country, the subject population first becomes bilingual and bicultural; then, through the prestige of the dominant group, later generations gradually are absorbed by or assimilated into the colonizing state. Although somewhat over-simplified and not always successful, this has been the pattern generally followed by both European and Asian colonial efforts.

In the case of Micronesia, the world's last mandated region, the United States as trustee has been much less concerned about the political effect of language than about its purely instrumental usefulness for administrative purposes. English is, and has been since 1945, the official language and the language of instruction beyond the primary level in the schools. The administering authority had no choice in the matter. A language of wider communication was, and is, obviously essential to the orderly governing of more than 2,000 islands spread out over a multilingual/ multicultural area as big as the U.S. mainland. Such a widely dispersed population, with extremely poor physical means of inter-island communication and with nine major vernaculars, is bound to present a serious administrative problem in any event.[2] None of the local spoken languages, which still lack a standardized written form, could possibly do the job, even if enough Americans could have been found who were willing to learn any one of them.

In the following pages, we shall look at some aspects of the language problem on Guam and in Micronesia and the importance of the *lingua franca,* English, in shaping the political future of these islands in the Western Pacific.

LANGUAGE AND DIALECT ON GUAM

Chamorro, the language of the original inhabitants of Guam and the neighboring Marianas, is, like the vernaculars of Micronesia, a spoken tongue. Few attempts to develop a written form were made before the nineteenth century except those undertaken by missionaries who used the Roman alphabet for Bible translation.[3] To date there is no literature in the sense of belles-lettres in Chamorro. Without a standard written form, or a formal literature to enshrine it, the language has been subject to such rapid change that relatively little of what might be styled "pure" Chamorro remains in the vocabulary. Remnants of its non-European origins are, nevertheless, retained in its structure. The prevailing influence on modern Chamorro is, of course, Spanish—a result of the more than 200 years (1668-1898) of domination by that country. Since America annexed Guam at the end of the nineteenth century, numerous English "loan" words have crept in and even a few Japanese terms were added during that nation's brief occupation of the island from 1941 to 1944. But characteristic syntactical patterns, such as a basic preference for the passive voice, lack a pronoun gender, and peculiarities of number and tense formation, mark the Pacific cultural imprint.

Although English has been the official language since the turn of the century, Guamanians continued to speak Chamorro as a mother tongue until a few years ago when the younger parents who were themselves postwar babies, seem to have decided that they would rear their children in what they saw as the language of the future—English. However, their determination to give their children a new mother tongue, although well-motivated, caused their offspring to speak a kind of Guamanian-English dialect which "stateside" elementary school teachers refer to as "broken English." Many of the parents of this era, originally mother tongue speakers of Chamorro themselves, had a poor command of spoken English. They inevitably passed this on to their children. Chamorro, which had experienced a sharp revival after its suppression under the Japanese, was their vernacular. They had learned English in school as a *second,* or even as a *foreign,* language; modern applied linguistics, and second-language methodology had not yet penetrated the American Western Pacific outposts. In spite of the fact that they spoke English haltingly and recognized their own deficiencies in the language, they were determined that their children should not suffer the same academic disadvantages they did when they had their own schooling in English, a language they seldom heard outside the classroom. These parents spoke to their pre-schoolers in the only English they knew—Guamanian English: American words appliquéd on Chamorro syntax. From this initiation, the youngsters have created their own language called Guamanian Dialect English (GDE), a melange of elements from both English and Chamorro.

In this context, the difference between a second dialect and a second language is a socially and politically significant one. Most Guamanian children of Chamorro parentage entering primary school in the seventies have GDE as their first language.[4] Even though Chamorro was the mother tongue of their parents (who had English as a second language), the children have been exposed constantly to English at home via television and radio. They identify more with the characters in "The Electric Company"[5] than with any heroic figures in their own folk lore. They think American. The adolescents, having had more time to pick up Chamorro, use it in speaking to each other as their private, teen-age language rather than as a means of cultural identification. Their values and desires—for jeans, beauty contest laurels, motor bikes, and plug-in guitars—are shaped as much by Hollywood and network advertising as those of any youngster in Chicago or Des Moines. They are Westernized. If they aspire to go to college, their first choice is a mainland U.S. campus, their second Hawaii, their last Guam. Many of them join the military services, and ROTC flourishes in the high schools. Their total behavior and their choice of life style reveal the much greater influence of their American-English language environment than that of their Chamorro heritage. They are clearly detribalized, and their "Western" perception of reality as well as their unconscious acceptance of American social and political institutions is facilitated by their cross-cultural English language school and media experience.

LANGUAGE AND EDUCATION IN MICRONESIA

Meanwhile Micronesia—its people wards, not citizens, of the United States— has much shorter exposure of only three decades to English (Guam has more than seven years exposure) as an official language. It has languished with a less developed public education system, fewer imported English-speaking teachers, and, of necessity, more schooling in the vernacular. The most recent UN Mission observed:

> The standard of spoken and written English, especially in the elementary schools, is still low and, in fact, most of the instruction is carried out in the vernacular, even beyond the fourth grade where, in theory, English should be the medium of instruction.[6]

No wonder, then, that even now so few Micronesians are able to complete college or survive the necessary training to prepare them for leadership roles in their own society. Their previous political fortune, or misfortune, as prey to a succession of foreign powers has given them a mottled language history and has shaped the political conservatism of the older segment of the population that continues to look to its traditional local chieftains as leaders.

In contrast to Guam, with its single language background, Micronesia speaks in many tongues and needs, even more, one language to tie it together. Carl Heine, one of Micronesia's most able commentators on the territory's political problems, has this to say:

> The fact that the English language is the only national vehicle of political unity in Micronesia, because it is used by the leaders, is little understood nor fully appreciated. It is disturbing that the language that is responsible for unifying the people of Micronesia is spoken by but a small proportion of the population.[7]

In the period of relative independence for Micronesia which lasted until the mid-seventeenth century,[8] education in the islands was an informal tribal transmission of essential learning from one generation to the next. In addition to this "natural" native tutelage, religious instruction was begun by missionaries under both the Spanish (1668-1898) and German (1899-1914) regimes. Their contribution included the teaching of reading and writing in the Roman alphabet and the production of a written form for several of the vernaculars so that the Bible might be translated into them. These efforts were directed more toward ecclesiastical than pedagogical or political goals.

Not until the Japanese occupation (1941-1944) was a public school system with a specific social/political goal widely introduced. The aim of this system was to provide a supply of general laborers and domestic servants—imperial colonial subjects—"who understood the Japanese language."[9] In spite of the fact that over half the school day was devoted to learning Japanese, only a few Micronesians acquired literacy in Japanese.[10] The foreign mission schools that were allowed to continue during this period were less intent in their Japanization program, so that a vestige of European language influence endured more or less underground.[11]

The advent of the Americans in 1945 saw the introduction of English-as-a-second-language in the third or fourth year of primary school. By 1948, an observer noted that English was already replacing Japanese as the *lingua franca* of the islands.[12] From 1945 to 1951, under the American naval administration, both Guam and Micronesia were closed to non-military personnel, so that 1949 school policy "preferred" local teachers who had learned English in mission schools. Nevertheless district teacher-training schools, "to educate natives in basic English," were staffed by Americans.[13] Even with the introduction of more "statesiders" as teachers after 1961 (including more than 500 Peace Corps volunteers in the late 1960s), and the use of English as the language of instruction in all subjects, Trust Territory students still suffered major disadvantages in their attempts to acquire a language of wider communication. Their isolation from the mainstream of American life (television has not yet been brought to the Trust Territory) inhibited the cross-cultural experience so necessary for functional bilingualism.[14] The fact that they seldom heard English outside the classroom made it, for them, a "foreign" rather than a second language. Lack of any scholarship tradition, or the literature that accompanies it, interfered with their appreciation and respect for learning in general and the literacy required to attain it.

The resulting pattern of academic failure has done little to contribute to better relations between "statesiders" and the indigenous population. It has served, in some cases, to lower the Micronesians' self-appraisal to the point where they react with: "Why do the Americans hate us so?" The longer Micronesians survive in the school system, the greater their resentment seems to be. As has been the case in emerging societies everywhere, the most articulate Trust Territory group, the university students, are the most hostile critics of administrative policy. During the last (1973) visit of the UN Trusteeship Council mission to the University of Guam, the Micronesian students had no hesitation in voicing their antagonisms to the United States.

LANGUAGE PLANNING

The posture described has been, to a great extent, the result of Washington officialdom's neglect. It may be only fair to add that this neglect has not been of Micronesia itself—although that too has been argued[15]—but of the opportunity for promoting the language of wider communication as a vehicle for interisland (intercultural) understanding and for political unification, or what sociolinguistics calls "language engineering." There is certainly some historical irony in the fact that the United States in the World War I period, before it had any administrative responsibility for these islands, worried so much about the communication threat to them, particularly to Yap where the cables to China, Southwest Asia, and Australia crossed.[16] More recently, as trustee, it has chosen to disregard the much greater political importance of stressing English as the means for island intercommunication and the unification of the territory's polyglot peoples. But such has been the case. Government concern with overall language planning has been notably absent since the United States took over jurisdiction of these Pacific Islands. Instead, it has followed the "cultivation approach," in which language problems are handled in a somewhat casual fashion by various private and public agencies without any coordinating body or plan.[17] The need for English has often been slighted in favor of the sentimental function of the vernacular. The practice of minimum disturbance seems to have prevailed. "Till recently, the concept of Micronesia as a *zoo* or *museum* flourished. . . ."[18] Evidently the United States has not wanted to seem repressive and has regretted the colonial pattern it followed in the Philippines; or perhaps it wishes to reverse the autocratic manner of the Japanese. Whatever the reason, the American administration has avoided establishing the necessary overall English-second-language policy for the islands.

This probably has been a sin of omission rather than of commission, and the responsibility for the negligence should be laid on Washington's doorstep rather than on the local administration's. There has always been too much to do with the limited budget allowed by an unconcerned Congress, which is generally indifferent to all unfranchised minority groups and especially to this small, distant, and powerless Pacific miscellany.

For lack of funds, salient components of improved communication in Micronesia have been disregarded. Thus, the United States has failed to be future-oriented politically in the very field in which it is most advanced technologically. It has failed to appreciate the enormous potential of English, with its supra-ethnic character, to ease internal communication and thus create unity and stability in the area. It would have been relatively simple. There is no Micronesian identity to be threatened.

> Micronesia is a pluralistic society. There is no Micronesian language and, thus no person can be called a Micronesian by virtue of the language he speaks. Collectively and culturally, there is a Micronesian person whose identity may be either Yapese or Ponapean. But there is no Micronesian identity. If Micronesia is politically established as a country, there may emerge a new identity.[19]

In these island speech communities that have no alphabet of their own, there is no resistance to the Roman alphabet. It is associated with the Bible, the literature they know best.

Young Micronesians want to learn English. They have no antagonism to it. For them, it is the language of technology, not the language of a single culture. They are aware that many Filipinos speak it as a mother tongue, as do Fijians and many other South Pacific islanders. It has great prestige. It is the language of government and of education. In this Christian region, it is also the language of religion. The Micronesian who has been educated recognizes, with Carl Heine, that

> Cultural and linguistic loyalties will present a problem in any future government. However, in view of the heterogeneity of culture and language, the future government of Micronesia will have to confine it-

self to the use of the English language as the official and common medium of communication throughout Micronesia.[20]

In view of the important social and political effect of English usage and the
aspirations of most young Micronesians to learn the language, it is regrettable that
such little attention has been given to such specific and important matters as the
development of basic English-second-language (ESL) texts for the schools[21] and
the recruitment of teachers with special training in Applied Linguistics or cross-
cultural experience in language teaching. Until recently, almost no attempt has
been made to prepare local teachers in the new methodology of second-language-
learning.[22] To begin with, no survey of the status of English in the islands has
ever been undertaken, so that there is no real data on which to build an ESL
program or policy.

In spite of numerous recommendations made by various researchers, conferences, and teams that came to study language policy, little has been done to
implement them. As long ago as 1961, the distinguished linguist Charles F. Hockett,
in his report to the Director of Education in Micronesia, made specific reference to
the need for coordinated ESL program supervision. He pointed out that the Department of Education should have a "Language Specialist" who visits the various districts; and that this person should be supplemented by language specialists for
each district. Under "Administrative Considerations," Dr. Hockett had this comment: "The ultimate return [on money spent] is not monetary or economic, but
friendship and good will, of inestimable importance in the world political scene."[23]
Central planning, he concludes, "ought to be possible for all of American Micronesia"
Such advice has, unfortunately, gone unheeded.

The Stanford Research Institute's Project Report, "Planning for Education and
Manpower in Micronesia," dated December 1967, sets forth in its conclusions a
proposal that, if put into effect, would have undoubtedly lowered the drop-out
rate that has been such a cause of disaffection for Micronesian college students.
The Stanford Report advises:

> A Territorywide college preparatory school should be established
> that will offer a one-year program stressing English language and
> study skills. A principal benefit of the school will be to increase the
> probability that Micronesian scholarship holders planning to study
> abroad will succeed.[25]

The Trust Territory Report to the Secretary of the Interior for 1972 refers to
the "several hundred" Peace Corps volunteers working as English teachers in
the islands. Of their achievements, it says: "The relative success of the English
Language (TESL) program, linchpin of Micronesian unity, is the most striking
example."[26] The Territory administration clearly expressed here its own awareness of the political importance of language but, without the necessary funding
from Washington, could do little to follow the recommendations made by the
various outside observers.

The doctoral dissertations on the subject of education in Micronesia, with no need to be impressive in reporting "achievements," are much more critical.[27] In referring to the TESL program on Ponape, a 1972 study condemns it: "This pedagogical process reinforces the indigenous imitative, rote style of learning."[28] The writer also faults the lack of cross-cultural preparation of teachers and the resulting effects on the students who muddle along with an "inadequate conceptual apparatus to accompany [their] new language skills."[29] For example, he mentions that Ponapeans see four colors in the rainbow while Americans see six, and that the concept of a *circle* for Ponapeans includes a sphere and a cylinder[30] while for Americans it is a flat continuous line. If these concrete matters offer such potential for misunderstanding, imagine the problems presented by more abstract concepts—like *equality, democracy,* and *freedom*—involved in the political process.

Unfortunately, the opportunity to use this uniquely powerful instrument of language to unify the diverse population of Micronesia has almost passed. Attitudes toward America have taken shape, and those that are already antagonistic will be difficult to change.[31] Although language is not specifically mentioned, the *Pacific Daily News* editorial for July 7, 1974, "Micronesian Unity— A Fragile Concept," sums up the present situation fairly well. Commenting on the existing disunity, it concludes:

> Things may have been done differently, if a long time ago, say ten years ago, the U.S. had decided that the islands would someday be independent, or a commonwealth tied to the U.S. and then worked in that direction with a strong program, including political education and a program of pulling the islands closer together through a strong communication and transportation system. This wasn't done, however. Instead, we decided to let them pretty much on their own, politically and, unfortunately, it may not work out. Moreover there doesn't seem to be any real way of going back, either. The sad part of all this seems to stem from a lack of a strong U.S. policy in the Pacific regarding the islands, a policy that would have been on-going and continuous. The U.S., because of this lack of a Pacific policy, will come in for criticism in the years ahead, at the way they botched up the Micronesians. This lack of policy was, in large part, created by differences of opinion between the Department of Defense, State, and Interior. We can sit back and blame the Micronesians for their split ups and lack of unity, but the United States government should have had the foresight to see what was going to happen. We didn't have that vision and we're certain that we'll come under increasing criticism for many years to come.

Washington is obviously as remote from Micronesia as London is from the West Indies, and the U.S. Congress evidently has as little concern for its wards as the British Parliament had for its overseas territories in the Caribbean before they began to clamor for their independence. Yet English could have been—and perhaps can still be—the means for unifying all of Micronesia into a single economic and social unit, if not a political one, as affirmatively inclined toward the United States as Guam is now.[32]

NOTES

1. Joshua A. Fishman et al., *Language Problems of Developing Nations* (New York, 1968), pp. 3-13.

2. Possibly the only comparable antecedent has been the British experience in the Caribbean.

3. Dr. Donald Topping of the University of Hawaii has recently published a grammar of Chamorro and has made important contributions toward regularizing its orthography. Attempts are also currently in progress to produce "readers" for use in the bilingual programs on Guam and Rota.

4. Unpublished report of the kindergarten survey made by the present writer under a grant from the Director of Research, University of Guam, Agana, 1972. Further research would likely establish that GDE has been the first language of many of the children born to Chamorro parents since 1965.

5. A very popular children's TV program aired daily by the Public Broadcasting System.

6. *Report of the U.N. Visiting Mission to the Trust Territory of the Pacific Islands, 1973*, p. 106.

7. Carl Heine, *Micronesia at the Crossroads* (Hawaii, 1974), pp. 110-111.

8. The Spanish gave little attention to the instruction of the autochthonous population in the first century of European hegemony.

9. J. L. Fisher, "The Japanese Schools for the Natives of Truk, Caroline Islands," *Human Organization* 20 (1961), p. 84.

10. Ibid.

11. Donald F. Smith, "Education of the Micronesian with Emphasis on the Historical Development" (Ph.D. dissertation, The American University, 1969), p. 13⅜

12. Elizabeth Converse, "U.S. as Trustee," *Far Eastern Survey* 18 (1948), 282.

13. Smith, op. cit., p. 40.

14. The principal contact that the outer islands (mainly atolls) have with "civilization" is the visit of the Trust Territory government field trip and supply ship on an irregular schedule three or four times a year. Other than this, they have a two-way radio that functions unpredictably at best.

15. In describing the Micronesians' reaction to the pace of American development programs, Heine remarks: "They came to realize that the United States policy of 'gradualism' was, in reality, a policy of neglect." Heine, op. cit., p. 56.

16. Roy W. Curry, *Woodrow Wilson and Far Eastern Policy, 1913-1921* (New York 1957), p. 258. Earl S. Pomeroy, in *Pacific Outpost: American Strategy in Guam and Micronesia* (Stanford, 1951), p. 7, also quotes Governor E. J. Born of Guam who wrote in 1911: "The object of taking Guam from Spain was primarily to secure landing for the trans-Pacific cable then in contemplation."

17. Joan Rubin and B. H. Jernudd, *Can Language Be Planned?* (Hawaii, 1971), p. xiv.

18. Heine, op. cit., p. 56.

19. Ibid., p. 49.

20. Ibid., p. 70.

21. The various districts have had to adapt materials, such as those designed in New Zealand (by Tate) for Polynesian speakers of British English or the Fries American English Series designed for Puerto Ricans.

22. *Pacific Daily News* of July 3, 1974, announced that a grant of $39,313 had been made available to the Trust Territory Department of Education to train Micronesian bilingual teachers. The *Pacific Daily News* of July 26, 1974, headline, "TT Language Grants Total $460,723," presents a classic example of "too late" if not "too little."

23. Charles F. Hockett, "Recommendations on Language Policy in the Trust Territory of the Pacific Islands and in the Territory of Guam" (unpublished, April 16-17, 1961), p. 7.

24. Ibid., p. 8.

25. "Planning for Education and Manpower in Micronesia" (Stanford Research Institute, SRI Project 6579), Conclusion # 16, p. 4.

26. Trust Territory of the Pacific Islands, *Report to the Secretary of the Interior* (Saipan, 1972), p. 36. TESL is the acronym for "Teaching English as a second language."

27. Smith, op. cit.; Nat Joseph Collelta, "American Schools for the Natives of Ponape" (Ph.D. dissertation, Michigan State University, 1972).

28. Collelta, op. cit., p. 118.

29. Ibid., p. 119.

30. Ibid.

31. It may be worth noting that the Mariana-Guam desire for closer affiliation with the United States represents that area in which the English language environment is strongest.

32. It may also be worth noting, as I have previously indicated, that:

> If the Micronesians are to enjoy communication with their fellow islanders in Oceania and the extended facilities for information and entertainment afforded by the mass media, they will need to understand the language of its dissemination. By all counts, that will continue for some time to be English.

See my article, "The English Language Imperative for Guam and Micronesia," *KIVUNG, The Journal of the Australasian Linguistic Society* (Boroko, PNG: University of Papua New Guinea, December 1972).

5

The Marshall Islands

In early February 1942, just two months after Pearl Harbor, American forces made the first offensive strike of the war against the Japanese. Carrier planes struck Japanese bases in the Marshall Islands, 2,000 miles south-west of Hawaii. The fighters attacked airfields at Milli, Kwajalein, Maloelap, and Wotje atolls and the Japanese Navy and seaplane base at Jaluit atoll and then retreated to the carriers.[1] The Marshall Islands would not see American bombers again until 22 months later, when they returned on a daily basis.

In late 1941, 26-year-old Ukukot Libokmeto sailed from his home atoll of Ebon to Jaluit atoll, about 75 miles to the north, to sell a boat and replenish supplies for sale at his general store. Unknown to Ukukot, the war was approaching, and the Japanese at Jaluit refused to let him return to Ebon; they forced him to work on the military installations at Jabor, Jaluit. On the morning of February 2, 1942, Ukukot, his wife, and son awoke to the sound of attacking airplanes. American pilots, unaided by intelligence reports and probably ignorant of the presence of Marshallese at Jabor, apparently were unable to distinguish military targets from other buildings. Ukukot Libokmeto was killed by an American bomb dropped on the Marshallese housing area at the northern end of Jabor Island.

From an American point of view, the February 2 incident is of minor significance in the history of World War II. For the Marshallese, however, it marked the beginning of thirty years of contact with the American military. The pattern begun in 1942 would continue; in succeeding years the Marshallese again would find themselves on the receiving end of military actions that were designed for the benefit of someone else, and that generally disregarded their wishes, aspirations, and rights.

BIKINI

The postwar world well knows the everyday meaning of the word "bikini"; but few people know the origins of the word and the history behind it. Bikini is an atoll in the northern Marshall Islands, consisting of 23 islands surrounding a 200-square-mile lagoon. A few of the islands have been inhabited for hundreds of years by a small group of Marshallese. In January 1946, the Pentagon announced that the United States had selected Bikini as the site for a series of atomic tests. A test site had to be distant from heavily populated areas, 500 miles from all air and sea routes, and uninhabited or containing only a few people who could be re-located.[2] The "few people" in this instance were the people of Bikini. They may have been "few" from the United States point of view, but from their own point of view they were *all* the people, not just a few. The Pentagon decision made no provision for the feelings, aspirations, or wishes of the few, and it was unthinkable that so few could defy the wishes of so many. The Bikinians, understanding lit-tle, faced by the awesome might of the United States, and having no other re-course, relented. Their *iroij* (chief) Juda told the United States that they could use Bikini if it would result in kindness and benefit to all mankind.

In March 1946, the Navy moved the 199 Bikini people to uninhabited Rongerik atoll, also in the northern Marshalls. Then the trouble began. Bikinians had long associated Rongerik with Libokra, an evil spirit who dealt in poisons. Many of the fish on Rongerik were in fact poisonous, and people became sick from eat-ing them. A report by a medical officer in July 1947 reported widespread mal-nutrition at Rongerik. A disastrous fire destroyed 30 percent of the coconut trees. The military investigated the situation, but nothing was done.

Fishing was difficult because the coconuts at Rongerik were of such poor quality that the Bikinians could not produce the sennit needed for lash-ing and rigging their outrigger canoes. On January 31, 1948, the only food on the island was one bag of flour, which was mixed with a little water and doled out to 167 people. In response to urgent messages, a doctor and emergency sup-plies were flown to Rongerik. The doctor examined the Bikinians and pronounced their condition to be that of a starving people.[3] At Bikini, 150 miles away, the military consumed vast quantities of steak and ice cream while serving at their testing ground hardship posts.

No one died from malnutrition at Rongerik, but it was clear that the Bikini people could not survive there much longer. The community was moved to the Navy base at Kwajalein, where they lived in tents for eight months, and then to Kili Island. Kili is a tiny speck of about 200 acres in the southern Marshalls. It is fringed by a reef; there is no lagoon; and heavy winds and tides isolate the island six months of every year. For a fishing people accustomed to a lagoon, Kili is a prison; the reef and surf isolate them and prevent access to the limited marine resources available beyond the reef. Serious food shortages occurred regu-larly before the implementation of a government food program in the 1970s. Then, and now, the Bikini people have an expression for Kili: *Kili enana*—"Kili is no good." As of 1976, the Bikinians have lived on their Kili prison, as they call it, for 28 years.

In 1946, when the Bikini people were first exiled from their home, the United States made no settlement with the people concerning Bikini. The military did not explain that the Bikinians had title to the atoll, and the Bikinians, even if they had such a concept in mind, were too intimidated to state it. They were told to move, and they moved.

In 1951, the government tried to settle the legal status of Bikini by trading some small islets at Jaluit, plus Kili, for Bikini. The military obtained the signature of a Marshallese chief, who claimed jurisdiction over the Bikinians, and of several lesser ranking landowners of the Bikini people. The Bikinians do not recognize the chief who signed the agreement, and in any case, the majority of the Bikini landowners refused to sign. As a legal matter, the 1951 agreement does not meet the requirements for transfer of an interest in land in the Marshall Islands because all those holding an interest in the land did not sign the agreement. In 1951, the United States was still trespassing, and testing, on Bikini atoll.

Although as recently as 1970 the Trust Territory government maintained that the 1951 agreement was valid and binding,[4] they clearly knew that it was not, for in 1956 they made another attempt to settle the legal rights to Bikini. Under pressure from Washington, the Trust Territory presented the Bikinians with a completed, non-negotiable document entitled "Agreement in Principle Regarding the Use of Bikini Atoll." The United States gave the Bikinians $325,000 and use rights to Kili, in return for use rights of an indefinite term to Bikini. About $25,000 of the money was taken to Kili in one-dollar bills; the remaining $300,000 was put into a trust fund. The enormous pile of dollar bills had the intended effect and the Bikinians signed the agreement. As for the trust fund, the principal had declined by $102,000 by 1972. The agreement included a clause stating that any future claims for the use or destruction of Bikini should be brought against the Bikini leaders who signed the agreement, and not against the United States or the Trust Territory.

By 1969, the Bikini people were ready to do something about their condition and the continued neglect by the United States. With the help of a young Peace Corps volunteer, they composed a letter to the High Commissioner of the Trust Territory:

> ... Kili is like a prison and unsuitable as a place for people to live.
> Our suffering on Kili is too much to endure any longer. ... On Bikini
> we were men responsible for our lives, but the United States Govern-
> ment chose to move us, taking the responsibility for our welfare in
> their hands. They have forced us to depend on their ships for our lives.
> We have been humiliated by being put in a place that forces us to beg
> for help. ... We trusted the Navy with our lives; are we to believe
> that the United States has turned away from that trust?[5]

The letter pointed out that the Bikinians never had lawyers to assist them in dealings with the United States; that the 1956 agreement was unfair and was signed ten years after the forced exile; and that portions of Bikini had been destroyed and other parts made radioactive. The letter asked for $100 million in damages for Bikini.

Ironically enough, it appears that the Bikinians had a much more accurate idea than the United States of the legal obligations under the "sacred trust" of the United Nations Trusteeship Agreement. Under the Trusteeship Agreement the United States is obligated to:

2. . . . Promote the economic advancement and self-sufficiency of the inhabitants, and to this end shall regulate the use of natural resources, encourage the development of fisheries, agriculture, and industries; protect the inhabitants against the loss of their lands and resources; and improve the means of transportation and communication; 3. Promote the social advancement of the inhabitants and to this end shall protect the rights and fundamental freedoms of all elements of the population. . . ."[6]

The High Commissioner never answered the authors of the 1969 letter. However, he apparently thought that the questions raised were serious enough to warrant an answer to his superiors in the Department of the Interior. His letter of May 7, 1970, asserted that the 1951 "agreement" was valid and then concluded that ". . . the government had the complete right to commit waste, make permanently unusable, alter and destroy the islands in the atoll, or portions thereof in the testing of nuclear weapons".[7]

Clearly the 1951 agreement is invalid, and even assuming its validity, it conveys no right to vaporize Bikini atoll. Furthermore, the 1956 agreement does not retroactively ratify the prior destruction or permit any destruction of Bikini at all. By 1970, Bikini had suffered 23 nuclear detonations, including detonation of several hydrogen bombs.[8] Although the yields of 16 of these tests are still classified, it is likely that Bikini has suffered under the explosive power of more than 100 million tons of TNT. In spite of this, the U.S. government, a trespasser on Bikini until after most of the tests, concluded that ". . . there is, in our opinion, no legal obligation to pay for said damages."[9] The Pentagon should reread Section Two of Article Six of the Trusteeship Agreement, where they made a solemn vow to "protect the inhabitants against the loss of their lands and resources."

In the late 1960s and early 1970s some events turned to favor the Bikinians. The government began to rehabilitate the atoll; it was cleaned of radioactive debris, coconut trees were planted on two islands; and forty concrete houses were constructed for the eventual return of the Bikinians to the atoll. These favorable signs should not obscure the basic facts of the thirty year "trusteeship" relationship between the people of Bikini and the United States military. The Bikinians have endured endless broken promises; three forced relocations; several occasions of malnutrition and near-starvation; unprecedented atomic destruction of their homeland and irradiation of their soil; deterioration of their social structure and loss of a sense of community; loss of many skills required for fishing on an atoll; isolation and rejection by the government; and the certain risk of living with the dangers of radioactivity should they return to Bikini. In return they have received a trust fund with a principal that has decreased in size and produces income of only ten dollars per Bikinian per year; some surplus USDA food; and an isolated and miserable island far from their home.

ENEWETAK

Enewetak atoll is a large, dry atoll in the northern Marshall Islands. Enewetak, like Bikini, had limited early contact with German, and later Japanese, copra boats and trading vessels.[10] In the early 1940s the Japanese fortified the atoll, and in February 1944, the Americans captured the island in a four-day fight. After the battle, the U.S. Navy established a huge advance base at Enewetak and fed and housed the Enewetakese on the smaller islands in the atoll.

In 1947, military strategists decided that Enewetak atoll was needed for atomic testing; Bikini alone was insufficient because it lacked established base facilities for logistical support and scientific instrumentation. On December 2, 1947, President Harry S. Truman approved the transfer of the Enewetakese to another atoll.[11] On December 3, the governor of the Marshalls flew to Enewetak to "propose" that the people move to Ujelang atoll. It would have been unthinkable for the Enewetakese to refuse the "proposal." The Japanese told the Enewetakese that the Japanese military was invincible, but the Americans overran the Japanese quickly and easily before Enewetakese eyes. The Enewetakese were awed by the American forces, and composed a ballad about them:

Why did the Americans come and shoot with rifles?
Oh why did the Americans come and machine gun, oh
No one is as powerful as America in all the world.
They fire guns
Are there any torpedoes stronger than the torpedoes of Americans
that destroy?[12]

They agreed to move and, three weeks later, the entire community of 147 people was located at Ujelang, where they professed to the Navy to be happy with an atoll that was much smaller in both land and lagoon size. The Enewetakese still live on Ujelang today, and in fact they have not ever been very happy about their exile. The two Enewetak chiefs told a government anthropologist:

We do not like Ujelang as well as our home atoll, Enewetak. It is not as good a place to live. . . . Ujelang does not have anywhere near the numbers of turtles, porpoises, and seabirds, as did Enewetak, our old home. However, there is nothing we can do about it. We are weak and powerless, so why complain? So we will just try to do our best here on this small atoll.[13]

The Enewetakese have perhaps suffered less from the military than the Bikinians, but such a state is hardly utopia. Enewetak atoll was wrested from its owners by military fiat and the people exiled, but they have not suffered several relocations or starvation. As with Bikini, the military attempted to legitimize the arrangement in 1956 by presenting the Enewetakese with $25,000 in one-dollar bills and a trust fund for $150,000 in return for their signatures on a document entitled "Agreement in Principle Regarding the Use of Enewetak Atoll." At the time, the people were not represented or advised by lawyers, their "trustee," or anyone else. The atoll itself has been ravaged by 42 known atomic blasts,[14] and is badly scarred by numerous small- to enormous-size craters. There are points on the atoll that are dangerously contaminated by radioactivity, plutonium, and berryllium. After the test-ban treaty stopped atmospheric nuclear tests, the atoll was used as a supersecret test facility for the dissemination of biological warfare agents by migratory seabirds; as a U-2 base; and as an impact point for missiles and satellites launched from California, from other Pacific islands, or from submarines.

In 1969, the Pentagon apparently decided that they would need Enewetak as an air base and test facility for many years to come. Following nine months or more of no food and no ships at Ujelang, the Ujelangese threatened to get on the first boat and sail back to Enewetak. Shortly thereafter the military presented the Enewetakese with an *ex gratia* payment of one million dollars. This money is now in a trust fund, and the interest from the fund provides a small income for the 400 or so Enewetakese. The money was given to forestall future protests and placate the angry islanders.

In April 1972, the United States government surprisingly announced that Enewetak would not be retained, after all, but would be returned to the Trust Territory government, as soon as another series of military tests at Enewetak were completed.[15] Legal services lawyers, representing the Enewetakese for the first time, soon learned that the tests involved large-scale attempts to duplicate the effects of atomic weapons with conventional explosives. The lawyers succeeded in enjoining further tests until an Environmental Impact Statement was prepared.[16] The Defense Nuclear Agency then decided that they did not really need to complete the tests after all. These events were landmarks for the Enewetakese, for they had demonstrated that the people were not as weak and helpless as they had assumed. They subsequently have taken an aggressive and active role in the planning for the clean-up and rehabilitation of their atoll scheduled to begin in the spring of 1975. The military, the Trust Territory government, and the Atomic Energy Commission (now the Energy Research and Development Administration) have now begrudgingly accepted the involvement of the Enewetakese in the planning for the future of the atoll. With some luck, decent and careful advisers, and wise leadership, the entire Enewetak community will be resettled on Enewetak by 1980. They will have new housing, with some chance for a viable economy based on subsistence activity, tourism, and scientific study at the marine laboratory that will continue to operate on the atoll. If so, it will show that partial repairs can be made to the cultural, physical, and psychological damage wrought by years of large scale and heavy-handed military presence in Micronesia. The people of Bikini, Kwajalein, and Rongelap atolls have not been so fortunate.

RONGELAP

The morning of March 1, 1954, was different from all other mornings for the 82 residents of Rongelap atoll in the northern Marshalls, for on that day the sun rose twice—once in the East once in the West. One hundred miles to the west of Rongelap, Joint Task Force Seven detonated "Bravo," America's second hydrogen device and the most powerful bomb yet tested (later estimated to equal 15 million tons of TNT).

Bravo consisted of 200 pounds of uranium-235, 200 pounds of lithium deuteride, and more than a ton of uranium-238. When it burst into being, it created a fireball three to five miles in diameter and produced a sun-like glow on the horizon at Rongelap. In two separate pulses, Bravo expended a third of its energy in X-ray and thermal radiation; half its force went into a high-pressure shock wave, which sped outward from Bikini site at more than 2,000 miles per hour. In the initial explosion, Bravo riddled the surrounding area with a small percentage of its energy in the form of neutron and gamma rays. The force of the explosion pulverized and vaporized several hundred million tons of the Bikini reef and lagoon, lifting it as water vapor and calcium oxide into a giant mushroom cloud that towered 21 miles into the sky within ten minutes of detonation. The remaining energy of Bravo was deposited as residual radiation in the uplifted water and coral.[17] The results of this last ten percent of Bravo's energy would hound the U.S. military and the people of Rongelap for the next twenty years.

When Bravo was detonated, Bikini atoll had been evacuated, and the ships of Joint Task Force Seven lay thirty miles to the east of the atoll. Shipboard observers knew immediately that something was terribly wrong. Bravo was considerably larger and more forceful than anticipated, and even worse, the wind began to carry the ominous mushroom cloud eastward toward the ships and Rongelap, rather than westward as predicted. Not only was Bravo a blast of monumental size, it was the first to utilize a fission-fusion-fission process, creating an exceptionally "dirty" bomb. The harmless-looking clouds, which the wind pushed eastward, contained water vapor and calcium oxide saturated with millions of rads (a rad is a measure of dosage, per unit mass, of radioactivity) of gamma and beta activity. The ships of Joint Task Force Seven turned southward at flank speed.

Prior to the detonation of Bravo, the military placed 28 RadSafe (Radiation Safety) monitors on uninhabited Rongerik atoll, about 30 miles east of Rongelap. Shortly after the blast, those men received word by radio that the radioactive cloud was heading eastward, and that they should put on extra clothing and remain inside their prefabricated metal building. Soon the decision was made to evacuate the 28 Americans, and 34 hours after the blast, the RadSafe crew was aboard ship heading away from the area. To reach Rongerik, ships of Joint Task Force Seven had to sail past Rongelap. The populace at Rongelap was not evacuated, in spite of the fact that the atoll was closer to Bravo than Rongerik.

At Rongelap the people saw the strange orange glow on the western horizon, heard the sound of Bravo and wondered if another war had begun. Several hours later a strange white ash began to fall on the atoll, and within several hours two inches of "snow" blanketed Rongelap. The next day some RadSafe monitors visited Rongelap by plane and told the people not to drink the water. Twenty-four hours later ships appeared in the lagoon, and the people were told that they must leave Rongelap or they would die. Sixty hours after the Bravo blast, all the people were evacuated by air or ship to Kwajalein. The Bravo blast and snow had been so powerful that the Rongelap people would not be allowed to return home for three years; even then the Rongelap environment remained radioactive and dangerous.

There was no RadSafe monitor on Rongelap in March 1954, so it will never be known how much radioactivity these people received. Based on later estimates, samples from the fallout at Rongerik, and recalculations from earlier data, the probable whole body gamma dose at Rongelap was 175 rads, plus or minus 25 rads. The minimum lethal dose for man is probably about 225 rads. At 500 rads, one-half of the exposed populace will die. On Rongelap several effects were immediately evident. Many people lost their hair and some skin, and everyone received beta burns of greater or lesser degree. Some radionuclides were ingested or inhaled by the Rongelapese, particularly nuclides of iodine and strontium. The thyroid glands of children received from 700 to 1400 rads, while adult thyroids received 160 rads.[18]

Since 1954, the Atomic Energy Commission has watched the exposed populace of Rongelap with interest. Each year the AEC—through the Brookhaven National Laboratory—sponsors a medical survey of the island. During the tenth annual survey, small thyroid nodules were discovered on three young girls. In spite of the fact that some growth retardation in exposed children had been noted in the earlier surveys, no thyroid medication for the exposed populace was administered until after the discovery of the thyroid nodules. Since 1964, similar problems have occurred in nineteen exposed Rongelapese. All have had surgery for removal of the thyroid nodules; in four cases the nodules were found to be malignant. There is no question that Bravo was the cause of the thyroid nodules. Treatment and removal of the nodules have been carried out at the expense of the AEC, and the whole exposed populace now receives thyroxine to retard the development of nodules. In spite of the belated administration of thyroxine, nodules continue to occur. Three more Rongelapese had nodules removed surgically in June 1974.[19]

In September 1972, 19-year-old Lekoj Anjain was examined on Rongelap and found to have a low white blood cell count. He was taken to Honolulu, and then to Brookhaven, where the diagnosis was acute myelogenous leukemia. Lekoj was admitted to the National Cancer Institute where he shared a room with columnist Stewart Alsop, who also was undergoing treatment for leukemia. Ironically, Alsop had originally reported on the Bravo detonation of 1954. Alsop wrote a graceful and poignant column for *Newsweek* (October 30, 1972) devoted to Lekoj and later included a chapter about him in his book, *Stay of Execution.* The stay of execution was for Alsop, not Lekoj, for America's first H-bomb victim died on November 15, 1972. Alsop wrote:

There was also the depressing feeling, hard to shake off, that I had somehow been responsible for Lekoj's death. There was the further feeling, as hard to shake off, that we Americans were responsible for his death—that we had killed him with our bomb. His was the world's first death from a hydrogen bomb, and the bomb was ours. And finally, there was the feeling of the desperate, irrational unfairness of the death of this gentle, oddly innocent young man. For some time, I found a line, I think from T. S. Eliot (though I can't find it), going through my mind: 'The notion of some infinitely gentle/Infinitely suffering thing.'

Before Lekoj died, I had long believed in my mind that the nuclear weapon, in its indiscriminate, unimaginable brutality, was an insane weapon, suicidal, inherently unusable. Now I knew it in my heart.[20]

Even before the death of Lekoj, there had been substantial concern in the Marshalls about the Rongelap people. When the Rongelapese were evacuated from their atoll in 1954, they were moved to a small island on Majuro atoll. There they were provided with subsistence and housing. Ten months after Bravo the United States gave Japan two million dollars compensation for injuries to the 23 crewmen of a fishing ship (the *Lucky Dragon*) hit by Bravo fallout and for losses sustained by fishing companies who could not sell fish caught in the Bikini area. The Rongelapese received some compensation twelve years, not ten months, after Bravo, and only then after a lawsuit had been filed and the problem brought to the attention of the United Nations.

In February of 1973 and 1974, a special committee of the Congress of Micronesia presented reports on the March 1, 1954 incident. The reports side-stepped any conclusion on whether the United States intentionally exposed the Rongelapese (as had been charged by Rep. Ataji Balos of the Congress). But it noted (1) the failure of the military to warn and educate the people in advance of the tests; (2) the failure evacuate Rongelapese at an earlier hour; and (3) the negligence or incompetence that led to lack of knowledge about upper atmosphere wind conditions. The committee was unstinting in assigning responsibility for the events of March 1, 1954:

> At the outset the committee wishes to note that unlike the Japanese in Hiroshima and Nagasaki who along with their countrymen were at war with the United States, and unlike the Japanese fishermen on the *Lucky Dragon* whose presence in Micronesia was unknown, the people of Rongelap and Utirik were innocent victims of error and negligence on the part of the United States.
>
> This is further compounded by the fact that the United States was acting as trustee at the time of the incident, a trustee which was charged with a 'sacred trust' and to promote the political, economic, social and educational advancement of the people of Micronesia and to also protect their lands, their health and foster their general welfare. The Rongelapese and Utirikese were not belligerents in a war and unlike the participants in the test series, they were uninformed, unadvised, unprepared innocent bystanders who were injured and affected as a result of the pursuit of certain national policies and programs by the United States government.[21]

KWAJALEIN

Kwajalein atoll is the largest atoll in the world, with 93 islands dotting a triangular reef that encloses a beautiful lagoon of more than 800 square miles. The largest islands sit at the corners of the triangle, and the U.S. military has exclusive occupancy of two of these three islands. Japanese forces occupied the same sites until they were wrested from them in five days of battle in 1944. The Marshallese landowners of Kwajalein have not had real access and use of these ancestral lands since the mid 1930s.

Kwajalein was a relatively quiet Navy base until the early 1960s, when it became part of the Pacific Missile Range. Missiles fired from California or elsewhere are targeted into or over the Kwajalein lagoon, where thay are tracked and often intercepted by anti-ballistic missiles launched from Kwajalein.[22] Missiles fired into the ocean, beyond Kwajalein, posed little problem for Marshallese residents of smaller Kwajalein islands. However, when the Pentagon decided to send missiles into the lagoon, it was clear that some Kwajalein residents would be exposed to falling debris from incoming or outgoing missiles. The military insisted on use of the comparatively shallow lagoon, for no other site permitted intact recovery of the missile warheads. The only solution was another relocation of Marshallese, this time to the already overpopulated island of Ebeye. The missile target area, a rectangle 32 by 180 miles, cuts a broad swath across the center of the Kwajalein atoll triangle and is officially designated the "mid-atoll corridor restricted area." The problems of relocation and support for this large group of Marshallese has plagued the military since 1964, and after a time the affected people simply became known as "mid-corridor" people.

Ebeye is a small (76 acre) island on the Kwajalein reef, about two miles north of Kwajalein Island, which is the largest island in the atoll and headquarters for the military and several thousand American missile technicians and their families. In the early days at the base, several hundred Marshallese were employed by the military and lived in a separate area of Kwajalein Island. In 1950, social friction and the shantytown appearance of the Marshallese labor camp caused the military to order the camp closed and the laborers relocated to Ebeye.[23] The Marshallese ghetto was moved out of sight of the military at Kwajalein, but it is never out of mind of those who have to live there. In 1974, the contrast between Kwajalein Island and Ebeye was still sharp and painful. Kwajalein Island has carefully clipped grass and a ring of tin around each of several thousand coconut trees to prevent rats from nesting in the fronds. Ebeye has precious little grass and only a few trees, but it does have plenty of rats. In 1961 and 1962, a polio epidemic swept Ebeye; it was carried along by overcrowding, shantytown housing, and total absence of sewage facilities. In 1961, Ebeye had 1,443 people;[24] by 1973 the number had grown to 5,124. The population density at Ebeye, which is without any multi-story buildings, is the equivalent of 51,240 people per square mile.[25]

In 1964, when the military told the Department of Interior that the mid-corridor people would have to be relocated to Ebeye, the Department of Interior balked in spite of a 1955 agreement that Interior would act as land acquisition agent for the military in Micronesia. Interior had come under fire from the United Nations for the squalid and unhealthy conditions at Ebeye—conditions that some viewed as a violation of the "protect the health" clause of the Trusteeship Agreement. Ultimately, the people were moved under an agreement signed by the United States and Trust Territory in 1964. The agreement provided for $25 per month subsistence payments to each exiled person, and although it was not part of the formal agreement, the military promised to build 300 dwelling units on Ebeye to upgrade the housing there. Twenty-eight of the units were to be occupied by mid-corridor people. Unfortunately, the mid-corridor agreement was doomed from the beginning.

The original mid-corridor agreement assumed that about 160 people would be evacuated. When relocation came, 395 people were taken off the target-area islands. Consequently, there was not enough money or housing to go around; 160 people did not fit easily into twenty-eight tiny 600-square-foot units, and 395 did not fit at all. Furthermore, the original agreement failed to account for numerous absentee owners of mid-corridor islands. These owners used their islands for copra production and food gathering, and were extremely distressed at the uncompensated denial of access to the islands. For several years the mid-corridor problems were debated between the Trust Territory and the military, each trying to claim that the responsibility was not theirs. A series of amendments were made to the original agreement, increasing either the subsistence payment or the number of eligible persons.[26] To the mid-corridor people, each amendment was considerably less than half a loaf.

By the late 1960s, the mid-corridor people were fed up with being landless paupers. A 1968 resolution, passed by the Congress of Micronesia, asked for return of the land or meaningful renegotiation.[27] A 1969 resolution created a Congressional committee to study the problem and warned that the mid-corridor people would reoccupy their islands if a solution was not found. Both resolutions were introduced by Ataji Balos.

Throughout 1969 and 1970, Ataji had told the Trust Territory and the military that the mid-corridor people would sail back to their islands unless a settlement was reached. Apparently his threat was not taken seriously, for he never received a single response to numerous messages. By March 1970, Ataji and his many supporters were ready with boats and supplies purchased from a special appropriation by the Marshall Islands Legislature.[28] On March 31, 1970, some of the islands were reoccupied, including Meck Island, a launch site for the Spartan ABM Missiles. The test series scheduled to begin that day was cancelled when the people refused to move even in the face of proposed missile launchings. By the end of the first week, 200 people had sailed back to their islands. Under increasing pressure, Ataji refused to end the "sail-in" until a fair agreement was reached. Public support from the United States did not appear, since news of the radical "sail-in" never penetrated military security. In the end, Ataji won the agreement he sought; the Army now pays the mid-corridor people a lump sum of $420,000 per year. The Army claims duress, but the Marshallese properly feel that the mid-corridor settlement is the first fair land agreement in their thirty years of dealing with the military.

Roi-Namur is the second largest island on Kwajalein atoll, and it forms the northern tip of the Kwajalein triangle. It was used as a U.S. air base during the early atomic tests; shortly thereafter it was left unused, and some landowners returned to live on the island. In 1960, they were ordered to move again to allow construction of a massive radar complex, which now supports the missile range. Throughout this period the Trust Territory believed it owned Roi-Namur by succeeding to the position held by the Japanese. The Trust Territory turned the island over to the military in 1960 without ascertaining who really held title. Various Marshallese, then living on Ebeye, filed ownership claims on Roi-Namur, and in 1964 a title examiner held public hearings on the matter. There was no evidence that the Japanese had purchased Roi-Namur, and the government presumption of title was baseless. Title was ruled to be held by the Marshallese.[29] The ruling was not appealed, modified, or even questioned, but the military continued its presence at Roi-Namur. The most complex radar and tracking installation in the world now exists at Roi-Namur, developed and manned by personnel from MIT's Lincoln Laboratory.[30] The United States reportedly has at Roi-Namur an investment in hardware that totals several hundred million dollars. The United States is trespassing on the land.

Beginning in 1965, the Marshallese owners of Roi-Namur have attempted to negotiate a settlement with the military. In the late 1960s the military finally offered a settlement of $400,000 for the 400-acre site, but the owners rejected it as too little and too late. The Army engaged a well respected land appraiser from Hawaii to appraise the island, and when the appraisal came in at $2.7 million for a 50-year lease (1944 to 1994), the military rejected the appraisal and then buried it so the landowners could not find out the appraised value of their property. This appraisal is the only one ever done in the Marshall Islands.

In 1971, the landowners asked the Trust Territory government to provide them with a lawyer to help in the negotiations. Despite the obvious conflicts of interest, the Trust Territory reversed its long standing policy of acting as a land acquisition agent for the military and agreed to assign an attorney. After the lawyer saw the appraisal and advised his Marshallese clients not to settle for $1,000 per acre, the military sent a special mission to the Trust Territory High Commissioner to tell him that the lawyer had seen "secret" information and should be removed from the case. Without asking what the information was, the lawyer was taken off the case, and the Marshallese were left once more without legal representation. The obligation to "protect the inhabitants against the loss of their lands and resources" apparently did not include the protection afforded by competent legal counsel in complicated real estate transactions. The people of Roi-Namur have now obtained other legal help, and negotiations may soon continue. If the military again negotiates in bad faith, Ataji Balos will call for another dramatic Marshallese "sail-in."

Right after World War II, the status of Micronesia was hotly debated at the upper levels of the American government. The Joint Chiefs of Staff argued for outright annexation and total control of the islands; they did not like the UN Trusteeship system then developing, and felt that Micronesians were incapable of ultimate self-government.[31] Harold Ickes, then Secretary of the Interior, accused the Navy of wanting an arrangement for Micronesia that would allow it to keep the administration of dependent peoples secret, saying that:

> Navy absolutism sneers at every Constitutional guarantee . . . the Navy is arbitrary, dictatorial, and utterly disregardful of civilian rights . . . the Navy is bent upon ruling these island people and it is determined that they shall not have those rights which the Charter of the United Nations guarantees.[32]

In the end, a trusteeship was established, albeit a "strategic trusteeship" that differed significantly from the eleven other UN trusteeships. In retrospect, it is clear that in his debate with the Pentagon, Ickes won the battle but lost the war, for the Marshall Islands have been used as the military wished in spite of the trusteeship agreement. The people of Bikini, Enewetak, Rongelap, and Kwajalein have all discovered that, as Ataji Balos says, "The Micronesians have the Trust, and the United States has the Territory."

NOTES

1. Samuel Eliot Morison, *History of U.S. Naval Operations in W.W. II* (Boston, 1960), pp. 225-268.

2. Robert Carl Kiste, "Changing Patterns of Land Tenure and Social Organization Among the Ex-Bikini Marshallese" (Doctoral Thesis, University of Oregon, 1967), pp. 100-106. See also Neal Hines, *Proving Ground* (Seattle, 1962), pp. 21-2.

3. The conditions at Rongerik in 1948 are described more fully in the Kiste thesis. The author has also discussed Rongerik memories with several of the Bikini elders.

4. Letter of May 7, 1970, from High Commissioner Johnson to Mrs. Elizabeth Farrington, Director of Office of Territories, U.S. Dept. of Interior, pp. 2-3.

5. Letter of December 14, 1969, from Kili Magistrate Lore Kessibuki to High Commissioner Johnson.

6. United Nations Trusteeship Agreement, Article 6.

7. May 7, 1970, Johnson letter.

8. Samuel Glasston, ed., *The Effects of Nuclear Weapons* (Washington, D.D., 1964), Appendix B.

9. May 7, 1970, Johnson letter.

10. See complete discussion in Jack A. Tobin, "The Resettlement of the Enewetak People: A Study of a Displaced Community in the Marshall Islands" (Doctoral thesis, University of California, Berkeley, 1967), pp. 20-7.

11. Hines, op. cit., pp. 80-81.

12. Tobin, op. cit., p. 29.

13. Tobin, op. cit., p. 230.

14. Glasstone, op. cit., Appendix B.

15. Joint announcement of Ambassador Franklin Haydn Williams and High Commissioner Johnson, April 18, 1972.

16. See *People of Enewetak* v. *Laird,* 353 F. Supp 811 (Dist. Ct. Hawaii, 1972).

17. *Report on the Medical Aspects of the Incident of March 1, 1954* (Congress of Micronesia, Special Joint Committee Concerning Rongelap and Utirik Atolls [Saipan, 1973]), pp. 65-78. The author is deeply indebted to this committee and Mr. Brian Farley for the information contained in their reports.

18. Dr. William S. Cole, *Report to the Special Joint Committee Concerning Rongelap and Utirik Atolls* (Congress of Micronesia, from the U.S. Public Health Service, Bureau of Radiological Health, Food and Drug Administration, Dept. of Health, Education and Welfare) p. 5.

19. *Pacific Daily News* (Guam), June 14, 1974, p. 5.

20. Stewart Alsop, *Stay of Execution: A Sort of Memoir* (Philadelphia and New York, 1973), p. 281.

21. *Report on Compensation* (Congress of Micronesia, Special Joint Committee Concerning Rongelap and Utirik Atolls [Saipan, 1974]), p. 36.

22. Kwajalein Missile Range Directorate, "Kwajalein Missile Range Historical Summary" (Huntsville, 1972) Vol. I, I-5 to I-8.

23. Jack A. Tobin, Memo to District Administrators Representative, Kwajalein, re Ebeye-Kwajalein, July 19, 1972, p. 3.

24. E. H. Bryans, Jr., *Life in the Marshall Islands* (Honolulu, 1972), p. 143.

25. *Pacific Daily News,* February 13, 1974, pp. 1 and 36, reporting release of 1973 Trust Territory census figures. The density of Brooklyn, New York, is 37,000 persons per square mile.

26. See the numerous memos, letters, and abstracts of meetings in Robert Haley's *History of Marshallese-Kwajalein Missile Range Relations* (Huntsville, 1970).

27. Congress of Micronesia, House Joint Resolution No. 35, Adopted August 3, 1968.

28. Marshall Islands Legislature (Nitijela), Bill No. 44, adopted October 14, 1969.

29. Determination of Ownership and Release 65-K-1 by Charles Hughes, Land and Claims Administrator, April 23, 1965.

30. For a description of some of the technical facilities at Kwajalein see Kwajalein Missile Range Directorate, "Historical Summary," chapters IV-VII, and Dale R. Gramley and Robert Erson, "Kwajalein Missile Range," *Army Research and Development News Magazine,* June, 1972, pp. 24-26.

31. Dorothy Richard, *History of U.S. Naval Administration of the Trust Territory* (Washington, 1953), vol. III, pp. 3-23.

32. Richard, op. cit., p. 19.

NOEL GROGAN

6

Dependency and Nondevelopment in Micronesia

The buildings of the Congress of Micronesia stand on the gentle slopes of Saipan's Mount Tapotchau in the midst of a former Central Intelligence Agency secret operations base. It has been suggested that the ghosts of CIA agents past, haunting the halls of the Congress, have been responsible for the generally submissive approach that body has demonstrated over the years in its relationships with the U.S. colonial administration. This atmosphere of acquiescence was temporarily shattered early in the spring of 1974 when the member from Ponape, Sungiwo Hadley, stood in front of his colleagues in the House of Representatives and charged that for 27 year the United States had willfully contravened the letter and the spirit of the United Nations Trusteeship Agreement covering Micronesia; it had denied the most fundamental of rights to 100,000 Pacific islanders by purposefully retarding the development of the area in an effort to establish a permanent dependency relationship designed to achieve the selfish and militarist ends of the American government.[1]

It is the purpose of this essay to develop an examination of Representative Hadley's allegations and to provide an accurate description of how and why the United States implemented its policy of nondevelopment and invalidated the international trusteeship system, which, ironically, two U.S. presidents worked to create

THE TRUSTEESHIP SYSTEM

To understand the role the United States has played in the development of inter national organizations in general, and the concept of trusteeship in particular, it is necessary to begin with a review of the expressions of American policy as presented by President Woodrow Wilson at the close of World War I. It was Wilson who developed the concept that the welfare of dependent peoples was the responsibility of the metropolitan nations, and the treatment of colonial possessions as simply private economic assets was no longer viable or permissible. He began working with this idea early in his career and hoped to see it become a national and international policy. As early as 1915 he said:

> We do not want a foot of anybody's territory. If we have been obliged by circumstances . . . to take territory . . . I believe that I am right in saying that we have considered it our duty to administer that territory not for ourselves but for the people living in it, and to put this burden upon our consciences—not to think that this thing is ours for our use, but to regard ourselves as trustees of the great business for those to whom it does really belong.[2]

At the Paris Peace Talks of 1919, Wilson presented his "principle of mandatories" to the delegates as the only reasonable solution to the management of territory formerly controlled by Germany. Despite considerable objection to Wilson's views, the main moral trust of his concept prevailed in the language of the mandate system of the League of Nations. Article 22 of the Covenant of the League states:

> To those colonies and territories which as a consequence of the late war have ceased to be under the sovereignty of the States which formerly governed them and which are inhabited by peoples not yet able to stand by themselves under the strenuous conditions of the modern world, there should be applied the principle that the well-being and develop-ment of such peoples form a sacred trust of civilization and that securities for this trust should be embodied in this Convenant.[3]

Under the mandates system, the Western Pacific islands north of the equator, which were formerly the possessions of Germany, were entrusted to Japan as a class "C" mandate on May 7, 1919. Under this arrangement, Japan was to admin-ister the Caroline, Marshall, and Mariana Islands (excluding the United States' territory of Guam) under the laws of Japan and as an integral part of Japanese territory.[4]

Japan's fortification of the islands, its withdrawal from the League of Nations, and the events of World War II are too well known to require additional comment here, except perhaps to note that a successful trusteeship system seems to need more than a strong moral base to be successful.

As American forces advanced across the Western Pacific in the 1940s, it became evident to President Franklin Roosevelt that he might soon face the same problem that Wilson had faced earlier in dealing with dependent territories at the end of a war. This time, however, there was a good chance that some of the spoils of war might be in the hands of the United States. In an attempt to meet this situation, a State Department group in 1943 prepared a "Draft Declaration by the United Nations on National Independence"; this proposed an "international trusteeship administration" to administer those areas still in a dependent status that would be taken from the enemy as a result of the war.[5]

Presentation of this concept to the British and the Russians at the Yalta Conference met with mixed feelings and is credited with sparking Prime Minister Churchill' famous comment that he had "not become the King's First Minister in order to preside over the liquidation of the British Empire."[6] The President, however, did not view Churchill's position as either reasonable or final; and this, together with Stalin's generally positive reception of the idea, encouraged him to pursue further the plan for international trusteeship.[7] Major resistance to the proposal finally came from within the United States rather than from the Allied Powers. By the time the actual negotiations for the creation of the United Nations got underway, the Secretaries of War, Navy, and Army, together with powerful members of Congress, were all taking very firm stands against the internationalization of the former Japanese-mandated islands and demanding that the United States maintain "*absolute,* undisputed control over our [military] base needs" in the Pacific.[8]

Faced with these sentiments, it appears that Roosevelt recognized that international trusteeship would be difficult to support politically in the postwar atmosphere where a direct confrontation with a military establishment, which had just successfully concluded a world war, would not be tolerated. In addition, the trusteeship issue was only a small part of the whole United Nations program. Roosevelt had a great desire to avoid President Wilson's dilemma and to see the concept of world organization become widely accepted in the United States.

In the compromise that resulted after Roosevelt's death, two specific types of trusteeships were developed in the United Nations Conference on International Organization, held in the spring of 1945. Chapters XII and XIII of the United Nations Charter (Articles 75-91) outlined the specific provisions of the trusteeship system.[9] Article Seventy-seven of the Charter (Chapter XII) stated that the types of territories to be covered by trusteeship are: those held under the League of Nations mandate system; those detached from enemy states as a result of war; and those voluntarily placed under the system by the states responsible for them.[10] The basic objectives of the trusteeship system were outlined in Article Seventy-six a the promotion of international peace and security; the promotion of respect for human rights and fundamental freedoms; and the equal treatment of all United Nations members in social, commercial, and economic matters.[11] Articles Eighty-two and Eighty-three outlined the terms of a strategic declaration that the authority administering a territory might make regarding all or a part of the territory. While territories *not* so declared would be established as trusteeships under the General Assembly of the United Nations, the territories declared strategic would be established under the Security Council.[12]

A Trusteeship Council was to be developed under the conditions presented in Chapter XIII of the Charter to handle the administrative and overseeing duties of the General Assembly in the case of non-strategic trusts, and to provide assistance requested by the Security Council in the case of strategic territories. The specific functions assigned to the Trusteeship Council were:

a. Consider reports submitted by the administering authority;

b. Accept petitions and examine them in consultation with the administering authority;

c. Provide for periodic visits to the respective trust territories at times agreed upon with the administering authority; and

d. Take these and other actions in conformity with the terms of the trusteeship agreements.[13]

On the surface, the United States, through working for the establishment of the trusteeship system outlined above, had seemingly accomplished both of its purposes. The system established a method for dealing with dependent territories in a way that was both consistent with the maintenance of international peace and security and with the promotion of the best interests of the dependent peoples. It also provided an element of supervision that was lacking in the League of Nations system. At the same time, it allowed the United States, through the strategic territory concept, to maintain almost absolute control of the Pacific islands formerly mandated to Japan. By declaring these islands a "strategic trust," the United Nations body responsible for them became the Security Council, where the United States had an absolute veto.

In all, eleven trusteeship agreements were submitted to the United Nations by 1949. Ten of these were submitted to the General Assembly as regular (non-strategic) trusts, and one—the Pacific Islands under United States Administration—was submitted to the Security Council as a strategic trust.[14] When the Australians granted independence to the Trust Territory of New Guinea (which joined with Papua as a single nation) in late 1974, the Trust Territory of the Pacific Islands became the last dependent area under the trusteeship system.[15]

THE TRUST TERRITORY OF THE PACIFIC ISLANDS

The proposed trusteeship agreement for the Pacific islands was submitted to the Security Council by the United States in February 1947.[16] In most respects the original draft conformed to applicable sections of the Charter, but a considerable amount of heated discussion ensued prior to the final approval of the amended document on April 2, 1947.[17] In the original draft of the agreement, the United States proposed to administer the area "as an integral part of the United States." During the discussions, this wording (which was included in the Japanese mandate) was deleted with the concurrence of the United States representative.[18] In addition, the original draft submitted by the United States stated that the administering authority (the United States) would assist the people of the islands in working towards "self-government." The phrase finally approved was "self-government or independence, as may be appropriate to the particular circumstances of the Trust Territory and its peoples."[19]

Another area of controversy that was to have importance later concerned the economic development of the territory. The United States included a provision in the draft agreement that gave "most favored nation" treatment to itself as administering authority. This was done, the United States explained, to protect the security of the territory and was consistent with Articles Eighty-two and Eighty-three of the Charter. The United Kingdom felt this was a violation of

Article Seventy-six of the Charter, which calls for equal treatment of all United Nations members in all social, economic, and commercial matters within trust territories. After much discussion of this point, the view of the United States prevailed.[20]

The only direct reference to strategic requirements in the original draft of the Trusteeship Agreement was contained in Article Thirteen, which allowed the administering authority to close any area of the territory for security reasons. This item, together with the requirement that the United States agree to any change in the agreement (or to its termination, as opposed to termination by the Security Council), brought about considerable debate regarding the wording and form of both provisions; both remained unamended in the approved agreement.[21]

From July 1947, when the trusteeship agreement became effective, until July 1951, the administration of the Trust Territory was under the U.S. Secretary of the Navy. A transfer of administrative responsibility from the Secretary of the Navy to the Secretary of Interior was accomplished under presidential order in July 1951. However, on January 1, 1953, the islands of Saipan and Tinian in the Mariana Islands temporarily were returned to Navy administration "for security reasons."[22]

UN VISITING MISSIONS

Despite the establishment of the territory as a strategic area, there has been no formal or overt attempt by the United States to limit the function of the Trusteeship Council in its consideration of the political, social, economic, and educational development of the area. Visiting missions organized by the Trusteeship Council for observation of the various trusteeships in the Pacific have included the Trust Territory of the Pacific Islands as one of their areas of investigation, and they developed comprehensive reports from each visit.[23] These Visiting Mission reports provide an unusually objective source of well-documented information on the U.S. administration of Micronesia. The non-partisan missions review and consider all pertinent debates, discussions, testimony, and reports as a part of their investigation. They are the *only* structure specifically designed to obtain an overview of the progress of the territory, and the only body that attempts to validate their findings through discussion with the subject peoples and substantial on-site investigation.

Seven visiting mission reports covering the period from 1951 through 1973 have been evaluated carefully for the purpose of writing this essay, and it has been determined that there are three consistent themes regarding the failure of U.S. development efforts in Micronesia running through all of these reports. The first of these three themes involves questions relating to land tenure, the problems of both public and private land use, the amount of land held as "public land," and the difficulties associated with the settlement of land claims. The second theme concerns the pace and style of development of local and territory-wide political institutions, the effectiveness of political education, the degree of authority granted to indigenous political bodies, and the problem of territorial-political integration. The final theme involves the pace and orientation of economic development programs, the degree of indigenous participation in economic planning, and the use or lack of development of comprehensive economic planning.

LAND TENURE AND USE

There exists a startling and disturbing similarity between the early reports and those of 1964, 1967, and 1973 regarding land problems within Micronesia. In the 1951 report, for instance, it was pointed out that the administration held some 450 square miles of land while indigenous inhabitants held less than 250 square miles. The administering authority had chosen to recognize all Japanese land transactions prior to the date of Japan's withdrawal from the League of Nations on March 27, 1935; as a result, much of the land held by the administration in 1951 had been declared "public domain" by the Japanese. The report goes on to point out that "the Japanese acquired such large holdings by simply declaring all unused land or land for which no title existed to be State domain and by the purchase of additional tracts."[24] The Mission recognized the questionable legality of the former method of land acquisition, the general dissatisfaction and resentment of the islanders at its implementation, and the fact that even in cases where a "sale" of the land took place there were elements of force and coercion involved.[25]

In the same report the Mission discussed the numerous unsettled land claims, the unavailability of the land records, and the lack of accurate survey and boundary information. The Mission concluded that in view of the fact that the hostilities had been concluded for more than five years, solutions to the land problems should be arrived at in a relatively short period of time.[26] Sixteen years later, in the 1967 Visiting Mission report, it is stated that "many, if not most, land boundaries are undefined and unsurveyed," and that land disputes were absorbing a major and increasing part of the time of the courts.[27] The Mission further pointed out that reform of the land tenure system(s) and settlement of land claims must be accomplished so that the land could be put into productive use. Additionally, it indicated that there were conflicts arising from the differences between traditional land tenure systems and the systems applied in the acquisition of land by both the German and Japanese administrations which the administering authority could not ignore. It observed that attempts to reconcile these problems in the past had met with little success.[28]

Finally, the report pointed to continued problems associated with the large amount of public land being withheld from use. In recommended the immediate development of comprehensive plans for public land use, urban zoning, and rural land development and utilization; development of a reformed tenure system and the final determination of land titles and boundaries also were advocated. It went on record as strongly opposing the recommendation of a recently completed comprehensive economic development study by an American firm that non-citizens of the Trust Territory be allowed to purchase land to create capital for local development projects.[29]

In an amazing echo of the 1951 Visiting Mission, the 1973 inspection group pointed out that there was still no visible progress on the subject of public lands after 26 years of trusteeship; that the question of the "dubious circumstances" under which the German and Japanese administrations had acquired part of the "public holding" has not been resolved; and that portions of the population held the mistaken notion that the public lands belonged to the United States rather than to the people of Micronesia.[30] While noting that attempts at solutions to the land tenure problem had been underway for some time, the Mission pointed out that there was still no brief and unambiguous description of land use and land tenure customs available, and that the approach being utilized to solve the problems of land tenure was one that "seems logical but is usually costly and often useless."[31]

MILITARY LAND USE

In addition to the problems outlined above, which in certain cases *might* be viewed as largely inherited from a confused situation existing at the end of World War II, there are land problems directly created by the administering authority; they have been the subject of both visiting mission reports and Trusteeship Council resolutions. A case in point is the "acquisition" of Kwajalein Atoll by the Trust Territory administration so that it could be turned over to the United States Department of Defense to be used for military purposes.

The 1961 Visiting Mission report presents a detailed account of the acquisition process and the difficulties it caused. Kwajalein, the largest atoll in the world, had been an important traditional holding of the Marshallese people. The composite land area, although amounting to only a little more than 600 acres, was capable of supporting a substantial population under traditional lifeways when combined with the rich marine resources of the large lagoon. In the dispute over the taking of the atoll, the Marshallese were asking for a return of twenty US dollars per acre, per month on a fixed period lease basis with a lump sum payment for past use by the military. The administration's offer was an outright payment of $500 per acre for something they defined as "indefinite use rights."[32]

In addition to the problem of the amount of payment for the area taken, the inhabitants of Kwajalein were re-located to the tiny island of Ebeye (76 acres) and were deprived of utilizing the atoll area for their livelihood (it was pointed out that some of them would be given jobs by the military). When the 1961 Mission visited the area, the situation had been without resolution for over a year, and no negotiations had been entered into for nearly that long. It was the Mission's view that land was the islanders' most precious commodity and that

. . . the views and wishes of the people concerning the basis for agreement on which their lands may be taken from them should not be ignored or over-ridden, and that in each case they are entitled to a fair compensation for the use of their lands by the United States Government for its military purposes.[33]

It was not until February of 1964 that a 99-year lease was finally agreed to by both parties. The lease provided compensation in the amount of $500 per acre for "past use" and an equal amount for future use. Thus it took nearly five years for this acquisition of private land rights to be completed. The 1964 Visiting Mission noted that the United States government had enjoyed full use of the land and had resettled the inhabitants "without due process of law and prior agreement among all concerned."[34] During the entire intervening period, in fact, the land had been used without any legal basis whatsoever.

The 1973 Visiting Mission found that the operations of the U.S. military continued to have negative affects upon the people of Kwajalein and neighboring Roi-Namur. They summarized the conditions they found on Ebeye as follows: "Unfortunately, because of overcrowding, and particularly by contrast with its neighbor island, Ebeye is a dismal and depressing sight, a slum occupying the whole of a Pacific island."[35]

POLITICAL DEVELOPMENT

The Trust Territory is divided into six administrative districts, soon to be seven, drawn roughly along cultural lines. There are at least nine separate and individual languages spoken in the territory.[36] Early Visiting Missions recognized the difficulties these limitations, and the geography of the region, placed upon the administration in building modern political institutions. Despite these limitations, however, as early as 1953 the visiting missions were pressing the administering authority for movement in establishing a territory-wide legislative body as it had proposed to do in 1950. The Mission in 1953 also pointed to the difficulty that would inevitably be encountered in trying to discuss political affairs on a basis broader than the district, "before a sufficient degree of advancement [was] reached."[37] (The High Commissioner is and was the chief executive of the government, and there is a District Administrator reporting directly to him in each district.) In order to speed up the process of political advancement, the Mission recommended the development and improvement of regional and district organs of local government and the granting of increasing amounts of authority to these bodies "until ultimately they may become fully responsible for local legislation affecting their districts."[38]

The 1953 Mission was also concerned with the political implications of separate administration by the Navy of a portion of the Mariana Islands. It cautioned against the creation of a feeling of total separation among the people of Saipan and Tinian islands and the negative long-run consequences for the territory as a whole.[39] Additional comments were offered regarding the negative aspects of having the administrative headquarters of the territory located outside of the Trust Territory. (At that time the High Commissioner's office was located in Honolulu, Hawaii, some 5,000 miles from the territory.)

In 1953, an inter-district conference was held in Truk District to allow Micronesian leadership to look at problems in a "broader-than-district" political context. During the visit of the 1956 Mission, the High Commissioner indicated his dissatisfaction with the inter-district conference; he said it had been of doubtful value and that he was reluctant to try another one in the same form. After a careful evaluation of all sides of the question, however, the Mission disagreed with this position and recommended that another conference be held at an early date.[40]

The 1956 Mission was impressed with the initial steps taken in five districts to implement local legislative bodies. They, like the previous mission, called for extending authority as rapidly as possible to these bodies; pointed to the continuing existence of the administrative headquarters in a temporary location outside of the territory (at that time located in Guam); and indicated the serious political problems that could develop from the split administration in the Mariana Islands.[41]

Considerable political advances by four Micronesian districts in the development of more viable local or district political bodies were noted by the 1961 Visiting Mission. They especially were satisfied with the fact that much of the leadership recently elected to local bodies consisted of younger and more formally educated men.[42] This Mission was somewhat more reserved, however, about the structuring of the district political bodies by the administration. They pointed out that, while the powers conferred by the charters to district legislatures seemed broad, the actual authority was limited by the fact that they could pass only on financial matters concerning local revenue, most of which went for the costs of elementary education. In addition, due to the meager operating budgets, sessions had to be quite short and careful consideration and preparation of legislation was impossible, or at best most difficult. The Mission called upon the administration to grant additional authority and to try to find a way to assist in financing the local law making bodies.[43]

This Mission also noted the establishment of an inter-district advisory committee to the High Commissioner, with members elected by local political bodies in each district. This body met, in conjunction with the members of the administration's headquarters staff, at the Trust Territory administrative headquarters for approximately one week each year to consider a wide variety of problems. The Mission was skeptical of the effectiveness of the role of this advisory committee and recommended "that the Administering Authority should give urgent consideration to the transformation of this body *into* a statutory elected Territorial Council with both legislative and fiscal functions."[44] Additionally in 1961, the Visiting Mission pointed to the continued separation of Saipan and Tinian from the rest of the territory as being counter to the objective of integrating Micronesia, a key goal of the United Nations. Not only did the splitting of the administration between American agencies cause serious communication problems and problems of identity, but the system also excluded the Saipan and Tinian delegations from full participation in the advisory committee. The full effect of the separation was clearly evident to the Mission when, upon their visit to Saipan, they were continually faced with the demand of the people for either annexation to the United States or integration with the United States Territory of Guam. The Mission issued a stern rebuke to the administering authority, indicating there was evidence that administration officials had added to the problem by unclear and slanted presentations of future possibilities to the people of Saipan.[45]

As a validation to the fears of the 1961 Visiting Mission, the 1973 Report noted that the United States had undertaken separate negotiations with the people of the Mariana Islands in the hope that they would join the United States as an unincorporated territory. They pointed out the favored position of the Mariana Islands during the period of trusteeship and suggested that negotiations for separate status be stopped until the future of the entire Trust Territory could be decided.[46]

THE CONGRESS OF MICRONESIA

The first territory-wide, popularly elected legislature was formed in 1965. Several key issues were raised by the 1964 Mission viewing the preparations for the first meeting of the legislature. The Mission questioned some aspects of the development of the executive order, which was to be the legal basis of the representative body. It expressed concern that there had been limited consultation with Micronesian leadership, and also that although the draft order might well represent the present wishes of most Micronesians, there was some question that it was broad enough in statement or flexible enough in form to provide for future growth of the body into a fully responsible legislative organ.[47] In this same context, the Mission pointed out that political advancement could not be geared to the "slowest or to those—the great majority in any country—who are little interested." Political advancement must follow those who are the most active, those who will be the new political leaders. In Micronesia, the Mission stated, there is no lack of new political leaders.[48]

The Mission offered some strong comment on the proposed relationship between the administration and the new legislature. It regarded the doctrine of a strict separation of powers as being of limited value in developing areas, although it might be quite workable in established nations. It voiced its concern that the administering authority was not always able to recognize the importance of this concept.[49] The Mission's view was that the misunderstanding of basic concepts by the administration must not do anything to discredit the new legislature, or to regard it as an irresponsible body unable to assume the full powers of legislation. "Legislative responsibility," the Mission stated, "cannot be portioned or it disappears."[50]

To avoid these problems, the Mission made the specific recommendation that the administration reconsider its entire position in the area of fiscal management and develop a fully realistic plan for turning legislative control for the entire Trust Territory budget over to the new legislature as soon as possible. The alternative to this, i.e., to retain an unyielding control in this area, the Mission observed, "will be to leave the territory an inert and politically lifeless burden on the [United States'] pocket book and . . . conscience."[51]

The afterview provided by the 1967 Visiting Mission indicates that many of the problems foreseen by the earlier report did in fact materialize. Out of a total territorial budget of nearly twenty million dollars, only $750,000 was under the control of the new legislature (officially designated the Congress of Micronesia); and this bicameral body required nearly $500,000 of this amount for its own operation. There was thus no effective control over administrative programs and although the Congress attempted to overcome their lack of real authority by passing resolutions with financial implications, this had only marginal impact.[52]

The 1967 Visiting Mission concluded its report with the following remarks on the future of Micronesia:

> The Mission considers that the initial work of the Congress of Micronesia has helped to sweep away one of the barriers to political progress by providing a force for unification and centralized leadership. The main obstacles remaining in the way of progress to political freedom and self-determination lie in the excessive economic dependence of Micronesia upon the United States and the lack of political understanding among the members of the public, particularly in the more remote islands, of the alternatives before them.[53]

The 1973 Visiting Mission, while noting the newly acquired power of approval over some executive appointments, concluded that the problems of earlier periods largely continued to exist, with the Congress still a dependent body subject to final control from the Executive branch. With regard to veto powers, the Mission specifically pointed out that the Trusteeship Council as a whole felt "the retention by the Administering Authority of the right of veto across the whole spectrum of possible legislation is no longer necessary or in principle desirable."[54] This Mission also sounded a critical note in regard to the behavior of the Congress and indicated that there was a serious gap between the Congressmen and their constituents, in both knowledge and material benefits. In their view, the Congress was not demonstrating an efficient and orderly exercise of its duties, and there was a certain lack of dignity in the Congress' treatment of questions such as their own salary levels without "an austere regard for the capacity of Micronesia to pay."[55]

ECONOMIC DEVELOPMENT

In discussions of economic development, the visiting missions have generally pointed to the lack of comprehensive planning and the lack of Micronesian involvement in the little planning that was done. They have also commented on the failure to attempt to exploit resources, especially in agriculture and fisheries, which were proven to be profitable under the Japanese administration. This question of agricultural and fisheries development is cited in some way in every report. In the early reports various general suggestions were made by the missions. In 1951 for instance, the Mission noted that the logical market for the product of a fisheries program, as well as the logical developer of the resource, was Japan. While the Mission understood the reason behind the administration's refusal to allow Japanese cooperation in this area, it pointed out the obligation to develop the area as an equally sound reason for bringing the Japanese in.[56] Agricultural development was always seen as a major possibility by the visiting missions, although they generally reported that their recommendations were met with a "that is not feasible" answer by the administration. This answer extended from suggestions about reestablishing the sugar industry in the Mariana Islands, to plantation development of copra and other tropical crops, to large scale cattle production, to large scale forestry development.

The problem of development planning was another area that the missions constantly attempted to solve, or assist the administration in solving. In 1961 the Visiting Mission, in discussing the need for economic planning with the High Commissioner, was told that the administration was currently awaiting the results of a major economic survey. The Mission subsequently found out that there was no survey underway, and in fact there was not even money provided in the budget for a survey. This Mission undertook some research on its own and found that a highly detailed and comprehensive study had been completed for the Navy in 1946 by an "eminent group of experts" and that this could well form the basis for sound planning.[57]

A strong recommendation was made for heavy Micronesian involvement in economic planning by the 1961 Mission, which submitted a detailed list of eleven specific proposals regarding economic program development and implementation. These recommendations included both the approach, cited earlier, of attempting to reestablish areas developed by the Japanese and several new concepts, such as separate development financing and budgets and working through the United Nations and other established international development agencies.[58]

The 1967 Visiting Mission was able to review the results of the first economic development survey prepared for the Trust Territory since its establishment in 1947. While the Mission positively viewed the undertaking as a whole, it expressed serious reservations about the recommendations concerning land, the labor force, and the orientation of future development. This study, which was conducted by an American firm (and is known as the Nathan Report), suggested that Micronesians be allowed to sell their land in order to obtain capital for development projects, and that project developments be accomplished through the importation of alien laborers. The Mission pointed out the basic conflicts with the trusteeship concept and the actual difficulties created for the Micronesian people by implementation of these plans; and they alleged they were of questionable relevance or value in terms of the long-run development of a large-scale tourist industry as the main source of economic advancement. It pointed out that while various visiting missions had suggested the development of tourism, it could never be thought of as the only or primary program, and that a truly viable economy could only develop from a balanced mix of all of the resources available.[59] This Mission went to perhaps greater lengths than any before in outlining the areas of development that might be open for the territory. It presented an especially detailed picture of agricultural and fisheries possibilities, citing Japanese production records and the results of various studies as evidence of the potential in several areas.[60] The presentation served, however, to indicate clearly just how little had been accomplished, as much as it did to point the way for the future.

The 1973 Mission Report clearly showed that the recommendations of previous missions had fallen on deaf ears. They concurred with the recent findings of a Congress of Micronesia Committee that the "existing state of marine resources development in Micronesia [is] 'pitiful'." They expressed hope at what appeared to be the more positive attitude of the administration in this regard, but pointed out that "the resources available under the budget continue to be very small compared with the size of the task to be done."[61] The same report responded to the administration's claim of new emphasis on agricultural development by noting that current expenditure on this item constituted only 2.5 percent of the budget with planned increases to only 3 percent by fiscal 1975.[62]

In order to illustrate the economic dilemma more clearly, it is useful to view private sector production against total government funding. For the fiscal year ended June 30, 1972, the total exports for the Trust Territory amounted to $2,637,000. For the same fiscal year, total government funding stood at $73,570,000. Of the latter amount, over $68 million came directly from the United States government and only about $4 million came from locally or internally produced revenue. Imports for the same year amounted to over $26,300,000, with food imports amounting to nearly $9.5 million and $13,906,000 spent for imported merchandise from the United States alone. In the five-year period between 1968 and 1973, government funding and costs of imported items have nearly doubled while the value of exports has been reduced to only 10 percent of the value of imports.[63]

CONCLUSION

It can be seen that the information developed by the United Nations visiting missions to the Trust Territory of the Pacific Islands in the areas of land administration, economic development, and political advancement strongly supports the charges made by Representative Hadley. Furthermore, in the three areas examined, the United Nations has had only marginal success in obtaining positive and timely action from the administering authority. In fact there is a strong suggestion of a deliberate pattern of response by the administering authority to criticism or recommendations by the visiting missions; that is, a pattern of creating "paper" solutions, which are never implemented.

In his 1950 study, Levi suggested underlying reasons for this pattern of relationships.

The trusteeship system well illustrates something that frequently happens. Overtly the nations seem to live up to their publicly confessed, high-minded aims; covertly a surrender to the demands of special interest groups has taken place. The structure of the trusteeship system is such that both purposes can be fulfilled.

The reasons why it was designed so equivocally are, first, that colonialism is not dead, and, second, that international rivalry for power and prestige drives nations toward territorial aggrandizement even when they admit that territorial possessions may be liabilities rather than assets.[64]

As Representative Hadley pointed out, the prime special interest group in Micronesia is the United States military establishment. As a validation of this, Rear Admiral William E. Lemos, Director of the East Asia and Pacific Region, in testimony before a Sub-Committee of the United States Senate on May 8, 1968, set the following parameters for the development of permanent dependency in Micronesia:

> The Department of Defense believes it is in the vital interests of the United States to continue to implement political, economic and social programmes which will provide the peoples of these islands with an opportunity to develop a way of life which would act as an incentive to identify their desires and aspirations with ours. We believe such actions would create an environment in which the Micronesians and the United States could work together towards mutually acceptable goals.[65]

A more explicit statement of this formula is found in a U.S. government document known as the Solomon Report. Prepared in 1963, but held secret until "leaked" to a Micronesian student group in 1971, this report candidly states that the overriding purpose of American administration of the Trust Territory must be internal political and economic manipulation to insure that the vote in a future plebiscite will make

> Micronesia a United States territory under circumstances which will: (1) satisfy somewhat conflicting interests of the Micronesians, the UN along lines satisfactory to the Congress [of the United States] ; (2) be appropriate to the present political and other capabilities of the Micronesians; and (3) provide sufficient flexibility in government structure to accommodate to whatever measure of local self-government the Congress of the United States might grant to Micronesia in later years.[66]

The report presents a wide variety of carefully detailed approaches to winning the plebiscite, including the use of increased U.S. appropriations for manipulation of elite groups; carefully selected development of capital improvements; the use of the Peace Corps as a means of pro-U.S. propaganda distribution; and the "general development of Micronesian interest in, and loyalties to, the US by various actions" including the "introduction in the school system of US oriented curriculum changes and patriotic rituals."[67]

The plans outlined in the Solomon Report proceed apace and the U.S. Office of

Information recently designed a system of not-always-so-subtle pro-American propaganda to be introduced throughout Micronesia as an education for self-government program.[68] This program is now being redesigned by a group of "local people" in the Trust Territory government and will be implemented throughout Micronesia.

The United States continues to negotiate separate status for the Mariana Islands and is proceeding with plans for a major "multi-service air base" that will utilize the majority of the island of Tinian and eventually will mirror the highly criticized Kwajalein missile project.[69]

Additionally, in what is termed a "major gesture of good faith," the U.S. Secretary of the Interior announced in November 1973 that he was approving the return of Micronesia's "public lands" to each district. Probably because this announcement seemed to most Micronesians to be the achievement of a long sought goal, little attention has been paid to the brief sentence on page five of the official communication specifying that title can pass to the owner(s) in the district only after an agreement is signed permitting the land to be used where necessary "to meet defense needs under the terms of proposed future status agreements with the United States."[70]

The twin goals of retarding the process of development and establishing a permanent system of economic and political dependence, which destroys self-respect and renders self-reliance impossible, are logical extensions of the militarism and paternalistic racism characteristic of American foreign adventures from the overthrow of the Hawaiian government to the recent colonial war in Southeast Asia.

While the Vietnamese have, at great cost, been successful in turning away American attempts at winning their hearts and minds, the Micronesians have allowed themselves to fall victim to the ambivalent patterns of gratitude and resentment that dependency generates.

The bitterness of Representative Hadley's attack on the United States is rendered impotent by the acquiescent attitudes of most of his fellow Micronesian leaders. As the 1973 Visiting Mission rather clearly suggested, the members of the Congress of Micronesia (and it may be safely assumed, most Micronesian members of the Trust Territory bureaucracy) now form an isolated elite fully dependent for their personal affluence and power upon the continued economic patronage of the United States Government.

So consumed with the search for their individual versions of the "good life" are these leaders, that they possess neither pride in cultural and national accomplishment, nor sufficient individual self-respect to successfully counter a quarter century of American domination.[71]

NOTES

1. *The Micronesian Independent* (Congress of Micronesia, News Service), March 2, 1974, p. 1.

2. Ray Stannard Baker, *Woodrow Wilson and World Settlement* (New York, 1927) vol. 1, 264.

3. *The Mandates System* (League of Nations [Geneva, 1931]), p. 4.

4. *Essential Facts About the League of Nations* (League of Nations [Geneva, 1939]), pp. 207-8.

5. *Postwar Foreign Policy Preparation, 1939-1945* (U.S. Department of State Publication 3850, Appendix 12 [Washington, 1949]), p. 472.

6. Edward R. Stettinius, Jr., *Roosevelt and the Russians: The Yalta Conference* (London, 1950), pp. 235-37.

7. Ibid., p. 238.

8. Arthur H. Vandenberg, Jr. (ed.), *The Private Papers of Senator Vandenberg* (Boston, 1952), p. 169.

9. *Everyman's United Nations* (United Nations [New York, 1968]), pp. 8-9, 568-70.

10. Ibid., p. 568.

11. Ibid., Article 76.

12. Ibid., p. 569.

13. Ibid., p. 570.

14. Ibid., pp. 372-73.

15. "PNG's Rapid Hand-Over, and So Much More to Think About," *Pacific Islands Monthly* 44 (December, 1973), p. 4.

16. *Annex to the Official Record of the Hundred and Thirteenth Meeting* (United Nations Security Council Official Records, Supplement 8 [February 26, 1947]), p. 69.

17. United Nations Security Council Official Records, Second Year, No. 31, 125th Meeting (April 2, 1947), p. 680.

18. Ibid., p. 644.

19. Ibid.

20. Ibid., p. 645.

21. *Annex to the Official Record* (Security Council), p. 69.

22. *Report on the Trust Territory of the Pacific Islands, 1953* (United Nations Trusteeship Council Official Records, Twelfth Session, Supplement No. 3 [June 16 to July 21, 1953]), p. 7.

23. Ibid., pp. 1-4.

24. *Report on the Trust Territory of the Pacific Islands, 1951* (United Nations Trusteeship Council Official Records, Eighth Session, Supplement No. 2 T/897 [January 30 to March 16, 1951]), p. 10.

25. Ibid.

26. Ibid., p. 11.

27. *Report of the United Nations Visiting Mission to the Trust Territory of the Pacific Islands 1967* (United Nations Trusteeship Council Official Records, Thirty-Fourth Session, Supplement No. 2 [May 29 to June 30, 1967]), p. 27

28. Ibid.

29. Ibid., pp. 27-8.

30. *Report of the United Nations Visiting Mission to the Trust Territory of the Pacific Islands, 1973* (United Nations Trusteeship Council Official Records, Fortieth Session, T/1641 [May 16, 1973]), pp. 50, 52.

31. Ibid., pp. 52-53.

32. *Report of the United Nations Visiting Mission to the Trust Territory of the Pacific Islands, 1961* (United Nations Trusteeship Council Official Records, Twenty-Seventh Session, Supplement No. 2 [June 1, 1961 to July 19, 1961]), pp. 82-84.

33. Ibid., p. 84.

34. *Report of the United Nations Visiting Mission to the Trust Territory of the Pacific Islands, 1964* (United Nations Trusteeship Council Official Records, Thirty-First Session, Supplement No. 2 [May 20 to June 29, 1964]), p. 19.

35. Trusteeship Council Report, 1973, p. 118.

36. *21st Annual Report to the United Nations on the Administration of the Trust Territory of the Pacific Islands* (United States Department of State [Washington, 1968]), pp. 1-5.

37. Trusteeship Council Report, 1973, p. 7.

38. Ibid.

39. Ibid.

40. *Report on the Trust Territory of the Pacific Islands, 1956* (United Nations Trusteeship Council Official Records, Eighteenth Session, Supplement No. 3 [June 7 to August 14, 1956]), p. 34.

41. Ibid., p. 35.

42. Trusteeship Council Report, 1961, pp. 6-7.

43. Ibid.

44. Ibid., p. 8.

45. Ibid., pp. 10-12, also Annex III. Editor's note: a majority of voters in the Northern Marianas approved of becoming a U.S. Commonwealth on June 17, 1975.

46. Trusteeship Council Report, 1973, pp. 127-29.

47. Trusteeship Council Report, 1964, p. 38.

48. Ibid., p. 38.

49. Ibid., p. 37.

50. Ibid., p. 40.

51. Ibid., pp. 43-5.

52. Trusteeship Council Report, 1967, pp. 38-40.

53. Ibid., p. 48.

54. Trusteeship Council Report, 1973, p. 42.

55. Ibid., p. 41.

56. Trusteeship Council Report, 1973, pp. 40-41.

57. Ibid., pp. 52-53.

58. Ibid., pp. 51-58.

59. Ibid., pp. 18-19.

60. Ibid., pp. 19-23.

61. Trusteeship Council Report, 1973, p. 59.

62. Ibid., p. 54.

63. *25th Annual Report to the United Nations on the Administration of the Trust Territory of the Pacific Islands* (United States Department of State [Washington, 1972]), pp. 271-72, 264-75.

64. Werner Levi, *Fundamentals of World Organization* (Minneapolis, 1950), pp. 160-63.

65. *Report of the Special Committee on the Situation with Regard to the Implementation of the Declaration on the Granting of Independence to Colonial Countries and Peoples* (United Nations General Assembly, A/7200/Add. 9 [November 14, 1968]), pp. 115-16.

66. Anthony M. Solomon, "Introduction and Summary" (Report of US Survey Mission), *The Young Micronesian,* 1 (March, 1971), p. 5.

67. Ibid., p. 10.

68. *Pacific Daily News,* September 29, 1973, pp. 1, 10.

69. *Pacific Daily News,* January 9, 1974, p. 1.

70. "US Land Policy Revealed," *A Dispatch to All District Administrators and Associated Agencies, Saipan, MI* (Office of the High Commissioner, The Trust Territory of the Pacific Islands [November 6, 1973]), p. 5.

71. For an excelient examination of the problems of dependency in the Pacific see: Ronald G. Crocombe, *The New South Pacific* (Wellington, 1973).

PART II

OCEANIA AND PACIFIC POWERS

C. HARTLEY GRATTAN   **7**

Australia and New Zealand and Pacific-Asia

Before one can discuss Australian and New Zealand policies in Pacific-Asia since 1940, it is absolutely necessary that the positions of the two countries be understood from the late eighteenth century. This requires one to pursue three inter-related lines of discussion: one that is essentially geographical, not least to define the Australian-New Zealand relation to Pacific-Asia; a second line concerning the involvement of the two countries in the British empire, and particularly as "dominions" from 1907, a status that constricted their capacity to deal with questions arising beyond their territorial limits in the international realm; and a third line focusing on the relative slowness of these dominions to take advantage of the enlargement of their capacity as self-governing dominions in the 1920s and 1930s and to engage in their own "persons" in foreign relations.

Of the two countries in question, New Zealand is wholly in the Pacific, while Australia, which bulks rather larger in the world's imagination, is of the Pacific because the economic and population heartland of the country consistently has been in the southeastern portion of the continent facing the Pacific Ocean. Although Australia's geographical reality began to be defined chiefly by the Dutch early in the seventeenth century, it was not until Captain James Cook inspected the Pacific coast in 1770 that any land was seen suggesting the possibility of European occupation. Eighteen years after Cook's visit, the British finally planted the first European colony in Australia (known as New Holland) and in the Southwest Pacific generally. The British did not claim the entire continent in 1788, partly because of a fairly total ignorance of the character of both the shore and the interior of the landmass; instead, they claimed everything east of the 129th degree of longitude and left the extension of their claim to the islands to the Pacific open and ambiguous. The British named their portion of the continent (as it proved to be) New South Wales, as Cook had proposed.

At that stage the islands to the east of "Australia" were also very imperfectly known, although they had been probed. Discoveries were made beginning with the Spanish operating from Peru in the sixteenth century, the Dutch in the seventeenth century, and the French and, above all, the British in the eighteenth century. The Dutchman Abel Tasman discovered New Zealand in 1643, sailing out of Batavia, and approached the Pacific by way of the Indian Ocean and to the south of New Holland. But it was the great British explorer James Cook who really put the country on the map in 1769 by brilliantly charting its coasts before he went on to the east coast of Australia.

To the pioneer British settlers in Australia, however, New Zealand was perceived for half a century as one of the more significant island groups to the east in the Pacific, in fact, as an integral part of Polynesia. It was not until 1840 that the British assumed sovereignty over New Zealand and set off a partition of the islands among the European powers that reached a short-lived equilibrium about 1900. Before New Zealand was absorbed into the British Empire, the British already had established their claim to the entire continent of Australia. However, they perceived the land resources inland from most of the southern, western, and northern coasts as enigmatic, problematical, or dubious; whatever was done by way of settlement and resource exploitation proved marginal or tributary to development in the southeastern "heartland" facing the Pacific.

Since the British settlers and governing authorities in Australia faced the Pacific, they early developed a possessive attitude toward the island groups east to the Marquesas and north at least to the equator. This attitude clearly was related not only to the island discoveries made by British explorers, but also to the indisputable fact that the British had initiated European settlement in the area. The Spanish pretension to exclusive rights in the Pacific was liquidated as far as the British were concerned at Nootka Sound in North America in 1790, two years after the settlement in Australia. The principal imperialist opponent in the Southwestern Pacific islands was France, until the Germans entered the picture late in the nineteenth century. For many years the Americans were a minor irritant, chiefly as resource exploiters and traders. They did not become aspiring claimants of territory until the end of the nineteenth century when they assumed possession of Eastern Samoa, and Guam north of the equator.

The British colonial attitude, first expressed in Australia and then in New Zealand after 1840, was that the British were unquestionably the predominant power in the Southwest Pacific and all other powers were therefore intruders into a British preserve. Early in the twentieth century the French publicist, Andre Siegfried, summed up the attitude as "Oceania for the Anglo-Saxons." In this imperialist struggle of the European powers for possession of the southwestern Pacific islands, which was territorial-strategical-economic in character, the Australians and New Zealanders participated only marginally because of their status in the British Empire. Nevertheless, one must rummage around in the story, for it is here that one will find the roots of the foreign (or more narrowly, the Pacific) policies of both Australia and New Zealand.

The ideas about the southwestern Pacific islands entertained both by the Australians and New Zealanders are close enough together to make generalization warranted. They believed that British possession of them was required *strategically* for the protection of the two countries against Britain's enemies—the idea of the islands as a *protective shield*; that British possession of the islands was required to guarantee that the fruits of exploitation would fall into British hands—an economic argument; and that they were needed to supplement with tropical products the basically temperate climatic resources of the two countries. The British authorities were always skeptical of the strategical arguments. The notion that the islands were rich because tropical soils suffered erosion over time proved false; and anyway, the islands as producers proved to be only marginal in the tropical economy of the world. The alleged complementariness of the islands to the economies of Australia and New Zealand, while in essence true, was often interfered with by both governments over time. Additionally, the relatively small economies of Australia and New Zealand could not absorb all the commodities the islands found it possible to produce. Inevitably Europe became the crucial market for the island products. Also, given the postures of the European powers in the international arena, decisions about the islands, particularly as to sovereignty, turned upon *European* perceptions and power relations, not upon those of the British Colonials in the Southwest Pacific.

While the colonists in Australia, and later those in New Zealand, early developed a possessive or covetous attitude toward the nearby island groups, over the years they were powerless to take action in their own "persons" to change the status of the islands, least of all to assume sovereignty over them. Even after the 1850s, when the eastern Australian colonies and New Zealand became self-governing under the forms of *responsible government,* they remained powerless to take such action. Although the gist of the evolutionary story of the British colonies to full autonomy is the progressive transfer of powers of government hitherto reserved to the Imperial authorities, the single power the Imperial authorities clung to most subbornly, from the colonial point of view, was that over "foreign affairs." The Imperial authorities defended the "diplomatic unity of the Empire."

Thus, while the colonists in Australia and New Zealand had ideas about the islands and were active in the European penetration of them, they were powerless to effect in their own "persons" any fundamental change in their status. They might contribute heavily to the creation of conditions that dictated a change, but they could not make the change. Only the Imperial authorities in London could do that. The colonial governments, who supported the adventurers in the islands, or opposed the alleged purposes of the Empire's imperialist competitors, could do little more than try to convert the decision-makers of the Empire to their point of view or function within the Empire either singly or occasionally jointly as pressure groups. This point can be illustrated by the colonial proposals and actions regarding Tahiti in the 1840s and New Caledonia in the 1850s. In both of these cases, the foreign competitor was France, which was victorious. Further illustrations are Fiji in the middle 1870s, where Britain won; New Guinea in the middle 1880s, where the British withdrew in favor of Germany and the United States on being given compensation elsewhere. In all these cases there was a clear conflict between the Australian or New Zealand view of what the destiny of the particular groups should be and the position the Imperial authorities in London regarded as best serving the interests of the Empire as a whole. In effect, then, the decision to take over control of the islands, whether in the form of a protectorate or sovereignty, was always in the end determined in Europe in the light of the then foreign political relations of the competing European powers.

The fluctuations in the concerns of the British colonists in the area need not detain us here; but we can view their successive expressions of policy with regard to the islands as exhibiting a continuing concern that the island groups, if they were to pass into European possession at all, should be British. This fundamental principle was not, as the record shows, entertained in Britain. The colonials gave their position classic expression at the end of 1883 at a conference in Sydney attended by spokesmen for the Australian colonies, New Zealand, and Fiji; they resolved "That further acquisition of dominion in the Pacific south of the Equator, by any Foreign Power, would be highly detrimental to the safety and well-being of the British possessions in Australasia, and injurious to the interests of the Empire."

Shifting our focus now to Asia, we may begin profitably by generalizing that while the Southwest Pacific is geographically "under the overhang of Asia" it rarely has been regarded by Europeans as an integral part of Asia, even when the area was generally called Australasia. At the time of the original European settlement in the Southwest Pacific, this area was as unknown to Asians as to Europeans. Over the succeeding decades, Asians—Chinese, Japanese, Javanese, Tonkinese (North Vietnamese), and Indians—appeared in the Southwest Pacific chiefly as imported laborers in European enterprises. As such, they were supplements to, or displacement of, the "kanaka" (the generic term for island indigenes) labor force, which was widely employed in the islands and in Australia. Only when the Asians were allowed to settle down as free workers did they become significant as segments of the permanent population; notable examples are the Chinese in Tahiti and, more importantly, the Indians in Fiji. In Australia itself, the Asian workers were seen as disastrous competitors with European workers, and from about 1860 efforts were made at the governmental level to exclude them or at least limit their intake. This effort achieved Australia-wide success early in the twentieth century when the new Federal Commonwealth of Australia passed an immigration law that implemented the so-called "White Australia" policy. This was to fortify the idea that the Southwest Pacific should keep Asia at a distance. Supporting this idea was all the more feasible because as producers and traders, and in financial, governmental, and cultural relations, Australia and New Zealand were strongly oriented toward and attached to the United Kingdom. The two countries were perceived by all concerned as outposts of Britain or Europe in the Pacific, not as countries significantly related to Asia. Nevertheless, the European imperialist power in Asia—southwest, south, southeast, and east—particularly British imperial power, is fundamental to any explanation of the success of the Southwest Pacific British countries in maintaining their positions of separateness from Asia.

Therefore the story of the rise of British imperial power in Asia from the late 18th century to World War I must be understood if the success of Australia and New Zealand in maintaining their separateness from Asia is to be understood. By the same token, the progressive decline of British imperial power in Asia from about

1900 to the present day must be understood if the emergence of Australia and New Zealand since World War II as significant participants in the political, economic, and cultural affairs of Asia-Pacific is to be understood.

Not only is the complex story of the British in Asia still under intensive study as a thing-in-itself, but also the study of it in relation to the history of the Southwest Pacific has yet to be undertaken. This is to say that the world-historical context of the rise of Australia and New Zealand is at present necessarily ill-understood. Yet anybody who has reflected upon the matter quickly becomes aware that from very early in the nineteenth century, the British imperial authorities related the guaranteeing of the security of the British in the Southwest Pacific to British naval power in Asia. At first it was the Imperial naval power of the India station, then the China Squadron, and finally between the two world wars the Singapore Base. Diplomatically, it was the British Foreign Office that absorbed the Asian protests against Australia's "White Australia" policy. And so on.

But while the British Imperial power in Asia underwrote Australian and New Zealand aspirations to maintain their isolation from Asia, it was not the only support they received. Several times I have pointed out that the Southwest Pacific became, around the time of the American Civil War, a "by-blow" in relation to the politics and economics of Pacific-Asia. The powers active in the Pacific, including the United States, focused their attention chiefly on the Pacific north of the equator and in Asia on the seaward rim from the Red Sea around to China—also north of the equator. The Southwest Pacific was perceived as something not only separate from the real arenas of interest but also as of very minor importance in a global perspective. If the Southwest Pacific was related to Asia-Pacific interests, non-British analysts did not count it for much in the power equations, while the British analysts regarded it as a dependent responsibility and not as a positive factor in calculating British Asian-Pacific strength. Therefore it appears that the desire of the Southwest Pacific to maintain its "separateness" from Asia was in some subtle fashion complemented by the willingness of the powers to discount heavily its significance in the power calculations regarding the Asian-Pacific arena north of the equator. It was taken into account, if at all, as an X-factor in the calculation of British power in Pacific-Asia, definitely ancillary to British power and really unweightable by foreigners.

Nevertheless the foregoing makes it more or less intelligible why the Australians came to regard themselves as a Pacific people. The New Zealanders were clearly of the Pacific Basin by virtue of geography, but this was not entirely true of the Australians. The long western coast of Australia facing the Indian Ocean figured little when it came to defining the Australian position. It was understood relatively soon after British settlement in the west in 1829 that the exploitable resources of the seemingly attractive southwestern portion of the western segment of the continent were thin, even for pastoral purposes. The idea that they nevertheless required protection was damped down to a low level by the understanding that from about 1815 the Indian Ocean was a "British lake" as a consequence of the settlement of affairs east of the Cape of Good Hope at the Congress of Vienna; this idea was fortified by later developments around the Ocean highly favorable to Britain. Even when the economic and other significances of the Australian west were upgraded—as by the establishment of an important sea-route to and from the United Kingdom via the Suez Canal after 1869, the rich gold discoveries of the 1890s, the successful establishment of a wool-wheat complex in the southwest a little later—no notion that the Indian Ocean coast required special attention in security terms was elaborated. That the Indian Ocean coast was vulnerable only began to be perceived in World War II. This perception intensified as the "British lake" concept began to dissolve in the postwar years. Yet even today, the Indian Ocean coast is regarded as a secondary problem of security for Australia, probably best resolved by an international agreement that the Ocean be made a "zone of peace,"[1] hopefully preventing it from becoming a place of confrontation for the navies of the United States and the Soviet Union. This solution is particularly appealing because it minimizes Australia's direct responsibility for the security of the Indian Ocean coast; even in collaboration with the American and the weakening British strength in the Indian Ocean and possibly South Africa, this security task might become exceedingly onerous. This position is held in spite of the fact that rich mineral resources have been discovered and actively exploited in the west since World War II, economically upgrading the area to a height hitherto unimaginable.

Equally, the northern coast of Australia has figured little in Australia's imagination of its fundamental orientation. Like the west, the north has long been seen as a low and highly problematical economic resource extending from the Pacific coast of northern Queensland, through the Northern Territory, to the Indian Ocean coast in northwestern West Australia, with the Northern Territory embracing most of it. Fundamentally this vast stretch of territory has been seen as a tributary pastoral area, with small spots of mining enterprise, whether as tributary to the southwestern area of the west, or to the infinitely more promising and highly developed southeastern heartland. At odd times in the first half of the nineteenth century, this curiously "blank" face that Australia presented to Asia was imagined to provide bases for possible British trading incursions into the Dutch-monopolized East Indies, but this came to nothing. The Territory soon settled into its character as marginal pastoral country useful chiefly for cattle (not sheep), whether governed from South Australia or, after 1911, by the Commonwealth. In the 1930s, when the then new air services to Europe via Asia began to make Darwin (the principal port on the northern coast and capital of Northern Territory) the place of initial landing in Australia and final departure from Australia, it was realized how shabby Darwin was and what an odd first impression of Australia it created for first-time visitors. Even so, because Australian attention was so strongly focused elsewhere, the vulnerability of Darwin and the northern coast generally was little discussed.

It took World War II to bring the security of the north actively to Australian attention. In defense terms, a great change came over its position after the fall of Singapore and the Netherlands East Indies to the Japanese. It was then clearly understood that the northern coast, distant from the southeastern heartland, was vulnerable by air, and possibly also by sea, to an enemy in possession of the Indies. And in fact, Darwin was subjected to numerous Japanese air raids during the war, the first of which gave the little town the dubious honor of receiving the first shots ever fired in anger by an enemy at Australia. Other points in the north were also raided by the Japanese Air Force. However, all this, in spite of its frightening import, did not change the Australian emphasis on its Pacific Ocean character. Neither in enemy practice nor in Australian theory was this where the Australian southeastern heartland could be menaced decisively. Rather it was expected that an invasion would involve a successful enemy occupation of New Guinea from the north, followed by a progress down the Pacific coast of Queensland with the objective of occupying the heartland south of Brisbane. This likelihood was first suggested by Lord Kitchener in 1913 before there was a coastal railway to support it. As a result, the first Japanese moves against the Australian-administered territory of New Guinea were interpreted as a signal of imminent invasion of the Australian continent.

It was only after the war was over that it was discovered that the Japanese strategy was different. What the Japanese actually tried to do was to isolate Australia, especially the southeastern heartland, from any succor from the United States by gaining control of the islands to the north, northeast, and east of Australia, thus cutting the lines of communication between North America and Australia. This accomplished, Australia could be left to "wither on the vine." Such a strategy clearly implied that the Japanese early became confident that the United States would come to Australia's aid if its security was menaced by Japanese action.[2] The Japanese strategy was frustrated, however, by the overextension of Japanese power that the effort represented, and by the success in battle of the Australian, New Zealand, and American forces, symbolized by the battles of the Coral Sea and Guadalcanal. Thus it came about that World War II was perceived by the Australians and New Zealanders as essentially a Pacific Ocean war, a Western Pacific war. They were confirmed in their long-standing assumption that they were menaced, if at all, from the north *in the Pacific.* It took the war and its consequences in Asia to bring home to them that their positions had to be radically modified.

From the foregoing it is, I hope, clear that the Australians and New Zealanders, while insuring their "isolation" behind the screen of islands in the Southwest Pacific, more or less informally accepted the Equator as defining the northern limit of their concerns. However, up to the end of World War I this notion of the Equator as a northern boundary can hardly be said to have hardened into a doctrine or policy. That the two peoples did on occasion entertain ideas about developments north of the Equator can be illustrated by, for example, the insistence of the Australians in the 1880s that their trading rights in Micronesia be protected by Great Britain against German interference; by the warning given in 1898 by Prime Minister Seddon of New Zealand to the United States that it should not take over Hawaii in disregard of British rights;[3] and perhaps most impressively by Prime Minister Alfred Deakin's proposal in 1909, addressed to the British Colonial Secretary for forwarding to the Foreign Office, that the British initiate negotiations for "an extension of the Monroe Doctrine to all the countries around the Pacific Ocean supported by the guarantees of the British Empire, Holland, France and China added to that of the United States." True, Deakin's proposal came to nothing, but it serves as a precedent for such actions as Prime Minister Joseph Lyons' proposal in 1937 for a non-aggression pact of the Pacific powers, and for the position of Dr. H.V. Evatt in the wake of the Cairo Conference of 1943 that Australia, as a primary Pacific power, must be consulted about any changes in sovereignty in all the Pacific as a result of the war. It is of very great importance to recall that lurking behind the proposals of Deakin, Lyons, and Evatt was the notion, widely entertained in both Australia and New Zealand, that to insure their security they must always strive to contain or frustrate the menacing forces they perceived as residing in the North. By 1900 this sense of being menaced by Asia had been pinpointed: it was Japan.

The notion that the Equator was somehow a dividing line for Australia and New Zealand in the Pacific was firmed up during the settlement of World War I at Paris. When World War I broke out, the Australians, on British cue, took over the German possessions in New Guinea and associated islands. (From 1906 they had been the administering power in the British portion of the island of New Guinea, the colony of Papua.) At the same time, the New Zealanders took over the German holdings in the Samoan group. Nauru, also south of the Equator, came under British control. At that time the Australians expected to go on and expel the Germans from the Micronesian Islands right up to the American posses- sion, Guam. In the operations against the Germans in the Pacific, the British not only commanded by right Australian and New Zealand cooperation, but also solicited the cooperation of their ally, Japan. Japan, to Britain's annoyance, elec- ted to enter the war as party against Germany and proceeded then to gather up what German spoils it could. Among the spoils, aside from those in China, were the Micronesian Islands south from Guam to the Equator. The British had to acquiesce in this Japanese action because they felt they had to have Japanese assistance in the Pacific and Indian Oceans, particularly for escorting Australian and New Zealand troopships to Suez.

In order to obtain Japanese naval assistance in the Mediterranean, the British in 1917 acceded to a Japanese demand that they be supported in getting sov- ereignty in Micronesia in any settlement after the war. This was also agreed to by France and Russia, and the documents became components of the "Secret Treaties" eventually revealed to the world by the Bolsheviks during their cam- paign to discredit the "imperialist" Allies after the Russian Revolution. At Paris, the Australians sought sovereignty over the ex-German portion of New Guinea, the New Zealanders sought to annex ex-German Samoa, and the Japanese ex- German Micronesia. This effort was spearheaded by Prime Minister William Morris Hughes of Australia. He was strongly supported by Prime Minister William Massey of New Zealand and tacitly by the Japanese. All were frustrated by President Woodrow Wilson's insistence that the territories be made mandates, eventually new and highly compromised mandates of the C-class variety. Hughes' case for annexation was based on a variety of arguments all of which had roots in the Southwest Pacific past: New Guinea was an integral part of the "island shield"; it was for the best that it be exploited economically by Australians and integrated into the Australian economy; and it was right and proper that Asians be kept out of New Guinea to insure that "White Australia" be preserved. (The Chinese community of old German New Guinea was not permitted to migrate even into the Australian colony of Papua, let alone to the continent of Australia, until after World War II.) It was as paladin of "White Australia" that Hughes "San" most egregiously affronted the Japanese, but that is another story. The net of the business is that Australia was installed in old German New Guinea on a basis that Hughes himself described as a 99-year lease as compared to a freehold; the New Zealanders got Western Samoa on the same terms; and Britain, New Zealand, and Australia got joint control of phosphate-rich Nauru, with the administration supplied by Australia. This disposed of the German holdings south of the Equator. North of the Equator, the Japanese were installed in Micronesia. Thus, in effect, the Equator became a *de facto* but not a *de jure* boundary between Australia and New Zealand on one side and the particular Asian country they conceived of as a menace on the other.

The Australians and New Zealanders were enormously disquieted, and their disquiet found many and various expressions between the wars. In the end it was from their Micronesian mandate (its status ambiguous, since the Japanese had left the League of Nations in 1935 and nobody had challenged their right to continue to control Micronesia) that the Japanese launched their assault upon New Guniea as a first step in a campaign to gain control of the islands south of the Equator and isolate Australia and New Zealand from North America, clearly a Pacific Ocean enterprise.

If the settlement after World War I left the Australians and New Zealanders with a sense that their northern boundary in the Pacific was, in effect, the Equator, this did not mean that they were not interested in what went on beyond the boundary. Because in the imaginations of the powers involved in the politics and economics of Pacific-Asia, it was what went on north of the Equator that was significant; Australia and New Zealand tended to be neglected, or left out of account altogether, in both the thinking and the action. In effect, only Great Britain had any interest at all in the possible repercussions of developments in the northern Pacific and Asia upon Australia and New Zealand. When Professor George H. Blakesley, of Clark University, wrote a paper for the U.S. State Department's top-secret briefing book for the Washington Conference of 1921-22 on Australian and New Zealand policy, his central point was that the two dominions were exclusively interested in the islands south of the Equator. Even well-regarded *ex post facto* accounts of the developments north of the Equator, like that by F.C. Jones (1954), barely acknowledge that Australia and New Zealand had any concern.

In its Pacific-Asia phase, the Washington Conference was an effort to provide a framework for the relations of the involved powers in the Pacific and East Asia; these relations had been disordered by World War I, the settlement at Paris afterward, and by developments in China, Japan, and Russia. The old framework for relations between the Western imperialist powers plus Japan and Pacific-Asia was assumed to be be beyond any useful rehabilitation; but it was nevertheless and paradoxically assumed that the traditional national interests of the United States,

Great Britain, possibly France, and Japan and China had to be protected in some new, but not revolutionary, fashion. "Wild" new factors, mostly to be contemplated with dismay, were recognized: the possible policies and actions of Germany, which had been expelled from Pacific-Asia as a result of defeat in World War I but was likely to make some kind of comeback; Bolshevik Russia, particularly in Manchu and maritime Siberia east to Lake Baikal; and China, particularly with regard to its intensifying revolutionary "nationalism." The United States, then on rather uneasy terms with Japan but heavily involved with it in trade, actively maintained its peculiarly intense interest in China, conspicuously its interest in the territorial integrity of the country and equality in economic affairs for foreigners. The United States wanted Great Britain to terminate its alliance with Japan (last renewed in 1911) to guarantee that Britain would neither assist Japan nor stand embarrassingly neutral if the United States and Japan got into a war. The United States also sought naval parity with Great Britain, but it would not concede it to Japan in the Pacific. The upshot was the 5-5-3 formula.

It was the question of the future of the Anglo-Japanese alliance that entangled the Australians and New Zealanders in what was generally understood to be a "north of the Equator" affair. Though the Anglo-Japanese Alliance, in either its 1902 or 1911 versions, had not diminished the Australian or New Zealand sense that Japan was the prime "menace" to them to the North, they had come around to the notion that it provided the means for Britain to moderate Japanese ambitions overseas, and probably to deflect them if they took a "southward" direction. The question of renewal or abandonment of the Alliance was debated at the Imperial Conference of 1921, at which Prime Minister Arthur Meighen of Canada put the United States case *against* renewal, while Prime Minister William Morris Hughes of Australia put the case *for* renewal. The Canadians regarded good relations with the United States as fundamental to their security. The British were also keenly interested in good relations with the United States. Hughes had no objection to good relations with the United States, but he regarded giving up the alleged British "brake" on Japan as too high a price to pay for them. They were not regarded by him as all that important to Australia, and anyhow they were Britain's concern. The argument, whatever its tenor and course, was adjourned, so to speak, by the American invitation to the Conference at Washington, issued in President Warren G. Harding's name by Secretary of State Charles Evans Hughes. At the Conference the Anglo-Japanese Alliance lapsed.

It was as a consequence of developments during World War I that the Australians and New Zealanders were involved in the debate over high Imperial policy in 1921. As World War I unfolded, the British dominions, particularly Canada, became more and more exercised by the British practice of making policy decisions of great importance for the dominions involving British disposition of their resources and manpower without full consultation with them. To meet the situation, David Lloyd George, when he became Prime Minister of the United Kingdom in 1916, convened an Imperial War Cabinet in London in which the dominion prime ministers had places when sessions were held to debate and decide policy matters and the decisions put into execution. This, in effect, realized the historical ambition of Australia and New Zealand alike to gain a recognized place for exerting direct influence on and responsibility for Imperial policy-making. They also willingly accepted the proposal that they have representation on the British delegation to the Peace Conference (Australia had two places, New Zealand one) and separate membership in the League of Nations. There Australia's and New Zealand's ambition, or nationalism, stopped; but that of the Irish, the South Africans, and the Canadians did not. Nevertheless, both the Australians and the New Zealanders accepted representation on the British delegation to the Washington Conference, though only after some fumbling with the question by Lord Curzon, then the British Foreign Minister. The Americans proved to be unexpectedly tolerant of the arrangement.

To pursue this question of the new international status of the dominions a step farther, we must recall that when the matter of formal redefinition arose at the Imperial Conference of 1926, the Australians and New Zealanders offered neither help nor hindrance. They did not share the intellectual passion of the Irish for as forward a formulation as could be achieved, nor the stolid unintellectual determination of the South Africans to achieve the same end, nor the strangely subdued approving position of the Canadians. The New Zealanders and Australians simply saw no justifying reason why status should be closely defined, legally or constitutionally. They felt they could do all they were likely to want to do as a result of the *implicit* redefinition reflected in their participation in the Imperial War Cabinet, the Peace Conference, the League of Nations, and their designation as mandatory powers in New Guinea, Samoa, and Nauru. In any event, they obtained exemption from the operation of Articles 2-6 of the Statute of Westminister, while the aggressive dominions used them to push forward rapidly toward fully autonomous positions. By 1944, a Canadian expert, Professor Frank Scott, was asserting the end of dominion status. But Australia and New Zealand remained an integral part of the Empire. In 1937, Robert Gordon Menzies, as Prime Minister Lyon's attorney general, tried and failed to get the Australian parliament to accept at last the rejected articles of the Statute by alleging a technical need to bring Australia into line with its fellows. Australia did not accept the articles until late in 1942 on the recommendation of a Labor Government and its attorney general, H.V. Evatt. New Zealand delayed acceptance until 1947. The significance of all this is that Australia and New Zealand faced the developments in Pacific-Asia during the 1920s and 1930s while they were still constricted, in theory, by the ancient dogma of the diplomatic unity of the British Empire. Hence, what they thought and said and did was important only as it had some effect upon the Britons who dealt with Pacific-Asia affairs. The Australians tried to improve their knowledge of, and presumptively their influence on, Imperial foreign policy decisions by appointing a liaison officer to London in 1924; his primary duty was to keep tabs on the Foreign Office, with what effect we do not yet know. (The officer, acting for Prime Minister Stanley Melbourne Bruce, was Richard Gardiner Casey, later Lord Casey.) The New Zealanders did not even do that much until the Labour Party won office and power for the first time in 1935. They then began to express particularistic views, using the League of Nations as a forum, since their policies were decidedly pro-League and in both fundamentals and details clearly different from the United Kingdom's views of the time. (The New Zealand spokesman at the League was W.J. Jordon, New Zealand High Commissione in London.)

It is a well-grounded suspicion that the Australians were quite consistently supportive of United Kingdom foreign policy right up to and including the climax of appeasement at Munich in 1938; and we know they went to war in traditional fashion the next year, not having been consulted at all about the guarantee to Poland. Similarly, we know that New Zealand, in spite of its spectacular and exhilarating dissent from Imperial policy in 1935-1938, also accepted the war with fervid declarations of loyalty to the Empire. The traditionalistic positions of Australia and New Zealand contrast oddly with the responses of Canada, South Africa, and Ireland to the war declaration.

The gist of all this is that between the two wars, Australia, which was ruled by conservatives up to 1935, gave little evidence at the government level of what their national political foreign policies in Pacific-Asia might be. Yet unquestionably, there was a significant movement of minds precisely about this Pacific-Asia matter, even in the 1920s, though it did not surface in publications until the 1930s. The relevant thinking and writing was, on present evidence, done chiefly by academic and extramural intellectuals and quasi-intellectuals, many of whom later had distinguished careers in academia and public service. The discussion emerged from an intensive consideration of the prospects of trade expansion in Pacific-Asia, a fundamentally important matter during the Great Depression, since trade was the field in which both dominions would be assertive and long had total authority. The dependence upon the export-import trade of the two dominions for economic viability was exceedingly heavy. Inevitably, however, as the foreign political situation in East Asia obviously worsened, the Australian and New Zealand concern about their Far Eastern political policies intensified, even if it was still assumed that they could be translated into actuality only by pressure upon the Imperial authorities in London. Inevitably some very harsh things were said about the underdevelopment of political foreign policies.[4]

After the event, it is very clear that this public debate was cribbed and confined by various implicit and explicit assumptions and ranges of ignorance. While the two dominions could do something about trade on their own, as traditionalists they were beset by the conviction that they must do nothing to jeopardize their close trade relation to the United Kingdom. This caused some shilly-shallying, which came to a climax in the so-called trade diversion episode of 1936 when Australia, to conserve and strengthen the United Kingdom tie, sharply offended both Japan and the United States. It was still assumed, at the governmental level particularly, that whatever they could do technically, they should not, in the light of the Australian assumptions about Imperial relations, do anything that implied breaching the diplomatic unity of the Empire. Implicitly, and often explicitly, it was assumed that Britain was still strong enough in Pacific-Asia to give positive effect, if it so chose, to Australian and New Zealand policy proposals; this, of course, involved a failure to understand or accept how the United Kingdom's power and authority in Pacific-Asia had declined markedly since World War I. While in Pacific-Asia the focus was properly on Japan, the hope and expectation in the dominions was that the difficulties could be resolved short of war by a powerful British diplomatic offensive, a misappreciation of Britain's actual position that continued to be entertained until 1941.

Even with regard to Japan, the perception was odd, particularly in Australia; the Australians were little concerned about the impact of Japanese policy and actions in continental Asia and little concerned about the impact on China, until the anti-British strain in Japanese action and thought began to appear. Even then, the overriding Australian anxiety was that the Japanese would veer away from the continent and turn south, menacing Australia's security. While the Pacific dominions had their eyes on Pacific-Asia, it was still the case after about 1936 that war might break out in Europe, thus summoning them to implement their traditional policy of supporting the Empire in "Europe" (which by definition included the Middle East and North Africa),[5] with an unknown impact upon the situation in the Western Pacific. In this context, the Singapore Base, which was the linchpin of British power east of Suez, came into the picture; and while on the one hand the official government position was that Singapore would keep the Japanese away from Australia, there was much scepticism about the likelihood of this, particularly if war should come simultaneously in Europe and Asia-Pacific. Finally, both Australia and New Zealand were bothered by their inability to define the probable role of the United States if the Western Pacific were to be plunged into an all-out war by Japan. In the 1920s it was orthodox wisdom that what the United States might do was of little interest or import to Australia. Only in the middle 1930s did speculation about America's probable or possible role in the Pacific Basin, and its impact on them, begin in Australia and New Zealand.

The foregoing discussions surfaced, as remarked, chiefly at the public level. In the parliaments of Australia and New Zealand, they were little in evidence although some of the dilemmas appeared in debate in a different dress and context, for the parliamentary debates were warmest in the field of defense. New Zealand and Australia both had long conceived of their defense policies in the context of Imperial defense, as conditioned by and supportive of Imperial defense. If anything, the New Zealanders were more "orthodox" in this respect than the Australians, for in Australia there was a disposition, which can be traced back to the early years of the 20th century, to argue that the fullest possible development of the domestic power to defend itself was the best possible contribution to Imperial security. These conceptions were held even though it was recognized that the ultimate situation Australia could not successfully defend itself against a powerful foreign enemy by itself—thus its final dependence upon Imperial strength.

In a way, the difference between the two dominions is well-symbolized by their response to the British decision after World War I to found its defense east of Suez on a great base at Singapore. New Zealand welcomed this proposal and made substantial money contributions to its realization that continued to be paid in full even during the Great Depression. It was, however, quite upset by the "go-stop-go" treatment given the project by the British. Only New Zealand

Labour expressed skepticism of the Base, and even it came around to supporting the Base in the end. The Australians, on the other hand, welcomed the idea of the Base and continued to regard it, even though on occasion with dubiety, as the fulcrum of British power in their geographical area; but they contributed no money to its building, rather emphasizing that their navy, which had come into being in 1913, was their contribution to sinewing Imperial defense in their vicinity.

In both countries defense expenditures were pared down to a low level during the first years of the Great Depression. In Australia it was not until 1934 that defense expenditures began to be returned to earlier levels. These then were increased progressively right up to the outbreak of the war in 1939, but only reached maximum possibilities during the war in the Western Pacific. During the pre-war defense debates, the conservatives, in office at the time, argued for a defense program which was lavish by the standards of the other dominions but definitely tilted toward sinewing Imperial defence. Labor, the official opposition, tried to develop the position that the emphasis should be on maximizing the country's capacity to defend itself, ultimate dependence upon Imperial power assumed. When war came in Europe, the conservatives (still in office) acted, after some hisitation occasioned by doubts about the position with regard to Japan in the Western Pacific, to put Australian power into the Imperial service with a concentration in the Middle East and North Africa. This was being orthodox, or "loyal," at extreme risk. Labor was uneasy about it, persistently arguing for a better balance of Australian defense power-in-being as between "Europe" and Australia.

As to the Near North (as the Far East was beginning to be called), the focus of concern was Singapore. The Australians and New Zealanders continued to regard it as an ultimate Imperial guarantee of their security, though doubts about both its adequacy and the prospects for decisive reinforcement in a crisis were rife. The doubts came to a climax after the fall of France in June 1940. Nevertheless, the Australians, especially, continued to "invest" in Singapore right up to its fall at the end of 1941; and about 15,000 Australians ended up as Japanese prisoners of war.

It was in this context of deep concern about the security of the two countries in the Pacific-Asia area that a subtle, but highly significant shift, was made to action at the diplomatic level to improve not only their information about developments but also to put them in a better position to influence policy formulation and action. It was decided by the Australian government that ministers should be exchanged with the countries chiefly involved in the Pacific-Asia imbroglio. In April 1939, Prime Minister Robert Gordon Menzies, reflecting discussions and soundings that had been initiated earlier under the predecessor government of Joseph A. Lyons and possibly also the public discussions of the immediately preceding years, declared in an oft-quoted public speech:

> In the Pacific we have primary responsibilities and primary risks. Close
> as our consultation with Great Britain is, and must be, in relation to
> European affairs, it is still true to say that we must, to a large extent, be
> guided by her knowledge and affected by her decisions. The problems

of the Pacific are different. What Britain calls the Far East is to us the
near north . . . . With this in mind I look forward to the day when we
will have a concert of Pacific powers, pacific in both senses of the word.
This means increased diplomatic contact between ourselves and the
United States, China and Japan, to say nothing of the Netherlands East
Indies and the other countries which fringe the Pacific.

In effect, this was to propose a move toward a new relation to Pacific-Asia, still
under the cover of the diplomatic unity of the British Empire; but it was also a
move to open the door to the emergence of Australia as an autonomous nation
under the ineluctable compulsion of events. It took Australia a full year to carry
out the intention Menzies announced. In the years 1940-1942, Australia dispatched
ministers to and received ministers from the United States at first, then Japan,
China, the Netherlands (its government-in-exile), and the Soviet Union. Acting in
a rather more leisurely fashion, New Zealand began a parallel development by send-
in a minister to the United States; he reached Washington shortly after Pearl Harbor.

Today, wise after the event, we know that Mr. Menzies' rhetoric was irrelevant to
the actualities of a deteriorating situation. It was not a pacific Pacific that was in
the cards but an appalling war. The worst suspicions of the Pacific dominions about
Japan were seemingly to be confirmed. But it must be kept in mind that those
Australian diplomats who reached their stations before the Pacific war broke out
had as their overriding concern the prevention of war. They tried hard to keep the
Japanese and the Americans talking. But assuming that war might nevertheless come,
the Australian minister at Washington was concerned to support the idea of British-
American collaboration to "stop" Japan, concentrating on convincing the Americans
that they should help reinforce Singapore; he suggested that the Americans might
find bases in New Guinea and Australia useful in backing up their position in the
Philippines and that the Australians had surpluses of raw materials the United
States might find useful. But while the Australian minister, Richard Gardiner
Casey, projected an attractive image of Australia to the general public, neither he
nor his colleague, the British ambassador, were able to modify essentially American
diplomatic or strategic conceptions about the situation in Pacific-Asia. Australia
figured very little in these conceptions. Only events, not propositions or arguments,
could change American ideas. At home, the Australians were concerned chiefly
that the Americans and Japanese keep talking, not lapse into fighting. This continued to be the Australian stance even after Labor had displaced both the conservative
Menzies government and its short-term successor of the same general complexion,
the Fadden government, from office in October 1941. Dr. H.V. Evatt, the Labor
Minister for External Affairs, emphasized the point in his first statement to Parliament. In the event, Evatt's first task as External Affairs Minister was not so much
foreign political as it was to get from the United States the material and manpower
to enable Australia and New Zealand to stop and roll back the Japanese. By that
time it had been decided by logic and the terrible events in Asia and at Pearl
Harbor that Australia was the base for any campaign to stop and roll back the
Japanese in the Western Pacific; and "appreciation" first was formulated by the

Australians. The same events, so appallingly disastrous to the British, had caused the assignment of primary responsibility for the Pacific war to the United States. Washington, therefore, by the logic of events became as significant a focal point of Australian concern as London had hitherto been. A revolution in the perception of the position of Australia and New Zealand in the Pacific was thus initiated by events which argumentation had proved powerless to set going.

Late in 1941, when the Japanese with a rapidity unanticipated by all parties involved, eliminated British, American and Dutch power from the Philippines to Singapore and south to the threshold of the Southwest Pacific, the Australians and New Zealanders confronted a condition and not a theory. Central to the condition was the assumption that an invasion of Australia was imminent, which would make New Zealand's position insupportable. With British power unavailable for the defense of Australia and New Zealand at the moment, the immediate problem was to obtain support from the United States as the only Pacific Basin nation with the requisite power prepared to act in collaboration with the two dominions. In this context the Japanese attack on Pearl Harbor was seen less as a crippling disaster for the United States than as a guarantee that the United States would act against Japan in a fashion that would serve the interests of Australia and New Zealand.

Whether the United States was to be regarded as a surrogate for the United Kingdom or whether the development was to be regarded as signaling a fundamental reorientation of Australian and New Zealand international relations was not then apparent. Neither was it clear whether the United States was coming to the "rescue" of Australia and New Zealand out of clearly magnanimous good will, or in response to the urgent American need for a base on which to mount a counteroffensive against Japan. As noted earlier, the Australian military strategists had anticipated the conception of Australia as the logical base for a campaign against Japan once American, British, and Dutch power to the north had been eliminated; in opposing the Japanese to the north, the Americans had tentatively, of necessity, explored the uses of Australia as a base.

Although the idea that in a war between Japan and the United States a stalemate would eventuate early in the North Pacific had been suggested by the British writer on naval strategy, Hector Bywater, in 1922, the idea had figured little in American strategic thinking. And certainly Bywater's corrollary, that to break the stalemate the Americans would have to go south of the Equator to roll up the Japanese forces established in the islands until the Japanese homeland could be assaulted, was clearly not in the American mind. But whatever the American motivation, or the interpretation of American action, it was decidedly in the interest of Australia and New Zealand to get on as intimate and intense a collaborative footing with the United States as they could manage.

While in a sense this had been a purpose of Australian policy (implicitly supported also by New Zealand) since it had exchanged ministers with the United States in 1940, the assumption all along had been that the collaboration would be between the United States and the British, with Australia and New Zealand obviously benefiting, and that the collaboration would keep any war to the north of the Equator well away from Australia and New Zealand. In the actual situation at the end of 1941, then, a hyperbolic, not to say hysterical, response from Australia was not unexpected. It was assumed that the British would hand over the desperate situation in the Western Pacific to the Americans, as actually happened, because it had been understood that for some time the power had been effectively in American hands.

But what now for Australia and New Zealand? Australia's initial response was clearly set out in a message to the world by Prime Minister John Curtin in late December 1941. Three major points in Curtin's message were:

(1) . . . the war with Japan is not a phase of the struggle with the Axis Powers, but is a new war . . . we refuse to accept the dictum that the Pacific struggle must be treated as a subordinate segment of the general conflict. . . .

(2) . . . Australia must have the fullest say in the direction of the democracies' fighting the plan.

(3) Without any inhibitions of any kind, I make it quite clear that Australia looks to America, free of any pangs, as to our traditional links or kinship with the United Kingdom.

Curtin's statement was that of a Labor Prime Minister who had been in office but two months, though Labor was to rule Australia for the next eight years. There were underlying ambiguities that were to persist in Labor foreign policy, ambiguities that have not been resolved finally to the present day.

How far were the points made Curtin's own or those of Labor parliamentary caucus, or were they derivative from the tradition of the Labor movement; and how far were they to be imputed to the Minister for External Affairs, Dr. Herbert Vere Evatt? The third point above, the one most offensive to the Australian traditionalists, who vividly expressed their outrage, served as a red flag to the great John Bull of the moment, Winston Churchill, a staunch traditional imperialist. It was an unnecessary point if designed to influence the Americans, who had learned something (though not too much) about dealing with British dominions in dealing with Canada. Certainly it is the case that John Curtin quickly beat a retreat from his statement and resumed his character as a believer in the organic nature of the Australia-Empire relation. Was the statement, then, a reflection of Dr. Evatt's views? He was not a believer in the organic relation thesis, but rather was an enthusiast for carrying on with the "devolution of powers" to the dominions until complete autonomy was achieved, leaving the Imperial relation a rather attenuated association.

Point One was also, and rather oddly, ambiguous. It implied a rejection of the Anglo-American interpretation of the war, which had been stated or implied again since Japan had joined the Axis in 1940. More importantly still, it implied either an ignorance or rejection of the global strategy of "Hitler (or Europe) first," which Roosevelt and Churchill had arrived at in secret meetings in Washington early in 1941 and which their armed forces advisers had accepted. Had not this been communicated to Australia by the Australian Minister at Washington? If it had, had it not reached Curtin and Evatt, then in opposition? Or had the possible significance of it to Australia been missed? At any rate, Evatt quite consistently maintained that he first heard of it, or at least first fully grasped its import, when he visited Washington in early 1942. The effect of this was that Evatt had to contend with the Washington authorities for Australia's defense needs from a position implicitly in contradiction to their definition of strategic realities.

On the other hand, Point Two did not tread so directly upon anybody's toes, but rather announced an Australian conception of its role in the war in the Western Pacific; it conceived of itself as a principal in its own "person," not as a small power by definition or subordinate to any Big Powers with which it was associated or allied. In this generalization was to be found Australia's protracted campaign for a voice in the highest counsels of the war and the postwar world. This was to posit that Australia was a fully autonomous nation. How this was to be worked out in practice, what exhilarating achievements, what debilitating frustrations this was to involve could only be determined pragmatically. As External Affairs minister, in effect, Dr. Evatt was to be the conspicuous public carrier of the ball during the eight ensuing years.

At this point the Australians and New Zealanders were, willy-nilly, launched upon the stormy seas that environ the global community of sovereign nations, and if not exactly cynosures of the world's attention, at least were more closely regarded than they ever had been before. It is not necessary to follow their progress step-by-step, but rather to try to epitomize the story with particular attention to Asia-Pacific. What is required here is less a chronological review of the specifics of foreign policy actions than an identification of the ideas behind the actions; and while the focus on Pacific-Asia must be maintained, attention must also be given to the conceptions entertained of Australia's and New Zealand's positions in the global community of nations. In this first round of foreign policy activity extending from 1941 to 1949, we shall assume that Evatt accurately reflected the Australian point of view and policy during the Labor Government's tenure of office, ignoring the controversy that swirls around precisely this proposition. We shall assume also that Prime Minister Peter Fraser, leader of the Labor government, and his own Minister of External Affairs, accurately reflected the point of view and policy of his government and country. It would be pleasant, but here rather irrelevant, to dwell at length upon the personal characteristics of these two men, but it is more to the point at this time to emphasize that while the similarities of the policies they forwarded are impressive, it is always necessary to stress the sometimes subtle and sometimes obvious differences.

First, Dr. Evatt: He was Australian-born. His prime "apparatus of the mind" and his doctorate were in the law. He had had a colorful and distinguished career at the bar, and he had also built up a considerable reputation as a constitutionalist, entertaining ideas about both the Australian federal constitution and the constitution of the British Empire. He had written Australian history and biography, both with distinction. He had become a justice of the High Court of Australia in 1931

and had resigned from the Court in 1940 to enter the federal parliament as a
Labor Party member. As a practicing lawyer he had participated in Labor Party
politics in New South Wales, and his return to politics in 1940 signaled one of
his fundamental characteristics—he used the law like a weapon to attack "privilege"
and defend the underdog. He was a libertarian and his views extended to the
Communists, anathema to the Labor Party, but to Evatt proponents of a legitimate dissent from bourgeois orthodoxy. He was quintessentially an Australian
nationalist, but he was intellectually an internationalist. Like so many men of the
twentieth century, he never quite reconciled the two positions. His normal
approach was the "adversary" approach of the lawyer, and this was given an
additional twist by his highly abrasive personality. Altogether he was a man of
impressive presence and force, but he was an indifferent politician and diplomat.
Suave conciliation was not in him.

   Peter Fraser was a very different person. He was a Scotsman by birth, and had
emigrated to New Zealand where he was a common laborer by occupation. He
appeared first on the New Zealand public scene as leader of a trade union of
"general workers" affiliated with a radical, anti-political federation of unions
popularly known as the "Red Fed." He subsequently had followed most of his
fellow "Red Feders" in abandoning the anti-political direct-action stance, and
he gradually had assumed the position that labor's objectives could best be
achieved through parliamentary politics. When the Labor Party first won office
and power in 1934, he was second in command to the party leader and Prime
Minister, Michael Savage, and slightly senior to a third conspicuous labor figure,
Walter Nash (subsequently New Zealand's first minister to Washington and, after
the war and the death of Fraser, a Labor Prime Minister). On the death of Savage,
Fraser succeeded to the prime ministership, with Nash as his deputy. Largely self-
educated, Fraser had a strong interest in education and the arts. An astute
politician of the "foxy-grandpa" variety, he was deeply conscious of the
fact that any New Zealand nationalism that there might be lying around was
overlaid by the prevailing New Zealand loyalty to the Empire. He was also far
more conscious of New Zealand's weak position in a world of Big Powers
than Evatt was of Australia's somewhat better but nevertheless still weak position.
Fraser and New Zealand, while definitely going in Evatt's direction, often acted
to moderate and to smooth the aggressive angularities of Evatt's policy proposals:
to keep the two countries clearly in their positions as associates of the Empire;
and to emphasize the international note rather than the national or regional ones.

   When Evatt was dispatched to Washington early in 1942, he had high on his
agenda two things: first, he wanted to arrange quick and heavy supplementation
by the Americans of Australia's terribly inadequate resources for stopping and
rolling back the Japanese; and he wanted to gain direct representation of Australia in the top-level circles where decisions about the war were being made.
He ran full tilt into the "Europe first" strategy and also directly into the resolution of the United States and Britain, of Roosevelt and Churchill, to keep the
fundamental direction of the war, both in Europe and the Pacific, in their own
hands. While by the necessities of its situation Australia commanded rather more

assistance than a strict interpretation of "Europe first" might have supported, its success over the long pull was less supported by Evatt's aggressive presentation of its case than by the fact that the American commanders in the Pacific demanded, and to an extent got, a broader interpretation of strategy than they had any right to expect. Australia thus benefited, rather unexpectedly, from the established American difference of emphasis as between a pro-Europe and a pro-Pacific-Asia orientation in global policy. All told, Australia did rather better in Washington than, on subsequently revealed evidence, it would have done had its dependence continued to be on London. But on winning for Australia a place at the table in the highest decision-making or executing councils of the war, Evatt suffered frustration and failure. Australia never made it. Evatt and Australia had to be satisfied with offering vigorous counsel and advice, with exerting pressure, with making loud noises. Symbolical of what eventuated was Evatt's success in having a Pacific War Council set up in Washington, downgrading the Council already existing in London under Churchill's thumb, and then discovering that it was nothing but an advisory council; often it was only a council ratifying policies handed down from on high, easily frustrated, and subject to having policies that it had accepted on cue from above set aside as new perceptions of the position in Pacific-Asia were felt to justify, to the Americans, a new line. Evatt, like so many Australian leaders, had a weakness for overcommitting himself to a line that suited his book, failing to keep in mind that his American associates, as confirmed pragmatists, were disposed to abandon a line that suited them at one moment, in favor of a new line as their perception of situations changed. Evatt's conspicuous lack of a capacity for adeptly adapting to shifts of position came to a climax during the dealings with defeated Japan after 1945.

In 1942, Evatt's experience in Washington tended to intensify his granitic nationalism and to raise by several octaves the stridency of his assertion of Australia's prerogatives as an autonomous nation. These prerogatives conspicuously included the right to a say-so about all actual and contemplated action not only in Pacific-Asia but also around the globe. Between 1942 and 1945, he moved with rather impressive inexorability from the position of a forceful asserter of Australia's rights and privileges to the position of the leading advocate of the rights of small nations as against the pretensions of the Big Powers in international affairs. What this meant was clearly revealed to all at the United Nations conference at San Francisco in 1945.

While it was not, at any stage between 1941 and 1949, Evatt's assumption that Australia's traditional ties to Britain were now in dissolution or that Australia was absolutely on its own, he did assume that Britain's power and authority east of Suez was (and was being) so drastically weakened that the primary responsibility for supporting Imperial interests east of Suez should pass to Australia. Recalling that the established definition of Britain's relation to the dominions was *primus inter pares,* Evatt saw the war as reducing Britain's stature in relation to its equals, not least Australia, and as sharply improving the equals' positions in relation to Britain. The assumption by Australia of responsibility for Imperial interests east of Suez seemed to follow logically, especially if one was a strong

Australian nationalist. As in the past, the prestige of Australia, whether as a congeries of colonies or as a dominion, had been enhanced by the Empire ties; so in the future, its position as an autonomous nation would be fortified in a new fashion by the Empire association.

It was not the case, however, that Evatt had any particularly accurate foreknowledge of what the war would do to the world east of Suez or elsewhere. His forecasts were as inaccurate as those of other men. But he had an expansive vision of the future of Australia. Unfortunately, any careful definition of Australia's relative power position in the world of nations was absent from his calculations. Rather than face up to vexing questions of relative power, he sought to evade them by stressing the theoretical equality of all sovereign nations. In emphasizing this proposition, he was seeking to exorcise the power politics that only the very biggest powers could hope to play successfully. His stance as a spokesman for the small powers against the big was at once both anti-power politics and an anti-big power gambit. As a moderate Laborite, Evatt believed that class conflict was and should be contained within the parliamentary system. He also believed that if all sovereign nations were taken as equal, it would be possible to defuse international power struggles by an improved version of the League of Nations. In such an international organization, the significance of Australia's deficiency of power would be minimized and its intellectual and moral authority could find free expression. A shorthand summary of Evatt's position was that the world should be organized on the pattern of the parliamentary system with the sovereign equality of the nations assumed; the end result would be the establishment of an international rule of law. It was Evatt's misfortune that the postwar world took shape in a way that made his ideal construct look like a flight from reality.

Thus Evatt's internationalism was deeply rooted in his Australian nationalism; his internationalism was designed to advance and protect the Australian national purpose as he, a Labor Party man, perceived it. As his adventure in foreign policy unfolded and he saw the world continuing in its evil but traditional ways, he emphasized more and more that Australia's international salvation as a small or middle power required that the United Nations be placed firmly at the center of Australian foreign policy. However, the unfolding situation also required that Australia's national interests be supported by other means than an ideal international organization. It was not only that Evatt was closely concerned with protecting the idea of national jurisdiction from invasion or erosion by inimical international pressures—like efforts to erode Australia's national right to determine the composition of its population (the "White Australia" policy) or its national right to determine its internal economic and social policies—but also that he was closely concerned with fortifying Australia's security on a regional basis as well as by association with the United States. Characteristically, he sought to counter the criticism of Australia's racist immigration policy by powerfully advocating the trusteeship principle for colonies and by exhibiting an active sympathy for colonies seeking to throw off imperial rule; he also sought to evade the charge of economic nationalism by advocating the universal acceptance of the full employment approach by the world's nations. He warded off criticism of his regional defense proposals by arguing that they would be within and supplementary to the global security system of the prospective United Nations.

Whatever balance between his nationalism and his internationalism Evatt may have attempted from time to time, there was never any doubt that he was aware of Australia's position in Pacific-Asia. This is particularly clear in the case of the Australia-New Zealand Agreement of 1944, an adventure in regionalism. However obscure the point may have been at the time, the Agreement was Evatt's contribution to the ancient Australian-New Zealand aspiration to take up a position separate from Asia and somewhat apart from the north-of-the-Equator Pacific. Unfortunately for clarity, other ideas were injected into the Agreement; some of them were clearly not relevant, like the proposal to internationalize air communications, which interestingly enough led nowhere and preluded the national enterprise Quantal and Air New Zealand air lines. Essentially what was attempted, however, was to define a security system for the Southwest Pacific that would place primary responsibility on Australia and New Zealand but would not exclude contributions from other Pacific powers, notably the United States, or the global security system of the United Nations, either direct or ancillary. The security systems would mesh, so to speak. But all this was clouded by a declaration that the building of bases during the war should not, directly or indirectly, give a right after the war to take sovereignty over the territory occupied. This was taken as highly offensive by many Americans, in and out of the government, who already were envisioning a global system of American bases in the postwar years. When the Americans defined a string of bases on islands off Asia in the Pacific after the war, they sought to inco porate a base in the Manus Island (part of New Guinea) that had been built during the war as a southern anchor. Evatt promptly asserted equality of access and use for Australia. The whole affair became a mare's nest, but the immediate consequen was that the Americans dropped Manus and cut off their line at the Philippines.

Equally contentious was the program in the Agreement for the Southwestern Pacific Islands. In essence two things were sought: to create an institutional forum called the South Pacific Commission to bring together the various nations holding sovereignty or other control in the islands (the Australians, the New Zealanders, the British, the French, the Dutch in western New Guinea, and the Americans in American Samoa and eventually Micronesia), and to initiate and coordinate develop mental projects of an economic, social, or cultural character, supported jointly and severally by the nations involved and also by international agencies of the United Nations. Implicit was an advanced view of metropolitan responsibilities for colonial peoples that was beyond the old League of Nations mandate system and looked forward to the "trust territory" approach of the United Nations. It was suggested that all dependent territories be brought under international supervision.

How the Australians and New Zealanders had moved from the rather lackadaisic concern for their dependent peoples that had been characteristic between the wars to this new and advanced position is now being closely studied by Professor W. Roger Louis. While in principle this new and advanced position was not especially objectionable to the Americans, it raised the hackles of the British who were then squaring away for a strong defense of the Empire. Slightly redefined, this Australian-New Zealand position became the basis of a powerful drive for a very liberal trusteeship system for the United Nations, conducted in close collaboration at San Francisco. Whether they foresaw the great postwar decolonization movement that dissolved the European empires is problematical, but it is noticeable that when Evatt contemplated developments in Asia during the last four years of his tenure of office, not only did he not uphold the imperialists but he definitely favored the decolonization forces, characteristically resolving the "issue" of whether those forces were communist or nationalist in favor of the nationalist position. Evatt was much concerned that the Asian peoples and nations recovering their sovereignty have the friendliest possible relations with Australia. The point is well-illustrated by the Australian action to advance the cause of the Indonesians against the Dutch and by Australia's highly sympathetic view of the Indian position against the British. But Evatt did not acknowledge that to conciliate the Asians, Australia would have to either substantially liberalize, or abandon, the highly nationalistic "White Australia" policy; some of his close associates, notably Macmahon Ball, did.

In his dealings with Japan, Evatt, who was clearly the dominant force, illustrated many of his fundamental attitudes. He was a firm believer in the established Australian doctrine that Japan was the enemy in Asia, and like so many believers in this idea he took it that the war in the Western Pacific certified the correctness of this position. Once the defeat of Japan was encompassed, Dr. Evatt was determined to "punish" Japan for its aggression and to make it impossible for Japan to threaten or embark upon aggression that was menacing to Australia ever again. His line was definitely "hard," and he firmly grasped and exploited every American policy formulation that, however temporarily, supported his position. His position not only included the idea of making any future Japanese aggression impossible by restrictions upon its power for action internationally, but also included measures for reordering Japan's domestic economic and social fabric to eliminate the capacity for supporting further aggression. The Australians also took a hard line with regard to Japanese war crimes and played a conspicuous role in the prosecution of war criminals both in their own territory and in Japan under victor's auspices. In these respects, Evatt came as near to being in harmony with majority opinion in Australia as he ever did, for the Conservatives were in essential agreement with him.

It was inevitable that as the Americans shifted their position toward Japan from that of an enemy to be punished to that of an ally to be mollified and reformed to serve American needs in the emerging anti-Communist Cold War in Asia (focused for the Americans on China and the USSR), Evatt should get more and more offside. It was not only that Evatt, in harmony with his libertarian view of communism, was extremely reluctant to accept the American rationale of the Cold War, whether in Asia or Europe; his view was more or less in harmony with the "revisionist" position that eventually emerged in the United States. But in the case of Japan, he thought the Americans were opening the way to the reconstitution of Japan "the Menace." All this came to a head when the Truman administration commissioned John Foster Dulles to negotiate a presumptively "liberal" treaty with Japan. By that time Evatt and the Labor Party were out of office and the conservative political groupings were in charge, with their own conception of how to manage Australia's international relations. New Zealand was similarly situated. As leader of the parliamentary Labor opposition, Evatt voted against the treaty with the Japanese; it passed the House because the conservatives accepted it for reasons to be explained in a moment.

Although Evatt got offside with the Americans on Cold War questions, including the future of Japan, he did not, as is sometimes alleged, abandon the idea that the Americans should play an extremely important role in supporting the security of Australia and New Zealand and in backing up any arrangements locally made to guarantee the security of South and Southeast Asia. However, Evatt's efforts in these respects were frustrated by the circumstances of Pacific-Asia and by the pause in American policy-making while "the dust settled."

In December 1949, the eight-year-old Labor Government of Australia fell in a general election, more for domestic than foreign policy reasons; nevertheless, it fell decisively. At about the same time, the 14-year-old New Zealand Labor Government also fell. While the Australian Labor Party was to be out of office at the federal level for the next 23 years, New Zealand Labor had a weak afterclap success under Walter Nash from 1957 to 1960. Not until December 1972 were the two countries again simultaneously in the hands of Labor administrations. In both countries, office and power were in the hands of parties of a conservative, or traditionalist, orientation, but too much should not be made of the word "conservative" in the politico-ideological context characteristic in the two countries. In Australia the government was a coalition of liberals oriented toward private capitalism as it found expression in the rural areas. At the head of the regime was the founder of the Liberal Party, Robert Gordon Menzies, and his strength was such that the era of his dominance, 1949-1966, came to bear his name. The three epigoni of Mr. Menzies (later Sir Robert Menzies), Prime Ministers Holt, Gorton, and MacMah, who held office for varying periods from 1966 to 1972, attempting only marginally significant foreign policy innovations, though Gorton's nationalistic bias colorfully ruffled the established synthesis. With regard to foreign policy, Menzies had once remarked that any agreement he had with Evatt's foreign policy actions was founded on different premises and was therefore coincidential.

Menzies was a "Queen's man," a loyalist of Empire by disposition, a traditionalist not an innovator, emotionally pro-British—to his bootstraps, as he was fond of saying. However, he was also a man of "kopf" (head), and therefore he was intellectually capable of adapting to the new conditions that environed Australia while his emotional loyalties remained constant. In New Zealand the situation was subtly different, not only because no clearly dominant figure like Menzies emerged, but also because the traditional New Zealand emotion of loyalty to the British was far more active and widespread among the voters than in Australia. The New Zealanders tried hard to sustain the assumption that the United States was indeed a surrogate for the United Kingdom, not a "permanent" replacement; but as the Pacific-Asia condition, not to mention the ever clearer evidence that the United Kingdom's world position was sadly diminished, dictated a redefinition of New Zealand's position, the New Zealanders reluctantly adapted to circum-

stances and gave the world the not entirely fair impression that they were following in Australia's wake. Although they were unknowingly confronted with nearly a
quarter century of conservative rule in 1949-1950, the Labor partisans of both
countries and the labor-oriented academic and extramural intellectuals were
naturally disquieted. They were strongly disposed to favor innovative adaptations
in foreign relations, and even if they were not exactly or wholly in favor of Evatt's
or Peter Fraser's "scenario," they certainly did not believe that *plus ca change plus
ca le meme chose* as they thought the conservatives assumed. In any event, the
Conservatives of both countries demonstrated that Grover Cleveland's principle
that conditions must prevail over theory was operative. In Australia during this
period the successive External Affairs ministers Percy Spender, Richard Gardiner
Casey, Garfield Barwick, and Paul Hasluck gave the most impressive performances,
while in New Zealand pride of place should apparently be granted to F. W. Doidge
and Sir Keith Holyoake.

Before attempting a synoptic account of Conservative foreign policy ideas, as
distinguished from a play-by-play report of foreign policy actions, it is necessary
to take a quick look at the economic environments of the two countries. In
Australia, the Conservatives, while not significantly modifying the general objectives of Labor's program for reconstruction, shifted away from Labor's effort to
achieve both viability and expansion by enlarging the public sector and intensifying
the government's controls over the total economy; the Conservatives moved toward
looser governmental controls and reliance upon the dynamic forces of private capitalism. The Conservative program also included an emphasis upon the encouragement of
foreign capital investment to facilitate a faster rate of growth than could be achieved
otherwise, thus reversing Labor's policy of keeping the economy under as tight
Australian control as possible. This later shift of emphasis encouraged an inflow
of investment capital, in the beginning heavily American in origin, which at times
reached such totals as to be embarrassing; in any case, it induced a dependence
upon foreign capital inflow to balance the international payments as imports rose
to meet the needs of development. In the beginning, the emphasized growing
point of the economy was the industrial sector, as by the agreement of all parties
it had been since the late 1920s; but considerable attention necessarily was given
to rehabilitating the pastoral and crop agricultural sectors, still the basis for commodity exports.

At a slightly later stage, the sense that Australia was on its way was intensified
by the discovery and exploitation of a wider range of mineral resources—coal,
iron, bauxite, copper, nickle, uranium, etc.—than anyone had imagined to be present before World War II. The net effect was a disconcerting pattern of boom and
recession, which was partly of domestic and partly of foreign genesis; it was handled by a freer use of governmental controls than had been anticipated, mostly
devised and administered by economists of the Keynesian persuasion.

Thus while impressive economic advances were made, the *rate* of advance was
such that Australia did not figure among the world leaders. The manpower needs
of the growth were met by considerably supplementing the natural increase of
the population with an inflow of immigrants, who were, by design, mostly
British but included also many of the European nationalities, thus moving Australia

nearer the pattern of national origins characteristic in Canada and the United States. At the same time the exigencies of international politics dictated a relaxation of traditional "White Australia" policy to also allow the entry of carefully selected Asians. This diverse inflow of population naturally, given the factory-industry emphasis, led to an intensification of the urbanization that had been characteristic all along, though the minerals boom did create new small clusters of people in the otherwise pastoral outback north and northwest.

Recalling that just before the outbreak of war in the late 1930s Australia had discovered that her export needs could not be met within the constriction of "Ottawa," it is hardly surprising that along with all this domestic change there was a carefully orchestrated effort to achieve a diversification of export outlets. This, over time and in conjunction with other factors, led to the diminution of the United Kingdom in the export-import trade and increased the emphasis upon the countries of Pacific-Asia, most significantly the United States and Japan. This was to give the necessary material base to the ideological perception of the 1930s that the future of Australia was in the Pacific. In essence, however, Australia remained what it all along had been, a country whose economic health depended upon the successful sale of surpluses of production over limited domestic requirements in markets overseas; in the earliest phase, these included pastoral products (wool predominant), then wool plus wheat from a crop agricultural industry, and now fibres, foodstuffs, and minerals. However, by putting it in this fashion, one should not ignore the impressive quantitative and qualitative changes—demographic, economic, and cultural—in the domestic life of the country as compared to the situation between the two great wars.

The economic situation in New Zealand was subtly different. The New Zealanders, like the Australians, thought the essence of their economic problem was marketing and not production, particularly with regard to exports. In the 1920s, to meet the interwar disorders then appearing, they had devised a system of producer syndicates to control marketing, and in the 1930s Labor had seized upon this and transferred executive control of the syndicates from the producers to the government as a major factor in the achievement of an *economie dirige* designed to insulate New Zealand from inimical world economic forces. Within this system, the emphasis was upon the idea of a consumption economy closely directed by the government rather than upon a capital-accumulating economy dedicated to growth on the basis of free enterprise. In the New Zealand perception, the principal external influence on the situation was the United Kingdon, which was their principal commodity market, source of finance, and object of political and cultural loyalty. Immediately after the war, Labor came under severe pressure from the Conservatives to loosen the controls across the board; they responded chiefly by transferring control of the producer syndicates from the goverment back to the producers themselves. However, Labor hung on to the fundamentals of their *economie dirige* with its nationalistic bias; this is symbolized by Labor's refusal to join the International Monetary Fund (IMF) and the International Bank of Reconstruction and Development (IBRD) because both were perceived as likely to undermine national control. But the position after the war was such that even when the "conservatives" won office, they could not achieve even the amount of emphasis on free enterprise that the Australians had accomplished; to meet the situation in which New Zealand found itself, they too simply had to "control." They could and did join the IMF and IBRD, but the political struggle, far more clearly than in Australia, turned not upon free enterprise versus an *economie dirige* but upon who could administer the economy most advantageously to the wayfaring New Zealanders. To be sure, the New Zealanders had no such scope for action as the Australians; they were dependent upon two islands, not a continent—islands with a population capacity of about 5 million, or roughly twice the current population, and with a much narrower range of resources and therefore less scope for growth. The economy had grown in the past, especially around 1900 as Britain's outlying farm, and was heavily dependent upon industrialized Britain as a market for its exports of, predominantly, luxury foodstuffs produced in pastures. With Britain in decline and showing clear signs of moving toward an anti-empire, *sauve qui peut* national policy, New Zealand had no choice but to look likewise to the protection of its interest as a sovereign nation, perhaps with the image of becoming a latter day Switzerland in the Southwest Pacific. It also had to diversify the outlets for its traditional exports, promote the exploitation of its exotic forests for papermaking and its hydroelectric capacity for processing minerals like bauxite from Australia, and all the time draw closer economically and politically to Australia without abandoning its natural sovereign identity. However, the absorption of New Zealand into the Australian federation, mooted since the 1890s, was assessed by Sir Robert Menzies in conversation in 1971 as a possibility "though not in my lifetime—or yours!" Meanwhile the New Zealanders cultivated an intensified sense that they were on their own in a difficult world.

The general expectation in early 1950 was that the return of Menzies to office and power (he had been Prime Minister earlier in 1939-1941) signaled a radical redefinition of foreign policy, describable as a second comprehensive effort to define a set of foreign political policies for a now indisputably autonomous Australia. It was expected that Evatt's formulation, as he had hammered it out in response to the challenges of wartime and immediately after, would be repudiated. The actual changes made during the next quarter-century did involve quite considerable redefinitions of guiding ideas, and a revolution in manners, but Evatt had had to face up to so many of the fundamentals of an Australia-based policy that many of the conservative redefinitions were simply different answers to the same questions. In sum, it was found that the volatile world in which Australia had to function almost inexorably required it to make *nationalistic* responses in both the economic and foreign policy fields.

The conservatives began by seeking to reestablish as fundamental the old conception of Australia as an isolated outpost of Europe under the overhang of Asia, still unable finally to defend itself out of its own resources and therefore still dependent upon a guarantor overseas. Confronting then the question of who now was the guarantor, they downgraded the United Nations from the primary position assigned to it by Evatt, but by no manner of means abandoned it. Then, while seeking to preserve as far as possible the traditional tie to the Empire, now redefined as the Commonwealth, they bowed to the realities and recognized that the final guarantor was indisputably the United States. Britain *and* the United States were, to employ the rhetoric of Menzies, to be Australia's great, good, and powerful friends overseas. Therefore it was a basic aspiration to establish an equilibrium between the United Kingdom on the one hand and the United States on the other which would serve Australia's purposes; help conserve the waning power and prestige of the Commonwealth; and forward the new close collaboration with the United States.

Again accepting the realities confronted, the conservatives particularly sought to localize this equilibrium in Pacific-Asia. Toward the newly independent Asian nations in their "Near North," they took what was in essence a sympathetic position, but one definitely tinged with regret that the imperialist powers, who had served Australian interests so well in the past, were there in full force no longer. They hoped that a British presence as powerful as possible could be preserved in Asia to insure a progressive stability in the region; and they hoped that the United States' Asian policy would support a progressive stability also. They promoted the policy of an American involvement in continental Asia as being against the American preference for a power stance based on offshore islands. As long as it was feasible, they supported the French effort to reestablish their authority in Indo-China; and when the Indonesian-Dutch showdown over West New Guinea came, they supported the Dutch as long as that was possible. The Conservatives, partly no doubt in response to the American analysis, emphasized communism over nationalism in assessing developments. With rather surprising agility, they transferred the focus of the old "Asia the menace" dogma from Japan to Communist China. The aspiration became to keep communism as far away from Australia as possible. In pursuing this line, they transferred their traditional conception of a forward defense area from the Middle East in support of Europe (the United Kingdom) to South East Asia in support of their national position in Pacific-Asia.

It must not be supposed that the Conservatives went directly from the Evatt positions to those just outlined. The complexities of the actual progress are necessarily obscured by a concentration on ideas rather than events. Moreover, throughout the period there was a difference of emphasis on this idea or that between individuals; and on occasion a fairly fundamental idea was demonstrated to be totally inadequate or irrelevant and had to be abandoned. The various ministers differed as to the weight to be given to strictly Australian national purposes and interests. In some the traditional pro-British orientation was stronger than in others. Few however would have had any use for Percy Spender's *jeu d' esprit* : "You can be anti-British if you like, provided you are pro-Australian!" And there was always the risk that an orthodoxy acceptable at home and abroad in one period might become an embarrassing impediment to a necessary shift of position in another. Under Prime Minister Menzies' influence the change in manners was decisive. No longer would Australia's arguments with its great and good friends be conducted in public, as Evatt with his passion for publicity in the media had done; but rather, they would be carried on behind the scenes and only accidentally become public knowledge. Menzies' position was based on the old Imperial practice. This was to have unfortunate consequences, probably equal to any damage Evatt's practices had caused.

There are always risks in selecting particular recent events for special emphasis, but it seems to me that in the present context primary emphasis should be given to the retreat of Britain east of Suez. This was steady, though, throughout these years, and it is not complete to the present time. In the conservative mind, British power was thought of as a positive factor favoring Australian interests and therefore should be supported. They placed great emphasis on maximizing British power east of Suez, with Australia as a backup collaborator, rather than conceiving of Australia as the heir to Britain east of Suez and Britain as its supporting associate. Therefore, every British move that clearly signaled a weakening of British power was "viewed with alarm" and sometimes near panic. An enduring equilibrium proved impossible to maintain. Early in this period, Australia illustrated a pro-American orientation by not recognizing Communist China as Britain and India had done, and the Labor Party is thought to have intended if they had won the election of 1949. The New Zealanders, entertaining similar objectives, accepted this also. It was followed up by the acceptance of the American-devised liberal peace treaty with Japan—fortunately favored also by Britain, even though it was really as unsatisfactory to the conservatives as to Labor. Labor, more consistently, voted against it in parliament. Again, the New Zealanders followed suit and accepted the treaty. The conservatives argued that though the treaty was unsatisfactory, Australia could not hope to do better by unilateral negoitations, a reflection of the conservative estimate of the country's power position. But in immediate sequence, a more decisively pro-American move was made: the Australians joined with the New Zealanders in engaging the Americans to support their security by treaty (rather than by tacit assumption) with the ANZUS treaty. Britain was not a party to ANZUS, and it strenuously protested its exclusion to no avail. Thus a conservative regime made a major shift of the equilibrium in favor of the United States. ANZUS soon became for all Australian and New Zealand parties the centerpiece of politico-security policy, and in spite of intensive scrutiny and criticism from Labor and the foreign policy intellectuals (some of it fantastic), ANZUS still after more than two decades survives intact, though in some respects redefined by glosses.

This, however, was not the end of the balancing act for there was the vexing question of policy in Asia (dealt with below); and there was the famous "Suez" episode of 1956, when the Tory regime in Britain, covertly in collaboration with the French and Israelis, attempted to counter the Egyptian nationalization of the Suez Canal by unilaterally resorting to force in defiance of the United Nations, the United States, and powerful opposition at home and in the Commonwealth countries. In this dramatic situation, the only solid support for Prime Minister Anthony Eden's policy came from Australia and New Zealand; in the Commonwealth, they alone maintained the old tradition of loyalty. In this context, this was more than an acceptance of power politics of the traditional kind, or a yielding to nostalgia for the good old days of British supremacy; it was decisive for Australia and New Zealand to unbalance the sought-after equilibrium in favor of Britain.

Before assessing the consequences of the stand on "Suez" to Australia and

New Zealand, let us look at their relations with Asia. We already have noticed that Labor sought to insure that an appealing image of Australia flourished in Asia by favoring the rebels against the imperialists and, in doing so, emphasize the nationalism of the rebels over their alleged communism. The Conservatives in their turn also sought good relations with the "new" and old nations of Asia; they accepted decolonization when it was *fait accompli,* but they favored maintenance of imperialist power when that appeared to be possible. The Conservatives also reversed the emphasis as between communism and nationalism in favor of a fervent anticommunism. For the Conservatives, communism was monolithic and conspiratorial. Its Asian habitation was clearly mainland China. Thus, when the Conservatives came to office, one of their first acts was to devise the Columbo Plan, in its earliest phase a Commonwealth assistance plan designed to fight communism by fighting poverty. But their bias was more forcefully illustrated by their policies with regard to Indo-China, Malaya, and Indonesia.

When war in the Western Pacific was becoming more and more likely in early 1941, Richard Gardiner Casey, then Australian Minister to Washington, pointed out to me in conversation that there was a great gap to the north of Australia between the American power base in the Philippines and the British power base at Singapore. Australia had, of course, a primary interest in closing that gap. As we know, the Japanese in due course not only took over control of the gap but also eliminated the American and British power bases too. However, Casey's perception survived the war, and when he became Minister for External Affairs in the Menzies government he particularly addressed himself to the task of cultivating friendly relations with the Asian nations with an eye on that gap. If American help in closing the gap was to be effective, it would involve acceptance of responsibilities, including possibly military action, on the Asian continent— something the Americans were then resisting. Therefore, in addition to cultivating good relations with the Asian nations, particularly those definitely not Communist, the Australian aspiration was to involve the United States in continental Asian affairs, particularly those of the gap region. Recalling that Labor had aspired to arrange a regional Asian security pact, which would be backed up by American power, the Conservatives sought a pact that would make American power primary with supporting British and French power, the power of such Asian nations as would abandon neutralism, and Australia and New Zealand. The focus of interest was Indo-China.

After the ANZUS treaty was signed, the Australians considered an Asian pact as the next step to be taken, but since it involved commitments on the continent, the Americans were wary. When the French effort to reassert their authority in Indo-China finally collapsed at Dien Bien Phu and the Indo-China question went to the Geneva Conference, the Australians, by working not as direct participants but on the sidelines, finally achieved their objective of involving the Americans in continental Asian affairs. The instrument was SEATO, the South East Asia Treaty Organization. Step-by-step, as we know, this led to "Vietnam" and all it symbolized for the Americans and the world. In the Vietnam enterprise, the Australians and New Zealanders collaborated (as they had earlier in Korea), but oddly neither at home nor abroad did they justify their action by reference to their strategic interest in "the gap"; rather they followed the American line of anti-communism or argued that participation was a premium payment on the insurance policy that ANZUS represented. An explanation of this may be given in the forthcoming official Australian history of the war in Vietnam. But for our present purposes, the point about SEATO is that it began as an effort to control an Asian situation by invoking non-Asian power, and that in due course it became a project primarily supported by the power of the United States. Thus Australia and New Zealand, as continuing participants, were edged further toward the American side in their search for equilibrium.

To facilitate this forward move into Asia, the conservatives had to deal with the question of manpower for employment in Asia. Before World War I, the Australians had hammered out a policy whereby only volunteers could be sent overseas, whether in the army, the navy, or the air force, while conscripts could be employed only in continental Australia. This worked quite well in World War I until the manpower crisis of 1916, when an effort was made to break down the policy. In plebiscites held in 1916 and 1917, the Australian people voted "no" both times against a proposal to abandon the distinction in order to meet the manpower needs as defined by the Imperial authorities. When war broke out in the Western Pacific in World War II, it was painfully apparent that conscripts would have to be employed outside continental Australia, so Prime Minister John Curtin took the lead in getting the Labor parliamentary caucus and the Party to draw a line near central Borneo up to which conscripts could be used. As a consequence, when General MacArthur's island-hopping policy carried him northward toward Japan across the Australian line, he assigned the Australian troops to the "dirty" task of cleaning out the pockets of Japanese he had left behind. Now the conservatives, in pursuit of their "forward" defense and political policy in Asia, made it legally possible to employ conscripts in its support. In the long run they paid a high price for their action.

Switching now to another phase of the "forward" policy in Asia, let us look briefly at the Australian and New Zealand involvement in the affairs of Malaysia. Prior to granting Malaysia independence within the Commonwealth, Britain was confronted with the task of resisting the efforts of Communist insurgents, chiefly Chinese, to take over the country. With the help of Australian and New Zealand's armed forces, the British successfully liquidated the insurgents. When independence was granted to Malaysia, the British assumed certain responsibilities for its defense, and the Australians and New Zealanders continued actively to support them. This was fundamentally a Commonwealth matter; but as it had an obvious relation to SEATO, Prime Minister Menzies obtained an OK of it from Washington. The arrangement went by the name of ANZAM: Australia, New Zealand, Malaysia. As the SEATO treaty led on to "Vietnam," so the ANZAM arrangement led on to the so-called "confrontation" between Indonesia, on the one hand, and Malaysia, on the other. Sukarno viewed the creation of Malaysia as an imperialist plot aimed at frustrating an expansionist Indonesia. His policy of "confrontation" involved violence and could lead to war. Britain, as guarantor of Malaysia's security, opposed

Sukarno; and Australia and New Zealand, as supporters of Britain, actively assisted in the resistance.

This caused a muted crisis in Australia's relations with Indonesia, Australia's nearest neighbor to the north. Although baffled by the Sukarno ideological excursions, with their pro-Communist component, the Australians all along had tried to keep on good terms with Indonesia. True they had been pro-Dutch in the West New Guinea dispute; true also they were defending Malaysia. But neither difference destroyed utterly the general policy of goodwill. (A phase of the Australian thinking about the West New Guinea question involved both a reassertion of the old "islands as a protective shield" doctrine and the conservative bias in favor of maintaining old imperialist powers in authority if possible. Moreover, the Australians did not want a land frontier with Indonesia in New Guinea, since they viewed the Sukarno regime with dubiety.) The Indonesians' government showed an unwonted, if cold, tolerance of Australian vagaries allegedly because they did not want a hostile Australia "behind" them. The resolution of the West New Guinea dispute taught the Australians a lesson, presumably first learned in earlier times: that a situation in their vicinity—historically, in the islands—was viewed differently by their great and good friends overseas. For in the resolution, the United States was a primary factor in devising a plan that gave control of West New Guinea to Indonesia. The Australians grumbled about digesting this, but they did; when the Sukarno regime fell with an accompanying liquidation of the Communists, ending the confrontation with Malaysia, they stepped up their efforts at a creative accommodation with Indonesia and had considerable success.

Going farther afield in Asia, the relations of Australia with Japan and China solicit attention. As to Japan, the Australians and New Zealanders accepted the Truman administration's liberal peace treaty with fatalistic reluctance and certainly with no expectation that before a decade was out Japan would emerge as a major trading partner. This relation, which was elaborated rapidly in the 1960s and 1970s, was founded on the economic booms in the two countries and especially in the circumstance that Japan was a resource-deficit country, heavily dependent on imports, while Australia was a resource-surplus country in foodstuffs, fibers, and minerals, and moreover was hungry for overseas markets and foreign investments. Thus the Australian-Japanese relation developed on an economic foundation, while the foreign political policy aspect necessarily remained obscure. Though Australia, New Zealand, and Japan were all dependent for their security on the nuclear umbrella of the United States, Japan had not developed a foreign policy beyond what was required to facilitate its heavy impor-export trade, while Australia and New Zealand had. It was an odd situation. It was also paradoxical that the relation should be so fruitful if one recalls the view of Japan entertained before, during, and after World War II. As the economic linkage strengthened, the ancient suspicions and hatreds relaxed.

As to China, the situation was different. Debarred from developing a political relation with China by non-recognition of the Communist regime—a very different thing from the Japanese reluctance to develop a full political foreign policy—the Australians nevertheless developed a trade with China that did not involve strategic materials (by the American definition), more or less after the fashion of Canada.

At the same time they exchanged diplomats with Taiwan and carried on trade with it also.

Reverting now to a comprehensive view of the Australian-New Zealand relation to Asia, it should be emphasized, without elaborating the point, that regional organizations of a political or an economic character were encouraged and where feasible participated in directly by the governments of Australia and New Zealand. The same attitude of encouragement was entertained toward the host of structured and unstructured private organizations. "Regional" has normally meant Southeast Asia, and Japan has been handled separately; the non-governmental private organizations have chiefly been spin-offs from the flourishing trade with Japan.

Thus preoccupation with Asia in all the phases mentioned here—in the cultivation of Asian studies in Australian and New Zealand schools and universities since the end of the war, and the admission of numerous Asians to their universities under the Colombo Plan or otherwise—raised the question, particularly in Australia, of whether Australia after all *was* by destiny *an Asian country*. This, obviously, was to go beyond the affirmation that the future of Australia would in large part be determined by what happened in Asia. Over the years the question has been discussed in speeches, essays, and books, but the more it was discussed the more obvious it became that while Australia was now, and would continue to be, deeply involved in Asia, and while the resident Asian component of its population would increase as the "White Australia" policy was relaxed or, ultimately, abolished, Australia was certain to remain a Euro-American-style country situated geographically under the overhang of Asia. In important part, its great and growing use to Asia and of Asia to it is rooted in that stubborn fact—a fruit of history.

Of New Zealand, where Asia is less portentously an issue, much the same can be said, with the difference that since the war it has added to its Polynesian-Maori population considerable numbers of Polynesians and other islanders by immigration. This calls attention to the fact that New Zealand—and Australia likewise—is, as traditionally, heavily involved in the islands. As mandatory of Western Samoa under the League of Nations, New Zealanders between the wars learned the difficulties of governing what have long been considered the most ardent and skillful politicians of all the island peoples. In accordance with the position toward subject peoples sketched earlier, the New Zealanders helped Western Samoans achieve independence in 1962, some of the first island people to regain their sovereignty. The New Zealanders also conceded self-government to the Cook Islanders, whose position was different from the Samoans' in that the Cooks had been within the official boundaries of New Zealand since 1900. Lately the New Zealanders have accorded separate self-government to the islanders of Niue—Captain Cook's Savage Island—long included in the Cooks. It is indicative of how New Zealand's relation to the islands is perceived by outsiders, that when Fiji had recovered its sovereignty from Britain in 1971, Tonga had shaken off the last remnants of the British protectorate established late in the nineteenth century, and Western Samoa was independent with important links to New Zealand, the United States should make its Ambassador to New Zealand also the non-resident Ambassador to Fiji, Tonga, and Western Samoa.

The newly independent, the self-governing, and others approaching the one status or the other, finding insufficiencies in the South Pacific Commission, have devised other organizations to meet their political, economic, and social (including sport) purposes.[6] The South Pacific Commission, headquartered in Nouméa, New Caledonia, still continues to function with Australia as the senior member and principal supplier of finance; but Australia's concentration of interest in the islands (though actually an Australian interest is present in all the groups south of the Equator) is on New Guinea. Making an even more radical adjustment of views than the New Zealanders, the Australians have sought since the war to prepare New Guinea for independence. They have combined the colony of Papua, taken over from the British in 1906, and the territory of New Guinea, the ex-German portion of the great island (formerly a mandate from the League of Nations, then a trust territory under the United Nations) into a single administration, with headquarters at Port Moresby in Papua. Beginning under the Labor government, a radical redefinition of policy was made which, while somewhat moderated under the Conservatives, has been carried forward to the present day. Complete independence for Papua New Guinea was accomplished in 1975, and it represents a more dramatic accomplishment than the granting of independence to the Western Samoans by the New Zealanders, because of the complicated fragmentation of New Guinea—geographical, tribal, linguistic—the degree of European influence, and the widely varying familiarity of New Guinea with European economic, political , and social institutions. The Australians have done their job well, even if Cromwell's "warts" are plainly there.

It seems to me that this all sums up to the conclusion that the conservatives tried to solve the Australian and New Zealand security problem—recognizing their common inability, as small and middle powers, to impose a foreign policy standing alone—by traditional means as modified by current circumstances: that is, by closely associating themselves with stronger powers overseas of presumptively like ideas. This involved a close relation with their longtime Imperial associate, the United Kingdom, now in decline, and also with the United States, surrogate for the United Kingdom in World War II but now more and more clearly the primary partner for the predictable future. Nevertheless, neither Australia nor New Zealand—New Zealand even less than Australia—wished precipitately to abandon the Commonwealth in favor of the United States, so the concept of "equilibrium" was developed. Unfortunately no stable equilibrium could be achieved, because while the United Kingdom's power, particularly east of Suez, waned, the ambition and power of the United States to sustain the "free world" against communism waxed. It was almost as though there were a cosmic conspiracy to throw Australia and New Zealand into the arms of the United States.

In this version of what happened, the disbalancing of the equilibrium known as "Suez" was at once a last throw of the dice in favor of the United Kingdom and the act that more than any other symbolized the decisive shift toward the United States. Once committed to the American side, seemingly irrevocably, the Australians, more than the New Zealanders, imported into the relation—to quote myself—"emotions traditionally supporting the UK relation, to the 'falsification' of a relation between two independent sovereign nations. By no

stretch of the imagination could the United States be a *full* substitute for the
United Kingdom. For Australia (and New Zealand) the U.S. was a friendly—even
very friendly—sovereign *foreign* nation, but never, never a 'mother country,' or
a benign imperial master or associate." In short, the relation to the United
States became overfervent and deferential, especially in the public view, because
of the Conservative practice of keeping disagreements with the Americans under
wraps, only occasionally documentable by careful, detective-like research.
Thus the Conservatives were jockeyed by events into heavy dependence upon
the United States. Their chosen way of handling the situation, imported
from their Imperial past, led inexorably to the accusation that they were nothing
more or less than satellites of the United States, an accusation seemingly supported by the fact that even the most sophisticated of the attempts at rationalizing their position, like those of Paul Hasluck, seemingly echoed American
rationalizations.

During the long dominance of the federal government of Australia and the
unitary government of New Zealand by the Conservatives, the Labor parties in
Australia and New Zealand were the official opposition, which while adhering to
the old adage that the duty of the opposition is to oppose, also sought, as traditionally, to impose an alternative vision for their nations upon the reality confronted. We should quickly lose ourselves in a murky maze of formidable proportions if we tried to give a full explanation of why the Laborites were at a
political disadvantage during the years of conservative domination. Suffice it to
say, then, that they were, and then immediately go on to generalize that the
gist of their indictment of conservative foreign policy was that it was shamefully
disregardful of the Australian national interest as they perceived it. This involved
not only objection to specifics but also to over-all orientation. It was not so much
that they were advocating a reversion to Evatt's nationalism-internationalism,
though he was leader of the Australian parliamentary party from 1950 to 1960,
as that they were seeking a new expression of nationalism-internationalism.
History may decide that the final expression of pristine Evattism was Labor's
vote against the Japanese peace treaty.

Thus Australian Labor, supported by many of the foreign policy intellectuals,
chipped away at the way in which the conservatives allowed ANZUS to be implemented, without even decisively repudiating the treaty, as a derogation from
Australian sovereignty. They opposed ANZAM as likely to offend and alienate the
nationalistic, neutralist Asians, but they were nevertheless very leisurely about
dissolving their hard position with regard to "White Australia." Above all they
made hay out of "Vietnam" although there was humor in the fact that the Labor
indictment reflected American ideas as clearly as the conservative defense. (The
distinctively Australian component was the attack on the conservative policy with
regard to conscription.) All this while domestically they expressed their social
democratic bias by their hankering to add to the weight of the public sector of the
accepting mixed economy, to subject the private sector to close control, to insure
that the national interest was supreme, and so on. And *mutatis mutandi* in New
Zealand. The result was that they made an obvious contribution to reinforcing the

conservative tendency to substitute rigid reiteration of established dogma for creative, adaptive thinking, especially during the years of the epigoni after Menzies resigned. The other side of the coin was that the initiative in proposing alternatives passed to Labor. The conservative inflexibility became rather close to paralysis when the Nixon Doctrine was articulated at Guam and the Kissinger diplomacy began to unfold. Taking advantage of the new climate, Gough Whitlam, Labor's leader, made a much-publicized excursion to the People's Republic of China in mid-1971 to engage in a dialogue, obviously preliminary to recognizing China if he should attain office and power. This was before Henry Kissinger's famous visit to Peking. Thus it came about that the conservatives had the limb on which they were sitting cut off, less in the final analysis by Labor than by the Americans. In the most general terms, what Labor was thinking was uttered by Whitlam in 1972 after he became Prime Minister:

> The general direction of my thinking is towards a more independent Australian stance in international affairs, an Australia which will be less militarily oriented and not open to suggestions of racism, an Australia which will enjoy a growing standing as a distinctive, tolerant, cooperative and well regarded nation not only in the Asian and Pacific region, but in the world at large.

Or as an Australian commentator put it after observing the moves made during the first six months of 1973:

> Mr. Whitlam's "more independent stance in international affairs" was based on a combination of maintaining those props of Australian foreign policy that were clearly in Australia's and the region's interest, but at the same time seeking a more positive middle power role.

Since the "props" in question were American props with ANZUS, Labor's ability to maneuver was heavily conditional by, first, the Nixon-Kissinger stance, and, second, by the global climate of international relations, especially the economic component. Australia might liberally interpret detente to mean not on establishing diplomatic relations with the People's Republic of China, with emphasis on expanding trade, but also with North Vietnam, North Korea, and East Germany. It might tighten and redefine its economic relations with Japan and even regularize cultural relations, leaving the political factor still to be clarified. It might switch to a more positive position in support of the anti-racist outlook, notably in Africa; but it still was not as free an agent as a Great Power could conceive itself to be. It still was, indeed, a secondary power—an ill-understood secondary power, true—required to maneuver within the constrictions of Big Power policies to effectuate its purposes. And, as it was the common assumption that the deterioration of the domestic and international situation was the Achilles' heel of the Nixon-Kissinger program, so Labor's new stance and its implementation could be fatally damaged if: (1) the global economy deteriorated into depression; (2) international inflation (Australia's rate is of the order of 16 to 20 percent per annum) proved not to be controllable; (3) the energy crisis (Australia is about 35 percent dependent on foreign oil but rich in alternatives like coal and uranium, not to mention solar energy) should force a radical redefinition of purpose on, for example, its great trading partner, Japan; (4) if the food crisis (Australia is an exporting food surplus country) destroyed international solidarity; or (5) all these, interacting, caused chaos. Thus while Labor's second effort to define a stance toward the country's international relations necessarily commanded close attention, the disturbing question was not how far it violated the conservative assumptions and ideas of the immediate past, but how far it went toward protecting Australia's interests in the terrifying future.

NOTES

1. This idea also enjoys the support of India, whose security motivated the British to develop the "British Lake" idea in the first place, with Australia as a secondary beneficiary, or perhaps tertiary beneficiary after South Africa, locale of the Cape of Good Hope, from which entry into the Indian Ocean from the Atlantic was controlled. In 1974 it was favored publicly by the Shah of Iran while on a state visit to Australia; and also by Prime Minister Tanaka of Japan later in the same year.

2. Exactly when the Japanese concluded that the United States would come to the aid of Australia if they menaced it in war has not, to my knowledge, been established; but it is certain that it was before American assistance to Australia became "inevitable" in late 1941 and early 1942. I myself became convinced that they had the idea firmly in mind in 1940 when I had a long conversation at luncheon in Sydney with Taijiro Ichikawa, then attached to the Japanese Consulate-General's office in Sydney and now a Japanese university professor with a special interest in Australia. I suspect that the Japanese strategists, having envisioned the elimination of American, British, Dutch, and French power in Southeast Asia, saw clearly that Australia would then become in the south a menacing base that must be neutralized. Or was this the logical alternative once the strategy of gaining control of Ceylon, Madagascar and the Indian Ocean in order to link up with the European Axis powers at Suez, became obviously impossible of realization?

3. Still symbolized by the small Union Jack in one corner of the Hawaiian flag.

4. MacMahon Ball said that the Australian position was "unworthy of desert tribesmen"; Hartley Grattan said that Australian foreign policy only existed "below the level of consciousness."

5. Implicit here is an idea that still works upon Australian and New Zealand security policy: that fighting to defend their security should take place as far away from them as possible. Hence, on the World War I precedent, World War II action was taken to aid the Empire in the Near East and North Africa. Hence, too, "Singapore" to the north of the Equator, was supposed to keep any enemy well away from the Southwest Pacific. A related idea in Imperial strategy was to the effect that if the "center" (i.e., the United Kingdom) held, all would hold. This idea tended to concentrate the attention of British leaders, not least Winston Churchill, in World War II on "Europe" and not on the Australian-New Zealand position on the periphery of Empire in Pacific-Asia. Hence the "Hitler First"

strategy of World War II, so objectionable to the Australians and New Zealanders when they became acutely aware of it after Pearl Harbor; hence, too, Churchill's failure accurately to "appreciate" the situation in Pacific-Asia right up to the fall of Singapore when "the baby" was handed over to the United States.

6. The cultural situation is, of course, paradoxical. The islands have been under European influence since the late eighteenth century, this involving the steady erosion of the indigenous cultures. Native sovereignty was all but extinguished during the nineteenth century. The idea that native sovereignty could be recovered was late in arriving in the Southwest Pacific, and when it finally arrived after World War II it was implicitly assumed that it would require the natives to Europeanize themselves further if they were successfully to "work" the necessary economic and political institutions that the contemporary world requires for the maintenance of sovereignty. Where this leaves the indigenous cultures is unclear, but still they are distinguishable, not only by anthropologists, one from the other. It is likely that some light will be cast on this problem by the University of Papua-New Guinea at Port Moresby and the University of the South Pacific at Suva.

8

Dilemmas of New Zealand
Defense in the Seventies

International relations as an academic discipline in its own right is relatively new, but already its practiioners have produced an embarrassingly extensive range of theories, which sometimes conflict considerably with each other. However there is one matter about which all the major theorists seem to agree, and that is the primacy of defense over all other means of serving the national interest. Thus, Hans Morgenthau defines "Primary Interests" as including the protection of the nation's physical, political, and cultural identity against encroachment from outside.[1] Again, Charles Lerche and Abdul Said have produced a very tidy model of the foreign policy decision-making process and its determinants.[2] The only catch is that none of these analysts seem to make any provision for exceptions to their rule, and in some ways, New Zealand, historically at least, is one such exception. This in part explains why, when the need to make decisions regarding defense was thrust upon it during the years immediately preceding World War II, New Zealand developed defense policies that now present it with unforeseen dilemmas.

Island nations tend to develop a strong sense of autonomy. New Zealand's remoteness and the small size and relative homogeneity of its population may reasonably have been expected to produce a vigorous sense of nationhood. But this was offset by the wholesale transference of British attitudes and the maintenance of strong economic ties with Britain. If we accept Hans Kohn's definition of nationalism as being a state of mind,[3] then it is clear that it was a state never achieved by New Zealanders as a whole. In fact, a fairly recent study by New Zealand scholars on the effects of remoteness on various aspects of New Zealand life bears this out.[4] If anything, New Zealanders of the late nineteenth and early twentieth centuries suffered from imperial fantasies in which they saw themselves as agents of British expansion in the Pacific, to the acute embarrassment of the Colonial Office.[5]

Fear of French, German, or Russian expansion in the South Pacific was felt only occasionally, and in any case these apparent threats were demolished by World War I; the British Navy was regarded as providing ample protection. Even following the emergence of Japan as an openly imperialistic power after 1931, New Zealand felt reasonably secure in the belief that the naval base at Singapore was sufficient for the British to fulfill their role of protector of white settlements in the South Seas. Only when that promise remained unfulfilled was there anything approaching panic fears of invasion by the Japanese; and after American successes in the battle of the Coral Sea, it was assumed that the United States had taken upon itself, at least for the time being, the role formerly played by Britain. However, when it became clear after the war that Britain had neither the desire nor the capability to resume protective functions, New Zealand felt the first stirrings of independent nationhood. The first political reflection of this was the conclusion in 1944 of the Canberra Pact with Australia; in 1947 the ratification of the Statute of Westminster finally freed the former dominion from the last vestiges of British metropolitan control over its policies. This was indeed a tardy acceptance of nationhood, since the Statute had been first enacted in 1931.

However, a century of tradition in the conduct (or rather the non-conduct) of its external relations dies hard; and the legacy it left has been analyzed by McIntyre as consisting of three inextricably interwoven strands that still influence the framing of policy today.[6] The first of these is the traditional link with Britain. As late as the Suez crisis of 1956, New Zealand continued to show an attitude of "where Britain goes we go," regardless of the justice or prudence of such a stance. Though considerably eroded since then, traces of this strand still are discernible. Secondly, New Zealand policy shows a marked streak of sentimental idealism in the form of a belief in the moral efficacy of collective arrangements for resisting aggression. This is seen in the attitude of the Labor Government toward the League of Nations during the period 1935-1939; subsequent championing of the establishment of the United Nations Organization, especially at the time of the China "incident"; and more recently in the view taken about New Zealand's participation in ANZUS, SEATO, or even ANZUK. There is also a fairly widespread belief in New Zealand's moral responsibility to Pacific Islanders of Polynesian race. However, McIntyre also sees a third strand of hard-headed pragmatism emerging, particularly after World War II; and in this lies the hope of less traditional and more practicable policies being espoused. On the other hand, it has yet to be demonstrated that new departures on these more rational lines have actually been made. There is plenty of evidence that both official and public premises, and advocacy of policies based on them, still reflect traditions of dependence on a strong protector; of favorable self-image as a small but loyal and dependable ally; and of a tendency to commit exiguous defense resources to the support of the protector in situations where New Zealand's national interests are barely involved, if at all.

Evidence of some official thinking on the lines mentioned is readily available, but it must be said here, though not in extenuation of New Zealand's intransigence, that similar premises and attitudes have been expressed and noted by Australians. For example the Prime Minister of New Zealand speaking on March 6, 1969, in Wellington said:

> We can only have good allies by proving ourselves a good ally. A good ally is not subservient; he has judgement and a voice and uses them; but he is also prepared to take up his share of the burden. Our voice can be all the more effective by having an accepted place with our close friends rather than sitting on the sidelines.[7]

This necessity for being an ally of a great power is voiced in rather more pragmatic tones by T. B. Millar writing of the Australian position: "We can lose nothing by insuring against the possibility of Chinese aggression. We could lose everything by not doing so."[8] Commenting on the psychological basis of the "good ally" belief in Australian society, D. Horne notes that "institutionalized in the suburbs is the belief in the Australian as a warrior, and the belief in Australia itself as some great power's best ally, somebody's brave and resourceful younger brother."[9]

Similarly the persistence of tradition in attitudes towards the deployment of forces is demonstrated by official New Zealand thinking about the importance of Southeast Asia as the focal point of threats to our safety. B. K. Gordon has noted that as early as 1939 the New Zealand Chiefs of Staff agreed that "the defence of New Zealand's interests lies outside New Zealand," and that Singapore was the most vital point for the defense of those interests.[10] More than twenty-five years later, on May 28, 1965, the Prime Minister, defending the commitment of New Zealand troops to Southeast Asia, stated in Parliament, "the fact that confronted us was that New Zealand's first line of defense is in Southeast Asia."[11] And on February 25, 1969, it was announced officially that New Zealand forces would be maintained in Malaysia and Singapore even after the withdrawal of British forces in 1971.[12] In a similar vein, Miller commenting on Australian defense thinking observes: "Wars at a distance, or a 'forward strategy' commend themselves to the Australian government."[13] All of this bears out the fact that the official view shared by Australia and New Zealand is fairly clearcut in regard to premises about the source of threats, the role of ally of a great protector, and the location in which that role may best be fulfilled.

However, a number of factors (some of fairly recent origin and others long anticipated) now make it imperative that both premises and policies based on them should be reconsidered if policy trends in the 1970s are to be adjusted in time to produce policies geared to the problems of the 1980s. The three most important imperatives are (1) the withdrawal of British forces from Southeast Asia after 1971, (2) the evident intention of the United States to achieve full disengagement in Southeast Asia at the earliest possible moment, and (3) the motions now being made by the People's Republic of China towards improving relations with the United States and its antipodean allies. These, in turn, may well produce changes in the policies of Malaysia and Singapore, making an ANZAC military presence there much less welcome than it is at present. (By longstanding tradition,

Australian and New Zealand forces have fought alongside each other in campaigns to which their British connection committed them—hence the term Australian and New Zealand Army Corps, abbreviated to ANZAC.) Other new threats can be associated with the open economic imperialism being practiced by Japan, and an increasing naval interest being shown by the Soviet Union in the Indian and Pacific Oceans. Finally there are the yet undetermined, and perhaps indeterminable, consequences of Britain's entry into the European Economic Community. If recently negotiated short-term safeguards for New Zealand's primary produce exports are not converted into permanent, or at least long-term guarantees, the economic consequences in the area of defense expenditure would be to force drastic reductions in New Zealand's capability to fulfill even its present limited role as good and faithful little ally of a powerful protector.

Before New Zealand can revamp defense policies or choose from a range of alternative options, it will be necessary to reconsider four major premises on which current policies are based. The first and most important of these is the assumption that Communist China has replaced Japan as an expansionist power threatening to impose an alien and unpalatable ideology on peoples conquered by it. Here the debate lies between those who support this new-traditional view, such as M. Halperin, who asserts: "With growing power [China] will pose an increasing threat to Western interests and to Russian interests over the foreseeable future";[14] and those like N. Maxwell who, without being a clearly identifiable Sinophile, categorically states that "China is not expansionist, aggressive, reckless and dangerous."[15] Maxwell bases his conclusion on Communist China's record since the end of the Korean War, reinforcing it with the argument that China is too occupied with Russia to have time for adventuristic policies in other areas.[16]

MacMahon Ball also advances the argument that "The Japanese government's assessment of China's foreign ambitions, and her capacity to achieve them by military measures, seems less alarming than the Australian government's assessment" he concludes that Australia may have a mistaken view of Chinese intentions. It seems reasonable, therefore, that some reassessment of the Chinese "threat" should be carried out before New Zealand continues to frame defense policies on the basis of the assumption that the threat is real and directed towards New Zealand.

The next assumption that needs to be reexamined is that the United States is as predictably reliable a protector as a small ally could wish. If the Nixon Doctrine is intended to be applied only to Asian members of SEATO, then the premise about its reliability may be right; but there is some evidence that the isolationist impulse, which some allies of the United States think they detect beneath the surface in U.S. politics, may reassert itself and logically compel the extension of the doctrine to white-settled states in the ANZUS pact. T. R. Reese quotes a *New York Times* editorial of July 16, 1968, as evidence that there actually is a new isolationist tide running in America, [18] and again quotes the same newspaper of July 7, 1968: "The most important task for the new President next January will be the redefining of America's vital interests and the reshaping of America's priorities to advance and protect those interests."[19] Reese also quotes the following statement by presidential adviser McGeorge Bundy: "The American commitment anywhere is only as deep as the continued conviction of Americans that their own interests require it."[20] Thus it is difficult to dismiss completely the suspicion that it may be unwise to rely too heavily on the Americans continuing to be affected forever by the Lafayette syndrome—a folksy belief that the Americans, still true to the heritage of their War of Independence, never let down a faithful ally under any circumstances. After all, at least some New Zealanders hold the view that such a breach of faith has already been made by Britain, which has much closer ties than the United States with New Zealand, and therefore we must not fail to take warning from the precedent set.

The third premise concerns Australia, which, though recognized as being a superior power to New Zealand, is regarded as having practically identical interests in defense matters. Many Australians hold a modified form of this view, since they regard New Zealand's security from attack as being ancillary to Australian security, whereas the security of Australia is essential for New Zealand.[21] Though this may be rather flattering to Australian *amour propre,* it is not necessarily correct. As a New Zealand diplomat has pointed out, Australia lies considerably closer to Asia, or at least to Oceanic Southeast Asia, than does New Zealand.[22] Therefore it is quite proper for Australia to pay greater attention to the influence neighboring Asian states may have on Australian affairs.

But New Zealand lies 3,000 miles farther south of Indonesia than does Darwin, and her proper sphere of interest ought to be Island Polynesia. In other words, while it is true that Asia is New Zealand's "North," it cannot be called its *"near* North" though this term applies to Australia. Therefore Australia may well absorb some Asian cultural influence while New Zealand by contrast may become increasingly Polynesian.

Again most of Australia's overseas trade went by a westerly route, especially before Suez was closed; but New Zealand's trade traditionally goes via Panama. Hence Singapore *is* important for Australia in a way that it cannot be for New Zealand, though it may be that Suva, as a major deepwater harbor in the most important island state in the Southwest Pacific, will come to have comparable importance for New Zealand. Thus the assumption that Australia and New Zealand have common interests needs to be reexamined in the light of evidence that these interests are more complementary than congruent, and New Zealand cannot therefore presume to predict what policies Australia may or may not follow in the future.

Finally, the widespread self-image of the New Zealander as being someone who is better beloved by far in Asia than Australians or Americans is basically untrue. Yet it is assumed that on this basis Asians welcomed the military presence of New Zealanders in their countries. Difficulties of language alone make it nearly impossible for New Zealanders to achieve any *rapport.* But if this is reinforced by the fatuous belief that Asians are quite happy to have their backyards turned into battlefields to prevent communism reaching New Zealand, then clearly New Zealanders simply have no idea how Asians feel about the prospect of seeing their respective countries turned into so many Vietnams.

If the foregoing assumptions are examined critically, it is possible to arrive at modifications that approach reality more closely than the original versions, and—

even tentatively—provide a more satisfactory basis for selecting defense options from the range available. In short, the revised assumptions would then be these: first, that China is not an indefinitely expansionist power; second, that United States interest in mainland Southeast Asia will be strictly limited in the future; third, that the Australian view of a defensible perimeter will vary from that necessary for New Zealand; and fourth, that Malaysia and Singapore will be increasingly reluctant during the 1970s to accept the indefinitely prolonged military presence of ANZAC forces on their soil.

In addition, there are other determinants that will influence New Zealand's choice of defense options. One of the most important is the rate at which U.S. disengagement takes place and the extent to which it will be carried out. One Australian authority suggests that "the U.S. may prefer, in an Asian situation, to rely on a deterrent exercised from afar, and to withdraw its troops."[23] In this case SEATO (with its component of Southeast Asia members) will become redundant, and ANZUS (basically a "white man's pact" and the cornerstone of Australian and New Zealand alliance systems) will become rather more tenuous than it appears at present. Similarly the extent to which Australia feels that Soviet naval interests in the Indian Ocean force its continued forward presence will influence New Zealand decisions to some extent. Millar, for example, sees Soviet naval pressure in the area as preventing the adoption of a "Fortress Australia" policy in the near future.[24] Bull also holds with this view: "The U.S. is unlikely to extend its naval responsibilities into the Indian Ocean area. It is likely instead to press its allies—especially Australia, New Zealand and Britain—to exercise the maximum influence possible, while hoping that the Soviet presence will not become too formidable."[25]

A corollary is the extent to which the United States proves willing to reinsure the ANZAC presence in Malaysia and Singapore, even if (as at present) they are there by invitation of the governments of those countries. If they should reconsider their situations vis-à-vis China and deem the danger slight, or reassess their own capability to defend themselves without external aid—a task they may well consider hopeless if the United States remains resolutely aloof—then one option at least will have ceased to exist, namely the defense of an advanced forward perimeter.

Again the costs of defense for New Zealand are severely limited by the size of the population, its taxable capacity, and its willingness to make sacrifices in peacetime. J. V. T. Baker estimates that it will be difficult to push defense expenditure above the current level of approximately $90 million or 2.4 percent of the GNP (gross national product), though a beleaguered New Zealand in 1943-1944 spent 42 percent of its GNP on defense. He concludes that "even under relatively favorable circumstances it would not be easy to restrain living standards increases in the interests of defense."[26] Thus New Zealand's capacity to maintain a forward defense policy, even in the 1970s, is going to be increasingly circumscribed, and the nation may be forced to fall back on one of the alternatives available.

Theoretically, the full range of options extends from acceptance of a status of complete clientage to the United States, or some alternative great protector; through participation in a subordinate states system, where it may expect some consideration to be paid to its wishes; to complete nonalignment at the other end of the spectrum. The last option can be either as a virtually unarmed and inoffensive state, or as a garrison state determined to defend its liberty unaided— a heroic but improbable posture because of New Zealand's resources of manpower, raw materials, and technology. If, as has been argued here, there is increasing likelihood of an over-the-horizon defense position being rendered progressively untenable during the 1970s, and a totally non-aligned position ruled out for practical purposes as an alternative, the remaining option is clearly a median position between these two. The question is: Where can a feasible defense perimeter be drawn? This will have to be seen in terms of practical strategic necessity, and of New Zealand's capacity to have some hope of holding it alone or in association with Australia, hopefully reinsured by a United States not totally withdrawn from Oceania.

It is interesting to see how some Australians view their own dilemma and their choice of options. One of them, M. Teichman, sees an Australia shaped on the Swedish model, armed and prepared (at a cost of 5 percent of the GNP) but proclaimedly neutral.[27] A Labor view expressed by L. H. Barnard rejects Robert Menzies' "forward policy" in favor of "a defense based on strategic frontiers rather than a line from Nui Dat to Butterworth to Terendak to Ubon . . . [without] renunciation of our commitments and alliances."[28] Both these positions seem rather unrealistic, though Teichman argues his case well, and Barnard fails to define his "strategic frontiers" (the implication is that they are synonymous with "natural boundaries"). The alternative for Australia, then, seems to be strengthening ties with the United States in the hope of its continued interest in Australia's welfare, and accepting a limited degree of responsibility (preferably underwritten by the United States) on the invitation only of Malaysia and Singapore and an independent Papua-New Guinea, but being prepared to withdraw if that invitation lapses.

New Zealand, on the other hand, has a quite legitimate and well-recognized interest in the arc of Pacific islands ranging from Fiji down through island Polynesia. A main article in the New Zealand *Foreign Affairs Review,*[29] and a major policy speech by the Minister for Maori and Island Affairs,[30] on December 19, 1970, leave no doubt about official interest in and commitment to the area. The Director of the New Zealand Institute of International Affairs has stressed the strategic importance of the South Pacific if either Russia or Communist China were to display an active military interest in it.[31] This is accepted by Millar, who recognizes the vulnerability of these island territories but also their usefulness as protective bastions:

> Despite their differences [in priorities allotted to areas of defense interest] Australia and New Zealand appear certain to co-operate in Vietnam and in Malaysia for the foreseeable future, and possibly elsewhere in Southeast Asia. It would be absurd for them not to co-operate on any defense arrangements made for the Southwest Pacific, which is closer to home for both.[32]

It is this Pacific perimeter, then, that provides the most promising option for the future; and there is possibly a shift already in official thinking towards redeployment of New Zealand's diplomatic resources, commencing during the 1970s, to produce in the 1980s a policy of the kind suggested. Recently the New Zealand Secretary for Foreign Affairs stated:

> I do not expect that we shall be threatened directly in the 1970's and our effort is likely to be turned towards ensuring that no threat develops in the 1980's that, in concert with others, we cannot meet. Because there is no immediate threat, we can, and should, pursue our defense efforts firmly in a framework set by our political interests.[33]

Of those most likely to act in concert with New Zealand, apart from Australia and the United States (and even in these cases with qualifications), the Polynesian islands are by far the best bet. They are linked to New Zealand by ties of language, trade, education, and, more recently, by substantial emigration. They are of a size and proximity that make aid something more than the drop in a bucket it appears to be in the Asian context. There is at least a reasonable possibility that it lies within the resource capacity of New Zealand, if husbanded by good planning, to meet the defense needs of the perimeter. In keeping with this, a recent Secretary of Defense suggests the rationalization of New Zealand armed forces to provide combined services task forces specifically trained for operations within the capacity of their size.[34] Australia could, on the same grounds of economic capability and military interest, undertake the manning of the western sector of this arc through Papua New Guinea and the Solomons to Fiji with New Zealand taking responsibility for the rest. All of this is contingent on the materialization of a threat from a source or sources as yet unidentifiable, and emphatically does not mean permanent garrisoning of these island bastions.

Alternative partners seem less attractive. Japan has a growing interest in the South Pacific, but as Larkin points out they have a qualified interest in New Zealand as a trading partner only and in no other capacity.[35] Moorhead puts forward the theoretically attractive proposition of a quadripartite alliance of the British-speaking peoples of the Pacific basin, Canada, the United States, Australia, and New Zealand;[36] but the probability of such an alliance emerging, except in time of crisis, seems remote. It has already been suggested that the Malaysian alliance is a rather fragile one, being based on the assumption that the ANZAC presence is both necessary and welcome, and this may well prove to be false before the 1970s draw to a close. In fact M. Stenson has argued ably that military withdrawal from Malaysia-Singapore does not mean a retreat into isolation, but rather that New Zealand has been too preoccupied with an area of which she is not a part.[37] Indeed, the 1970s and 1980s are the period during which New Zealand must decide on its identity—Asian or Polynesian—and the answer is only too clear.

New Zealand in the 1970s is at a decisive stage in the formulation of defense policies for the 1980s. Clearly she cannot abruptly terminate current commit-

ments, but political realism demands that at least she could make prudent provision for progressive change during the decade. For the present, despite diver-
gences in interest, history seems to press New Zealand in the direction of
Australia, and both towards the United States—all this notwithstanding the
beginnings of a Sino-American diplomatic thaw. Protection need not mean clientage; indeed, this is recognized (at least in theory) by some Americans, for
President Richard Nixon, speaking in Bangkok on July 29, 1969, conceded that
"if domination by the aggressor can destroy the freedom of a nation, too much
dependence on a protector can eventually erode its dignity."[38]

Though a small nation like New Zealand must accept, at least partially, a subordinate role in the expensive task of defending the area in which it is placed, it
can do so without loss of independence through the exercise of prudence and
foresight, which are, after all, the bases of political realism. Protectors and allies
a small nation must have. As Ramsay MacDonald observed in a speech to the
League of Nations in September 1924, "The certain victim of a military age is the
small nation which trusts to its moral claims to live."[39] The choice of protector
and the price to be paid, however, are matters too weighty by far to be decided
hastily or by proxy, lest the protected nation ends up as a sacrificial victim on the
altar of misplaced trust. Fortunately there is recently a new interest abroad in
New Zealand in the problems of foreign policy and defense, and what was once a
non-issue politically is now the subject of debate and demonstration. It is by no
means impossible that this new public awareness may prove the stimulus that
brings about official reconsideration of New Zealand's defense dilemmas. The
result, hopefully, may be the adoption of policies more realistically within the
capabilities of a remote island nation, to replace those inherited from a past characterized by imperialism-by-association and occasional traces of delusions of
grandeur. Such defense policies, in conjunction with supportive economic and
diplomatic ones, would be more in consonance with the logic of New Zealand's
geographical position and historical associations than current postures.

The election of a Labor government to office in November 1972 was expected
by some of its supporters to presage radical changes in alignments. In fact such
diplomatic moves as have occurred were predictable and are indeed moderate
when compared to the record of Gough Whitlam's regime in Australia. The simul-
taneous establishment of diplomatic missions in Peking and Moscow reflects the
pragmatic style mentioned earlier. Continued token defense commitments to
Southeast Asia, despite British and Australian withdrawal, is regarded as being
supportive of bilateral trade, aid, and immigration agreements and terminable
at the behest of the host country. A solid swing in the direction of shouldering
New Zealand's obligations in Polynesia is reflected in a substantial increase in
aid and greatly liberalized immigration policies. Finally, there seems likely to be
a fairly radical revision of the organization of New Zealand defense forces and the
role envisaged for them. A move towards integration on the Canadian pattern is
not unlikely, and, since the notion of setting up combat task forces in the absence
of any palpable enemy is slightly ludicrous, the new role is that of providing peace-
keeping units under international command, relief teams for areas struck by

natural disaster, particularly in the Southwest Pacific, and training units for allies who may request them under bilateral agreements. All of these lie within New Zealand's resource capabilities in men and material. At the same time, while the SEATO link is regarded as having little defense significance, the ANZUS pact still holds good and the continued U.S. presence in the Pacific and Indian Oceans provides the New Zealand people with some sense of still being safeguarded from military disasters of an order with which they could not possibly cope.

All in all these policies, though not dramatically changed, are sufficiently in consonance with the needs of the 1970s to appear credible, and they therefore hold the hope of better serving New Zealand's national interests in a confused and critical decade.

NOTES

1. Hans J. Morgenthau, *Dilemmas of Politics* (Chicago, 1958), pp. 50-51; also Morgenthau's analytical conspectus is summarized in Thomas W. Robinson, "National Interest," *International Politics and Foreign Policy,* ed. James N. Rosenau (New York 1969), pp. 183-84.

2. Charles O. Lerche, Jr. and Abdul A. Said, *Concepts of International Politics* (1963), pp. 59-68.

3. Hans Kohn, "The Nature of Nationalism," *American Political Science Review* 33 (1933), 1001-21.

4. K. Sinclair, ed., *Distance Looks Our Way* (Auckland, 1961).

5. A. Ross, *New Zealand Aspirations in the Pacific in the Nineteenth Century* (1964).

6. D. McIntyre, "The Future of the New Zealand Systems of Alliances," *Landfall* 84 (December 1967), 327-45.

7. K. Holyoake, *A Defence Policy for New Zealand* (Wellington, 1969), p. 13.

8. T. B. Millar, *Australia's Defence* (Melbourne, 1965), p. 51.

9. D. Horne, "Australia Looks Around," *Foreign Affairs* (April 1966), p. 447; quoted in T. R. Reese, *Australia, New Zealand and the United States* (London, 1969), p. 342.

10. B. K. Gordon, *New Zealand Becomes a Pacific Power* (Chicago, 1960), p. 111.

11. *New Zealand Parliamentary Debates* (1965), p. 342.

12. *Report for 1969-70* (Ministry of Foreign Affairs), p. 48.

13. J. D. B. Miller, *India, Japan, Australia—Partners in Asia?* (Canberra, 1968), p. 207.

14. M. Halperin, "China's Strategic Outlook," *China and the Peace of Asia,* ed. A. Buchan (London, 1965), p. 108.

15. N. Maxwell, "The Threat from China," *International Affairs* 47, No. 1 (January 1971), 44.

16. N. Maxwell, "Russia and China: The Irrepressible Conflict," *Pacific Community* (July, 1970).

17. W. MacMahon Ball, *Australia and Japan* (Sydney, 1969), p. 145.

18. *New York Times,* July 16, 1968, p. 56.

19. Ibid.

20. Ibid.

21. T. B. Millar, ed., *Australian-New Zealand Defence Co-operation* (Canberra, 1968), p. 109.

22. F. H. Corner in *New Zealand's External Relations,* ed. T. C. Larkin (Wellington, 1962), pp. 146-47.

23. J. D. B. Miller in *Britain's Withdrawal from Asia,* ed., T. B. Millar (Canberra, 1967), p. 104.

24. T. B. Millar, "Australian Policies Towards Asia" (lecture delivered to the International Congress of Orientalists at Canberra on January 11, 1971).

25. H. Bull, "Security in the Indian Ocean," *Modern World* 7 (1969), 61.

26. J. V. T. Baker, "The Economics of New Zealand Defence," in T. B. Millar, *Australian-New Zealand Defence Co-operation,* p. 40.

27. M. Teichman, *Australia—Armed and Neutral?* (Melbourne 1966), p. 21; also "Non-Alignment—A Policy for Australia," in *Aspects of Australia's Defence,* ed. M. Teichman (Melbourne, 1966).

28. L. H. Barnard, *Australian Defence: Policy and Programmes* (Melbourne, 1969), p. 52.

29. *Foreign Affairs Review* 21, No. 1 (January 1971), 3-8.

30. Ibid., pp. 9-15.

31. B. Brown, "New Zealand's Approach to Asia and the Pacific," *Pacific Community* 8, No. 3 (1970), 549-63.

32. T. B. Millar, *Australian-New Zealand Defence Co-operation,* p. 109. The phrase in brackets is the author's.

33. G. R. Laking, *Foreign Policy in the 1970's* (Wellington, 1970), p. 28.

34. J. K. Hunn in an address to the Economic Society of Australia and New Zealand, Wellington, August 25, 1966.

35. T. C. Larkin, *New Zealand and Japan in the Post-War World* (Wellington, 1969), p. 24.

36. Quoted in J. H. Moore, *The American Alliance* (Sydney, 1970), p. 226.

37. M. Stenson, *New Zealand and the Malay World* (Wellington, 1970), p. 17.

38. Quoted by B. Grant in Laking, *op. cit.,* p. 49.

39. Quoted in *New Zealand Herald,* January 20, 1968.

9

Western Samoa: A New Zealand Experiment

New Zealand is a Pacific power. As such, it has always been interested in the South Pacific region, most markedly from the latter part of the nineteenth century When World War I broke out in 1914, Britain asked a willing New Zealand to occu German Samoa and on August 29, 1914, New Zealand troops reached and seized th territory without a shot being fired. Thereafter, New Zealand administered Western Samoa militarily from 1914 to 1919; then as a mandate of the League of Nations from 1920 to 1945; and finally as a trust territory of the United Nations from 1945 to 1961.

Before 1939, the New Zealand administration was marked by conflict between the Western-oriented administration and the indigenous, nationalistic movement called the Mau. In a sense, Western Samoa was an experimental station for New Zealand's expansionist interests in the Pacific. During and after World War II, the relations between the two were more cordial, with the New Zealand government at that time openly espousing the nationalistic movement towards independence. The radical change in the New Zealand government's attitude towards the Samoan was largely due to the new liberal and humanitarian policies toward Samoa adopte by the Labor Government both before and after World War II. With some realization that the experiment had failed, New Zealand withdrew on January 1, 1962, with Western Samoa's friendship; but it left behind a country full of political, administrative, cultural, educational, legal, and economic problems.

In retrospect, New Zealand's involvement in Western Samoa was almost accidental, the result of World War I. Being a Commonwealth country, New Zealand aligned itself with British military interests and obeyed the motherland's call to seize German Samoa. But deeper down, New Zealand's interest in Western Samoa had already been long established. Western Samoa, one of the most internationally famous of the South Pacific island groups, was to be the testing ground, the spearhead, so to speak, of New Zealand's leadership role in the South Pacific. New Zealand's interest in Western Samoa was due largely to larger interest in the South

Pacific region as a whole. Neighbors have always affected the politics of every country, and New Zealand's South Pacific neighbors are no exception. Today, for instance, thousands of Pacific islanders residing in New Zealand are having a deep impact on New Zealand's politics, economy, and way of life. Many of them are voters assiduously wooed by both the labor and National political parties.

Economically, the Pacific islands represented a sizeable market for New Zealand goods. Their proximity entailed cheaper services. Additionally, the Pacific islands were a source for manpower urgently needed by New Zealand manufacturing industries. Because of the low rate of increase in the New Zealand population, there were not sufficient unskilled laborers to man the booming industries and New Zealand had to import them from elsewhere. Militarily, the South Pacific islands ringed New Zealand, and these could be used as military bases by New Zealand's enemies. It was thus in New Zealand's interests militarily to befriend the governments of these island communities. On the other hand, the islands formed an outer ring that could be utilized by New Zealand for defensive purposes against external enemies; this was yet another reason why New Zealand needed to gain the friendship and cooperation of the island governments. Thus, strategically, from a geographical as well as from an ideological point of view, New Zealand had no alternative but to take an active part in the affairs of the South Pacific. The New Zealanders gladly came to Western Samoa, but, as history records, their experience in Western Samoa was far from being a happy one.

The experience would have been successful but for a number of factors. These include the poor caliber of men put in the top administrative posts in Western Samoa. With one exception, these men, who served from 1914 to 1949, had all excelled in the military services of the Commonwealth; but they were more suited to ruling soldiers than civilians. To them, the law was the law and there could be no deviation from it. This was hardly suitable to the Samoans who were accustomed to a typical Polynesian way of life characterized by a carefree attitude. But despite their shortcomings, these "military" administrators were men of fine character who were basically well-meaning. They wanted to give their best in their new employment but were in turn restricted as to what they could do by both their superiors in Wellington and by the terms of the mandate. As a result, they occasionally found themselves at odds with the locals over certain issues. The liquor question, for instance, aroused a lot of ill will on the part of the locals and part-Europeans towards the administration. Under the terms of the mandate, liquor could not be sold to the "natives." The part-Europeans, especially, thought that this prohibition was unfair, and they constantly badgered the administrators to lift it. But the administrators, though generally sympathetic to the part-Europeans' inclinations, pointed out that the liquor prohibition was the responsibility of the League of Nations. This dissatisfaction over the liquor question was one of the basic causes of the Mau movement, which affected Samoan politics for decades.

During its formative years in the 1920s, the Mau was led by part-Europeans, but principally by Mr. O. F. Nelson, the leading Apia merchant at the time. Before going into this subject much further, perhaps it would be opportune here to point out that the Mau movement has oversimply been viewed as a struggle by "natives" against a basically exploitative colonial power, New Zealand. This is not totally correct as J. T. Gill has demonstrated.[1] It was much more than a simple "rebellion" against authority. Though the causes of the movement were deep, the movement need not have been actualized but for a couple of important factors: one, the part-Europeans' dissatisfaction with the administration over matters like the liquor prohibition, the administration's patent discrimination (the "natives" were generally favored in matters of policy and the part-Europeans felt left out), and certain trade restrictions that were keenly felt by merchants such as Nelson; two, the dynamic leadership and organizational skill of the Mau leaders. The part-Europeans' complaints were to be the spark, or the immediate cause, that generated the movement.

The Mau movement was started during the administration of Brigadier G. S. Richardson (1923-1928). Richardson, after several years in Samoa, had achieved international standing as the prototype of a successful administrator. An Englishman who had distinguished himself in the Commonwealth's military machine, he instituted many reforms in health, education, and public works. His aim was to bring Western Samoa into the twentieth century under the League of Nations. His refusal to see the Samoan Legislative Council as a potential body that could be developed to take on more self-government functions, however, colored his policies and brought complaints against him.

Other complaints had to do with Richardson's hiring of "too many" officials, the consequent costs of supporting the administration, the imposition of a medical and poll tax, to be paid by both *matai* (chiefs) and commoners, and the effects of the Samoa Act, which dangerously affected many Samoan customs and traditions. An example of the latter was the prohibition of common law marriages, a basic part of Samoan social life.

But all these measures were made in good faith by the administrator in accordance with his established policies for the advancement of the country. And for this reason, neither the administrator nor his superiors in Wellington regarded the complaints seriously. In fact Richardson came to be regarded as a successful modern colonial administrator, and he was even knighted for his services in 1925.

But already storm clouds were gathering, for there were others who still felt deeply hurt over the prohibition and trade restrictions. They were quite prepared to do something about their complaints. And the way they went about it was novel, if not outright radical, in many ways, for they were prepared to bypass the Legislative Council, which was primarily an advisory body to the administrator, and hence rightly regarded as a mouthpiece of the administrator. Instead, the opposition led by Nelson (who was himself a member of the Legislative Council and once a trusted personal adviser of the administrator), were determined to appeal directly to the people. Their excuse for bypassing the administrator was that he had proven himself despotic and that, therefore, it was their duty to introduce a democratic form of government to Western Samoa. In the atmosphere of those times of iron-willed colonial rule, such a move could only be regarded as subversive by the administration, especially as the interests of the administration and of the nationalistic movement appeared in conflict. That open conflict was inescapable in the end was hardly surprising.

A lot of academic research has gone into the origins of the Mau. Was it an accidental event that took place and was carried through by its own momentum? A lot of evidence shows that the Mau movement was not an accidental product of some dissenting minds, but rather a carefully planned organization set up to achieve certain objectives. Its activities were, therefore, well under the control of the Mau leaders and their arch-leader, Nelson. In 1925 Nelson had gone on a business trip to Sydney, Australia, and while there he received reports of serious maladministration (on the part of Richardson) in Western Samoa. Returning via New Zealand, Nelson had consulted with New Zealand cabinet ministers and managed to persuade the government to send a minister to have a first hand look at the social and political situation in Western Samoa. Back in Samoa, Nelson urged some of the leading Samoan chiefs and part-Europeans to hold a public meeting, more or less as a public rehearsal for the forthcoming visit of the minister. This meeting was consequently held on October 15, 1926, and a Citizen's Committee was formed. The formation of this committee was an important step for Nelson, at least, for it meant the establishment of an organization to fight for Nelson's and the Samoans' rights. The Committee was to have a constitution. Later it was to be renamed the Mau movement as its aims became more nationalistic and its control came more under "native" Samoan leaders.

At this meeting, the leaders of the dissenting movement presented a number of papers dealing with the group's complaints on matters dealing with the Legislative Council, finance, labor, agriculture, and prohibition. The atmosphere of the meeting thoroughly influenced a number of Samoan leaders, who commenced open propaganda against the administration. In large part, this was due to Nelson's skillful maneuvers as much as to his dominating personality. He had a thorough understanding of motive psychology, enabling him to assure the local leaders that the part-Europeans' interests were theirs also. No doubt, Nelson saw that for the part-Europeans and himself to get somewhere, the support of the Samoans had to be obtained. And he got enough of this to engage in bolder plans.

The meeting was a peaceful one, called to enable the public to discuss "public" issues. Subsequent meetings were called with this aim in mind, but increasingly these meetings came to have undertones of subversion, at least from the administration's point of view. Members hardly made any effort to conceal their disgust with the administration's more unpopular policies. In short time, the committee's administrative machinery had extended to almost all of Western Samoa, and there was increasing anti-government feeling among large segments of the Samoan population. The committee's open purpose was to replace the administration's machinery with that of its own, and as a result the committee represented a kind of shadow government. Whether this was legal is not the point here, but merely that the committee's objectives seemed to have received widespread support from Samoans. Samoans were told not to obey the administration and instead to follow the dictates of the committee through its agents in the districts. By the end of 1926, a passive resistance movement had started in many parts of the biggest island, Upolu. Samoans began to refuse to meet the administrator on his regular visits to the districts, to pay taxes, or to obey regulations concerning beetle collection, the cleaning of villages, or the repairing of fences.

Surprisingly, Richardson's reaction to these developments at the start was rather mild. Apparently, he had not foreseen the serious consequences that were yet to come. But as time went on, he realized the seditious affects the Mau was having on the population in general, and he threatened punitive action against Mau leaders. The New Zealand minister's visit on June 2, 1927, did not help matters either. It appeared the minister had bungled any chances of reconciling the Mau by tending to see the problem too strongly from the administrator's point of view. Richardson's subsequent attempts to suppress the Mau proved futile. Clearly there had to be more than a superficial probe into the problems between the administrator and the Mau.

Accordingly, New Zealand appointed a Royal Commission to investigate the problems in the mandate. It began hearings in September 1927 and heard testimony from 155 witnesses in sessions in both Upolu and Savaii. The Mau complained to the commission about a great number of items: government interference with the copra trade (which was one of the main things that turned Nelson against the administration); the lack of "native" representation; the overwhelming official majority in the Legislative Council; excessive expenditure on public works and on administration; the lack of satisfactory control of "native" funds; the continuation of liquor prohibition; and illegal threats to cancel trading licenses.

On the question of the administration of "native" affairs, the Mau also complained about the lack of the administration's consideration for "local" customs, beliefs, and wishes; its disregard for the "natives' " social and political system; and its illegal application of measures depriving "natives" of titles and banishing them without trial. Above all, the Mau complained about the lack of channels for airing grievances and the use of intimidation by the administrator. This was perhaps an unintended result of Richardson's *modus operandi*—his relative seclusion in Government House at Vailima—and the consequent loss of touch with the people. There could hardly be any doubt, however, concerning Richardson's good intentions from his vantage point. On the other hand, counsel for the administrator sought to convince the commission that the Samoans' unrest was caused by the machinations of a group of European traders led by Nelson, and that these traders were stirring up trouble mainly because their economic aspirations were threatened by the administration.

In the end, the commission vindicated Richardson and condemned the action of the European members of the Citizen's Committee for the resulting unrest. But, as Gill has commented, the commission had reached its conclusions by examining superficial evidence.[2] It should have dug deeper. As a result, the Mau leaders, Nelson, Gurr, and Smyth, were deported—Nelson and Gurr for five years; Smyth for three years.

As an epilogue to this whole episode, the bitterness resulting from the deportation of the intellectual element that had dominated the Mau's early existence slowly faded; but new leaders, though less effective, took the place of the old, and Nelson continued to offer his advice from New Zealand. Now, however, the

Mau's objectives became the recall of the deported leaders, and the granting of independence.

After Nelson's deportation, relations between the Mau and the administration grew worse and led to drastic measures by New Zealand, which at one time sent sailors and marines to arrest members of the Mau who were picketing stores in Apia. And for a long time, scores of New Zealand policemen were semi-permanently based in Samoa to deal with the Mau. The hostilities between the Mau and the police climaxed in a famous event, the Black Saturday of December 28, 1929, when the New Zealand police fired on a procession of Mau supporters and indiscriminately killed eleven Samoans and one New Zealand policeman. The Mau supporters were parading to welcome back Mr. Smyth who was returning from exile. When the police tried to arrest a number of wanted men in the procession, a fist fight ensued. In the confusion, the police used their pistols, and a police machine gun also opened fire, fatally wounding Tamasese and seriously wounding Tuimalealiifano and Faumuina, then the highest ranking leaders of the Mau. Ironically, these leaders were trying to bring order to the procession. Tamasese's "death, and that of ten others, added a new note of bitterness to the attitude of the Mau towards New Zealand rule and finally confirmed its dedication to the object of full self government."[3] Many years later, a direct descendant of the fallen Mau leader, Tapua Tamasese Meaole, was to raise (together with the present Head of State, Malietoa Tanumafili II) the flag of the new independent state of Western Samoa on January 1, 1962.

The conflict between the Mau and the administration continued until 1935 when it lessened somewhat. The main reason was the Labor Party's victory in the general elections. The new Labor Government, New Zealand's first, was basically anti-colonialist and had adopted a conciliatory policy towards the Mau. In 1936, it sent a good will mission to Western Samoa, and proceeded to abolish many unpopular laws and policies made in Western Samoa by the previous administrator.

In 1947, the Labor Government again pushed Western Samoa forward on the road to independence when it introduced many significant reforms. The New Zealand Parliament passed the Samoa Amendment Act giving Western Samoa a large measure of self-government. There was to be a Council of State consisting of a High Commissioner (formerly the administrator) and the three *Fautua* (the highest chiefs, used as advisers by the colonial administrations) and a Legislative Assembly comprising eleven Samoans, with not more than six official members. The Legislature was not merely an advisory body to the administrator as before, but a fully pledged law-making authority. But as yet, it could not legislate on matters pertaining to defense or the Crown's title to land. At the same time, the Samoan Public Service Commission was made more independent of the New Zealand State Services Commission. Thus, all decisions to be made regarding Western Samoa's future would henceforth be made only in Western Samoa and not in Wellington. This was "a break-through of a kind rather unusual in the annals of colonial development, since it had ensured that the political future would not be planned in Wellington—as the future of so many other dependencies have been, and are still being, planned in London, or Paris, or Canberra—but in Western Samoa itself."[4]

From here on, it took another fifteen years for the transition to independence to take place. Throughout it all, the New Zealand government was behind the plans for independence being made by the Samoan leaders in Parliament, in business, and in the districts. New Zealand became Western Samoa's trusted adviser, a role that survived Western Samoa's independence in 1962, and a role that was formally recognized in the Treaty of Freindship signed by Prime Minister Fiame Mataafa and the New Zealand High Commissioner to Western Samoa, Mr. J. B. Wright. The treaty formally recognized the ties of friendship existing between the two countries, and enabled New Zealand to represent Western Samoa diplomatically overseas. The treaty is a landmark of New Zealand's eventual success in Western Samoa, after decades of trouble with the Mau.

The manifest motives for New Zealand's withdrawal from Samoa were such things as bitter, nationalistic Samoan feelings against what Samoans considered "unfair" colonial administrations, a reformist Labor Government policy on colonial matters, and world wide opinion against colonialism. A latent reason for New Zealand's withdrawal, however, was to ensure that many of the reforms which the Western Samoan government and people needed would not be carried out, at least for quite a long time. For instance, the land tenure system remained largely unchanged. In an age when more Samoans are leaving their villages for the urban areas every year, the land tenure system is becoming more out of date. While over eighty per cent of Western Samoa's land is customary land, thousands of Samoans are crying out for land in Apia. The usual signs of the ghettoes are evident: overcrowding, squalor, and crime.

Another area in which reform was lacking is the voting system. Only the chiefs (*matai*) could vote in the general elections, and only they could be candidates. Though in theory it has been argued that the *matai* are representative of the people, in practice such a political arrangement has the effect of creating a government of *matai*, by the *matai*, for the *matai*—a strange contrast with democratic principles. In practice, such a group tends to promote its own interests at the expense of the public or national interest, and generally does its best to discourage or outlaw the emergence of opposite interests, much to the disadvantage of the country as a whole.

In the sphere of economic development, New Zealand achieved outrageously little during its 48 years in Western Samoa. At the time of independence, for instance, industrialization was practically nil. What industrialization was there, was largely the work of local entrepreneurs like E. A. Coxon, O. F. Nelson, I. H. Carruthers, and E. F. Paul. Even then, these businessmen and others dealt mainly with the wholesaling, retailing, and service industries. It was only after independence that a number of small industries (producing beverages, biscuits, concrete, and soap) were set up. The New Zealand administration's expenditure was mostly on infra-structural development (which was minor in comparison with post-

independence development) and on meeting administrative costs. It would appear
that New Zealand had followed a hands-off policy, that is to say, to interfere
with the local economic life (largely subsistence) as little as possible; or in other
words to leave the "natives" as much as possible to themselves except as the administration dictated during the Mau troubles. What New Zealand hoped to gain from
this policy is not certain, but it is quite unattractive by modern standards and insufficient by the standards now adopted by Samoans themselves.

On the cultural level, New Zealand policy appeared to favor leaving Samoan
customs and traditions alone. Again this appeared to be a matter of convenience,
rather than any deeply felt love for Samoan culture. But, of course, the administration always had the power to intervene in cultural matters, as was amply
demonstrated with the passing of laws that cut across Samoan customs and traditions. This was one of the causes of the Mau rebellion.

The one area, however, in which New Zealand excelled was in education.
From 1945 onwards, New Zealand has provided scholarships at universities and
technical schools for Samoan students. In the 1950s, New Zealand money financed
the construction of Samoan College, now the leading secondary school in the country, and New Zealand was also instrumental in the establishment of the Alafua
College of Tropical Agriculture. Education is an area in which New Zealand's
influence will long be felt.

It could be argued, of course, that New Zealand could, and should, have carried
out extensive reforms in the political, administrative, cultural, legal, and economic
spheres. That these were not done is not entirely New Zealand's fault. In some
areas, for example land and local government, New Zealand tried to effect reforms but was not successful. Also the Mau troubles indirectly retarded Western
Samoa's economic development as the Mau and the administrators fought out
a political battle. However, New Zealand must share at least part of the blame.
In the political sphere, for instance, New Zealand must be blamed for giving the
chiefs too much political authority—an authority that should not belong to an
elite or elites, but to the people as whole men and women, titled and untitled,
rich and poor, full Samoans or half-castes. The interests that New Zealand catered
to were pseudo-nationalistic ones, for true nationalism must comprise the rank and
file of the people.[5]

But now with New Zealand gone, it would appear that the reforms that will
have to be carried out eventually must now come from the Samoans themselves.
Already, young educated Samoans, and those who have lived overseas for some
time and have had the opportunity to compare life in Samoa with those in other
places, are beginning to clamor for reforms in many areas. But it is an up-
hill fight all the way. Samoans must now be pitched against their own government,
against the establishment as represented in Samoa by such strong, ultra-conservative
groups as the *matai*, the churches, and the merchants. New Zealand could have at
least given the true nationalists a favorable advantage before independence.

In conclusion, while it seems that New Zealand has finally gained her objectives
in Western Samoa, on the other hand, Western Samoa has yet to gain her own in-

ternal objectives. The issue of bringing Western Samoa into the twentieth century, abandoned by New Zealand, is now a burden to be carried by the Samoans themselves. And in the end, it could be asked, "Who has really gained?"

NOTES

1. J. T. Gill, "The Administration of Major General Sir George Richardson in Western Samoa 1923-1928" (Master's thesis, Victoria University, Wellington, 1964) pp. 93-94.
2. Ibid., p. 90.
3. J. W. Davidson, *Samoa Mo Samoa* (Melbourne, 1967), p. 137.
4. Ibid., p. 187.
5. Frantz Fanon, *The Wretched of the Earth* (London, 1969).

BIBLIOGRAPHY

Lee, John A. *Simple on a Soap Box*. Auckland: Collins, 1963.
Masterman, S. *An Outline of Samoan History*. Nelson Memorial Library, Apia.
Mead, Margaret. *The Coming of Age in Samoa*. London, 1943.
Stevenson, R. L. *A Footnote to History*. London, 1892.
Watson, R. M. *A History of Samoa*. Wellington, 1918.

10

Toward a Papua New Guinea Foreign Policy: Constraints and Choice

On September 16, 1975, Papua New Guinea, after nearly seventy years of Australian colonial control, received its independence. Although now politically a single country, it was in fact two separate countries. Papua, which occupied the southern and southeastern parts of the country, was acquired by Australia in 1906 and until independence was Australian territory.[1] New Guinea, which occupies the northern and northwestern parts of the country, was a Trust Territory, administered on behalf of the United Nations Trusteeship Council by Australia with the ultimate objective of preparing the territory for self-government.[2] During World War II, when Papua and New Guinea became a battleground between Japan and the Allied Powers, Australia administered the two territories jointly.[3] After the war, this joint administrative arrangement was continued until 1949 when it was formalized permanently under the Papua and New Guinea Act passed by the Australian Parliament.[4] After independence, the name Papua New Guinea was retained despite some parliamentary sentiment in favor of Niugini. In many cases, the nature of Australian colonialism with regard to Papua and New Guinea will leave its imprint on the future relations that independent Papua New Guinea will have with the rest of the world. The purpose of this paper is to evaluate the constraints Papua New Guinea must confront now that it has shed its formal colonial strings and must embark on its own unique relationships with the international community.

AUSTRALIAN COLONIALISM

Until the mid-1960s, Australian colonial control of Papua and New Guinea could be characterized as tardy and negligent vis-à-vis the object of ultimate independence for these territories.[5] Even after World War II, when colonial movements in the Third World were beginning to bring concessions for independence, Australian administrators were predicting that Papua and New Guinea would not be ready for anything like self-government for another hundred years.[6] The spirit was one of protracted and almost indefinite rule.

It appears that during this phase between World War II and 1960, the objective of Australian colonial administration was not to prepare the countries for an existence outside the Australian Commonwealth.[7] On the contrary, the policy seemed to be oriented towards "integration" of Papua and New Guinea.[8] This would have been easy in the case of Papua, which was Australian territory; but in the case of New Guinea, which was a Trust Territory entrusted to Australia "to promote the political, economic, social and educational advancement of the inhabitants" and to advance "their progressive development towards self-government," this would have been a bit more difficult, but not impossible.[9] It was perfectly legitimate under the Trusteeship arrangement for a self-governing New Guinea to opt for some sort of association with Australia.

The critical point, however, is that Australian policy was not oriented to a swift transfer of power to the territories. Australian delegates at the United Nations continued to stress the need for "preparing" the colonies to undertake self-government perhaps 100 years later.[10] "Preparation" evidently was intended to be a tardy affair.[11] To be fair to the Australians, it must be stressed that after World War II they did undertake to administer Papua and New Guinea with increasing subsidies from Australia to improve the welfare of the inhabitants. Earlier it had been the colonial policy of the Australian government to make the territories pay for their own administration through revenues collected from them.[12] Post-World War II policy stressed "welfare" and "subsidy"—albeit a mere trickle initially as compared with the finances which would be committed in the late 1960s.[13]

Australia's colonial foot-dragging received a jolt from the successful anticolonial movements in Africa and Asia in the 1950s. In 1960, the United Nations passed the Declaration on the Granting of Independence to Colonial Countries and Peoples. In the same year, the British Prime Minister made his famous "wind of change" speech. These events culminated in a dramatic speech made by the Australian Prime Minister, Robert Gordon Menzies, in late 1960. In what was a clear reversal of the old Australian colonial approach to self-government, he said: "I think the prevailing school of thought today is that if in doubt you should go sooner, not later. I belong to that school of thought now, though I didn't once."[14] But while the Menzies speech articulated the new independence approach, Australian policies thereafter still continued until the mid-1960s to stress practices suggesting that independence would not come until about the year 2000. In 1962, the United Nations Visiting Mission to New Guinea, which was headed by the ex-British colonial administrator, Sir Hugh Foot, called on the Australian government to accelerate the involvement of Papua New Guineans in the process of government decision-making.[15] In 1961, the Australians introduced a Legislative Council with a restricted franchise, and consequently an indigenous minority representation, but by 1964 universal adult suffrage was introduced and the First House of Assembly inaugurated.

But even at this point, Australian policy was still backward, and change was brought about only by a United Nations condemnation of Australian tardiness in decolonizing the territories.[16] At this stage, Australia still appeared fairly indecisive as to what eventual status was intended for Papua and New Guinea. Indications were that Australia wanted some sort of close association with its territories after independence. A statement by Charles Barnes, Minister for Territories, to the Australian House of Representatives, on May 5, 1965, underlined this point:

> There is no fixed path which a dependent territory must travel on the
> way to self-determination or independence. Nor is independence as a
> separate sovereign country the inevitable or pre-determined result of
> political development. . . . While internal self-government is the minimum
> and sovereign independence the maximum in political development, there
> are a variety of arrangements which could be made within these two
> positions if the people desire a continuing relationship with Australia.[17]

"Partnership" and "Seventh Statism" became the key concepts at this stage, but these would be soon eliminated. On June 23, 1967, Barnes, under increasing pressure from the UN Trusteeship Council and a newly formed independence movement, said he did not see as "a practical possibility the absorption of Papua and New Guinea in the Australian Commonwealth at least on the same terms as the other states."[18] As late as 1968, however, Barnes still did not predict independence until 20 to 30 years later.

It is important to note that the major influences thus far responsible for Australia's slow and reluctant accession to future independence for Papua and New Guinea had come from outside. These influences included the successful anti-colonial movements in the Third World, pressure from the UN Trusteeship Council, and finally one other factor not mentioned earlier—that is, the growing insignificance of Papua and New Guinea as part of the Australian strategic defense calculus.[19] This re-evaluation of Papua New Guinea's strategic importance is partly traceable to the termination of the confrontation that occurred between Indonesia and the Netherlands over the other "half" of the island, West Irian.[20]

Late in the 1960s, the impetus towards accelerated decolonization in Papua and New Guinea came mainly from internal sources. An embryonic nationalist movement was emerging. Its principal instrument was the Pangu Pati (formed in 1967),[21] which demanded immediate self-government for Papua New Guinea.[22] Other events in the territories included the establishment of the House Committee on Constitutional Development;[23] but even more important was the agitation that the Mataungan Association spearheaded in the Gazelle Peninsula.[24]

Internal turmoil was beginning to tax the Australian colonial administrators' capability to govern without the consent of the people and without the use of force. In response to these pressures, Prime Minister Gorton of Australia said, in a statement of equal significance to Menzies' statement a decade earlier, that further devolution of political authority would be transferred to Papua New Guineans.[25] He added, "We don't want to remain in the Territory one week against the wish of the majority of its people."[26] But even Gorton, in speaking about self-government, did not contemplate the swift constitutional changes that were to follow. He said, "I think it is quite impossible with any responsibility to set a particular date. I don't myself think it will be too long delayed, but certainly not by 1972, and certainly not by 1973 or 1974."[27]

At this stage the preponderant decolonization influences swung back from internal Papua New Guinea sources to Australian sources. Elections were forthcoming in Australia with the Labor Party making a strong challenge to unseat the Liberal-Country Party Coalition, which had governed Australia for the previous two decades and which had been responsible for the very conservative colonial practices of Australia. The leader of the Labor Party, Gough Whitlam, visited Papua New Guinea and promised that if his party should win the forthcoming Australian federal elections, Papua New Guinea would receive its independence under the Labor government's rule.[28] This was the first time that a fixed period was set for Papua New Guinea's independence. To add to this factor, the House of Assembly's Committee on Constitutional Development submitted a report recommending early self-government and independence.

The Labor Party won the Australian federal elections, and with it the wheels of the independence movement accelerated dramatically. Prime Minister Whitlam, intent on altering the Australian image in the international community, noted: "Our conduct in Papua New Guinea is the matter on which, more than anything else, we are being judged by other nations."[29] Whitlam was determined to give independence to Papua New Guinea, as he had promised, during the first term of his party's tenure in office regardless of whether Papua New Guinea wanted it or not. Internal self-government was granted on December 1, 1973, and the announced date of independence, exactly a year later, was only frustrated by certain internal wranglings among the coalition government in Papua New Guinea. Independence was finally achieved in September 1975.

Looking back on the entire stretch of Australia's colonial relationship with Papua and New Guinea, this introductory overview has described the suddenness of the Australian decolonization process that took meaningful form in the early 1970s. One commentator described the transition as follows:

> What is immediately striking is how rapidly perceptions of the role of the territory—and indeed of the whole island—in Australian defence and foreign policy have changed; and the changes have consistently been in the direction of downgrading its importance.[30]

> It was considerably less than twenty years since Menzies was declaring that Australia was in New Guinea to stay.[31]

The legacy of colonial Australian administration has left certain severe constraints on the formulation of an independent Papua New Guinea foreign policy. This is so partly by virtue of the nature of what colonial relationships tend to be and partly by virtue of the suddenness of Australia's devolution of political authority to Papua New Guinea. Throughout the rest of this paper, the possibilities within which Papua New Guinea will have to relate to the international community will be discussed in relation to the problems posed by and constraints created by Australian colonial practice in Papua New Guinea.

A THEORETICAL FRAMEWORK FOR THE STUDY
OF CONSTRAINTS ON A PAPUA NEW GUINEA
FOREIGN POLICY

In order to organize and present the data on the constraints limiting the choice of a Papua New Guinea foreign policy, a simple, but hopefully illumina- ting, framework has been adopted.[32] The concepts and categories used to express the relationships between the variables in the framework are also simple and famil- iar to students of international relations. The variables can be separated into two categories, namely (1) isolationism, (2) nonalignment, and (3) diplomatic coalitions factors related to the choice of one of these strategies.

A state's foreign policy orientation may be conveniently classified into three categories, namely (1) isolationism, (2) nonalignment, and (3) diplomatic coalitions and military alliances.[33] A state that chooses a particular foreign policy strategy does so because it feels that its national interests, whatever they are, will be best served by this orientation. However, this choice is not entirely within the latitude of decision makers without constraints imposed by external and internal factors. At least four factors within the domestic and international environment will be isolated analytically as strong determinants of a final choice of policy. These are: (1) the structure of the international system; (2) the social, political, and economic characteristics of the state; (3) external threats the state faces; and (4) geographical contiguity factors.

A state that chooses an isolationist foreign policy strategy intends to limit its interaction with the international community to a low level of involvement. But, for a state to choose this policy it must satisfy the four requirements enumerated above. In this case, an isolationist policy is best made under the optimal condi- tions described in Table 2.

By this framework, it is clear that an isolationist position can be met optimally when the objective conditions support a choice such as is found in Table 2. A totally unrealistic isolationist orientation would be represented by Table 3. It from the arena of great power conflicts. These are the optimal conditions. Stated differently, a state could pursue a fairly realistic foreign option of isolationism when the objective conditions support a choice such as is found in table 2. A totally unrealistic isolationist orientation would be represented by table 3. It will be very difficult in the contemporary world for any state to embark on, and successfully implement, such an isolationist foreign policy, although several states have done this in recent history.[34]

A state that pursues a policy of nonalignment refuses to commit itself militarily to the objectives of another state, and although it may from time to time provide diplomatic support on issues that another state may espouse, it is not bound in

TABLE 2

CONDITIONS FOR A REALISTIC ISOLATIONIST POLICY

	INTERNATIONAL SYSTEM		INTERNAL/EXTERNAL FACTORS		THREATS		CONTIGUITY	
	Diffused	Polar	Self-Sufficiency	Dependency	No	Yes	Remote	Close
1. International System	X							
2. Internal/External Factors			X					
3. Threats						X		
4. Geographical Contiguity Factor								X

TABLE 3

CONDITIONS FOR AN UNREALISTIC ISOLATIONIST POLICY

	INTERNATIONAL SYSTEM		INTERNAL/EXTERNAL FACTORS		THREATS		CONTIGUITY	
	Diffused	Polar	Self-Sufficiency	Dependency	No	Yes	Remote	Close
1. International System		X						
2. Internal/External Factors				X				
3. Threats						X		X
4. Geographical Contiguity Factor								

the future to a particular pattern of support for a country, alliance, or bloc. Nonalignment, which is a policy undertaken by a state through its own wish, must be distinguished from "neutrality," which refers to the legal status of a state that has been collectively imposed by outside powers.[35] Unlike an isolationist foreign policy strategy, a policy of nonalignment is not locked rigidly within the four factors that influence its choice. The range of choices within the four factors is wider. However, an optimal condition may still be defined (see Table 4).

Optimal conditions for a strategy of nonalignment occur when (a) the international structure is diffused, (b) a country is not self-sufficient but depends upon other countries for such things as access to markets and aid, (c) a threat to the state security is absent, and (d) the state is remote from struggles among great powers.

It is important that a nonaligned state, to project credibility for its foreign policy posture, avoid entering into any military arrangements, such as providing military bases to another country, particularly one of the great powers. Further, it must show that its nonaligned policy has the support of the major parties or

TABLE 4

CONDITIONS FOR A NONALIGNED POLICY

	INTERNATIONAL SYSTEM		INTERNAL/EXTERNAL FACTORS		THREATS		CONTIGUITY	
	Diffused	Polar	Self-Sufficiency	Dependency	No	Yes	Remote	Close
1. International System	X							
2. Internal/External Factors				X				
3. Threats						X		
4. Geographical Contiguity Factor							X	

TABLE 5

CONDITIONS FOR DIPLOMATIC COALITIONS OR MILITARY ALLIANCES

	INTERNATIONAL SYSTEM		INTERNAL/EXTERNAL FACTORS		THREATS		CONTIGUITY	
	Diffused	Polar	Self-Sufficiency	Dependency	No	Yes	Remote	Close
1. International System		X						
2. Internal/External Factors				X				
3. Threats						X		
4. Geographical Contiguity Factor								X

power groups in its own country and that it has a reasonable amount of political stability so that it does not easily invite external intervention or subversion. A policy of nonalignment may also win credibility when over the long run the state's behavior shows shifting support for different blocs or states from issue to issue.

A state that enters into a diplomatic coalition or formal alliance with another state or states does so because it believes that its national aims are best served by such a collective arrangement. Sometimes, a state aligns militarily with another state or bloc of states to improve its domestic strength and maintain itself in power. Such an alliance may also serve to dissuade internal revolution or dissidence.[36]

The optimal conditions under which diplomatic coalitions or military alliances may be entered into are set forth in Table 5. Such conditions occur when (a) the international system is polarized and a country's choice may very well be dictated to it from outside; (b) states share common domestic needs that can be met by a collective approach; (c) states perceive a common threat; and (d) states are physically in the middle of an actual or potential fray.

Collective arrangements vary with regard to subject matter and scope. In the case of a diplomatic coalition, states consistently and openly pledge support to each other at international conferences such as the United Nations. This could be the scope of the collective agreement, although it is likely to spill over to economic and social areas. A military alliance occurs when countries pledge to assist each other militarily when they are threatened. The nature of this arrangement may vary from an "automatic" military response to a "consultation" process prior to military action. In either case, the state has committed its military resources to another country's use under certain circumstances. It is not isolationist or nonaligned but allied.

CONSTRAINTS ON THE CHOICE
OF A PAPUA NEW GUINEA FOREIGN POLICY

Papua New Guinea has about 2,500,000 people who inhabit one of the most mountainous and topographically chopped up areas of the world. After nearly a century of colonialism under German, British, Japanese, and Australian control, about 85 percent of the people still live in villages. Within recent years, since Australia began accelerating its aid program to Papua New Guinea to prepare the country for a more viable survival as a sovereign entity in the international system, more and more persons have left the rural areas for the town; and increasing numbers of schools have become available to service the modernized sector of the country.[37]

Accompanying the changes in economy are social and political strains, which render unchallenged control of the government very difficult. Secessionist movements, cargo cults, rising unemployment, a growing school drop out population, urban slums—all part of the paraphernalia of most Third World countries—are becoming painfully evident in Papua New Guinea. These factors together limit the domestic decision makers in formulating and implementing a foreign policy.

To be realistic, a country's efforts to formulate an independent foreign policy must take cognizance of the structure and capability of the economy in supporting that orientation. Especially with ex-colonial countries, such items as foreign investment, aid, and trade, plus the availability of skills and control of the public sector are critical variables in evaluating how a country may relate to the international community.

The traditional Papua New Guinean economy, like that of all the Melanesian countries, was based in "small villages separated by long distances and difficult terrain and often by problems of language and traditions of warfare . . ."[38] The villagers subsisted mainly on Kau-Kau (sweet potato) or sago, until the first foreign intruders arrived looking for slave labor to recruit, tropical products to trade, or gold to mine.[39] Thereafter massive disruptions and transformations occurred in the Papua New Guinean economy; but basically the country was turned into a dependent, export economy controlled by foreign investors. H. C. Brookfield summarized the colonial legacy in Papua New Guinea and the rest of Melanesia as

. . . essentially satellitic economies, with strongly skewed patterns of resource endowment and domestic production. The export industries of all are to a great degree enclave economies, supported by heavy foreign investment. All depend on foreign funds, public and private, for growth. Not only is there lack of integration between territorial economies, but also within them. Significant parts of all territories are economically stagnant or suffering from backward effects.[40]

Brookfield added that so much of "growth centers and new industries [is] in the hands of foreign enterprise" that if a Melanesian nation's capital and industrial center were burnt to the ground, it would lose nothing "but the records of [its] debts."[41]

In Papua New Guinea the facts of economic life dramatically illustrate the accuracy of Brookfield's observation. To begin with, it has been estimated that about 60 percent of the gross monetary sector is controlled by Australian individuals and companies.[42] In the private sector dealing with agriculture, forestry, and fisheries, Australian enterprises contributed in 1971-1972 about $24 million (Australian)—or one-third—to the total value of output.[43] The principal agricultural products in Papua New Guinea are cocoa, coffee, copra, rubber, and tea. In each of these areas Australian influence or control is strong. Estimated Australian control of the cocoa industry is 55 to 60 percent, and in the coffee industry 20 to 25 percent.[44] In the copra industry, Australian expatriates accounted for about 80 percent of the total commercial production.[45] In the tea industry, expatriate land holdings account for 90 percent of all acres planted in 1970.[46] In the case of rubber, practically all production was in nonindigenous hands.[47] Nearly all of these agricultural items are produced for export market and expatriate-owned enterprises produce 60 percent of all export crops.[48] The most striking point about the agricultural sector, in spite of the strong Australian influence, is that it is the economic area of least Australian influence.[49]

Continuing with the private sector, in commerce and manufacturing, Australians control about 75 percent of the output.[50] In manufacturing, where expatriates control all but 1 or 2 percent of manufactured goods and most mining output, Papua New Guineans simply do not have the capital to make great inroads in this sector.[51] It is estimated that of the approximately 700 factories operating in Papua New Guinea, only about 50, mostly very small scale, are owned by indigenous persons.[52] Papua New Guinean nonagricultural enterprise is limited to a few hundred small businesses such as trade stores, small-scale building and construction, truck transport of freight and passengers, gold sluicing, and production of handicrafts.[53]

Commerce is dominated by three Australian companies (Burns Philip Ltd., W. R. Carpenter Ltd., and Steamship Trading Co.), which enjoy close to monopoly conditions in urban areas.[54] It is estimated that 85 percent of retail trade is conducted by Australian firms. [55] Of the 2, 376 locally registered companies and 572 foreign companies, in 1971, about 2,500 were owned by Australian individuals or companies.[56] In the area of hire purchase, insurance, and real estate, practically all were in Australian hands. [57] In tourism and associated industries, such as hotels, motels, and restaurants, Australians owned about 90 percent.[58] Together, about 87 percent of all these investment facilities was in expatriate hands. [59] These facts point not only to dependency of an overwhelming sort, but attest to the eleventh hour speed of the Australian decolonization process that transferred formal constitutional power to Papua New Guineans while leaving control of the private economic sector in expatriate hands. Papua New Guinea is a veritable economic region of Australia. But, this severe picture of dependency is also found in the public sector.

In most developing countries, including Papua New Guinea, the public sector plays a very significant role in the country's economic life. This is so partly because foreign aid grants and loans tend to be channeled through the public service for project and general implementation. A second reason points to the socialist or semi-socialist economic philosophies that most of these countries adopt, resulting in greater reliance on public corporations and enterprises to initiate and carry out productive economic activities. The overall consequence is that the government's budget tends to be inordinately large in relation to the size of the private sector.

In Papua New Guinea, revenues to support a large public budget cannot be adequately raised from local sources. It is vital that the gap between public expenditure and local sources of revenues be met by foreign aid. Over the last few years, Australia provided about 55 percent of public sector spending.[60] In 1974, Australian aid was A$187 million, up about A$9 million from the 1973-1974 grant.[61] Earlier in 1974, in anticipation of independence, Gough Whitlam, the then Australian Prime Minister, promised A$500 million for the three years after 1974-1975 for "development and social welfare" projects;[62] Papua New Guinea would be given first call on the Australian foreign aid program [63] to the tune of almost one-third of the total amount allocated for assisting developing countries.[64]

The Australian aid program has had three components: (1) a direct grant to the Papua New Guinea budget; (2) special grants to cover broad spectrums of activity such as agriculture; and (3) aid for specific projects.[65] Papua New Guinea, like all recipients, is interested in obtaining aid in the form of outright grants. Australia, on the other hand, as the Minister of External Territories said in 1973, would have to account to Parliament and to the Australian taxpayer about the specific purposes for which aid monies are allocated.[66] It is sufficient to note at this point that Australian aid to Papua New Guinea is on "soft" terms, is mainly in grant form (among Development Assistance Committee countries, Australian aid has the highest grant element),[67] and will be converted increasingly into project aid.[68]

At least two components of Australia's foreign aid program need to be sorted out for special attention, namely skilled personnel and defense. In the area of skills, it is clear from the great amounts of aid to be administered that trained personnel will be in great demand. As of 1970, there were very few or no indigenous architects, engineers, accountants, doctors, or dentists.[69] Most of the skilled labor requirements of the country were met from the 40,000-strong expatriate population, many of whom are leaving. Expatriates account for approximately 97 percent of

the professional and managerial manpower throughout the economy, and 75 percent of technical, subprofessional, and middle-level managerial personnel.[70] In the
public sector, Australian public servants have been transferred to Papua New
Guinea. Together, the Australian aid for these defense commitments amounted to
organized into the Australian Staffing Assistance Group (ASAG). The Finance
Minister in his annual budget speech summed up this source of dependency:

> As in 1973-74, Australia will still meet the full costs of the salaries
> and allowances of the members of the Australian Staffing Assistance
> Group. The estimated cost in 1974-75 is A$60 million, compared with
> actual expenditure of A$53.9 million.[72]

In the area of defense, Australia has borne the cost of maintaining these forces,
spending about A$23.5 million in 1973-1974.[73] From December 1974, special
grants to cover certain parts of defense costs, amounting to one-half of the total
defense budget, had to be borne by Papua New Guinea.[74] Thereafter, Australian
defense aid had to be restricted to pay the cost of Australian servicemen with the
Papua New Guinea Defense Force, of training Papua New Guinea servicemen in
Australia, and of certain "mutually agreed" upon major projects in Papua New
Guinea. Together, the Australian aid for these defense commitments amounted to
about A$8,030,500.[75] When independence arrived, some A$60 million in military
installations and other assets were turned over to Papua New Guinea.[76]

Until September 1974, Papua New Guinea's armed forces were an integral
part of the Royal Australian Navy and Military Forces.[77] Because of the suddenness of the Australian decolonization process, little was done until just before
independence to gear the Papua New Guinea army for an independent existence.
For example, training of indigenous officers for the future Papua New Guinea
Defense Force did not begin until 1963; by 1974 only two senior officers existed
to serve in positions of high authority in the Defense Force.[78] Professor Robert
O'Neill wrote in 1970 that the—Papua New Guinea (PNG) government would probably
have to speed up promotions—losing some efficiency thereby—but still continue to
depend heavily on Australian officers after independence:

> The rate of indigenization of senior ranks depends partly on the degree
> to which the PNG government is prepared to sacrifice short term
> efficiency and partly on the numbers of experienced officers available.
> There are only five indigenous army officers of six years commissioned
> service or more. The senior two are company commanders and, after
> receiving some staff training and experience, should be ready to become
> battalion commanders before independence. There are also many
> technical postings which will be difficult to indigenize for several years.[79]

The situation is similar in the Navy. The Papua New Guinea Division of the
Royal Australian Navy will require several years before indigenous captains and
commanders will be able to assume responsibility for the coastal patrol boats and

training facilities in the Papua New Guinea Navy.[80] "Even further off is the technological independence from the Royal Australian Navy. Major servicing of patrol boats may be an Australian responsibility for their entire operational lives."[81]

In the case of the air force, there is no indigenous section. No plans to date have been announced for training local air force personnel, so that "PNG will be dependent for several years on an external power for the air mobility which has become an integral part of the Army's deployment system."[82]

Overall, then, although the Defense Department is under the final control of a Papua New Guinean civilian Minister for Defense and a Papua New Guinean civilian Secreta and the armed forces are under a Papua New Guinean commander (the Army and N units were formerly under the control of a Joint Force),[84] financial and personnel requirements to sustain the military establishment continue to be heavily dependent Australia after independence.

SOCIO-POLITICAL FACTORS

Political factors within any country can facilitate or retard the effectiveness with which foreign policy objectives of the state are formulated and carried out. Papua New Guinea is at a very propitious juncture in its political history. It has recently achieved political independence, but the experience of other Third World countries has shown independence to lead to struggles between groups and forces for either "pre-eminence" or "protection." In Papua New Guinea, the "pre-eminence objective" is caught up in the battle between the new radical elites who in their rhetoric, but not in their westernized life style, emphasize the virtues of village life, self-sufficiency, and national control of the country's resources against predatory foreign investors and the combined forces of the old colonial aristocracy, who are largely expatriate business and plantation owners, and the new pragmatic elites who, like the radical elites, are bourgeois in life style but who see the rising demands of the people unattainable without foreign investment.[85] Prior to independence, the "radicals" and "pragmatic elites" clashed over the future structure of the country's constitutional framework, with the latter winning very convincingly.[86]

The "protection" objective in Papua New Guinea has so far been pursued primarily by secessionist movements. With over 700 linguistic groups in a very socially and geographically fragmented country, several units view their future with uncertainty in independent Papua New Guinea. The secessionist threats have come mainly from Papua, which as pointed out earlier was an Australian territory. Josephine Abaijah, the leader of the secessionist Papua Besena Movement, bases her demand for a separate and independent Papua on the fear that New Guinea, which is more densely populated and economically developed, will dominate Papua and reduce it to a vassal state.[87] Secessionist threats of equal credibility have also come from the copper island Bougainville and from the Gazelle Peninsula.[88] The Australian government firmly discouraged secessionists from believing that independence would be granted any separate entity apart from Papua New

Guinea as a united country. However, the central government that now governs independent Papua New Guinea has had its resources severely taxed to maintain the integrity of the state from persistent challenges to the legitimacy of its authority.[89]

Together these two main socio-political factors, which are gathered around "pre-eminence objective" is caught up in the battle between the new radical elites determine the question of political stability. In the event that the radical group in the first category should take control of the government, and should it live by its creed, one can safely expect rapid and ruthless alteration of Papua New Guinea's economic structure. This is not likely to be done without opposition. Indeed, it could very well lead to great bloodshed in which a military coup d'etat might be the saving solution. Similarly, should the secessionist Papua and Bougainville movements successfully organize and mobilize their forces, the seams of the state might have to be held together by the coercive apparatus, namely the army and force alone.[90]

The problem will revolve around the capability of the state to cope reasonably well with the demands of all major groups so that none is totally frustrated. This means that the articulative and aggregative political institutional structures, such as pressure groups and parties, must be well developed and given ready access to the decision-making bodies of the state.[91] It will also mean that existing sources of revenue necessary to meet the demands from the various groups must be preserved and expanded. This cannot be done immediately from internal sources, but over the long run, when its abundant resources are developed, Papua New Guinea should be able to assume responsibility for meeting its own demands. But, both the socio-political problems and the heavily dependent financial resource base point to heavy constraints, which will limit the freedom with which Papua New Guinea can conduct its relations with Australia and the international community.[92]

THREATS

The formulation of any country's policy must, first and foremost, attend to its immediate security needs. Perceived threats must be eliminated, deterred, or mollified. Papua New Guinea, living under the Australian defense umbrella, has thus far shared Australia's friends and enemies alike. Since independence, however, theoretically it has been free to realign its relations to fit a different set of interests and calculations.

In practice, however, Papua New Guinea's relationship with Australia would appear to define the new country's friends and enemies. There is no question that Papua New Guinea will remain in the Western camp if only by virtue of the kinds of economic and military connections that are maintained with Australia. However, this will not necessarily mean that Papua New Guinea's enemies are to be the Soviet Union or China. Papua New Guinea probably will simply stay away from such a definition of the world, which in any event will be remote from its affairs.

If a potential threat to Papua New Guinea is to be named, it is more than likely to be found somewhere on its contiguous borders. The adjacent countries are Indonesia, the British Solomon Islands Protectorate, and Australia. Of these, Indonesia is seen by some as the most likely future threat. The basis of the Indonesian fear originated from the period of confrontation between Indonesia and the Netherlands over what was called West Irian, now Irian Jaya. Australia, for most of this crisis, allied itself indirectly but unambiguously with the Dutch arguments for the retention of West Irian under Netherlands rule.[93] Since the time of the settlemen in 1962, which was finalized in 1969 after the "Act of Free Choice," two events have led to a lessening of tension between Australia and Indonesia over the entire island of New Guinea. First, President Sukarno of Indonesia was overthrown and replaced by a friendly military regime; and second, Irian Jaya was placed firmly in Indonesia's control as an integral part of its territory.

Papua New Guinea, however, continues to share the New Guinea islands with Indonesia's Irian Jaya. While good relations prevail currently, many Papua New Guineans fear that with another Sukarno, Indonesia's expansionist desires may spread east-ward. This point becomes real when Papua New Guinea weighs two salient facts of political life: First, Indonesia with its 135 million people, overcrowded population, and powerful military establishment, could easily overwhelm Papua New Guinea in any military conflict. An incentive for this could be the disparity in living standards between the two parts of the island. Second, while the Australian relationship with Papua New Guinea will in the short run be protective, in the long run Australia will have to consider whether it gives greater priority to Papua New Guinean or Indonesian friendship. It is easy to visualize a scenario in which a radical Papua New Guinean government invites trouble from Indonesia through encouraging the "Free Papua Movement" (see below) with the consequence that Papua New Guinea, in Professor Hedley Bull's words, may become "a net strategic liability" to Australia.[94]

Presently Papua New Guinea's relations with Indonesia over Irian Jaya are good.[95] Before independence, Australia allowed Papua New Guinea to partake in negotiating agreements between the two countries when they affected Papua New Guinea. Two of these agreements are noteworthy. First, Irian Jayanese who cross into Papua New Guinea seeking political asylum may be granted "permissive residence" on condition that such persons do nothing inimical to Indonesian interests while residing in Papua New Guinea.[96] Because a small "Free Papua Movement" made up of Irian Jayanese continues to harass and periodically kill Indonesian troops in Irian Jaya, this agreement became necessary so that Indonesia could be assured that Papua New Guinean bases would not be used as launching pads against Indonesian territory. The second agreement relates to permission given to villagers whose traditional lands straddle the border to be allowed to move back and forth freely.

Papua New Guinea has also opened an embassy in Jakarta, and limited cultural and trade contacts have already occurred. The Papua New Guinean strategy, like the Australian, seems to be oriented toward warm friendly relations with Indonesia.[97] The necessity to maintain peace with Irian Jaya at all costs will impose a major restraint on Papua New Guinea's foreign relations with Indonesia, especially if the two countries continue to have very different political systems.

GEOGRAPHY

Although a minor factor at present, one must be reminded that during World War II, Papua New Guinea became part of the Pacific arena where Allied Forces fought the Japanese. Many Papua New Guineans were killed as well as villages destroyed. Numerous war relics, graves, and caves remain today to attest to the need for Papua New Guinea to evaluate its geographical position in terms of any widespread warfare in the future.

Unless one gives credibility to the practicality of limited warfare, it appears that, given the evolution of sophisticated nuclear technology, it simply would not matter where you were during a war between the East and West. In terms of Papua New Guinea's geography, it seems that Chief Minister Michael Somare's call for a neutral zone in the Pacific and Indian Oceans on both sides of Papua New Guinea makes sense. Australia's attitude toward this proposal is uncertain. The most Papua New Guinea could do at present is to keep nuclear and other bases off its soil. Previously, Australia had a naval base on the Papua New Guinean island of Manus. Its usefulness today seems to be restricted to training and refueling purposes of the Australian Royal Navy.[98]

Overall, it is noteworthy that Papua New Guinea geographically is in the middle of an encircling set of Western-oriented countries. To the west is Indonesia, to the east the British Solomon Islands, to the south Australia, and to the northwest the United States Trust Territory of the Pacific. Geopolitically, while these national perimeters are not determinative of the choice of foreign policy, they may suggest limits to Papua New Guinea's experimentation with policies very alien or provocative to its neighbors.

THE NATURE OF THE INTERNATIONAL ORDER

The strong bipolar politics that emerged after 1945, when the East faced the West, has now given way to what is termed a "bipolycentric" international order instead of a multipolar order.[99] Bipolycentrism asserts that an essentially bipolar system prevails, but it is not as rigid as it was previously when countries were forced into unambiguous alignments with either the United States or the Soviet Union.[100] The preoccupations of these superpowers with their own problems, the prevailing détente, the assertion of some measure of independence by both Western and Eastern European countries via-à-vis the United States and the Soviet Union, respectively, and the emergence of the People's Republic of China as a potential superpower, have combined to loosen the bipolar order.

The implications of bipolycentrism are that rivalries, mainly around economic questions, have become prevalent among allies of a single pole. This, in turn, is reflected in previously subservient allies, such as France and Czechoslovakia, formulating not only fairly independent, but challenging foreign policies to that of the superpowers. The challenge, in most cases, has not been military. Economic rivalries, however, are strong.

Given its fresh experience with the war in the Pacific and its demonstrated dependence on American help (the same could be said of the Western European powers), it is not surprising that Australia followed the American foreign policy line closely after World War II. During the brief period under Whitlam's Labor government, Australia redefined its friends and enemies. Today, under the Frazer Liberal-Country Party government, Australia will probably freely return to closer relations with the United States.[101]

For Papua New Guinea, this "loosening up" of the bipolar world order must be welcomed because, in the light of its economic and military connections with Australia, under a strict bipolar arrangement its ambit of choice is circumscribed tightly. With this new order, Papua New Guinea can now risk diplomatic and economic relations with such countries as China, the Soviet Union, Vietnam, and North Korea without necessarily incurring the intervening wrath of the United States and its ally, Australia. It would seem that the prevailing bipolycentrism would allow Papua New Guinea a wider latitude of foreign policy options than it would have had up to as recently as six years ago when the United States redefined its own relations with the People's Republic of China.

THE AVAILABLE CHOICES OF A PAPUA NEW GUINEA FOREIGN POLICY

As discussed above, the choice of a Papua New Guinea foreign policy orientation will ultimately be dictated among others, by these factors: (a) the nature of the international order; (b) Papua New Guinea domestic social, economic, and political factors; (c) external threats; and (d) geopolitical factors. Additionally, the ideals or ultimate objectives of Papua New Guinea foreign policy must be considered. Some of these objectives were articulated by the Chief Minister, Mr. Somare in a seminal speech given on April 16, 1974, to the Australian Institute of Foreign Relations. In it, Mr. Somare emphasized that he did not want his country's heavy dependence on Australia to be "interpreted by other nations as neocolonialism or an 'Uncle Tom' relationship."[102] To this end, Mr. Somare said:

We wish to diversify our resources for aid, and in fact, we have already started on this program. Australia has assisted us in locating these sources. We have had favorable response for aid and investment from countries such as New Zealand, the United States, Japan, Great Britain and other European nations. The indications are encouraging and it is on foreign investment, trade and technical assistance that the basis of our future ties with these countries will be made. We have assured trade links with Great Britain, for some time yet. New Zealand has already made available technical assistance and we see as important her involvement with the Pacific region.[103]

The Chief Minister's objectives must be considered brave words, for the record to date shows that the countries he has named as alternative sources of aid have contributed very little indeed. In the case of New Zealand, Papua New Guinea will receive over the period 1974 to 1977 about A$5.5 million.[104] The British government for its part has offered to provide Papua New Guinea with technical assistance to the value of A$80,695.[105] The United Kingdom will also be able to help diversify Papua New Guinea's foreign economic interests because Papua New Guinea joined the Commonwealth after independence. [106] Mr. Somare said that "PNG has obtained a standstill arrangement on the tariff treatment of PNG products on the United Kingdom market."[107] With regard to the United States, no aid package has yet been arranged.

The country that appears to offer the best alternative to Papua New Guinea's dependence on Australia is Japan. Although Japan's promise of aid to date has been described as "large, vague, benign but not specific," in other areas it has made dramatic inroads already.[108] In the area of trade, Japan's share in Papua New Guinea's total imports increased from 8.3 percent in 1965 to 17.1 percent in 1971.[109] Its share in the export sector expanded from 3.6 percent to 11.8 percent during the same period.[110] In 1972, Japan imported from Papua New Guinea six times as much as the previous year and exported to Papua New Guinea twice as much as the previous year's exports. Japanese interests are focused mainly on such primary products as lumber, veneer logs, prawns, lobster, tuna, and mining. There is no reason, short of an international crisis, to suppose these trends and interests will not continue into the future.

The Japanese economic influence, however, has received mixed reactions from both the government and the public. Mr. Somare has looked at it as being benign.[111] Certain members of the House of Assembly, however, have warned the government about overextending Japanese investment influence.[112] This sentiment is becoming widespread among the educated elites who, paradoxically, are the highest beneficiaries in services provided from tax revenues, which must come increasingly from profits of foreign companies.

The other region that appears to have some promise for diversifying Papua New Guinea's dependence on Australia is the Melanesian countries of the South Pacific. (Indonesia, according to Mr. Somare, will have essentially a political relationship with Papua New Guinea.)[113] However, because of the similarity in the export primary crops produced by these countries (there are a few exceptions, such as sugar and rice produced in Fiji, which can be imported to Papua New Guinea), trade relations will be minimal. To be sure, political and limited economic regional cooperation through the South Pacific Forum and the South Pacific Commission will be actively pursued,[114] but basically Papua New Guinea's relationship with the South Pacific will be cultural. There may even be some rivalry between these islands for the same markets, and certainly there is fear of Papua New Guinea dominating its smaller South Pacific neighbors.

The implications of these limited successes at diversifying aid, trade, and investment sources are that realistically Papua New Guinea will be neocolonially related to Australia for some time to come. The options open to it, however, should be reevaluated before a final judgment is passed. The three strategies available, as pointed out earlier, are isolationist, nonaligned, and diplomatic coalitions and alliances.

The isolationist strategy is obviously not practicable. It would require a revolution of a backward looking type to reinstate the old patterns of life which are nowadays glorified as the "Melanesian way." Once the ball of modernization starts moving, it can only be slowed and perhaps directed, but it cannot be stopped.

The nonaligned or the coalition-military alliance strategies are the competing orientations from which Papua New Guinean decision-makers must choose. It is clear from Mr. Somare's attitudes that neocolonial relationships are not desired or desirable. This is a very emotional issue where symbolic aspects are very significant for salving the identity crisis of a Third World country. Nonalignment and independence are cherished especially by those who have just severed their connections with their colonial masters. Understandably, pressures are usually put on decision makers to destroy all remnants of colonial control in their societies.

On the other hand, as the facts of political, social, and economic life both on the national and international scene have shown for Papua New Guinea, it cannot hope to be free from its dependency relationship with Australia in the short run. The swiftness of the decolonization process, and its concomitant consequences on locally owned industries, has left Papua New Guinea in a position to continue building its social, political, and economic infrastructure until some time in the future when it may choose to declare its own unique and domestically determined foreign policy strategy for itself. But as of now, and for many years to come, one can expect at international forums to hear Papua New Guinea using the rhetoric of a Third World postcolonial country as it continues having what hopefully will be a dignified dependency relationship with Australia that does not have to be detrimental to the promotion of Papua New Guinea's national interests. If properly used, Papua New Guinea's relationship with an affluent neighbor could reap bountiful rewards at a price that some nationalists may still consider exorbitant. A realistic Papua New Guinea foreign policy will be *de facto* one of alliance, but carefully camouflaged by the symbolic rhetoric characteristic of a foreign policy of nonalignment.

NOTES

1. Lucy Mair, *Australian in New Guinea* (Melbourne, 1970), p. 11.
2. Ibid., p. 22.
3. Ibid., p. 18.

4. Ibid.; see also, J. R. Mattes, "Constitutional Development—A Short History," *New Guinea Quarterly* 7 (June-July 1972), 10-12.

5. See Chapter XI, *Charter of the United Nations,* "Declaration Regarding Non-Self Governing Territories," for a description of Australia's obligation to New Guinea, a trust territory.

6. For a discussion of this protracted policy see Merze Tate, "Australia and Self-Determination for New Guinea," *The Australian Journal of Politics and History* 17 (August 1971), 249-50.

7. Ibid., p. 251.

8. Ibid.

9. See Article 88, *Charter of the United Nations and Statute of the International Court of Justice* (New York 1968), pp. 46-47.

10. Tate, *op. cit.,* p. 251.

11. For a stimulating discussion of the "preparation" concept as a means of delaying independence see B. B. Shaffer, "The Concept of Preparation," *World Politics* 18 (October 1965), 42-67.

12. See Brian Jinks, *New Guinea Government: An Introduction* (Sydney 1971), pp. 95-97. See also the change of policy statement, which was announced by the Minister for External Territories, Mr. Ward, in the House of Representatives on July 4, 1945, in *A New Guinea Brief,* ed. Ian Grosart (Sydney 1967), Extract 6, pp. 10-12.

13. Ibid.

14. Ibid., Extract 11, p. 18.

15. "Report on New Guinea of the United Nations Visiting Mission to the Trust Territories of Nauru and New Guinea," in Grosart, Extract 18, pp. 31-38.

16. *Resolutions and Decisions of the General Assembly at its Twentieth Session, September 21-December 21, 1965* (UN Press Services, Office of Public Information, Press Release BA/1360, December 21, 1965, Resolution 2112 [XX]), pp. 50-1.

17. Tate, *op. cit.,* p. 251.

18. Ibid., p. 253. See also the article written by Oala Oala Rarua, a co-chairman of the Pangu Pati, in *Australian Quarterly* 39, No. 4 (1967), 30-33.

19. See Robert O'Neill, "Australia's Future Defence Relations with Papua New Guinea," *Australian Outlook* 26 (August 1972), 200; also, Hedley Bull, "Australia's Involvement in Independent Papua New Guinea," *World Review* 13 (March 1974), 5.

20. For a general bibliography of the Australian role in the Netherlands-Indonesia conflict, see William Henderson, *West New Guinea: The Dispute and Its Settlement* (New Jersey, 1973), p. 270.

21. See David Stephen, *A History of Political Parties in Papua New Guinea* (Melbourne-1972), p. 17. See also Ralph R. Premdas, "The Case Against the No-Party State in Papua New Guinea," *Social Science and Humanities Journal* 1 (November 1974).

22. Premdas, *op. cit.,* p. 1; see also E. Wolfers, "A History of Political Parties in Papua New Guinea," *The Politics of Melanesia,* ed. Marion Ward (Canberra, 1970), pp. 444-46.

23. Tate, *op. cit.,* p. 255.

24. For a brief description of the actions taken by the Mataungan Association, see Claire Clarke, "Independent Papua New Guinea," *Australian Foreign Policy: Towards a Reassessment,* ed. Claire Clark (Melbourne, 1973), pp. 102-103.

25. Tate, *op. cit.,* p. 256.

26. Ibid.

27. *Post-Courier* (Port Moresby, PNG) November 30, 1973, p. 28.

28. Tate, op. cit., p. 257.

29. See Owen Harris, "Australia and an Independent Papua New Guinea," *Spectrum* 2 (October 1973), 38.

30. Ibid., p. 34.

31. Ibid.

32. This framework has been adopted from K. J. Holsti, *International Politics: A Framework for Analysis* (New Jersey 1967), pp. 97-121.

33. Ibid., p. 98.

34. Ibid., p. 101 (for a list of these countries).

35. Ibid., p. 103; see also, S. N. Anabtawi, "Neutralists and Neutralism," *Journal of Politics* 27 (1965), 351-66.

36. Holsti, *op. cit.,* p. 110.

37. See John Conroy and Richard Curtin, "Migrants in the Urban Economy," *Oceania* (December 1973); see also Ross Garnaut, "Exploring Why Some People Come to Town," *YAGI-AMBU* 1, No. 5, pp. 71-78.

38. Ross Garnaut, "The Melanesian Economies in the International Community" (Paper presented at a Seminar on Papua New Guinea's Foreign Economic Relations, November 19, 1972, University of Papua New Guinea), p. 7.

39. See C. D. Rowley, *The New Guinea Villagers* (Melbourne, 1964).

40. H. C. Brookfield, *Colonialism, Development and Independence: The Case of the Melanesian Islands in the South Pacific* (Cambridge, 1972), p. 141.

41. Ibid.

42. *The National Times,* November 19-24, 1973, p. 8.

43. Ibid.

44. Ibid.

45. Ibid.

46. Ibid.

47. Ibid.

48. John V. Langmore, "A Critical Assessment of Australian Economic Policy for Papua New Guinea Between 1945 and 1970" (Mimeo, Economics Department, University of Papua New Guinea, August 1972) p. 5.

49. *The National Times,* November 19-24, 1973, p. 9.

50. Ibid., p. 8.

51. Langmore, op. cit., p. 5.

52. *The National Times,* loc. cit.

53. Langmore, op. cit., p. 5.

54. *The National Times,* loc. cit.

55. Ibid.

56. Ibid.

57. Ibid.

58. Ibid.

59. Langmore, op. cit., p. 5.

60. *The National Times,* November 19-24, 1973, p. 8.

61. *Post-Courier,* September 18, 1974, p. 1.

62. Speech by Mr. Whitlam in Port Moresby, February 18, 1973; for the text see *Australian Foreign Affairs Record* (February 1973), p. 105.

63. Ibid.

64. *Post-Courier,* March 19, 1974, p. 2.

65. Ibid.

66. See Papua New Guinea Department of Information, News Release, No. 1042, April 27, 1973.

67. O. Mendelsohn, *Australia's Foreign Aid: The Perception of Parliamentarians* (Canberra, 1973), p. 3.

68. *Post-Courier,* loc. cit.

69. *The National Times,* November 19-24, p. 9.

70. Langmore, op. cit., p. 5.

71. *Post-Courier,* loc. cit.

72. "Budget Speech 1974/75" delivered by the Minister for Finance, Mr. Julius Chan, to the PNG House of Assembly on September 24, 1974 (Port Moresby 1974), p. 22.

73. *Post-Courier,* September 18, 1974, p. 1.

74. "Budget Speech 1974/75," p. 21.

75. *Post-Courier,* loc. cit.

76. Ibid.

77. Robert O'Neill, "Australia's Future Defence Relations with Papua New Guinea," *Australian Outlook* (August 1972), 193.

78. Claire Clark, op. cit., pp. 88-9.

79. O'Neill, op. cit., p. 194.

80. Some improvement in this situation occurred in October 1974, when a PNG lieutenant commander was appointed to command a PNG-crewed patrol boat. *Post-Courier,* October 4, 1974, p. 3.

81. O'Neill, op. cit., p. 195.

82. Ibid.

83. A civilian secretary was appointed in early October 1974. *Post-Courier,* October 4, 1974, p. 4.

84. Ibid., October 30, 1974, p. 3.

85. For a more elaborate description of the conflict between these two groups, see Bill Standish, "Papua New Guinea Review," *Australian Quarterly* (September 1974); see also *The National Times,* August 5-10, 1974, pp. 48-9.

86. *Post-Courier,* October 4, 1974, p. 1.

87. *The National Times,* July 30-August 4, 1974, p. 8.

88. Claire Clark, op. cit., pp. 101-103; see also T. Scarlett Epstein, "Economics and Politics in Papua New Guinea: Separatism and the Mataungan Association," and B. J. A. Middlemiss: "Napidakoe Navitu," *The Politics of Melanesia,* ed. Marion Ward (Canberra, 1970), pp. 47-63, 100-104.

89. See Ralph Premdas, "Towards a One-Party State in Papua New Guinea: Some Problems and Prospects," *Australian Outlook* (August 1975), p. 170.

90. For a discussion of the role of the military in an independent PNG, see Ralph R. Premdas, "Keeping the Military Out of Papua New Guinea Politics," *New Guinea Quarterly* (April 1975); U.L.F. Sundhaussen, "The Army—A Political Role?" *New Guinea Quarterly* 8, No. 2, 29-40.

91. Premdas, op. cit., pp. 13-19.

92. PNG is rich in natural resources, and presently the copper mine on Bougainville has earned profits almost equal to the country's Gross Monetary Sector Product. When PNG is able to obtain a higher percentage of the profits (in 1973 PNG received about 20 percent of the A$158 million profit the company made; the profits may double in 1974), it would enable PNG to become more

financially viable but it will still depend on foreign investors for capital formation and economic growth of any significance.

93. See footnote 20.

94. Bull, *World Review* 13, p. 5; for a discussion of the reasons for PNG's decreasing significance to Australia, see Harris, *Spectrum* 2, p. 35.

95. Michael Somare, "The Emerging Role of PNG in World Affairs" (Unpublished) pp. 14-15.

96. J. B. Miller, "Papua New Guinea in World Politics," *Australian Outlook* 27 (August 1973), 193.

97. Somare, op. cit., pp. 14-15.

98. O'Neill, op. cit., p. 195.

99. John Spanier, *Games Nations Play: Analyzing International Politics* (London, 1973), pp. 81-82.

100. Ibid.

101. W. MacMahon Ball, "The Foreign Policy of the Whitlam Government," *Australia's Neighbors* 4 (April-June 1974), 1-4.

102. Somare, op. cit., p. 7.

103. Ibid., p. 8.

104. *Strategies for Nationhood 1974* (Port Moresby 1974), p. 277.

105. Ibid.

106. Somare, op. cit., p. 10.

107. Ibid.

108. Miller, *Australian Outlook* 27, p. 196.

109. Hisao Kanamori, "Japan and the Developing Countries with Special Reference to the Foreign Economic Relations of Papua New Guinea" (Paper delivered at the University of Papua New Guinea, November, 1973), p. 11.

110. Ibid.

111. Somare, op. cit., p. 11.

112. For example see *Post-Courier,* September 11, 1974, p. 3.

113. Somare, op. cit., p. 14.

114. Ibid., p. 12.

JOHN KEARSLEY THOMSON

11

Economic Development in the South Pacific: Some Problems and Prospects

The potential for the development of the natural and human resources of the South Pacific is enormous, but there are equally large problems to overcome and changes that must be made on the path to economic progress. Merely by looking at any map of the Pacific Ocean one can visualize the magnitudes involved: The land masses are but tiny dots of islands, sometimes too small to be identified by name, separated by thousands of miles of sea. This essay attempts to outline the distinctive features of some of these island economies and to explore the possible directions future developments may take.[1] In terms of geographical coverage, this survey concentrates on those countries in the South Pacific that are either already independent or self-governing, or are likely to become so within the next four years.

One of the most important periods in the economic history of the region, since the coming of the European settlers in the first half of the nineteenth century, began on January 1, 1962, when Western Samoa became the first independent sovereign state. Samoa was followed by the republic of Nauru in 1968, the Dominion of Fiji in 1970, and the republic of Papua New Guinea in 1975. The Kingdom of Tonga also is recognized internationally as an independent nation, and, at the time of writing, the Cook Islands have attained self-governing status. Promises of independence have been given to the Solomon Islands, Niue, and the Gilbert and Ellice Islands by Britain and New Zealand. Britain and France jointly administer the New Hebrides. This group of islands was established as a condominium by an agreement between the two colonial powers in 1906 after menacing German interests had tried to secure a foothold in the group. Only the French seem disinclined to the concept of independence for their island territories in the South Pacific, these being New Caledonia, French Polynesia, and the Wallis and Futuna Islands. And the French-speaking inhabitants of these territories are reluctant to break with their Continental brothers for obvious cultural and economic reasons. None of these three territories, nor the three governed by the United States, will be considered here as part of the "region."

This era of political change offers a great opportunity for a fresh assessment of the assumptions and objectives of economic thought and development policies as applied to the South Pacific. It should be made clear from the outset that the meaning of "economic progress" in the region is by no means synonymous with "economic growth" as interpreted by Western capitalist theory. The quality and pace of life in the Pacific are unique, and the traditional structure of island communities can be maintained only if economic progress is shared by all. The prospects of such progress are severely limited by the special circumstances of these small, developing islands. In the words of the Chief Minister of Papua New Guinea, "we are moving away from past policies that emphasized economic growth as the basic goal, and moving towards a more well-rounded program with the basic aim of improving the lives of Papua New Guinean people."[2] This means development solutions, which may be suitable for the problems of larger developing countries, cannot be easily transplanted into the Pacific without prior evaluation of their relevance. The undesirable consequences of economic growth in industralized societies can also afflict the developing world. In the Pacific, priority attached to economic progress must in future be balanced against the preservation of the environment simply because the livelihood of the majority of Pacific islanders is dependent upon the yields of the soil and the sea.

FROM VILLAGE SUBSISTENCE TO MONETARY SUBSERVIENCE

Most of the South Pacific islands are small either in terms of area, population, or wealth. As indicated in Table 6, Papua New Guinea has by far the largest population and land area; but in terms of per capita income and productivity it is smaller than most of the other countries. Generally, the smaller a country the more specialized is its economy, and the more dependent it is upon trade. While the Pacific islands have attempted to diversify their economies, they still rely mainly on two or three agricultural exports. This traditional export trade has in the past been subject to severe fluctuations in world commodity prices, irregular and expensive shipping services, and irregular and devastating hurricanes. As examples of this, citrus fruit, copra, and bananas have, in most years, provided 90 percent of Cook Island export earnings; copra, cocoa, and bananas 90 percent of Western Samoa's exports; land copra and bananas 80 percent of Tonga's exports. Nauru is an exception because of its phosphate resources, and more recently Papua New Guinea, because of a newly established copper ore trade with Japan.

This export specialization has meant that development of both employment and capital in the islands has relied heavily upon a growth in trade. Today, each economy has a large external sector, and governments are finding it virtually impossible to effect any control over internal prices. The countries of the region have on average been experiencing consumer price increases of approximately 12 percent per annum.[3] In Tonga the consumer price index for food items (based

TABLE 6

SOUTH PACIFIC ISLAND ECONOMIES

Country	Land Area in Square Miles	Population[1]	Annual Population Growth Rate[2]	GDP at Market Prices[1] (Aust. $'000)	Visible Trade Balance[1,3] (Aust. $'000)
Cook Islands	93	20,500(73)	-3% (2.6%)	8,000(70)	-3,070(70)
Fiji	7,095	551,000(73)	1.9%	247,300(72)	-97,000(73)
Gilbert & Ellice Islands	376	57,960(73)	3%	13,666(72)	+3,062(73)
Nauru	8.5	6,927(71)	3%	24,000(68)	+24,318(70)
New Hebrides	5,700	86,000(71)	3.5%	n.a.[4]	-10,500(73)
Niue	100	4,988(71)	-8%	n.a.[4]	-584(73)
Papua New Guinea	178,260	2,581,198(72)	3%	650,000(72)	-140,080(73)
Solomon Islands	11,500	160,998(70)	2.6%	29,000(71)	-1,658(73)
Tonga	269	92,360(72)	2.6% (3.1%)	13,320(71)	-4,600(73)
Western Samoa	1,133	146,461(71)	2% (3%)	17,000(71)	-13,000(72)

1. Figures in parentheses represent years.
2. Percentages appearing in parentheses are natural growth rates.
3. Visible trade balances equal total exports minus imports
4. Not available.

on September 1972) jumped from 117 points in December 1972, to 158 points in December 1973, representing a rise of almost 35 percent during 1973. One of the largest components of this external inflation is taken up by freight charges. By the middle of 1974, transport costs had escalated out of all proportion largely because of the increasing price of petroleum. These developments have had a two way effect on the island economies. In simple terms, the local cost of imported goods equals world prices plus freight, while export revenue equals world prices minus freight; this in turn inflates domestic prices and erodes foreign exchange earnings.

Many of the islands have a high population density together with a high population growth rate. For instance, should growth patterns continue in the Gilbert and Ellice Islands, it is predicted that over the ten years between 1973 and 1983 the population will increase by 40 percent.[4] And the same can be said for the populations of the New Hebrides, the Solomon Islands, and Tonga. For the Cook Islands, Niue, and the Tokelaus, large-scale emigration to New Zealand has reduced the effects of high natural population growth rates. However, most of the countries in the region are still without a cohesive program to control population growth;

only in Fiji have the efforts of a family planning campaign shown some encouraging signs of success.

Prospects for further development along the traditional channels of trade expansion are lessening, simply because of an increase in the ratio of labor supply to land resources. Any increase in population, and in particular the supply of labor, will only increase unemployment totals and pressures for overseas immigration. This distressing situation is aggravated by the fact that over 50 percent of the population in the region is under seventeen years of age.[5] These growing populations are placing an increasingly heavy burden on the development of large public sector infrastructure and community and social services, such as urban housing, hospitals, water, sewerage, and schools. It is possible that with the added effects of imported price inflation, per capita incomes in real terms will either remain stationary or will decline in the South Pacific over the next few years.

As already mentioned, economic activity in the South Pacific has generally centered upon subsistence agriculture, fishing, and the maintenance of a few crops, and sometimes handicrafts, for exports. Even today the effects of rising consumer prices and growing unemployment have little impact upon the lives of the many Pacific islanders who are still part of a self-sufficient village community. For exampl figures for 1966 show that over 90 percent of Papua New Guinea's economically active population was engaged in subsistence agriculture; and the proportion in the New Hebrides and Western Samoa was just over 60 percent.[6] On the other hand, in some cases such as Nauru, it is negligible. The movement into cash economics has been associated with the movement of village people into the urban areas. The fact that these new town dwellers demand and pay cash for agricultural produce brings those remaining in the village into the expanding monetary sector.

With independence and the right to self-determination, the aspirations of island people and the meaning of money to the community have come into question. There is a conflict between custom and money, particularly in the more isolated rural areas of the region. The development of a cash economy has led to a loosening of the ties binding the individual to the village community. The opponents of this development usually have appealed to the moral and social values of the traditional island way of life, which emphasizes generosity and a fair distribution of wealth. It is often claimed that economic growth runs counter to these values, and that economic growth is inherently selfish as it disregards a man's duty to his neighbors. In pre-European times, each village was self-sufficient and the people had the satisfaction of working in their own community where land resources and natural beauty were plentiful. Civil warfare, warfare, natural disasters, or migration corrected the population balance when a ceiling was reached on land resources.

Rivalry and competition have always existed in the village community, particularly in regard to land rights and chiefly rank, and there were always some who took pride in accumulating small amounts of wealth. Traditional Polynesian societies had their own form of incentives to induce people to work hard and show initiative. Both men and women competed for prestige and rank by displaying their ability to produce tangible goods, such as food and handwoven mats. Today, however, people who work all day in an urban environment are not so eager to use part of their earnings to support relatives who have remained in the village or who remain unemployed in the same town.

The local customs of South Pacific societies have, to a great extent, inhibited development both inside and outside the traditional fields of economic activity.[7] Land tenure systems in many of the island countries are very rigid, and it is clear that greater agricultural output can only come from an increase in the efficiency and intensity of land use. If arable land is not to become a salable asset, then it must be distributed equitably amongst the men who are prepared to work and reap the benefits from the communal land. In most cases, the main difficulty with the production of two or three export crops is not the actual marketing of the produce, but rather in obtaining sufficient quantities of a certain quality and transport to meet the market opportunities that already exist. This is particularly true of the two major exports from the region, bananas and copra. New Zealand is prepared to import as many bananas as the South Pacific islands can export, but in fact this trade decreased from 25,100 tons shipped in 1967 to 7,700 tons in 1972.[8] Over the twelve months of 1973, the prices paid to copra producers in most of the islands tripled, and yet there was no corresponding increase in copra exports. In part this lack of response is because of the fact that once planted, a coconut tree takes five years to mature and bear its first nuts.

In the short run, because the majority of copra workers from part of the rural subsistence sector of the economy, any increase in the price they receive will mean that they can exchange fewer bags of copra for their usual quantity of imported goods at the "company store." However, many are now aspiring to material well-being, particularly in those areas where the "demonstration effect" of tourism has been strong. Currency transferred from wealthy relatives who have emigrated to better paid jobs also discourages production; for example, in the Cook Islands net external money order transactions handled by the Post Office alone during 1973 came to $280,000 (New Zealand); while the total value of two of the three most important exports—bananas and copra—was only NZ$290,000.[9] In Western Samoa, provisional planning figures for 1973 indicated that funds remitted from New Zealand and American Samoa were more that $3 million (Western Samoa), while the value of the major export—copra—was just under WS$2 million.

The economic dependence of the islands on two or three export crops, whose growth has been stagnating over recent years, has prompted governments to look at the potential for diversification into a variety of local industries in order to promote employment. However, because of the small size of their domestic markets and their isolation from overseas markets, the economic losses through diversification may be too costly. If export specialization is to continue in the South Pacific, and if there is to be any stability in development programs, countries should favor international commodity price agreements, preferably tied to imported rates of inflation. All other things remaining equal, stable and balanced trading arrangements with a variety of other countries would allow the island economies to enjoy, in theory, a stable internal situation as well.

In practice, trade suffers from price instability and takes place with a few developed countries—Australia, Britain, France, New Zealand, or the United States—because of past and present colonial connections. Although Japan has no historical links with the South Pacific islands, it has, since the early 1960s, developed strong economic ties with the area in order to obtain stable supplies and additional sources of vital resources such as copper, timber, and fish. Present trade figures indicate that Japan supplies approximately 15 percent of the region's imports and takes 25 percent of the exports.

Another major constraint on development in the region has been the link between an increase in local production and income and an increase in imports. For example, a rise of 1 percent in gross national produce may lead to an even larger percentage increase in imports. Of those countries listed in Table 6, only Nauru and the Gilbert and Ellice Islands have favorable balances of payments. Both countries are dependent on the extraction of phosphate deposits; but in the latter case, these deposits, which in 1973 contributed 90 percent of the country's export earnings, are likely to be exhausted by 1977.[10] In most of the other countries of the region, exports have been growing, but nowhere near as fast as imports.

For a long time the traditional export crops served only to finance the importation of a few non-essential consumer goods. Now with the movement away from subsistence agriculture, people are relying more and more upon imports even as a source of food. The growing number of tourists in the region with their rarefied appetites for sterilized foods has added fuel to this change. In 1972, for the first time in Western Samoa's trading history, the amount of money spent on imported foodstuffs alone exceeded total export revenues. These imported processed foods are relatively expensive owing to the additional charges for freight and the small size of consignments. Hence, marginal gains in income made from rising export price have been eroded. It is obvious that future development policies must be geared towards expanding food production in the region if trade is ever to be balanced with the outside world.

THE EXTENT OF NON-TRADITIONAL ECONOMIC ACTIVITIES

The agricultural sector has without doubt failed to provide the necessary impetus for greater development in the region. It would appear that the future employment and living standards of the growing populations of the islands will be increasingly dependent upon development in the following economic sectors.

Small-Scale Manufacturing Industries

The manufacturing sectors in all the countries of the region are still in the early stages of development and are at present restricted to a few small industries, usually processing local materials. The Cook Islands process and can much of their citrus and pineapple crop for export to New Zealand. In Tonga, a small factory has been established to desiccate coconut for markets in Australia, New Zealand, and the United Kingdom. The Solomon Islands have been manufacturing cane furniture for export, and in Western Samoa a pineapple processing and canning factory has been operating on and off since 1967. Over the same period, Fiji and Papua New Guinea have experienced a comparatively rapid growth in small-scale manufacturing industries. In Fiji the expansion of this sector—including brewing, matches, paint, tobacco, and cement manufacturing—has surpassed the expectations of the Sixth Development Plan (1971-75), with an average growth rate of 6.2 percent per annum up to 1973.[11] This growth has been encouraged by the Fiji government's industrial concessions policy, which aims at developing, and where necessary protecting, local industry. However, such concessions for small industries can lead to price inflation and not necessarily an improvement in the balance of payments, as the island consumers are deprived of cheaper foreign products. So protection of local industry through import barriers involves cost disadvantages because economies of scale or external economies are difficult to obtain within such small domestic markets.

In manufacturing, import substitution objectives can be achieved through the establishment of either resource-based processing industries or those industries that enjoy a strong geographical protection because of freight differences. As already indicated, with the growth of population and the development of a cash economy, the region is increasingly relying on imports, even as a source of food. It is hoped that government policy in this sector will concentrate on creating more opportunities for labor-intensive food processing and for other competitive import substituting and export-oriented manufacturing using local resources.

The largest export earner in the region is copra—the dried flesh of the coconut—which is processed into coconut oil, copra meal, and cake. Within the region, only Fiji and Papua New Guinea have their own copra crushing mills. There are distinct possibilities of establishing a regional crushing mill for the other countries, which are at present shipping unprocessed copra to Australia, New Zealand, and Europe.[12] There is also potential for setting up other industries using coconut by-products such as coir, for the manufacture of chipboard, brooms, and brushes. Fiji could begin refining its raw sugar for markets both within and outside the region. Opportunities for fish processing are being studied in most of the islands with a view to achieving a high degree of self-sufficiency in fish. At present, despite the fact that the resources of the ocean are enormous, only the Solomon Islands, Papua New Guinea, and the New Hebrides have a net trade surplus in fish. Above all, commercially profitable prospects for industrial development can be found in those areas that use local raw materials, and, in particular, where the transport costs for competing imports are excessively high. Individually, the countries will not be able to support large-scale manufacturing enterprises simply because of the size of their home markets. Policies of developing import substitution industries could most effectively be implemented at the regional level, employing a large variety and quantity of resources and producing for a far greater market.

Tourism

The tourist "industry" has now become an integral part of the diversification programs of several Pacific islands. Nearly everywhere the tourist dollar is seen as a means to offset large visible trade deficits. North of the Equator, there can be no denying that tourism has been the predominant feature of the Hawaiian economy for over a quarter of a century. Within the past few years, the economies of Guam and Saipan have been changed dramatically by the rapid growth of Japanese tourism in the area. Farther south, in Fiji and Tahiti the industry has expanded greatly over the past ten years largely through foreign investment actively encouraged and sought after by these countries. Now other countries like Western Samoa, Tonga, and Papua New Guinea are also constructing hotels and revovating airports to cater to the seemingly endless supply of holiday-makers from North America, Australia, and New Zealand. Niue Island, which, until its airport was built in 1972, was one of the South Pacific's most isolated communities, has launched a tourism development program with the construction of a forty-bedroom hotel financed by New Zealand aid funds. With the opening of Rarotonga's international jet airport in January 1974, and the introduction of duty-free shopping, the Cook Islands will soon penetrate Fiji's unrivaled position of regional supremacy in the tourism industry.

Indeed, the growth of this unique industry has been so rapid that concern is being expressed about the detrimental social and economic effects of tourism. In practice a large proportion of the industry's inputs in the form of duty-free goods, hotel staff, and foodstuffs is being imported. In Fiji, experience has shown that the net foreign exchange earnings from tourism are marginal and that the tourist income multiplier has remained at less than unity—approximately 0.7 to 0.8 from 1966 until 1971—while the industry has grown over the same period at an annual average rate of 20 percent, causing an imbalance in the economy. "Pressure on building and construction, infrastructure, and agricultural employment are, in large part, due to tourism and to urbanization resulting from growth in the tourist industry."[13]

It is frequently argued by travel promoters that tourism encourages tradition and culture, but in fact the opposite has been experienced in the Pacific. When the industrial revolution hit Western Europe two centuries ago, the human misery and suffering was enormous because those societies could not cope with such a rapid change. For some communities in the South Pacific, the tourist industry creates the same sort of social crisis. Consumer prices are inflated, and employment for locals is usually available only at the bottom end of an industry, which is run by detached expatriate staff. Large numbers of village dwellers abandon their vegetable farms to take up more lucrative jobs as porters, barmen, and guides, and taxi drivers in overcrowded areas. In fact the unique Pacific way of life is likely to be smothered rather than stimulated by tourism. By demonstrating higher spending patterns and vastly different social habits, foreign holiday-makers (with their paradoxical demands for home comforts in an adventure away from "Western civilization") often cause irreparable damage to the very "paradise" they have come to explore.

However, it is equally wrong to talk of preserving or protecting the Pacific way of life simply for aesthetic or historical reasons. When economic growth is too rapid, it can be the most powerful force for social disruption. But through careful planning, the tourist industry could have a beneficial impact on the economies of the South Pacific if its development is linked to increased production of local inputs and a greater sensitivity and respect for custom and culture.

As tourism is a highly capital-intensive industry, many governments in the region have provided liberal tax incentives to encourage investments in hotel development. In the near future, however, countries could begin to compete for airline patronage and tourists as well as for investors, and a vicious circle could evolve with one country being played off against another. On the other hand, governments could co-ordinate tourism policies at the regional level by preparing investment guidelines designed to maximize economic and social benefits for all the islands.

It is also in each country's interest to promote tourism on a regional basis as the South Pacific is and will remain one of the most expensive tourist destinations. The tourist who journeys so far from home naturally wants to see as many sights and visit as many countries as possible. International tourist agencies find it more profitable to promote "all-inclusive" tours, which are easier to manage and publicize than individual travel arrangements. If countries in the region could co-ordinate planning for both the development and promotion of resorts, the South Pacific tourist industry could provide a strong force for development in other economic sectors. Intra- and extra-regional air and sea transport, which is discussed in the section below, is also required to facilitate this development process.

Civil Aviation and Shipping

Geographical isolation and a dependence on trade and tourism make transport an indispensable part of development planning in the region. At present, the majority of routes served by airlines and shipping companies are based on traditional trading links with the developed world. In the air transport industry, a few American and British Commonwealth airlines have a virtual monopoly over trans-South Pacific air services. Many airfields now in use were in fact originally Allied and Japanese air force bases during World War II, and they have now been restored and upgraded to international transport standards. Others have been specifically built to cope with the growing tourist traffic.

As well as constructing runways and international terminals, some of the island countries have now built up their own national airlines. Given the small size of intra-regional passenger traffic, it was originally envisaged that there would only be enough business for a single regional air carrier. Accordingly, Air Pacific was created in 1971 out of the Fiji Airways consortium owned by Qantas, BOAC, and Air New Zealand. With this new regional airline, additional equity shares were taken up by the governments of Fiji, the Solomon Islands, the Gilbert and Ellice Islands, Nauru, Tonga, and Western Samoa, and regular services commenced between these countries. However, the overseas airlines retained a majority shareholding in the regional venture; and the governments soon came to realize that while they were concerned with providing an essential service, the airlines were interested only in feeding passengers at a profit into the Qantas/BOAC/Air New Zealand worldwide network at Nadi Airport in Fiji.

With large foreign exchange reserves accumulated from phosphate exports, Nauru bought its own Fokker jet aircraft, established Air Nauru, and withdrew from the Air Pacific consortium early in 1972. In Western Samoa, the government gave financial backing to Polynesian Airlines, which now competes with Air Pacific for traffic between Fiji and Western Samoa. At the beginning of 1974 the King of Tonga announced that Tonga would soon have its own airline as well— Friendly Islands Air—which would be financed and run by pilots from Japan. One of Air Pacific's two BAC 1-11 jets is to be leased because the Tonga Government felt unable to grant the airline landing rights for a service between Fiji and New Zealand via Tonga. One would expect to see the newly formed Air Niugini, based in Papua New Guinea, soon competing with Air Pacific for landing rights in other parts of the region. With such fundamental problems, it appears that unless a new shareholding arrangement can be settled between the airlines and the governments, Air Pacific's increasing financial difficulties, encouraged by rising fuel costs, could spell disaster for the concept of a truly regional carrier.

The importance of shipping to the region in terms of trade cannot be overemphasized. By comparison, the region's air freight industry is still in an embryonic stage mainly because large-scale trade in fresh fruit and vegetables has been inhibited by largely obsolete quarantine regulations.[14] As has already been pointed out, economic development in the South Pacific has in the past been dependent upon an increase in extra-regional trade. And intra-regional price inflation has to a large extent been generated by relatively high and rising freight rates.

Most South Pacific cargo and passenger shipping services are provided by shipping companies owned and operated from outside the region. Of the island nations, Nauru and Tonga both have national shipping lines; the Nauru Pacific Line now owns five ships and charters three, while Pacific Navigation of Tonga owns four and charters two. The Cook Islands and the Gilbert and Ellice Islands also operate ocean-going vessels, but these were obtained with public capital primarily to provide essential services and not necessarily to operate as commercially profitable concerns. The other countries in the region have been reluctant to become involved individually because of a lack of finance and local skills in this field. However, since 1970 there have been various collective moves to float a regional shipping line, the first being the Pacific Island Producers' Association (PIPA) proposal to base a regional line on the existing services of Pacific Navigation Line. After receiving an unfavorable accountant's report on the financial position of the line, the governments concerned made no attempt to implement the original recommendation, and so in September 1972, the matter was referred to the South Pacific Forum at its third meeting in Suva. The newly established South Pacific Bureau for Economic Co-operation (SPEC) was then commissioned to undertake a study of the operation and financial structure of a regional shipping line.[15]

Compared to separate national ventures, a regional shipping line could enjoy a number of economic advantages, including access to a greater variety and quantity of finance and a greater efficiency of services and cargo space. The report to the South Pacific Forum, which was completed in August 1973, recommended that the regional line should operate on several routes throughout the region. Apart from regional profits accruing from the operation, this shipping line's two essential objectives would be to create greater island control over freight rates and to promote trade between countries of the region. In doing so it would also improve communications generally between participating countries and give birth to a greater independence and interdependence for the region. This multi-national shipping enterprise would draw on the manpower resources of all its member nations. At the top of the management structure, and at ministerial level, would be the Regional Shipping Council, which would discuss all aspects of shipping in the South Pacific. At the second management level would be the Regional Shipping Corporation, commercially operating the line along the guidelines laid down by the Council.

In the West Indies, a Regional Shipping Council and Shipping Corporation were established in 1961 by the West Indies Federation. Although the Federation was disbanded in 1962, the Corporation continued to operate its island-hopping service throughout the 1960s with two mixed passenger and cargo vessels under the authority of the Council. The service was revitalized in 1968 when the Carribbean Free Trade Area was launched in a move towards closer economic integration.

In the South Pacific, for obvious reasons of national pride and independence, the Governments of Nauru and Tonga are reluctant to relinquish control of their fleets by participating in a regional shipping venture. With the collapse of regional cooperation in the field of civil aviation, other countries are hesitant to commit themselves to financing another joint enterprise. However, at its 1974 meeting in Rarotonga, the Forum did agree to establish a Regional Shipping Council which would commission, through SPEC, further studies concerning the setting up of a shipping venture as a basis for a subsequent decision by the South Pacific Forum. As an initial step towards a more integrated regional service, it would appear that Tonga and Nauru would be prepared to join some form of "pooling" arrangement. This would be a more politically acceptable form of regional cooperation in shipping as it would not necessarily involve any loss of "national flag" and international identity.

Foreign Aid and Investment

Because of their limited domestic capital structures, development in the island economies requires an injection of overseas finance in the form of private investment, loans, and official aid. All the countries in the region are faced with the question of whether or not they should pursue official policies that actively promote foreign private capital. The natural tendency of foreign capital in the South Pacific has been, in the first place, to find investments having a potential for high profits. Local and foreign companies have been able to establish small-scale processing industries by demanding generous, and in some cases excessive, tax and tariff concessions.

Commerce in most of the islands is operated by a few large foreign multi-national companies. Local businesses have either been taken over by foreign-owned rivals, or they have been prevented from entering a profitable industrial sector because of the scale of financial involvement and technical and marketing experience of the overseas firms.[16] In this way development decisions are in the hands of non-nationals whose objectives of maximizing profits may conflict with the host country's objectives of maximizing social benefits.

As a result of the doubtful benefits of some private foreign investment, greater importance is now attached to capital aid and loans from overseas governments and international banks. For example, in Western Samoa and Fiji, approximately half of government revenue for capital works is obtained from external sources in the form of loans, grants, and bilateral aid schemes. Similarly, the greater part of capital for Tonga's development planning since 1966 has come from United Kingdom aid and grants from international agencies. The Australian Government is committed to a five-year aid plan to support Papua New Guinea's own improvement program. Total external aid for this newly independent country in 1974 was estimated at A$200 million.[17] New Zealand's financial assistance to the Cook Islands runs to something like NZ$4 million per annum, and direct United Kingdom official grants support colonial administrations in the Gilbert and Ellice Islands and the Solomon Islands.

Island governments have also called on the capital resources of the international development banks, particularly for large infrastructure developments such as new roads and water supply systems. The major disadvantage of the World Bank Group and the Asian Development Bank as sources of finance is the time-consuming and costly preinvestment procedures to be fulfilled before funds can be made available for projects. These and other problems have led some countries to support the South Pacific Commission's proposal to establish a regional development bank staffed by people from the South Pacific.[18] It is argued that such a bank would pay more attention to the particular financial problems of the smaller island countries, which have difficulty in obtaining loans from international banking agencies for their small but important development projects.

In theory, economic growth requires large amounts of capital and thus the major constraint to the economic expansion is domestic savings. Foreign aid and investment have enabled governments and the private sector in the islands to spend more on current expenditure. In certain sectors there have been obvious short-term economic benefits, for the indigenous community, radiating from foreign capital. More often there has been an overdependence in the South Pacific on such aid and investment, and in future it would seem prudent for countries to encourage, wherever possible, joint-equity ventures between foreign and local sources of capital and management with the eventual possibility of a complete localization or "nationalization" of the equity. Donor countries would be providing the region with a more productive service if their assistance were redirected into encouraging island exports by offering protective import quotas and price incentives.

Aid from the developed world, although usually given in good faith, will never generate development and fundamental reforms in the South Pacific. Instead it can have demoralizing effects for the recipients and should only be accepted for temporary hardship relief. This conflict between a dependence on foreign capital and a loss of self-determination is an eternal problem for the poor half of the capitalist world.[19]

Planning for Development

Development planning is accepted by most countries of the South Pacific region as an essential tool to promote national progress. In general, these programs stress the importance of expanding and diversifying agricultural production, the development of processing industries using local raw materials, and the need to develop new growth industries, in most cases based on either tourism, fishing, or forestry. They all recognize that economic growth is essential if employment is to be provided for the increasing labor force. The Nauruan strategy for economic development is somewhat different simply because its economy is dependent upon the mining of phosphate deposits, which are expected to be exhausted in twenty years time. The large foreign exchange reserves amassed from this single industry have enabled the Nauruan government to build up a shipping fleet, a jet airline, and a portfolio of lucrative investments overseas.

Although these past development programs have concentrated on improving the agricultural and rural structure of island economies, they have achieved little success in this direction. For instance, Fiji's Sixth Development Plan (1971-75) projected that the agricultural sector would grow at an annual average rate of 3.5 percent; but in fact agricultural output declined by an average annual rate of 3.8 percent in 1971 and 1972.[20] In Tonga, production in agriculture, forestry, and fishing declined by 3.5 percent over the year 1969-70 to 1970-71.[21]

Development programs in the South Pacific are at fault both for their failure to take account of migration from rural to urban areas and emigration from the islands, and for their failure to provide adequate alternatives for diversification away from the traditional one or two export crops, quantities of which have been dropping off in many cases. For example, 1972 export receipts for copra in the Gilbert and Ellice Islands were a third of what they were in 1971, and for the New Hebrides and Western Samoa, nearly half of what they were in 1971. The South Pacific island producers' share of the New Zealand banana market dropped from 90 percent in 1967-68 to 44 percent in 1971-72.

Inevitable vital political and social issues are involved in economic development. Many of the island countries, although nominally independent, are still fettered by their economic ties with former colonial powers. In practice most local politicians have shown little enthusiasm for the preparation and implementation of the very development programs necessary to shrug off these bonds with the past. However, with independence a reality, the leaders of Papua New Guinea have shown an impressive awareness of concepts for social equality, self-reliance, and rural development. Their government's economic planning machinery is being completely overhauled to strengthen coordination at the national level and to allow more scope for decision-making in the rural areas of Papua New Guinea. Planning at the national level will concentrate on increasing that proportion of the economy under the control of individuals and firms. It will be interesting to observe how the new government carries out these promises, and whether it does in fact localize the country's assets.

The cornerstone of any policy of self-reliance in the South Pacific should be the localization of employment throughout the economy. Developing countries must learn to face up to their own problems, otherwise they will continue to be swamped with more and more schemes run by foreign experts on international standards and at international costs. Foreign aid can most productively be channelled into building up local technical skills. A survey conducted by the United Nations Development Advisory Team in the South Pacific estimated that in 1972 nearly half of all higher level manpower in the island governments was staffed by expatriates.[22]

The smaller countries in the region faced serious difficulties in maintaining a balanced supply of skilled labor. Because of their size, it is not feasible for them to establish local training institutions, and so technical skills have to be acquired in other countries. Foreign-educated graduates are often reluctant to return to their small island communities, and this perpetuates a "brain drain" to Australia, New Zealand, and North America.

Part of the answer to these pressing problems could be found in regionalism. In 1968, the University of the South Pacific, based in Suva, began offering degree courses in social science, education, and natural science. Today it has a total undergraduate population of over a thousand. Similarly, the University of Papua New Guinea has developed curricula and facilities adapted to the needs of the region. However, regional cooperation can play a more important role in educating people in technical skills—engineers, architects, and accountants—the people who will make development policies practical. The present dependence on foreign skills will never be rectified by talk alone. Eventually it may be possible to allow intra-regional mobility of skilled manpower to create a large and flexible labor market. More attractive employment opportunities for a greater variety of skills will reduce the incentive to emigrate.

THE POTENTIAL FOR REGIONAL ECONOMIC INTEGRATION

Experiences during World War II prompted various administrators to seriously contemplate regional economic management based on the pooling of national resources. As a result, the colonial governments formed the South Pacific Commission (SPC) in 1947 to coordinate consultation and advice on economic development, health, and other social services among the island territories.[23] The Commission, with its headquarters in Nouméa, has been a useful channel for international aid and technical assistance at the regional level. In addition, the Commission first fostered the concept of island cooperation, and as a result other regional bodies have a place in the South Pacific today.

The independent nations of Western Samoa, Nauru, and Fiji, which are now legitimate members of the organization, have shown a growing awareness of the need for island voices in regional decision-making. All have voiced strongly worded protests over recent French nuclear tests on Mururoa Atoll; they have indicated their determination to alter the traditional set-up of the Commission and to remove the paternal stigma of the colonial governments. At the thirteenth South Pacific Conference and the thirty-sixth session of the Commission, held jointly in Guam during September 1973, compromising proposals were put forward by Australia to revitalize the organization and merge the Commission and Conference sessions. By May 1974, these recommendations had been provisionally approved by the other participating governments. It is difficult to envisage how the Commission will continue to function smoothly as, under the present structural and political instabilities, managerial direction of the organization's activities will soon become difficult. Already the French have threatened to withdraw from the Commission with their "three and a half" Pacific territories, and should this happen, at the very least, the headquarters of the SPC would have to be relocated.

Brighter horizons may lie elsewhere: three other regional organizations have emerged from the structural failures of the SPC and the demands of the new island leaders for self-determination. The first of these, the Pacific Islands Producers' Association (PIPA), was established in 1965 largely through the initiative of the Cook Islands, Fiji, and Western Samoa. A permanent secretariat was set up in Suva, Fiji, and the three initiators were joined by the Gilbert and Ellice Islands, Niue, and Tonga. The organization would, it was hoped, provide a basis for cooperation on regional trade and represent the interests of the island producers in the marketing of bananas and copra.

The South Pacific Forum was the second of these three regional organizations to be formed, this time by heads of government from Australia, the Cook Islands, Fiji, Nauru, New Zealand, Tonga, and Western Samoa, who met for the first time in Wellington in August 1971.[24] Discussions took place in the Forum on a proposal for a "Trade Bureau" to study such matters as regional trade and shipping and to make recommendations back to the Forum. At its fourth meeting in Apia during 1973, the Forum formally agreed to establish the South Pacific Bureau for Economic Cooperation (SPEC). As a result, PIPA was disbanded in 1974 and its functions were absorbed by SPEC.

SPEC differs from PIPA and the Commission in that it has a governing body that can make economic decisions and implement recommendations at the highest political level. During its first year of operation SPEC produced, among other things, three reports for the Forum on the establishment of a regional shipping line, on the prospects for an expansion of trade between island countries, and on the European Economic Community negotiations for associate status for Fiji, Tonga, and Western Samoa.[25] Australia and New Zealand have stated that their participation in SPEC is based on their desire to contribute to the region's development. In addition to meetings of the Forum, held usually once a year, regular consultation takes place between senior officials from all member governments at SPEC Committee meetings. SPEC has established its headquarters in Suva with a permanent secretariat of seven professional staff headed by a director.

Previous sections of this essay have stressed that because of the size of the island economies it is difficult to diversify production and to compete effectively in world markets, and that these small economies must export what few crops they can competitively produce in order to earn foreign exchange and raise levels of domestic capital. One of the tasks handed down to SPEC from the Forum is to carry out investigations into the development of free trade among its island member countries. In the West Indies, such a scheme has achieved promising success under the Caribbean Free Trade Association, which brought together twelve developing Commonwealth countries. CARIFTA, as it came to be called, was founded upon the basic principle of an abolition of tariffs and other trade barriers on products originating in the region. A special agricultural marketing protocol was built into the CARIFTA agreement to favor the less developed members of the group because of their substantial integration-induced trade imbalance with the more developed members. Moves are now afloat to expand the Association into a Caribbean Common Market to strengthen economic integration in the region.

By comparison, regional trade between the island countries of the South Pacific has been almost non-existent. Irregular and indirect shipping services, strict quarantine regulations, and identical basic exports have not helped past efforts in interisland trade. Because of Suva's position as an entrepôt for cargo shipments in the region, and as a center for small-scale manufacturing, Fiji has obtained more benefits from regional trade than all the other islands combined. If a free trade scheme is ever developed among the island member countries of SPEC, net benefits must flow equally to all member countries. For instance, the East African Community has devised a transfer tax for this purpose, involving fiscal compensation for regional trade imbalances.[26] In the Caribbean, the provision of CARIFTA'S "guaranteed markets scheme" was not sufficient, but under the new common market proposal, arrangements have been designed to make it easier for the less developed member countries to sell a given product. In the Pacific, SPEC has been instructed to "investigate the scope for regional development planning aimed among other things at a rationalization of manufacturing and processing industries and the achievement of economies of scale in certain regional enterprises."

In terms of economic cooperation and integration, the islands of the South Pacific are a decade behind their Commonwealth partners in the Caribbean. Not only do West Indians share a common language and cultural background based on European economic and psychological domination, but they already have a history of regional cooperation in sport and education. In contrast, each Pacific island has its own distinctive culture to preserve. Yet, until the Pacific nations wholeheartedly accept the concept of an economic community of islands, they will never attain the significant degree of economic independence necessary to shrug off the same history of foreign domination from which the West Indies has turned. Unfortunately, politicians who are elected in the short term to serve their particular country are by their very nature reluctant to support long term regional policies.

The economic progress that will be necessary to meet the needs of growing populations in the South Pacific can be achieved by regional policies aimed at coordinating development programs including population and emigration control, harmonized tourist and foreign investment policies, efficient transport systems, and regional trading arrangements for specific products and industries. Complementary rather than competitive development strategies are the essence. Although some depressing production and population trends have been noted in this survey, economic prospects for the South Pacific in the year 2001 are not gloomy. Despite the present worsening world food shortage, and the ominous rising cost of fuel and other essential imports, the potential for development and diversification in the South Pacific is still very real. The islands are surrounded by the world's richest ocean, whose latent mineral and aquatic resources still remain largely untapped. Productive foreign technological assistance is available on favorable terms. Energetic and determined leadership that instills in the people of the region a new spirit of self-reliance and unity can harness and mobilize these natural and human resources.

NOTES

1. Any views expressed in this essay, other than those specifically referred to, are those of the author. They should not be interpreted as reflecting the views of any organization or the official opinion or policy of any government. The author is grateful to his wife, Lorna, and two obliging friends, Kenneth Piddington and Fa'amatala Toleafoa, who helped to clarify several points in this essay.

2. Michael Somare, "New Goals for New Guinea," *Pacific Perspective* No. 1 (Suva, 1973), p. 1.

3. Refer to *Statistical Bulletin No. 4: Retail Price Indexes 1973* (South Pacific Commission, Nouméa), p. 12.

4. The Gilbert and Ellice group is already becoming overcrowded: On the main island, Tarawa, the population density in 1968 was 2.6 per acre. Refer to *Development Plan 1973-1976* (Central Government Office, Tarawa), p. 20.

5. This figure is derived from an average of the most recent census reports, summaries of which are contained in *Statistical Bulletin No. 1: Population 1972* (South Pacific Commission, Nouméa).

6. Refer to *Statistical Bulletin No. 3: Economically Active Population 1973* (South Pacific Commission, Nouméa), Table 3.

7. Often, through local arrogance and a pride in traditional ways, there is a bias against the introduction of new methods. These national feelings are manifested in at least three South Pacific languages: "fa'a Samoa," "faka Tonga," and "vaka Viti" for Fiji.

8. In part, this fall in the banana trade was caused by the fixed price New Zealand offered to the island producers between 1966 and 1974. During the same period the average price of New Zealand's exports to the islands rose by 60 percent. In March 1974, the New Zealand Government announced a temporary 25 percent price increase to be financed out of official aid funds. The banana exporting countries of the region are the Cook Islands, Fiji, Tonga, and Western Samoa.

9. Refer to *Quarterly Abstract of Statistics, December 1973* (Statistics Office, Rarotonga), p. 28.

10. Refer to *Development Plan 1973-1976, First Annual Review* (Central Government Office, Tarawa [1973]), p. 42.

11. *Review of Fiji's Sixth Development Plan* (Ministry of Finance [Suva, 1973]), p. 88.

12. The proposal for a regional copra crushing mill was put forward at the Seventh PIPA Conference and, at the time of writing, a feasibility study is being undertaken by the Tropical Products Institute of London.

13. *Review* (Suva, 1973), p. 113.

14. Experience has shown that quarantine regulations intrude in many potential areas for trade within the region. There is the ironic case of Tongan tomatoes, which have at times been shipped an extra 3,000 miles via New Zealand to Suva in order to avoid Fiji's stringent quarantine regulations on produce originating from other tropical countries. However, some progress is now being made to improve and coordinate regional quarantine services in the interests of trade between the islands. At the time of writing, a two year pests and diseases survey in the region is about to be undertaken by a small team of United Nations experts.

15. The framework and history of these three regional organizations is covered in the final section of this essay. The report referred to here is *The Establishment of a Regional Shipping Line* (SPEC [Suva, 1973]).

16. For a detailed discussion of this topic refer to Michael Ward, *The Role of Investment in the Development of Fiji* (Cambridge, 1971), p. 314.

17. Refer to *Compendium of Statistics for Papua New Guinea, October 1973* (Department of External Territories, Canberra).

18. Refer to *South Pacific Regional Development Bank* (United Nations Development Program, Report of the Mission to Study the Proposal [Sydney, 1972]).

19. Perhaps the most thorough analysis of this dilemma is given by Andre Gunder Frank, *Capitalism and Underdevelopment in Latin America* (London, 1971).

20. *Review* (Suva, 1973), p. 47.

21. Derived from GNP figures in *Statistical Abstract 1972* (Statistics Office, Nuku'alofa), Table 10.

22. Refer to *Higher Level Manpower in the South Pacific* (UNDAT [Suva, 1973]), p. 20.

23. The original member governments of the Commission were Australia, Britain, France, the Netherlands, New Zealand, and the United States. In 1962, after President Sukarno had "Indonesianized" Dutch New Guinea, the Netherlands withdrew from the organization.

24. Having attained self-governing status, Papua New Guinea was admitted to the Forum at its sixth meeting in Rarotonga, 1974.

25. Refer to *Director's Annual Report 1973/74* (SPEC Suva).

26. Refer to Peter Robson, *Current Problems of Economic Integration* (UNCTAD, 1971), p. 25.

27. *Agreement Establishing the South Pacific Bureau for Economic Cooperation* (SPEC [Suva, 1973]), Article 1 (c).

PART III

METROPOLITAN POWERS AND OCEANIA

W. DONALD McTAGGART

12

New Caledonia and the French Connection

Amid the territories of the Pacific, New Caledonia is unique. Its uniqueness is not only demographic—the fact that it became a "colony of settlement," and now has a large proportion of Europeans in its population—but also economic. New Caledonia is the only Pacific island having an abundance of economic resources, especially mineral resources. By all the available statistical parameters the territory must be considered to be "developed"; it boasts a mining industry of considerable sophistication, intense capital investment, and a high material standard of living.

The wealth of the island makes it a valuable possession in the eyes of the government of France, and by the same token sustains fears that other powers in the South Pacific may want to take it over. The original annexation of New Caledonia in 1853 was carried out in the face of hostility from the Australians and the British. And periodically since then, there have been crises in New Caledonia's relationship with her distant "mother country." During World War II, New Caledonia depended for defense, sustenance and trade upon "Anglo-Saxon" Pacific powers, including the United States, Australia, and New Zealand. Currently, New Caledonia imports much of its foodstuffs from nearby Australia; and there has always been pressure of various kinds to expand contracts with near neighbors. Yet France has always resisted the total identification of New Caledonia with the region in which it is located and has insisted on the maintenance of a policy that stresses its "French" character.

The policy of maintaining the "French connection" in New Caledonia is more complex than may appear at first sight. It is not a simple matter of the assertion of metropolitan French proprietary and economic interest in the face of New Caledonian separatist politicians; it is not simply a call for French cultural purity and vitality in a region long dominated by English-speaking nations. Rather it is a sinuous story of conflicting and shifting poles of interest within New Caledonia, each with different goals, and each seeking to derive different benefits from the strengths and weaknesses of the French connection. The connection has proved to be durable not so much because of the obvious strength of sentimental attraction, but because practically every political and economic element in New Caledonia has at some stage had reason to regard the connection positively.

Unfortunately, the preoccupation of political and economic management with the question of the relationships between New Caledonia and France has diverted attention from some of the fundamental problems that exist within New Caledonia. The French connection has permitted the maintenance of a condition of social and economic dualism, a separation between the rich export-oriented economy of the European sector of the population and the poor, backward Melanesian subsistence sector. The result is that New Caledonia, for all its wealth and prosperity, has failed to grapple adequately with the problem of how to initiate self-sustaining economic and social change locally. Its prosperity remains conditional upon its willingness to constitute itself as an appendage—an appendage to a wider political and economic system that alone can guarantee the resources of political stability and investment capital, but an appendage that does not seem able to offer to the Melanesians a role which they feel is compatible with their dignity as a people.

In the terminology of one writer, New Caledonia has an economy that is "peripheral."[1] If we regard an economy as composed of four primary sectoral elements—an export sector, a mass consumption sector, a "luxury consumption" sector, and a capital goods sector—it is evident that for most countries that have reached a state of economic development, the principal mechanism has been the interplay of the second and fourth sectors. Goods produced by industry and agriculture have circulated throughout the economy; profits or savings thereby generated have become the primary means whereby new investment has been created, so leading to an expansion of the productive capacity of the economy as a whole. In most colonial countries (and New Caledonia is no exception) this important linkage between the second and fourth sectors never takes place. As a rule, the economy is geared to the production of commodities (raw materials) for export. Capital investment in these export industries derives from outside. Instead of a "mass consumption sector" creating further economic development, consumption takes the form of purchases of high value imported goods by the elite groups in the population. The economy thus remains peripheral—linked to the fortunes of an economy somewhere else. And although it may appear to prosper and although the level of economic activity may be very high, it has failed to initiate a process of local development that will keep the economy viable if and when the relationship with the outside power is terminated.

In the New Caledonian context, the export sector has grown wealthy with the export of nickel ore and metallurgical products. These make up virtually the totality of exports from the island. All other economic activities depend on the export sector—trade and industry in the island's capital at Nouméa, service industries, even government and administration. The export sector dovetails with the larger economy of France, and to a certain extent with that of Japan, Australia, New Zealand, the United States, and Canada. From these countries is derived the vast array of imported goods necessary to sustain the high living standards of the New Caledonians.

Intersectoral linkage between the export sector and the Melanesian sector in New Caledonia is minimal. The bulk of the Melanesian population continues to live in reservations and to indulge in agriculture with only a modest component of cash cropping. Wage labor, though by no means unknown, is of only minor importance. The Melanesians, in other words, are largely irrelevant to the New Caledonian export economy, because they have been evacuated from the lands that are capable of being mined for nickel. And just as the Melanesians do not share in the export economy to any great extent, they do not share in the consumption of imported "luxuries."

Both sectors have their hopes as far as the French connection is concerned. The export sector requires the maintenance of access to markets and sources of capital, along with reasonable guarantees of political stability. The Melanesian sector hopes for assistance towards the initiation in New Caledonia of a political settlement which will end the invidious dualism and permit the Melanesians to become part of the mainstream of national life. In the following pages we shall examine the record for recent years and endeavor to gauge to what extent these differing goals have been attained.

EVOLUTION OF THE SOCIO-ECONOMIC STRUCTURE
OF NEW CALEDONIA

The territory of New Caledonia, comprising the main island of New Caledonia of the "Grande Terre," the Isle of Pines, and the Loyalty group, amounts to some 7,475 square miles (19,360 square kilometers) in area. The islands are situated just north of the Tropic of Capricorn, some 684 miles (1,100 kilometers) east of the coast of Queensland. The island of New Caledonia itself—much the largest component of the territory—stretches from northwest to southeast for a distance of about 250 miles (400 kilometers), and is about 30 miles (50 kilometers) wide. It is fringed by reefs along either coast, more continuously on the southwest side than on the northeast. The island is made up of a central mountainous core or spine, rising in places to over 4,920 feet (1,500 meters), and dropping sharply to the coast on the northeast side. Along this coast, only limited areas of lowland exist in the lower valleys of the short rivers that drain towards the sea. On the southwest side, the drop to the sea is more gradual; and the western littoral margin of the island is occupied throughout much of its length by a series of enlarged river basins, offering substantial areas of level terrain for agricultural or pastoral development. Scattered down the western coast, and completely filling the southern portion of the island, are areas of peridotite massif, an important geological formation in the economic history of the island. Although virtually useless for agricultural purposes, these massifs, under their heavy capping of summit lateritic material, contain beds of nickel enrichment, which amount to almost half the proven nickel resources of the non-communist world.

The Isle of Pines and the Loyalty Islands (Ouvea, Lifou, and Mare) consist of uplifted blocks of coral limestone. Unlike the Grande Terre, their relief is only moderate and for the most part consists of flat table-like structures. The Isle of Pines, in addition to its uplifted coral, has a peridotite core at its center.

New Caledonia lies in the Trade Wind belt of the Southwest Pacific. Its climate is sufficiently tropical to sustain the Melanesian agriculture, based on yam, taro, coconut, sweet potato, sugar cane, and plantain. Temperatures range in the lowlands from a cool season 68 degrees Fahrenheit (20.1 degrees Celsius) in August to 79 degrees Fahrenheit (26.2 degrees Celsius) in the hottest month, February. Rainfall is around 40 inches (1000 millimeters) per annum in the drier parts of the western coast (sheltered from full exposure to the Southeast Trades) and almost 120 inches (3000 millimeters) on the eastern coast, and in parts of the higher mountainous terrain.[2]

Inhabited at the time of first European penetration of the region in the eighteenth century by a collection of Melanesian tribes, New Caledonia was largely left alone. Its fringing reefs made close navigation dangerous, and the tribes had a reputation for hostility. However, in the 19th century traders began to exploit its resources of sandalwood, *bêche de mer,* and trochus shell; and eventually an English trader established a station on the Ile Nou, close to the present day site of Nouméa.

New Caledonia was annexed by the French in 1853, with the intention of its being used as a site for a penal colony. Penal settlements of differing kinds existed at one time or another at Nouméa (Ile Nou), on the Isle of Pines, and at several points along the western coast of the main island.[3] The penal centers established in the interior of the Grande Terre constituted a form of agricultural settlement or colonization, with convicts eventually being granted rights in land to a small peasant-sized holding, which they could farm for subsistence and cash crops.

Economic and related social development proceeded along several directions. The penal settlements and associated military presence lasted until the end of the century when Feillet (the first civilian governor of New Caledonia, holding this office from 1894 to 1902) succeeded in stopping further transportation. He wished to see the territory settled by accelerating the flow of free peasant farmers, drawn from France, and he encouraged experimentation with various crops that might serve as a basis for this settlement. His name is particularly associated with the popularization of coffee cultivation.

Pastoral development, along the lines of Queensland cattle stations, also took place, especially on the western coast where the topography was more suitable. The initial market was the military establishment and the penal settlements, but ultimately some export trade was begun.

Mining, especially of small deposits of copper, gold, and other minerals in the northeastern part of the territory, began in the nineteenth century. However, in the long run, nickel and chrome were to become the mainstays of the mining industry in the twentieth century. Convict labor was used in the early phases of mining, but proved to be totally unsatisfactory; by the time the twentieth century opened, moves were afoot to organize the importation of indentured labor from other Pacific islands and from parts of Asia. In this way, important components of the population were introduced, including Japanese, Vietnamese, and Javanese.

While these developments were taking place in the evolution of an export-oriented sector, the Melanesian population was being relocated. A policy of confining the Melanesians to reservations was adopted by the French administration at an early stage. A decree of 1868 declared Melanesian property in land to be communal or tribal and incapable of being alienated; but at the same time it implied the necessity to delimit Melanesian property. In 1876, a further decree specified the manner in which designation of Melanesian lands was to proceed; the commission that began to work on land delimitation shortly afterwards became a tool whereby Melanesians were confined to an ever-shrinking patchwork of restricted lands. In 1878, the Melanesians on the western coast resorted to armed revolt; they were ultimately crushed and the reservation policy continued.[4]

The policy of confinement to reservations had a profound impact on the Melanesian population. In the first place, it seriously undermined the basis of their economy by removing them from their best lands and leaving them with insufficient space for the conduct of shifting agriculture. Allocation of land to individuals within the heterogeneous tribal groups, which found themselves thrown together to share a reservation, proved to be immensely troublesome and generated intense conflict.[5] In the second place, it destroyed the texture of their concept of social space—an essential component in the social structure of the Melanesians. Clans and other groupings were bound together in an inter-weave of criss-crossing relationships that were functional, religious, political, and spatial all at the same time.[6] It is significant that reestablishment of whatever remained of these relations has been a high priority for the Melanesians from the moment the confinement on reservations was ended.

By the 1930s, the socio-economic and political structures in New Caledonia had begun to assume the forms they now display. In 1936, the census figures showed that of the total population of 53,254, 32 percent were Europeans, 54 percent Melanesians, and 13 percent of Asian origin. The Europeans predominated in the town of Nouméa, but were also scattered along the west and east coasts of the mainland where some of them were engaged in agricultural, pastoral, or mining activities. The Melanesians were also entirely confined to their reserves (see maps of Melanesian reserves), either on the mainland or the islands. The Asian population, derived from the indentured workers brought primarily for work in the mines or the nickel smelter near Nouméa, were located wherever their work demanded. Some were in Nouméa, others in the mining centers of the interior; a few had been released from indenture and had undertaken a variety of occupations in commerce or agriculture.

The economy was dominated by the export of nickel and, to a lesser extent, other mineral products. Some coffee was also exported, derived partly from European smallholders, partly from Melanesians who had recently been encouraged to adopt cash cropping.[7] The major company involved with the export of nickel was the Société le Nickel (SLN), which had emerged from the post World War I reorganization as the strongest single entity. This company had close ties (through its shareholding structure) to the Rothschild financial empire in France, and consequently was associated with the territory's one and only bank, the Banque de l'Indochine. Through control of credit sources in New Caledonia, the Banque de l'Indochine effectively controlled the activities of the major trading houses.

WORLD WAR II AND PORTENTS OF CHANGE

The events of World War II had a profound impact on New Caledonia. But although some of the institutional arrangements implicit in pre-war New Caledonia were finally altered, the basic dualism of economic purpose remained.

With the collapse of France in May 1940, a crisis arose in New Caledonia. Adherence to the Pétain regime, established that year at Vichy, was scarcely feasible, given the distance from France and the proximity of Australia. New Caledonia opted to join de Gaulle's Free France, following an upsurge of political feeling against the pro-Vichy governor and administration in New Caledonia. Thereafter the main threat came from Japan, and in March 1942, New Caledonia was "invaded" by a large American force, which used the island as a base for the remainder of the war in the Pacific. The presence of this large American force stimulated social and economic change on a wide front. Europeans both in Nouméa and in the agricultural regions of the interior were attracted by the employment opportunities created by the American presence. The Americans also employed considerable numbers of Melanesians, and this was the first time members of this group had been employed freely and paid high wages.

In the aftermath of the war, social changes were consolidated. The reformist governments that held power in metropolitan France favored policies of emancipation. Indentured contract labor was banned. Melanesians were freed from the restrictions that confined them to the reservations. New Caledonia thereupon entered a period not of transformation, but of adaptation. If the broad outlines of the prewar conditions were to be perpetuated in the economic sphere, if the distinction was to be maintained between an advanced and productive mining and export sector on the one hand and a backward somnolent Melanesian sector on the other, a new set of political and institutional arrangements would have to be worked out. Essentially, the political and social history of the post-World War II period is the story of how, despite substantial disagreements as to how the policy should be carried out, and what should be the role of metropolitan France, the export sector of the economy has been nurtured, and the Melanesian sector has been fossilized.

CONSERVATISM IN POST WAR NEW CALEDONIA

Factors of adaptation and conservatism in New Caledonia may be examined for the post war period under three broad rubrics—land ownership (and associated population distributions), economic organization, and political behavior.

Land Ownership and Population

As suggested earlier, land policy in the nineteenth century centered on the establishment of settlement areas for European immigrants. Whether for pastoralism or for smallholding agriculture, land was held to be available in large quantities for Europeans. Concessions made to companies, which professed their willingness to establish land settlement schemes, sometimes bordered on the absurd.[8] The Melanesians, on the other hand, were gradually compressed into ever smaller areas, and before the end of the nineteenth century there were confident forecasts that sooner or later the Melanesians would be extinct; all their lands would thus become available for white settlement. In point of fact, this demographic forecast proved to be false, but pressure to reduce the Melanesian reserves continued until well into the twentieth century.

By the late 1930s the Melanesian reservations on the Grande Terre amounted to some 311,220 acres (126,000 hectares).[9] During the postwar period, despite substantial efforts by Melanesian political figures, and by others interested in Melanesian welfare, the area of these reservations has not been increased greatly. By 1960 some 37,065 acres (15,000 hectares) had been added, making a total of about 348,285 acres (141,000 hectares). This is the equivalent of just over 8 percent of the area of the Grande Terre; in addition, the Loyalty Islands and the Isle of Pines are Melanesian reservations. The total area of such reservations in 1969 was 917,926 acres (371,630 hectares).[10]

The ready access to land enjoyed by the non-Melanesian population is reflected in the fact that they own or rent a much larger area than the Melanesians. In 1950, it was estimated that Europeans held 1,353,440 acres (552,000 hectares) of land, 58 percent of it in some form of ownership.[11] Much of this land took the form of large concessions, offered to cattle station operators. But little of this land is intensively used, either for stockrearing or for arable agriculture.

Examination of the population distribution figures given in Table 7 serves to draw attention to the fundamentally different patterns that apply to the Europeans and the Melanesians. Although Melanesians have been free since 1946 to settle wherever they wish and to seek whatever employment they wish, the figures show that, as a rule, the Melanesians have not deserted their reservations. The number of Melanesians in Nouméa has increased in the period 1956-1969 both absolutely and as a percentage. Nonetheless, the proportion of the Melanesians resident on a reservation either on the Grande Terre or on the islands is still high—76.3 percent, compared with 85 percent in 1956. The percentage of Melanesians living in parts of the Grande Terre outside the reservations, and not including Nouméa, has in fact remained almost stable. By contrast, the

TABLE 7

DISTRIBUTION OF MELANESIANS AND EUROPEANS IN
NEW CALEDONIA, 1956 AND 1969

PLACE OF RESIDENCE	MELANESIANS				EUROPEANS			
	1956		1969		1956		1969	
	Nos.	%	Nos.	%	Nos.	%	Nos.	%
Nouméa	2,432	7.0	7,073	15.3	15,188	60.4	26,252	63.6
Grande Terre Off reservations	2,842	8.1	3,873	8.4	9,887	39.3	14,836	36.0
Reservations	17,711	50.7	21,716	47.0	—	—	—	—
Islands	11,979	34.3	13,538	29.3	85	.3	180	.4
Totals	34,964	100.0	46,200	100.0	25,160	100.0	41,268	100.0

Sources: Institut National de la Statistique et des Etudes Economiques
            (a) Recensement général de la population de la Nouvelle Calédonie, 1956
            (b) Résultats statistiques du recensement général de la population de la
            Nouvelle Calédonie effectué en Mars 1969

Europeans show heavy concentration at both dates, but significantly the degree of concentration is increasing.

Some idea of the overcrowding on the Grande Terre reservations may be gained from the fact that their population density is 15.4 per square kilometer (1.39 per square mile). This compares with a figure of 5.9 per square kilometer in the Loyalty Islands and the Isle of Pines. The overall density of population for the Grande Terre outside Nouméa was 2.6 per square kilometer.

The land tenure situation thus has its counterpart in population distribution. The Melanesians, who own or occupy little land, do so at very high density. The European sector of the population, owning or occupying much larger quantities of land, is nonetheless concentrated in the urban center. Their non-urban land is not used intensively at all. Despite an increase in the total number of Europeans living in the interior of the Grande Terre, the numbers reporting their occupations as "agriculture" or "forestry" fell from 1,282 in 1956 to 1,193 in 1969.[12]

In the context of the present political situation in New Caledonia, there is no obvious solution in sight. On numerous occasions proposals have been put forward to rectify the imbalance, but none have proved practicable. To purchase European-owned land and return it to the Melanesians would be difficult, not only on account of the cost but also because of the profound feeling of political insecurity it would cause among the non-Melanesian population elements. In addition, the land as seen by the Melanesians does not constitute simply an economic asset. The Melanesian agricultural system is not geared to the production

of cash crops, and, in any case, the potential for a rapid increase in New Caledonia's exports of cash crops such as coffee and copra is limited. To the Melanesians, the land has value as the land of their ancestors; thus social reasons for
wanting its return are as powerful as the economic.

Despite some discussion at the political level, all parties in New Caledonia
seem to have accepted that the continuation of the connection with France im-
plies a maintenance of the present land tenure situation. There is widespread
recognition of the need for fundamental land reform,[13] but no one believes that
it can be initiated either by the local assembly in New Caledonia or by the government in France.

Economic Organization

Hopes that New Caledonia would become a flourishing agricultural colony
have not materialized. Attempts were made to introduce sugar and cotton as
well as coffee, but only the last has survived as a crop of any significance. Coffee
(some of which is grown by the Melanesians) and copra are the only forms of
agricultural produce regularly exported from New Caledonia, but they account
for less than one per cent of the value of exports, and even this modest level is
supported by a territorial subsidy.

In recent years cereal production in New Caledonia has been virtually non-
existent.[14] Only about 4,000 to 5,000 tons of fruit and vegetables from New
Caledonian farms have been marketed, and this is much less than the volume of
these products imported from neighboring countries at considerable cost. Although there were 1,032 cattle stations, with some 109,000 head of cattle
(augmented by approximately 11,000 in the Melanesian reservations), meat still
had to be imported on a large scale.[15]

Tourism has been suggested as another possible industry that could flourish
in New Caledonia. Some 15,000 visitors per year have been coming to New Caledonia
as tourists in the past few years. But they have often found that the costs are high,
and the boycott of French territories (a response by Australians and New Zealanders
to the French nuclear tests in Polynesia) has had an adverse effect on numbers.

Overshadowing all else in New Caledonia is the mining and metallurgical industry,
particularly the nickel industry. In 1973 nickel ore and metallurgical exports were
valued at 13,906 million francs CFP.[16] About 15 percent of the island's work force
is directly employed in mining or metallurgy. Direct taxation of exports of nickel
provides about fifteen percent of the territorial budgetary revenue.

Two structurally contrasted elements participate in the mining and metallurgical industry. On the one hand stands the giant Société le Nickel (SLN), and on the
other the independent miners, or the *petits mineurs* as they are sometimes egregiously designated. Hitherto, only the SLN has carried out any processing of ore
locally from its own mines—actually open cast workings high on the peridotite
massifs of the interior of the island—or has shipped ore by sea to Nouméa, where
the Doniambo smelters have converted it to *mattes* or *fontes,* ready for shipment
overseas. The *petits mineurs* have had to sell their ore either to the SLN or to pur-

chasers overseas, and the Japanese have been virtually the only buyers of untreated ores. Of the nickel exported in 1973, some 26 percent was accounted for by ore (and therefore emanated from the *petits mineurs* almost entirely) and 74 percent was accounted for by processed products from the SLN smelters.

The SLN has always maintained close ties with the French government, and these have become a factor in some of its New Caledonian operations. For example, during the years 1958-1969, the metropolitan French government paid a subsidy on refined nickel that helped the SLN through a period of extensive development and investment in its New Caledonian plant and equipment.[17] In March 1962, the governor of New Caledonia—an appointee from metropolitan France—supported the request of the SLN to have its produce exempted from territorial export duties in view of the difficulties it was having in selling its nickel.[18] Although that request resulted ultimately in a compromise, a subsequent request in 1973 for similar relief was agreed to, part of the price being a subsidy from the French government to the territorial budget.[19]

In 1970, nickel exporters in New Caledonia were surprised by the sudden imposition of a quota on exports of untreated ore to Japan. The French government, in explaining the ban, argued that some control would be needed on exports of ore in order to ensure that sufficient supplies were made available to smelting works in New Caledonia. At the time there was only one (the SLN plant at Doniambo), other projects having been slow to get off the ground. The independent miners in New Caledonia complained that their reputation for reliability as suppliers to the Japanese was compromised by this high-handed governmental action from Paris, and they said it was unnecessary to hold back exports of ore when little enough was being done to get new smelters installed.[20]

But the main issue over the future direction of development of the mining sector has been that of allowing non-French companies to compete with the SLN in the field of nickel processing. The independent miners have always felt they were at a disadvantage in not having an alternative smelting outlet in New Caledonia. Either they accepted the conditions of the SLN over the sale of their ore, or they sought sales to the Japanese (and the Japanese could be irregular buyers, varying their sales enormously from year to year). According to legislation passed in France (and France invariably has refused to grant New Caledonia the power to control mining activities in her own territory), only French citizens or companies could invest in such mining and metallurgical enterprises. This limitation effectively barred any competitor from entering the field in New Caledonia, since there was no French company large enough and wealthy enough to be able to break into the nickel smelting business.

Persistently, from the early 1960s onwards, the independent mining community tried to bring pressure to bear on the administration to permit foreign companies, notably the Canadian company International Nickel (INCO), to invest in processing facilities in New Caledonia. But the French government remained cool to the prospect of allowing foreign, especially North American, capital to exploit any portion of the mineral wealth of New Caledonia. Encouragement was given, however, to the establishment of new factories under some form of joint venture which would enable the French partner to retain control over the management of the enterprise.

Several such proposals have managed to reach the operational stage, and others are proceeding. The SLN embarked on a phase of expansion, developing its mining facilities at Nepoui in the central part of the western coast of the island. The smelting plant at Doniambo, producing about 38,000 tons of nickel in 1968, was expanded to a capacity of 60,000 tons by 1974, and may be producing 80,000 tons per annum before the end of the decade. In these projects the SLN has been assisted by technical and financial participation by Kaiser Aluminium, an American corporation.[21] In the southern part of the island arrangements involving Freeport Minerals, along with Aquitaine, and AMAX, in association with the French Pennaroya company, have been discussed. Significantly, these are projects in which either the French government (Aquitaine) or the SLN (Pennaroya) has a substantial holding interest.

A number of other projects for joint ventures have run into obstacles, usually the failure of one of the parties to raise sufficient capital. In the southern part of the island, INCO proposed a joint venture (referred to as COFIMPAC) to exploit the lateritic ores and process them in a smelter to be built nearby. After years of hesitation the French partners had to withdraw, and INCO was left to restructure its proposals and proceed on its own. The French government ultimately agreed to this, and current proposals envisage factory construction taking place between 1974 and 1977, with output in 1977 amounting to 20,000 tons of nickel; a subsequent rise to 50,000 tons is intended, with the possibility of reaching as high as 100,000 tons.[22] In the northern part of New Caledonia, a major scheme was proposed for the exploitation of the ores at Poum and Tiebaghi, and the construction of a smelter at Koumac. Initially this proposal involved some SLN participation, some local New Caledonian capital, and the Patino Corporation (North American); Japanese loan capital was also considered. By late 1972, the scheme had changed somewhat, and what was then proposed was a partnership between Patino and the French group Pechiney-Ugine-Kuhlman, under the name COFREMMI.[23] By March 1973, a development schedule was announced, providing for the first production in 1975, and an annual capacity of 36,000 tons of nickel.[24]

In all these developments the reluctance of the French government to open up New Caledonia to non-French corporations is evident. Whether justifiable or not, local New Caledonian interests, especially mining interests, have perceived their advantage to lie in the most rapid development of alternative outlets for their produce, and have therefore pressed for the admission of foreign corporations. The SLN and the government in Paris have followed a policy of trying to conserve control as much as possible in French hands, while at the same time allowing for development at a rate commensurate with the growing demands of the world market.

Political Behavior

If the interplay of competing forces, local or external, has been observed in the spheres of land tenure and economic development, it is only to be expected that it will assume an important role in politics. In New Caledonian politics we can observe the changing constellations of interest groups, and the appearance and disappearance of particular issues. But we can at the same time detect the long-run patterns, the reappearance of the old issues and conflicts under new guises, and continuing attempts to enforce the old solutions.

The fundamental proposition concerning political evolution in New Caledonia is that, in keeping with the initial structural economic analysis that we have made, the health and strength of the export sector is a prime objective of the politically dominant groups. The wealthiest, most articulate, and politically most sophisticated elements in New Caledonia have been involved with its export activities ever since the time the export economy emerged in its present form at the end of the nineteenth century. Agreement in principle therefore exists between two important elements in New Caledonia, despite the fact that they have frequently contended openly; these elements are the metropolitan French interests on the one hand (the governor, the appointed administrators, and the externally based economic institutions such as the SLN and the Banque de l'Indochine), and the larger local European interests on the other (*petits mineurs,* cattle raisers, independent commercial traders, etc.). Their contentions have centered repeatedly on the issue of "centralization" or "autonomy." The metropolitan interests have fought for the maintenance of a strong "French connection," while local interests have frequently espoused more local decision-making responsibility. But basically their objectives are similar, and they differ only over means.

The Melanesian component is of a different nature. Melanesian life, social, economic, and cultural, bears little relation to the economically motivated export sector. Melanesians remain apart from the mainstream of New Caledonia's "international" lifestyle. They enter the European world selectively and often for only brief periods. Although assimilation is not prevented, it does not take place to any marked extent. But it is not yet clear to the Melanesians what their real political interests are. They were crushed and subdued in the nineteenth century, and the legitimacy of their interests was denied. The period since their technical and legal emancipation in 1946 has been one of a vague searching for an identity.[25] They have never called in question the whole principle of the French presence, or denied the right of the immigrant section of the population to conduct economic activities. But they have begun to question whether present arrangements concerning the internal distribution of resources, especially land, in New Caledonia are equitable. They are beginning to articulate the view that since present land ownership and settlement patterns reflect the fact of conquest, they are no longer appropriate for an age that must accept the Melanesians as a post-conquest people.

Politically speaking then, the problems faced by the Melanesians concern their role in the future New Caledonia. There are uncertainties in their minds as to what direction they must follow, the extent to which they can cooperate with non-Melanesian elements, and how they should relate to the already existent tensions between metropolitan and local Caledonian interests. They are aware that pressure for the policy of emancipation in 1946 came from metropolitan France, and that it was resisted in some quarters locally. They are also aware that, in the Gaullist era, the metropolitan government has been a conservative factor. Hence Melanesians have at times found common cause with European elements of the New Caledonian population who, like themselves, experience frustration before the seemingly monolithic economic and land control of big business.

Although municipal government came to the European population in New Caledonia as early as 1979,[26] with the establishment of a commune at Nouméa, political activity did not reach a high level before the period of the governorship of Feillet (1894-1902). Feillet introduced a general council for the territory, with electoral participation by male French electors, and also introduced rural or mixed communes in various parts of the interior.

From the early years of the twentieth century until World War II, the pattern of political activity remained essentially the same, despite variation in its details. Local European interests fought to increase their share in the processes of decision-making, and they harassed the governor continuously. In particular, they fought against the imposition of an elaborate and costly bureaucracy staffed by persons from France to be paid for by New Caledonia; France argued in return that there was no way New Caledonia could manage on its own, and that, in any case, metropolitan support for the territorial budget was generous.

After World War II, there were a number of changes, but they were not as far reaching, in their initial stages, as had been hoped for. In 1946, the Constitution of the Fourth Republic allowed for the representation of overseas territories such as New Caledonia through the medium of delegates to the various assemblies in Paris—the National Assembly, the Council of the Republic (the Senate) and the French Union Assembly. The Paris government still retained control over New Caledonia through its power to appoint the governor and some other high-ranking administrators; its control over certain types of budgetary expenditure; and the restricted nature of the powers accorded to the General or Territorial Council. The structures established in 1946 were not intended to be a permanent settlement of the constitutional position of the overseas territories; but in any event, it was 1956 before they were replaced for New Caledonia by a more permanent *loi-cadre.*

Only a small number of Melanesians qualified as voters in time for the General Council elections in New Caledonia in 1946. But a major shift occurred in 1951, when the franchise was greatly extended among Melanesians. As a result Maurice Lenormand—a metropolitan Frenchman drawing support from the newly enfranchised Melanesians—won the election for the position of Deputy, and thus embarked on a political career notable both for its flamboyance and for its significant role in the politicization of the Melanesian people. By 1953, the Melanesians were strong enough electorally to bring to power in the General Council Lenormand's party, the Union Calédonienne, an alliance of Melanesians and lower income Europeans.

The local New Caledonian European political establishment found it difficult to adjust to these developments. Initially there was talk of a complete break with France. Proposals were put forward in 1951, at the time of the enfranchisement of the bulk of the Melanesians, for the severance of the "French connection" altogether, and for an alliance with Australia or the United States.[27] Somewhat less extreme were the proposals for electoral reform in such a way as to introduce a "double-college" system, and hence prevent the Melanesians from assuming command of the politics. In due course, however, it became clear that the metropolitan business interests were as interested in preventing the "radicalization" of New Caledonian politics as were the New Caledonian conservatives. The SLN, for example, was concerned lest taxation policies of the New Caledonian government should get out of hand and become a threat to the viability of their nickel business; they argued that the passing of political control to a section of the population that paid no taxes was frought with danger. The only way to maintain stability in New Caledonia was to ensure that the newly emergent political forces did not have the power to "legislate" disruption of the existent economic structure.

Consequently, when a *loi-cadre* was finally established in 1956, it provided for few far-reaching changes in the structure of the government of New Caledonia. France still retained power, appointed the governor and senior administrators, and retained control over important resources such as mineral rights. New Caledonia still influenced central government policy only through her delegates to national parliamentary bodies in Paris. The only significant change was the creation of a loc "council of ministers," elected by the General Council (henceforth to be known as the *Assemblée Territoriale* or the Territorial Assembly); but the powers of the "ministers" were quite limited.

In 1957, at the first election following the adoption of the *loi-cadre,* Lenormand party captured eighteen out of thirty seats. Altogether, thirteen Melanesians were elected, and of the eight members of the Union Calédonienne selected to constitute the "council of ministers," two were Melanesians; in 1958 Michel Kauma, a Melanesian, presided over the Territorial Assembly. The Union Calédonienne thereupon found itself assuming the mantle of the party crusading for Caledonian autonomy, a role formerly played by the local conservatives. The latter quickly found themselves close to the position adopted by the national government, favoring the maintenance of a strong French position.

The hand of the conservatives was greatly strengthened by the Algiers *coup* of May 13, 1958, and the return of de Gaulle to power in the Fifth Republic. An attempt was made at that time to force the resignation of Lenormand, and although it did not succeed, conservatives were encouraged to believe that there might be some chance of effecting a split in the Union Calédonienne. De Gaulle's government in Paris soon cooperated. It was common knowledge that de Gaulle believed in and had proclaimed the French destiny of the Pacific territories, and in 1959 Laurent Péchoux was sent as governor, one of his tasks being to effect a weakening of those forces opposed to a strong French influence. In practice, he would have to break Lenormand, and destroy the influence of the Union Calédonienne, whose policy of economic reform and social advancement was atracting increasing numbers of lower paid European wage earners and small-holders into a posture of alliance with the electorally powerful Melanesians.

The policy of reducing the political power of New Caledonia under the 1956 *loi-cadre,* and of Maurice Lenormand as the leader of its strongest political organization, was carried out in several stages. The referendum of 1958, following de Gaulle's ascent to power, bluntly required the overseas territories to vote "yes" or face immediate total independence without any financial assistance. Even the Union Calédonienne did not desire to go as far as this, and so it recommended a positive vote. In 1963, the French Parliament passed a bill that reduced the powers of the New Caledonian "council of ministers," leaving them only the function of "tendering advice to the governor." In 1964, Lenormand was implicated in a bomb threat (on somewhat dubious evidence it seems) and stripped of his civic rights; in this way he was forced into political oblivion, at least for the time being. In 1967, the French government passed a series of laws–the Billotte Laws–greatly extending its degree of control over the mining industry in New Caledonia.

At the same time, a series of measures were undertaken to placate local business interests. The steps taken to allow entry into New Caledonia by foreign mining corporations have already been mentioned. The monopoly of the Banque de l'Indochine was also ended, and a series of other French banks came to set up branches in Nouméa. Finance has been forthcoming for a number of projects, including several in and around the city of Nouméa. Such financing has the ultimate effect of enhancing real estate values, an area of business in which many of the local conservatives have significant interests.

Nevertheless, the persistent underlying issue of the role of metropolitan France in the affairs of New Caledonia has not been solved. After a period in the 1960s in which it appeared that de Gaulle's designs had succeeded, and after the fall of Lenormand and the fragmentation of the Union Calédonienne, the autonomy issue has again come to the forefront. Metropolitan interests still favor strong ultimate control from Paris, typified in recent years by the pro-French style of Governor Verger. But local European interest groups are no longer so adamantly opposed to the "autonomist" line, once the preserve of the Union Calédonienne. They have seen what they believe is "electoral politics" in an administration that seeks to encourage a continued flow of immigrants from France (when jobs are scarce in New Caledonia) as a device to ensure enough loyal voters.[28] And they have come to oppose the heavy-handed control over the economy, which, despite appearances of decentralization they still believe is controlled in France. The Melanesians, their voting power weakened in the 1960s by dissensions and defections, seem as a result to be less feared by the European sector. They have come forward with no far-reaching revolutionary demands, and by now it is clear that a decade of their political participation has not had the dire effects once predicted. Their concern is still with the problem of their way of life and their lands; and there is some real awareness that unless their legitimate grievances are adequately handled, more revolutionary forces subsequently may emerge.

The Union Calédonienne was held together in the later years of the 1960s by Rock Pidjot, a Melanesian closely associated with Lenormand. Although New Caledonia was represented in the Senate in Paris by a member of the local business elite–Henri Lafeur–Rock Pidjot continued as Deputy. He held together the remnants of the Union in the Territorial Assembly after the eclipse of

Lenormand. And in more recent elections, he has continued to hold his position, despite the divergent tendencies frequently observed within the Melanesian community itself.

By late 1971, the Union Calédonienne, which had initially held twenty-two seats in the Territorial Assembly out of a total of thirty-five, had been reduced through defections to twelve.[29] In the assembly, the Union Calédonienne joined with the Union Civique (one seat) to form the Front Calédonienne pour l'Autonomie. But this was insufficient to offset the preponderance of the anti-autonomists. These comprised the Entente, including the Union Démocratique (centering upon Georges Chatenay, a prominent lawyer), the Entente Démocratique et Sociale (centered upon Roger Laroque, Mayor of Nouméa, and Henri Lafleur), the Liberals, and the Union Multiraciale. The Liberals included a number of former members of the Union Calédonienne who had split over the issue of autonomy and moved to the anti-autonomist camp; the Union Multiraciale consisted mainly of Melanesians whose attitude towards autonomy was ambivalent; later its leader, Yann Celene Uregei, was to come out as anti-autonomist. Significantly, Lenormand himself, having emerged from obscurity, was by this time again playing an important role within the Union Calédonienne.

In the elections held towards the end of 1972 for the Territorial Assembly, something of a stalemate resulted. There were sixteen members returned who were convinced anti-autonomists, and two more who were likely to join with them for crucial votes. Twelve seats went to the Union Calédonienne, and five to the Union Multiraciale, which at that time was still prepared to demand at least some form of decentralization for the territory. Voting patterns showed that the southwest, including Nouméa, returned a majority of anti-autonomist candidates, while the interior areas and the islands returned a majority of autonomist candidates.[30]

Some months later, in March 1973, elections were held for the Deputy, to be returned to Paris. The conservative elements teamed up to support Jean Léques, a former president of the Territorial Assembly, and an anti-autonomist. The opposition groups, instead of fielding one candidate, fielded two; both were Melanesians—Rock Pidjot, running with the support of the Union Calédonienne, and Yann Celene Uregei, running with the support of the Union Multiraciale. Clearly, the fact that there were two Melanesian candidates would have the effect of splitting the important Melanesian vote, and this is what happened. Lèques led the field on the first ballot, but failed to gain an absolute majority, and had to face a run-off against Rock Pidjot. In the runoff election Rock Pidjot won, but the vote distribution was indicative of the polarization of New Caledonia. Nouméa, with its European population and large numbers of recent European immigrants, gave 65 percent of its votes to Lèques, whereas the interior gave 64 percent of its vote to Rock Pidjot.[31]

In the Territorial Assembly itself, subsequent realignment of members led to changes in the balance of parties. There were defections from the anti-autonomist groups, and by May of 1973 a count put the balance at 20-15 in favor of autonomists. Nonetheless, the assembly is in no position to implement any policy in respect of autonomy, and the administration has continued to treat New Caledonia in accordance with the wishes of the government in Paris.

Political life has thus come round in a circle. The electoral process has achieved what it is always capable of achieving—a majority for those in favor of autonomy. But it cannot give them the power to implement any such policy. Continuance of the way of life as it is known at present in New Caledonia depends on mining and metallurgy, not on politics. So long as this is the case, politics is likely to continue as it is at present, a form of "dependent politics" where political life adapts to what is permitted by the "realities" of the situation.

CONCLUSIONS

In its early days as a French colony, New Caledonia operated on the premise that it would become a wholly European colony of settlement and that the Melanesian population would in due course disappear. The goal, in other words, was a unitary society, not a dual one. No provision was therefore made for the accommodation of the Melanesian society and economy of the territory. Even when it became obvious that the Melanesian population was not going to disappear, there was no attempt to determine what kind of society New Caledonia would need to develop in order to accommodate all of its population.

Guiart has also shown convincingly that the assimilation of Melanesian social structure and political relationships into the form required for participation in a European type of society and economy is quite improbable.[32] White and black thus gaze at each other across a vast chasm. For the European population there is no conceivable likelihood of adapting to any Melanesian set of values. For the Melanesians there is a dilemma; Melanesians have the political strength to use the electoral system and move in upon the European economic structure, at least insofar as it remains amenable to local political manipulation, but this would imply a renunciation of their present status. On the other hand, they have the option of trying to maintain a Melanesian form of life and culture, at the price of accepting their virtual exclusion from the process of exploiting the wealth of their own land. Possibly the only way a Melanesian form of life can survive and develop is through the denial of European forms of economic rationality. Hitherto, the process of historic evolution in New Caledonia, at least since the Second World War, has neatly illustrated the proposition that change is not necessarily change; the more it changes the more it is the same thing. Separate social systems have been maintained side by side, in a kind of harmony. But this harmony conceals the fact that there are major differences, and that the aspirations of all groups and classes cannot be satisfied under the conditions in which they are maintained. The prospects for the future, though bright for the short run, are less certain in the longer perspective. Neither the political nor the economic system operative at present in New Caledonia seems capable of generating real change, and time alone will tell if other means will have to be found.

NOTES

1. Samir Amin, "Le modèle théorique d'accumulation et de développement dans le monde contemporain," *Tiers Monde* 13, 52 (1972), 703-26.

2. J. Giovannelli, *Le climat de la Nouvelle Calédonie* (Nouméa 1953), pp. 15, 29.

3. Jean-Paul Faivre, "Vue générale de l'histoire calédonienne," *Journal de la Société des Océanistes* 9 (1953), 13.

4. Roselène Dousset, *Colonialisme et contraditions; étude sur les causes socio-historiques de l'Insurrection de 1878 en Nouvelle Calédonie* (Paris, 1970), pp. 76-79.

5. Jean Guiart, "Un problème foncier exemplaire en Nouvelle Calédonie: la Vallée de Tchamba," *Le Monde Non-Chrétien,* No. 55-56 (1961), 182-96.

6. Jean Guiart, "Carte du dynamisme de la société indigène à l'arrivée des Européens," *Journal de la Société des Océanistes* 9 (1953), 93-97.

7. Alain Saussol, "Le café en Nouvelle Calédonie; grandeur et vicissitude d'une colonisation," *Les Cahiers d'Outre Mer,* 20 année, No. 79 (1967), 275-305.

8. Dousset, op. cit., p. 77.

9. Virginia Thompson and Richard Adloff, *The French Pacific Islands* (Berkele 1971), p. 379.

10. J. Angleviel, *Note de conjoncture, Mars 1974* (Nouméa, 1974), p. 38.

11. Thompson and Adloff, op. cit., p. 381.

12. *Recensement général de la population de la Nouvelle Calédonie 1956: tableaux statistiques* (Institut National de la Statistique et des Etudes Economique [Paris 1962]), p. 122; and *Résultats statistiques du recensement général de la population de la Nouvelle Calédonie, effectué en mars 1969* (Paris, no date), p. 85.

13. Thompson and Adloff, op. cit., p. 382.

14. Angleviel, op. cit., p. 38.

15. J. Angleviel, *L'importation des produits alimentaires en Nouvelle Calédonie, 1965-1972* (Nouméa 1973), p. 34-35.

16. Angleviel, *Note de conjoncture,* pp. 30, 33.

17. *L'activité minière en Nouvelle Calédonie, 1960* (Service des Mines, Nouméa) pp. 12-14.

18. Thompson and Adloff, op. cit., p. 313.

19. *Pacific Islands Monthly* (Sydney), December 1973, p. 10.

20. Ibid., November 1971, p. 34.

21. Ibid., June 1971.

22. Ibid., March 1973, p. 113.

23. Ibid., July 1972, p. 101.

24. Ibid., March 1973, p. 113.

25. Apollinaire Anova-Ataba, "Deux exemples de réflexions melanésiennes," *Journal de la Société des Océanistes* 25 (1969), 201-19.

26. W. D. McTaggart, "Nouméa: A Study in Social Geography" (Canberra, 196. p. 23.

27. Thompson and Adloff, op. cit., p. 292.

28. *Pacific Islands Monthly,* November 1972, p. 22.

29. Ibid., August 1971, p. 34.

30. Ibid., October 1972, p. 27.

31. Ibid., April 1973, p. 7.

32. Jean Guiart, *Structure de la chefferie en Melanésie du sud* (Paris, 1963).

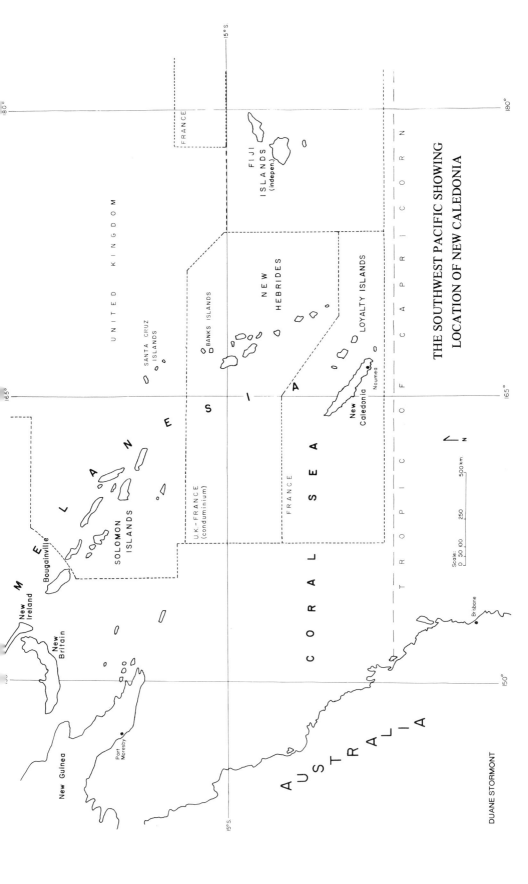

THE SOUTHWEST PACIFIC SHOWING
LOCATION OF NEW CALEDONIA

DUANE STORMONT

DUANE STORMONT

ISLE OF PINES

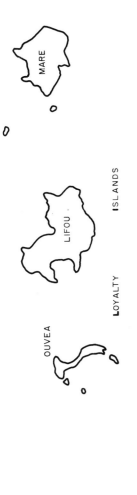

MARE

LIFOU

ISLANDS

OUVEA

LOYALTY

ADMINISTRATIVE DISTRICTS OF
NEW CALEDONIA

100 km.

N

YATE

MONT
DORE

NOUMEA

DUMBEA

PAITA

THIO

BOULOUPARIS

CANALA

LA
FOA

SARRAMEA

FARINO

MOINDOU

BOURAIL

HOUAILOU

POYA

PONERIHOUEN

POUEMBOUT

KONE

PONDIMIE

TOUHO

VOH

HIENGHENE

GOMEN

POUEBO

OUEGOA

KOUMAC

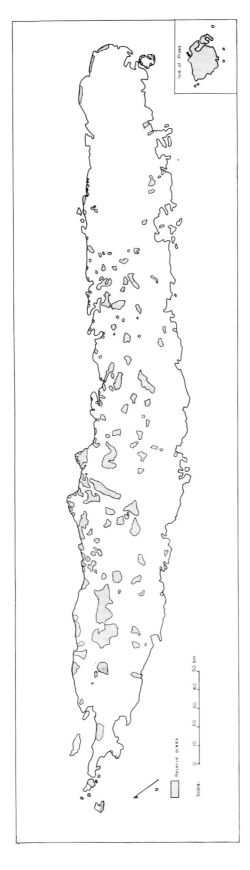

DUANE STORMONT

Isle of Pines

Scale:
Reserve areas
0 10 20 30 40 50 km

MELANESIAN RESERVES ON THE GRANDE TERRE AND ISLE OF PINES

Source: Jacques Avias, "Evolution de l'habitat indigène en Nouvelle Calédonie de 1843 à nos jours," *Journal de la Société des Océanistes* 9 (1953) 129-50.

WILLIAM E. TAGUPA **13**

France, French Polynesia, and the South Pacific in the Nuclear Age

Efforts to create a French nuclear force began ambiguously in 1945 with the establishment of the *Commissariat à l'Energe Etomique* (CEA) as a public corporation with an "industrial and commercial character . . . concerned in the main with the military uses of atomic energy."[1]

> Though it was never said that the CEA should manufacture atomic bombs, it was implicitly assumed that the activities of the CEA were of interest to national defense. At that time the direct applications of atomic energy were unknown, civilian use was non-existent or hypothetical.[2]

Officials of the Fourth Republic realized that there was an immediate need for an adequate and well-prepared national defense program in order to prevent a repetition of events that preceded both world wars. It was, therefore, not surprising that the question of constructing an atomic arsenal became an integral part of French government policy even during the declining years of the Fourth Republic. By April 1958, Premier Félix Gaillard authorized the manufacture of an atomic bomb to be first tested by 1960. It was not, however, until the advent of Charles de Gaulle's Fifth Republic that French nuclear policy began to take positive and more discernible form. In his noteworthy *écoles militaire* speech, De Gaulle enunciated the fundamental principles outlining the new concept of a French nuclear strike force (*force de frappe*):

> . . . the idea of a war . . . in which France would no longer be herself and would not act on her own accord, following her own objectives . . . is unacceptable. . . . Consequently it is evident that we must achieve in the forthcoming years a force which is capable of acting on our behalf which is conveniently called a *force de frappe* capable of being deployed at any moment and at any place. . . . In the area of defense, this will be our greatest task in the coming years.[3]

The policymakers of the Fifth Republic, as well as the public in general, were well aware of recent international events in which French interests and policies failed to receive support from the Atlantic community, particularly from the United States. The Indochina and Algeria wars and the Suez crisis provided convincing proof that military dependency on the United States was impractical where "... the vital interests of the United States were not at stake."[4] It would not, however, be accurate to assume that the *école militaire* speech marked the exact beginning of French nuclear policy, but rather its political crystallization. Evidence suggests that French nuclear policy was an accumulation of smaller decisions that preceded and continued through the Fifth Republic. The military aspect of the atomic programs had commenced as early as 1956 when responsibilities concerning the construction of an atomic arsenal were divided between the CEA and the military services, with the former being responsible for "... conducting the preliminary studies for the experimental atomic explosion ... supplying the necessary plutonium ... for making the prototype ... for carrying out experimental atomic explosions."[5] The armed forces, on the other hand, would be responsible for the "... preparation for experiments concerning nuclear explosions."[6]

Though parliamentary opinion gradually grew in favor of an atomic arsenal, the CEA and the military sustained the impetus needed for the formulation of an effective *force de frappe.*

> The action of responsible political leadership was lost in a long chain of events—a response to a protracted internal pressure combined with the force of the external military and political environment. Guidance and direction for nuclear policy came not from the French government or the French Parliament, but from a small, dedicated group of administrators, technocrats, politicians and military officers whose activities centered on and emanated from the CEA. This group exhorted successive governments ... to prepare the groundwork for an eventual decision to create an atomic arsenal, and their persuasion increased in direct proportion to the decline of French influence and prestige in the international environment.[7]

Gradually, the need for an atomic capability became identified with the need to pursue an independent course in international diplomacy. The concept of the *force de frappe* fitted well with the Gaullist vision of a greater and independent France. On February 13, 1960, the first nuclear device was detonated at the Reggane Firing Ground in the Sahara, and France officially entered the international nuclear cartel. Pierre Messmer, then armed forces minister, remarked:

> We have just taken a very important step, but we have not yet attained our goal. We will continue to work in order to give France a *force de frappe* disposing of both nuclear warheads and the necessary means to transport them, thus giving our armed forces the capacity to accomplish

their permanent mission which is to insure respect under all circumstances of national independence.[8]

With Algerian independence, however, France was soon deprived of her Saharan testing site and another location had to be found.[9]

The atolls of Mururoa and Fangataufa in French Polynesia were chosen as the new test sites because the area was French, uninhabited, situated outside of maritime and airline routes, capable of supporting scientific equipment, and relatively distant from populated areas.[10] The decision to relocate the nuclear testing site created a sudden furor of debate in the French Pacific territory.[11] Debate over the issue centered upon three major points: (1) the effects of radioactivity upon the biota and human population of the territory; (2) the political morality of conducting such tests without consulting public officials or conducting a public referendum in the territory; (3) the socio-economic effects resulting from the mass influx of civilian and military personnel and the migration of rural population into the urban area.

The members of the Territorial Assembly were most concerned about the long-term affects of the test upon the island ecosystem. The Assembly had been informed continuously about the results of the British atomic experiments at Christmas Island and had been most critical about the tests in 1962. Consequently, when the Assembly President, Jacques Tauraa, returned from Paris that year with the news that de Gaulle had approved the decision to relocate the test site to French Polynesia, the Assembly members became noticeably alarmed and perplexed. Though the response to the issue generally followed party and political affiliation, it was apparent that even the most faithful Gaullist supporters were alienated.[12] Assemblyman Jean B. H. Céran-Jérusalémy led the CEP opposition and severely criticized the Gaullists for being conspicuously acquiescent on the issue.[13] Other political critics voiced dissatisfaction with government explanations concerning safely measures against radioactivity, citing that Algeria had protested a possible Mediterranean site. A resolution was passed by the anti-CEP faction in the Assembly in 1963 protesting the installation of the CEP in the territory.[14]

Concern over the radioactive effects of the test, particularly that of strontium 90 was the most pervasive topic of debate. The CEP opponents indicated that the harmful effects of radioactive by-products on the population could threaten the health of children and the well-being of future generations.[15] Furthermore, the opposition asserted the fallout from the atoll tests could be carried on the ocean currents, and its effects on schools of migrating tuna could not be accurately monitored. John Teariki indicated that the populations of five islands in the Tuamotu and Gambier archipelagoes would be affected by the fallout pattern. French governor Aimé Grimald, speaking in behalf of the CEP, replied to Teariki's charges, affirming that "absolute security of the population and all possibilities even the most improbable have been envisaged by responsible authorities."[16] Teariki expressed no confidence in the governor's remarks and later urged his colleagues in the Territorial Assembly Permanent Commission to pass a resolution to that effect.[17]

The issue of adequate protection from radiation was raised again during the 1963 session of the Assembly. Anti-CEP forces submitted a proposal requesting that a special team, consisting of competent individuals in the field of radiology from the United States, France, Japan, and New Zealand, serve as observers with the *Service Central de Protection contre les Rayonnements Ionisants* (SCPRI), the CEP agency responsible for the monitoring of radioactivity in the territory. The resolution was ignored by Paris on the basis that the CEP was part of a national defense project and that international scrutiny of its operations would be completely unacceptable.

Local politicians also debated the possible sociological effects that would result from the influx of military personnel into the territory. Anti-CEP partisans criticized the assignment of the two Foreign Legion companies to Tahiti, indicating that some friction would likely result.[18] Governor Grimald cautioned the Assembly that the issue of the Foreign Legion, like that of the CEP, was the prerogative of the metropolitan government and therefore was not a fit subject for discussion in the local Assembly.[19]

One major unforeseen effect of the CEP was the rapid immigration of rural populace into Papeete and environs, seeking employment suddenly created by the labor demand for CEP projects. Several *quartiers* of the Papeete urban zone became overcrowded with immigrants, some living in quite deplorable conditions.[20] Moreover, the most serious effect of such a situation was the marked depopulation of certain rural areas, especially in the Tuamotus, and the subsequent effect on local agriculture.[21]

The presence of civilian and military personnel in Tahiti (estimated between 15,000 and 16,000), argued pro-CEP factions, would prove economically beneficial to the resident population and to the territorial economy. Independent party assemblyman Frantz Vanizette was the most active proponent of this point of view: "I estimate that the installation of the military [in the islands] should bring all the advantages of practical investments . . . if we know how to manage it."[22] Gaullist assemblyman Gérald Coppenrath echoed Vanizette's sentiments in commenting on the construction of a new airstrip on Hao atoll: ". . . there may be a day when the CEP will have no reason to remain . . . there could be . . . an international airport which would be an extraordinary advantage for tourism."[23]

The economic advantages of the CEP were undeniable and perhaps greater than anyone had originally anticipated.[24] Interisland airstrips, a new hospital at Mamao, and massive subsidies to the territorial budget were among the newly gained advantages attributed directly or indirectly to the CEP—obvious facts that the anti-CEP partisans could not deny. The intensity of their political arguments, however, did not diminish. Teariki conducted a virulent anti-CEP campaign through his party organ *Te Here Ai'a*. The campaign emphasized radioactive pollution and contended that the new facilities, especially the Fa'a'a airport and interisland airstrips, had military priorities and that civilian use was only incidental.[25]

During de Gaulle's visit to the territory in 1967, Teariki, then French Polynesia's deputy, obtained a private audience with the French president at which the Tahitian nationalist articulated his views about the CEP.

Looking at it over the passage of time, it seems clear that this policy has been conceived and followed with the principal objective of insuring that your government has the free use of our territory for its nuclear tests. . . . The creation of this thing and its presence here among us without the Polynesians having first been consulted in any way, although their health and that of their descendants was at stake, constitute a serious violation of the contract which binds us to France. . . . Your propaganda strives to deny evidence, by pretending your nuclear and thermonuclear explosions carry no danger to us.[26]

There was no question that the autonomist faction wished that the CEP issue be submitted for a public referendum in the territory. It was, however, made clear from both the *métropole* and the governor's mansion that national defense projects were outside the purview of territorial politics, much less a public referendum.[27] The *métropole* made every effort to publicize the amount of funds available for public works and social programs. Cabinet official Michel Inchauspé emphasized this point during his 1968 visit to Tahiti:

Some wish to believe that France does not take interest in Polynesia because of the CEP. However, how do they explain the considerable investment in the area, particularly in the area of education. . . . Polynesia is a part of France with all the rights and assurance that such a relationship is entitled to.[28]

Political skeptics, nonetheless, remained unconvinced at the pronouncements made by metropolitan officials. The issue was again debated in 1972, when a research mission was sent to the Marquesas Islands by the French geological research unit, the *Bureau de Recherches Géologiques et Minières* (BRGM). This induced speculation that the CEP was planning to establish an underground test site at Eiao island.[29] French government officials were subjected to intense questioning by the members of the Permanent Commission on the matter. Since the territorial *Service des Travaux Publics* was not included in the mission, the Permanent Commission was convinced that the CEP was attempting to determine whether Eiao was feasible as an underground site. Secretary-General Jean Tissier explained to the Permanent Commission that such research projects were état prerogatives and that he was not in a position to discuss any questions *vis-à-vis* the BRGM mission.[30]

Teariki proposed another anti-CEP resolution during the mid-1972 session of the Permanent Commission. He was encouraged by the outcome of the Stockholm Conference on Environment at which atmospheric testing of nuclear weapons was condemned. Teariki's resolution demanded that the Territorial Assembly obtain "the definitive cessation of nuclear arm experiments in French Polynesia."[31] Teariki's proposal was thus the boldest protest against the CEP since its inception. The Tahitian assemblyman spoke forcefully at great length, citing the numerous reasons for the cessation of the tests, and not hesitating to point out that several Pacific and South American states had likewise demanded similar action. In spite of the opposition voiced by CEP sympathizers, Teariki's resolution was passed.[32]

As an important sequel to this resurgence of protest, Deputy Francis Sanford, rising to the forefront of protest, went to the United Nations, in July 1972, to protest the tests; while there he requested that the United Nations send an investigation team to Mangareva and Tureia to inquire about the living conditions of the Polynesian inhabitants residing there. Sanford asserted that the islanders were being adversely affected by the excessive use of potable water by the CEP installations.[33] Senator Pouvana a Oopa, himself a long-time adversary of the French government, likewise participated in the protest by sending a telegram to UN Secretary-General Kurt Waldheim stating that:

> In the name of the inhabitants of French Polynesia I request that you accept and transmit our warmest thanks to all the governments who voted on the resolution in Stockholm, requesting the ultimate cessation of nuclear bomb experiments in Polynesia and the entire world.[34]

The surge of protest gained significant momentum in 1973. French Deputy Jean Jacques Servan-Schreiber, France's most active opponent of the bomb, arrived in Tahiti with six members of the so-called "Battalion of Peace" with the intention of conducting demonstrations against the CEP. Subsequently, a mass demonstration was organized, with the help of local anti-CEP partisans, the size and cope of which Tahiti had not seen in years.

> It was a typically Tahitian crowd with pareus, guitars and children, who surrounded the immense square of the city hall to listen to their mayor Mr. Tetua Pambrun, their senator, their deputy and six members of the "battalion of peace" for two hours under the hot sun . . . on the tabu subject . . . the bomb.[35]

Deputy Servan-Schreiber, as well as other members of the "Battalion of Peace," wrote a series of articles for the local press, explaining their objectives and purposes. In one article, directed exclusively at the local populace, Servan-Schreiber said:

> Your problems and that of nuclear armament are joint problems. I have already received criticism . . . asking me what will follow if the CEP is removed? Nuclear armament is not even an integral part of French Polynesia. You know that the bomb will not be here forever . . . and French Polynesia has many other means of development without adhering to nuclear armament.[36]

The French deputy was severely criticized by the new Gaullist-Independent coalition majority in the Territorial Assembly.[37]

> Mr. Servan-Schreiber . . . searches for ways of provoking . . . disturbance and anxiety as well as attempting to upset the political equilibrium in favor of the autonomists. . . . We will see to it that the territory will overcome the grave economic and social recession that will fol-

low the departure of the CEP. . . . We deny Mr. Servan-Schreiber
the right to speak on the economic and political future of the territory. We ourselves can assume our own responsibility without
resorting to the miracle remedies of a bourgeois reactionary who
. . . makes a stage for his pretentious demonstration.[38]

Though the activities of the "Batalion of Peace" failed to effect any changes
in French nuclear policy, it at least managed to give France "its most well-
organized, precise demonstration of the French nation's feelings about its own
bomb."[39] Anti-CEP figures, like Pouvanaa, seized the opportunity to chastise the
CEP sympathizers in his classical form of Polynesian rhetoric:

We regret that certain of our compatriots unknowing of the danger
or seduced by the CEP money, still follow the evil shepherds who
sacrifice our public health and betray our Christian faith in the
service of a satanic enterprise. . . . To defend the CEP is to sell
Polynesia and the health of our children to the merchants of death.[40]

Totally frustrated by the adamant attitude of the *Métropole* against changing its
policy, Sanford and Pouvanaa announced that they intended to demand a public referendum for independence. The referendum petition said in part:

We are driven into a situation where we can do nothing but to submit
a choice to the French government. . . . The choice is the bomb or
Tahiti. The government prefers the bomb. From this day forward,
we will work for independence.[41]

It is indeed difficult to estimate the chances of success for independence
even at the height of anti-CEP sentiment, for at least one reality has remained
in French Polynesian politics and that is the careful distinction between being
anti-CEP and anti-French. There is no doubt that the employment of local
residents by the CEP and the various economic advantages attributed to it are at
the crux of the problem. It is also true that the associated agencies working in
conjunction with the CEP, such as the oceanographic research unit *Centre
National d'Exploitation des Océans* (CNEXO), have contributed much to the
territory's economic development. It has been difficult for anti-CEP partisans
to separate the desirable benefits of the nuclear testing program from its more
objectionable aspects. It appears, however, that defense priorities have made
the continuation of the CEP experiments a national goal beyond the possibility of arbitration or compromise. The ultimate question remaining for those
still opposed to the test series is whether it is possible to pursue an anti-CEP
campaign while maintaining amicable relations with the *métropole.*
    Debate in French Polynesia over the CEP issue has been a ten-year record
of divided and increasingly complicated political debate. Outrage against the
tests initially was quite vocal, primarily because of the uncertainty over radio-

logical pollution. Opposition to the tests began to abate and fluctuate when the economic advantages became more apparent.[42] This is not to say that public opinion in Tahiti changed to any great extent, but rather that it became less alarmist in nature. It is today quite evident that there still exists strong sentiment against the CEP by many island residents. This segment of opinion, however, has been frustrated by a feeling of futility and resignation. It would be quite correct to say that almost everyone in French Polynesia, though some considerably more than others, has benefited directly or indirectly from the economic by-products of the CEP. Conversely, however, it would also be true to say that others have preferred to see the other side of the issue while others have remained blind. Vanizette admitted the existence of a dichotomous controversy in one particular statement:

> I have never denied the disadvantages of the CEP installations in the territory, but I have always said that it is the advantages which seem to me to be superior and that these advantages will become more important if we regulate . . . the situation and the problems posed by the installations.[43]

For others like Teariki, Pouvana, and Sanford, the CEP is another example of a long and tedious list of instances where national policy was made at the expense of territorial interests. The CEP is a major issue which in part has given political impetus to the rise of resistance movements in French Polynesia since 1963. Though political activists have attempted to make the CEP issue a separate dispute, capable of being settled through public referendum, the intransigient policies of the *métropole* have made this prospect illusory. Political conservatives in French Polynesia have chosen to accept the CEP (as well as its generous economic remittances) as a political price to be paid for maintaining ties with France and have succeeded in convincing many voters into thinking likewise. On the other hand, anti-CEP activists have deemed such a relationship with France to be morally and politically intolerable. They, however, have not been able to "crystallize public sentiment into any kind of overwhelming popular tide against the CEP."[44] At present, the sociological drift toward urbanism and proletarianism is decidedly in favor of maintaining the status quo.[45] Though CEP critics have constantly stressed the possible *future* effects of the tests in their arguments, many island residents have decided upon accepting present *economic* realities.

Protest from the Pacific community against the French tests was slow in achieving note-worthy proportions, but Australia and New Zealand, morally reinforced by the signing of the Partial Test Ban Treaty by the United States, the Soviet Union, and the United Kingdom, began issuing a series of formal protests against the tests because of the "potential danger to health" and the hindrance to the "attainment of an effectual international agreement to stop testing."[46] However, these protests lacked a great deal of credibility at that time. Australia had allowed the use of portions of its territory for British atomic tests between 1952 and 1957. Similarly, New Zealand manifested negligible concern over the British tests at Christmas Island, a site not very distant from the New Zealand-administered Tokelau archipelago. In addition, both Australia and New Zealand evidenced little concern over the Soviet tests that were conducted during that particular period.

France was quick to indicate these facts in rebuttal.[47] France also noted that New Zealand had stated during the July 1954 session of the UN Trusteeship Council that the American tests in Micronesia were "compatible with the maintenance of peace and international security."[48]

After the 1966 commencement of the French tests, New Zealand policy began to take a more active course.

> The New Zealand Government's objection to the continuation of the
> French testing programme as it is to the development of nuclear weapons
> by Communist China . . . is that it flies in the face of the clear interna-
> tional trend in the last few years towards limiting the spread of weapons
> of mass destruction.[49]

Aside from the international implications connected with the French tests, New Zealand was also concerned with the possible hazards posed by radioactive fallout on its Pacific island dependencies. In order to survey the level of radioactivity in the Pacific, New Zealand established monitoring stations in Fiji and the Cook Islands. Though scientific opinion in New Zealand concluded that the French tests would not present "a significant health hazard to the people of New Zealand or the Pacific Territories," the New Zealand administration continued its opposition to the possible polluting effects of the tests.[50]

On the subject of radioactive pollution, the French *Livre Blanc* asserted that the French monitoring system employed a method of "rigorous surveillance of radioactivity" by stations located in Reunion, Guyana, Bolivia, Chili, Columbia, Ecuador, and Peru.[51] Furthermore, the *Livre Blanc* stated that the results gathered from the monitoring stations were forwarded to the United Nations' Scientific Committee for the study of the Effects of Radioactivity. A June 1972 report from the South American stations verified that "radioactive contamination was not significant."[52] Not all scientific opinion, however, reached the same conclusions. Dr. Gordon Baines, a biologist at the University of the South Pacific in Fiji, claimed that the amount of strontium 90 in the South Pacific region had increased five-fold since 1966.[53]

The tide of protest did not abate but continued to spread. During the September 1970 Tenth South Pacific Conference of the South Pacific Commission, an unprecedented move was made when chairman S. M. Koya of Fiji allowed debate to proceed on the nuclear test issue. Disagreement arose between the two French Polynesian delegates, Henri Nettre and Romuald Allain, the latter a member of the autonomist *Te E'a Api* party. The debate became so incensed that Nettre boycotted the proceedings. Allain later stated that if some change in French nuclear policy was not forth coming, an appeal to the United Nations would be contemplated.[54] The conference issued a statement expressing

... their concern at the potential hazards that the atmospheric tests
pose to health and safety and to marine life, which is a vital element
in the island's subsistence economy, and addressed an urgent appeal
to the government of France that the current test series should be
the last in the Pacific area.[55]

A similar regional organization, the South Pacific Forum, also issued a strongly
worded resolution making known its "determination to use all practical means to
stop the bomb tests."[56] During mid-1973, the forces of protest gained significant momentum. Boycotts against French goods, mail transportation, and tele-
communications were instituted in Australia and New Zealand by the Australian
Council of Trade Unions, the Union of Postal Clerks and Telegraphists, the New
Zealand members of the International Confederation of Free Trade Unions, and
the New Zealand Federation of Labor.[57] The Fiji Trades Union Congress also
joined the boycott against French-owned UTA airlines.[58] A counter-boycott
against the Australian and New Zealand airlines, Qantas and Air New Zealand, was organized by the French Polynesian labor organization, *Federation des Syndicats de la
Polynésie Francaise.* Federation leader Charles Taufa, also a Government Councilman, accused the Australians and New Zealanders of attempting to deny French
Polynesia its rightful "place in the sun" and wishing to monopolize the South
Pacific region.[59]

In June, Prime Minister Norman Kirk of New Zealand ordered the frigate *Otago*
into the French designated "danger zone." "What we aim to do is to publicize
what is happening in this remote part of the world, so as to stimulate world
opinion still further and attract wider support for the rights of smaller
nations."[60] Private protest vessels sailed into the restricted zones, and in two
cases, the crew members of two such vessels became involved in a confrontation
with the French military. The members of the protest yacht *Fri* were escor-
ted to Papeete, whereupon several of them staged a much publicized hunger
strike.[61] Canadian Daniel McTaggart of the *Greenpeace III* also received publicity when he claimed that he was forceably seized by the French military while in
international waters, beaten and taken to Papeete, and deported after a short
stay in a military hospital there.[62] Though disapproving of the presence of the
activist vessels in the area, New Zealand issued protest notes to France upholding
the right of the vessels to enjoy the freedom of the high seas and denying the
right of France to "suspend international navigation . . . for the purpose of testing
nuclear weapons."[63]

The culmination of embarrassment for France came in May 1973, when
Australia, New Zealand, and Fiji filed legal briefs with the International Court
of Justice contesting the legality and morality of the tests.[64] New Zealand insisted that diplomatic appeals made to France during the previous year had proved
to be fruitless. In its brief, New Zealand stated that:

... it has a special concern with the nuclear testing ... which represents a potential hazard to life, health and security of the people of New Zealand. . . .

The French Government also made it plain that it did not accept the contention that its programme of nuclear testing . . . involved a violation of international law. There is, accordingly, a dispute between the Government of New Zealand and the French Government as to the legality of atmospheric tests in the South Pacific region.

Having failed to resolve through diplomatic means the dispute that exists between it and the French Government, the New Zealand Government will seek a declaration that the conduct . . . of the nuclear tests in the South Pacific constitutes a violation of New Zealand's rights under international law and that these rights will be violated by any further such tests.[65]

In ruling on the Australian case in September, the International Court of Justice rendered the opinion that ". . . the French Government should avoid nuclear tests caused the deposit of radio-active fall-out on Australian territory."[66] The French government responded to the decision and ". . . informed the Court, as it had notified the two Governments concerned, it considered the Court was manifestly non-competent in the case and that it could not accept its jurisdiction."[67] French Foreign Minister Michel Jobert, in an October meeting of the UN General Assembly, assailed the various actions of protests as "slanderous campaigns" and reiterated the two-decade-old *raison d'être* of French nuclear policy:

The past and geography have taught us lessons that we are not likely to forget. We are like a too-often-stalked prey that the hunter can no longer approach. Illusions, then wars, more illusions and again war, such has been our fate. Henceforth, we count foremost on ourselves in our own efforts. . . . France provided herself with nuclear armament, not in order to indulge in dreams of vain greatness, but because her very existence was at stake. Alone, we covered the ground of difficult research, with a considerable time lag. And today some are indignant that we dare tread this path, presumably the royal way reserved to those in power today.[68]

The final outlook and conclusions concerning the ramifications of the French test series are almost as ambiguous as the events during the formative years of the issue. What is certain, however, is that the issue is another example of the long continuum of events wherein decisions of vital concern to the inhabitants of the South Pacific were made in the context of international considerations, without specific reference to the wishes of the local communities and states of that region. French determination to procure a respectable nuclear strike force was effectively sustained by a well-motivated group of military, scientific, and political figures. Neither metropolitan pacifists, territorial autonomists, nor even the Pacific community could effectively reverse one of France's most important defense projects.

Such decisions, however, are not without important residual effects. Metropolitan protest was apt to be occasional. The French public, though increasingly aware of the effects of radioactive pollution, was ignorant of ". . recent events in the Pacific and . . . the . . . wide concerns of nuclear explosions at Mururoa."[69] The diplomacy of Australia and New Zealand was equally futile, as was protest emanating from French Polynesia. The ineffectiveness of seemingly kindred action was due in a large part to the lack of concert and coordination of all those concerned and their failure to stir the consciousness of the international community, particularly that of the United States, Great Britain, and the Soviet Union.[70]

The most far-reaching effects of the tests are those directly affecting French Polynesia. Divisive political opinion over the CEP evidences the already fragmentary nature of French Polynesian society itself. It is not conceivable that the CEP could cause any serious hemorrhaging of the socio-economic status quo of the French Overseas Territory; however, the hope for long-term solutions for progressive agricultural development and demographic stabilization would have to be postponed for the immediate future. It is evident that new fields of economic and scientific development such as tourism and marine resources exploitation have owed much to the existence of the CEP. It is questionable, however, if such developments can solve the long-term problems of French Polynesia and close the widening socio-economic gap within the local society.[71] The modern phenomenon of rising expectations has not escaped the sun-drenched islands of Polynesia. It would be simple to overemphasize this aspect for past experience has shown that the Tahitians (as well as their other Polynesian neighbors) have weathered a great deal of political and social trauma. In some cases, justifiable solutions have resulted regarding internal problems provided that the distance between problem and solution did not reach irreconcilable proportions. The remaining question is whether the socio-economic gap created by the CEP has reached an irreversible dimension. The remaining decades of the twentieth century will quite likely provide the much anticipated answers.

NOTES

1. F. Ridley and J. Blondel, *Public Administration in France* (New York, 1969), pp. 78-79.

2. Christian de la Malène and Constantin Melnik, "Attitudes of the French Parliament towards Nuclear Weapons" (Rand Corporation, RM2170-RC, Santa Monica, California), May 14, 1958, pp. 32-33.

3. Jean Lacoutre, *Citations du President de Gaulle* (Paris 1968), pp. 128-29.

4. Wolf Mendel, *Deterrence and Persuasion; French Nuclear Armament in the Context of National Policy 1945-1969* (New York, 1970), p. 103.

5. Wilfred Kohl, *French Nuclear Diplomacy* (Princeton, 1971), p. 141.

6. Ibid.

7. Lawrence Scheinman, *Atomic Energy Policy in France Under the Fourth Republic* (Princeton, 1965), p. 215.

8. Kohl, op. cit., pp. 103-104.

9. "Algerian independence did not hinder the continuity of the tests. But it was evident that they could not continue on foreign soil. The Pacific was the only disposable area." *Le Monde,* 14 Juin, 1972, p. 1.

10. *Livre Blanc sur les Expériances Nucléaires* (Paris, 1973), p. 5.

11. The *Centre d'Experimention du Pacifique* (CEP) was established by the *Conseil de Défence* on July 27, 1962, as a major agency responsible for the supervision of the nuclear test series in the Pacific. Construction of the CEP installations began in the following year.

12. Faithful Gaullists like Eli "Nedo" Salmon and Gerald Coppenrath obviously were torn between their affiliation with Paris and their concern for the welfare of the territory. Their ambivalent attitudes changed when they were compelled to defend metropolitan policies against the attacks made by opposition parties.

13. *Assemblée Territoriale de la Polynésie Française, 1ère Session Extra-ordinaire Budgetaire 1962/1963,* 1ère séance, Decembre 1962, p. 112. The leading opposition party at this time was the *Rassemblement Démocratique de Populations Tahitiennes* (RDPT) of which Jean B. H. Céran-Jérusalémy and John Teariki were the most vocal members. Céran-Jérusalémy later formed his own splinter party, *Te Pupu Tiama Ma'ohi.* After both parties were dissolved by presidential order in 1963, Teariki formed his own party, *Te Pupu Here Ai'a Te Nuna'a ia Ora,* for the purpose of joining the internal autonomy effort by Francis Sanford and his party, *Te E'a Api no Polynesia.* Both Teariki and Sanford spearheaded the anti-CEP campaign.

14. Ibid., p. 115.

15. *Assemblée Territoriale de la Polynésie Francaise, Session Administrative de 1963,* 23 Avril-4 Juillet, 1963, p. 73. Resident correspondent James Boyack accurately described the Tahitian attitude towards radioactive pollution. "The Polynesians instinctively know of the test dangers; they connect the widespread fish poisoning with the blasts. The fact is, however, they, like most of us, can't say for sure what the real dangers are." *Pacific Islands Monthly,* August 1973, p. 9.

16. *Assemblée Territoriale de la Polynésie Française, Session Administrative de 1966,* 7ème séance, 25 Mai, 1966, p. 206.

17. Ibid., 8ème séance, 31 Mai, 1966, p. 54. The Territorial Assembly's interim administrative body, the Permanent Commission, ceded the Mururoa and Fangataufa atolls to the CEP after a prolonged debate. See *Assemblée Territoriale de la Polynésie Française, Commission Permanente, Session Ordinaire de Février 1964,* 1ère séance, 6 Février, 1964, pp. 22-26.

18. *Assemblée Territoriale de la Polynésie Française, Administrative Extra-ordinaire de 1963,* 2ème séance, 27 Juin, 1963, p. 718.

19. Ibid., p. 668.

20. *Assemblée Territoriale de la Polynésie Française, Session Budgetaire,* 12 Décembre, 1967 pp. 722-23. For more detailed information on the socio-demographic change resulting from the influences of the CEP, see G. Ringon, "Les Changements d'une Commune de Tahiti entre 1960 et 1970; Faaa," *Cahiers ORSTOM* 9, no. 1 (1972), p. 1; J. Fages, F. Ravault, G. Ringon, C. Robineau, "Tahiti et Moorea, Etudes sur le Société, l'Economie, et l'Utilization de l'Espace," *Travaux et Documents de ORSTOM,* No. 4 (Paris, 1970), p. 3; B. M. Grossat, "L'Emploi en Polynésie Française," *Journal de la Société des Océanistes* 29, Septembre 1973, 241-61.

21. A report compiled for the Territorial Assembly expressed such a concern for the economic situation of the farmer who ". . . could in no way resist the demand for labor generated by the CEP. . . if he should desire to earn more liquid capital quickly." The report also cited a situation at Ana'a atoll in the Tuamotus where thirty-six laborers were recruited for work on Mururoa whereas only six could be persuaded to remain on Ana'a to work on the copra crop. *Assemblée Territoriale de la Polynésie Française, Session Budgetaire de 1963,* 3ème séance, 31 October, 1963, p. 3.

22. *Assemblée Territoriale de la Polynésie Française, Commission Permanente, Session Ordinaire,* Févroer 1964, p. 33.

23. *Assemblée Territoriale de la Polynésie Française, Commission Permanante,* 22 Avril, 1965, p. 34.

24. The CEP employed approximately 5,508 residents in 1973. In addition, the *Fonds d'Investissment pour le Development Economique et Sociale* (FIDES), the metropolitan subsidies for public works and programs, increased from 115.8 million CFP in 1966 to 363.5 million CFP in 1970. *Les Nouvelles,* 31 Juillet, 1973, p. 1. *Bulletin de Statistiques* (Secretaire Général Adjoint, Bureau d'Etudes de Statistiques, Service du Plan, Polynésie Française, 1970), p. 5.

25. *Te Here Ai'a,* 8-15 Avril 1969, pp. 2-9.

26. "French Polynesia and the French Nuclear Tests: The Submission of John Teariki," *The Journal of Pacific History,* II (1967), 153-54.

27. *Assemblée Territoriale de la Polynésie Française,* (Session Administrative de 1963), 23 Avril-4 Juillet, 1963, p. 211.

28. *Les Nouvelles,* 18 Septembre, 1968, p. 4.

29. *Assemblée Territoriale de la Polynésie Française, Commission Permanante, Session du Mois d'Août,* lère séance, 22 Juin, 1972, p. 1357.

30. *Ibid.,* p. 1719. Owing to subsoil weakness, Eiao was found to be unsuitable as a test site. *La Dépêche de Tahiti,* 4 Juillet, 1973, p. 1.

31. *Assemblée Territoriale de la Polynésie Française, Commission Permanante,* 3ème séance, 22 Juin, 1972, p. 1357.

32. Ibid., p. 1381. By the virtue of their assembly majority, the autonomist parties were able to raise the CEP issue at opportune intervals.

33. *Le Journal de Tahiti,* 29 Juin, 1972, p. 3. Sanford's mission met with only nominal success, but he did manage to attract some attention to the CEP operations.

34. Ibid., p. 4. Pouvana, the one-time head of the defunct RDPT, returned to Tahiti after an eight-year term in exile in France in 1968. He was subsequently elected *senateur* in 1971. Pouvana is considered to be the most vocal anti-French political figure in postwar territorial history.

35. *L'Express,* 2-8 Juillet, 1973, p. 14. The periodical reporter estimated the crowd to be approximately 5,000 in number. Ironically, only a year earlier reporter James Boyack prematurely remarked that: "There has been less furor over the tests in Tahiti than anywhere else in the Pacific. The autonomist Territorial Assembly majority remains opposed in principle to nuclear activity but public manifestations of its stance have been lethargic and infrequent. There are no slogans on the walls, and, since the first blasts six years ago, no one has taken to the streets with placards of displeasure. Frankly, I don't think the Tahitians give much of a damn about them." *Pacific Islands Monthly,* July, 1973, p. 6.

36. *Le Journal de Tahiti,* 22 Juin, 1973, p. 6. Sanford had allied himself with

the *Mouvement Reformateur* of Servan-Schreiber and French Senate President Allain Poher during the March 1973 National Assembly elections in which Sanford was narrowly re-elected. For a detailed account of the elections see William Tagupa, "The 1973 National Assembly Elections in French Polynesia," *Pacific Viewpoint*, November 1973, pp. 189-92.

37. The autonomist majority in the Territorial Assembly was upset in the 1972 elections by a coalition of local Gaullists and independents.

38. *Le Journal de Tahiti*, 28 Juin, 1973, p. 5. Only one month previously, Gaullist Territorial Assembly President Gaston Flosse, while in Paris, requested that metropolitan officials ". . . maintain the CEP in the territory as long as possible. . . . This center is one of the most important elements of our economy due to the employment of local labor, rural commerce and to the expenditures by its personnel." *La Dépêche de Tahiti*, 16 Mai, 1973, p. 1.

39. *Pacific Islands Monthly*, July 1973, p. 14.

40. *Le Journal de Tahiti*, 22 Juin, 1973, p. 6. Sanford extended this demand for independence to include the other French Pacific dependencies, New Caledonia and the New Hebrides, in a proposed resolution at the World Conference against Atomic Bombs. *Les Nouvelles*, 12 Aout 1974, p. 12.

41. *Le Journal de Tahiti*, 3 Août, 1973, p. 4.

42. A case in point which illustrates this fact is the defection of Céran-Jérusalémy to pro-CEP factions. He figured prominently in the formation of the pro-CEP party *Union Polynésienne*, which affirmed that the army and the CEP were "absolutely indispensible" to the economy of the islands. *Le Journal de Tahiti*, 29 Juin, 1972, p. 5.

43. *Assemblée Territoriale de la Polynésie Francaise, Session Budgetaire 1963-1964*, 27 Janvier 1964, pp. 1150-51.

44. *Pacific Islands Monthly*, August 1973, p. 8.

45. Daniel Guérin, "Tahiti Maladie de la Bombe," *Les Temps Moderne*, Novembre 1972, No. 316, pp. 787-91.

46. *New Zealand External Affairs Review*, May 1963, p. 23.

47. *Livre Blanc* . . . , pp. 8-23.

48. Ibid., p. 14.

49. *New Zealand External Affairs Review*, August 1968, p. 48.

50. Nigel Roberts, *New Zealand and Nuclear Testing in the Pacific* (Wellington, 1972), p. 18.

51. *Livre Blanc* . . ., pp. 6-7.

52. Ibid.

53. *Pacific Islands Monthly*, July 1970, p. 33.

54. *Fiji Times*, September 24 and 25, 1970, p. 1.

55. *New Zealand Foreign Affairs Review*, August 1971, p. 7.

56. *New Zealand Herald*, April 19, 1973, p. 1.

57. Ibid., April 30, May 14 and 25, 1973, p. 1; *Sydney Morning Herald*, May 1 and 5, 1973, p. 1.

58. *Sydney Morning Herald*, May 5, 1973, p. 8.

59. *La Dépêche de Tahiti*, 26 Juillet, 1973, p. 1.

60. *New Zealand Foreign Affairs Review*, July 1973, p. 19; June, 1973, p. 82.

61. *New Zealand Herald*, August 20 and 30, 1973, p. 1; *Pacific Islands Monthly*, September 1973, pp. 6-7; *La Dépêche de Tahiti*, 13, 14 and 17 Août 1973, p. 1.

62. *New Zealand Herald*, August 30, 1973, p. 1.

63. *New Zealand Foreign Affairs Review,* October 1973, p. 22.

64. The Australian brief chose to emphasize the potential effects of radioactive pollution on its citizens, affirming that ". . .radiation from the French tests already carried out could cause cancer and deformation in future generations of Australians." New Zealand, on the other hand, preferred to ". . .dwell on world condemnation of atmospheric tests. . ." in its brief. *New Zealand Herald,* May 22 and 25, 1973, p. 1.

65. *New Zealand Foreign Affairs Review,* May 1973, p. 10.

66. *UN Monthly Chronicle,* August-September, 1974, p. 86.

67. Ibid., June 1973, p. 55. For a legal appraisal of the case see L.F.E. Goldie, "The Nuclear Tests Cases: Restraints on Environmental Harm," *Journal of Maritime Law and Commerce* (April 1974), pp. 495-505.

68. "Address by His Excellency Michel Jobert, French Minister of Foreign Affairs, before the 28th Session of the United Nations General Assembly on October 10, 1973" (Ambassade de France, Service de Presse et d'Information, New York), pp. 3-4.

69. Australia and New Zealand even failed to gain the support of the United Kingdom in the matter. *New Zealand Herald,* April 6, 1973, p. 1.

70. Colin Dyer, "French Attitudes to Nuclear Experiments in the South Pacific 1971-1973," *Australian Outlook* (February 1973), p. 172.

71. Jacques Derogy, "La France vue de Tahiti," *L'Express,* 16-22 Juillet, 1973, p. 15. Daniel Guerin, op. cit., pp. 791-2.

14

Tropical Torpor: The United States in the South Pacific Commission

In a burst of unrestrained internationalism following the Second World War, the United States committed itself to participation in a large number of multinational organizations. Not all these organizations have survived and many have not achieved much prominence, but perhaps of all these bodies still in existence today none is less well known in the United States than the South Pacific Commission (SPC). Despite being the only regional instrument for the expression of American policy in the Pacific and despite its own more than respectable image among the local leadership, the SPC enjoys a remarkably low salience in Washington. This paper will briefly outline the major characteristics of American membership in the SPC. It will also argue that this style of participation has limited the capacity of the United States to play a creative role in the regional body.

ORIGINS AND STRUCTURE

Initially advanced by Australia and New Zealand early in 1944, the idea of a regional organization covering the South Pacific islands was revived after World War II, and it found ready acceptance among the other four metropolitan powers— the United States, the Netherlands, Great Britain, and France—invited to attend a South Seas Conference in Canberra in January 1947. Within eight days of the Conference's opening, the basic charter of the new organization was drafted and signed. The celerity with which the entire operation was completed is attributable in part to the excellent preparatory work carried out by Australia and New Zealand and in part to the fact that the two host countries had modeled their proposals along the lines of the Caribbean Commission, a body already established by the other four participating states.

There was one significant departure from the original 1944 Australasian proposals in the charter (known officially as the Canberra Agreement Establishing the South Pacific Commission), and that was a deliberate eschewal of any reference to political development. France, in particular, was reluctant to have such a goal as a tenet of the organization.[1] As an alternative, the United States suggested that the protection of "human rights" could be placed within the ambit of SPC concerns, but this was rebuffed on the grounds that such a provision would permit the discussion of some political matters; in the end agreement was reached on accepting the more specific phrase "social and economic rights."[2]

The Pacific organization created at the South Seas Conference was designed to perform an advisory and consultative role by providing a reservoir of expertise on South Pacific problems. Its function was not to supplant the efforts of the territorial administrations but quite the contrary. It was to support, complement, and supplement their efforts through research and by facilitating the rapid exchange of information on common problems across the Pacific. In short, it was to be a "clearing house for ideas" rather than an active agent for the execution of common policies among the metropolitan powers and their territories.

The SPC's role as merely a catalyst for development in the South Pacific has not changed since its inception. Unimaginative direction from the metropoles and a limited budget, even today only slightly under $2 million (Australian), militated against more grandiose aspirations. Nonetheless, the organization has served a useful function in the South Pacific's regional development. In the early years, the SPC was unsure of itself, and of the needs of the islands, and therefore tended to favor basic research. A Review Conference in 1957, however, resolved that the resources of the SPC ought to be directed much more towards a practical, problem-solving work program. Since the late 1950s, the SPC has provided a wide variety of training courses, professional seminars, pilot projects, and the like to satisfy expressed needs in the islands. In addition, it has served as a common room for itinerant specialists who visit the islands on scheduled rounds or by request. These activities have been particularly important to the smaller territories, as they rarely require, and even more rarely can afford, permanent, full-time expert advice in such areas as breadfruit pathology, mental health, and sanitation.

Formally, the SPC is composed of four distinct elements: the South Pacific Commission; a permanent Secretariat; and two auxiliary agencies, the South Pacific Conference and the Research Council. This original framework has not been maintained however, and at the present time one would have to say that the Conference is coequal with the Commission proper.[3] These two elements along with the Secretariat now make up the functional parts of the current organization. Although it is somewhat confusing, the term "South Pacific Commission" is commonly used both to refer to the body of Commissioners within the organization as well as to the entire organization.

The Commission proper consists of not more than two Commissioners or their alternates from each of the eight member governments participating in the SPC. Where a member state is represented by two Commissioners (the usual number), one of its Commissioners is designated the Senior Commissioner and it is this representative who casts the delegation's vote. Meetings of the Commission were held biannually until 1953; since then annual meetings have been the rule.

Initially, the six member countries in the Commission were metropolitan powers with dependencies in the South Pacific region. In 1962, the Netherlands was forced to give up Western New Guniea, and the Dutch, therefore, were obliged by the wording of the Canberra Agreement to retire from the Commission. For a time it was thought that Indonesia might want to assume the vacated seat, but Indonesia, although interested, refused to view West Irian as a dependency. After the Netherlands' departure from the organization, three local states—Western Samoa in 1964, Nauru in 1969, and Fiji in 1971—entered the erstwhile exclusively metropolitan club. This fundamental change was made possible by a formal redefinition of the basis for membership so that any former area dependency could join on becoming independent.[4]

Internally, the Commission is regulated by two sets of formulas. One establishes the budgetary contribution imposed on each member government. At present, the United States pays 20 percent of the budget assessed participating governments (which is not to be confused with the total budget, since there are voluntary contributions from the territories and member governments, income from the sale of books, and similar additional inflows of money that go into making up the total budget of the SPC). Australia contributes the most at 31 percent, while both the United Kingdom and New Zealand pay 16 percent, France 14 percent, and each of the three local states is assessed 1 percent. The second formula weights the voting strength of each member government. The United States, New Zealand, and France each are entitled to four votes; Australia and the United Kingdom have three votes; Western Samoa, Nauru, and Fiji cast a single vote each.[5]

In addition to a Secretary-General, the SPC's Secretariat is composed of three Program Directors (one each for the fields of Health, Economic Development, and Social Development) and a modest-size staff of professional, administrative, and service personnel. Most of the staff are headquartered in Nouméa. There is also a small SPC Publications Bureau in Sydney, which is responsible for preparing and disseminating the organization's publications. The Secretariat's staff is internationally recruited although the Secretary-General and the Program Directors are appointed by the Commission only from participating countries and territories.

It was expected originally that the Research Council, composed of eighteen nominated members (three from each member country) and six drawn from the Secretariat, would be the heart of the SPC, for the organization was, as noted above, envisaged not as a policy-executing body but as a clearinghouse for ideas. In fulfilling this purpose, the SPC's auxiliary body was "to maintain a continuous survey of the research needs in the territories, to make recommendations on research activities." And during the first decade, the Research Council's proposals generally did become the basis for the Commission's Work Program. After the 1957 Review Conference, however, it was decided that the SPC would wind down its exploratory research surveys and concentrate more on practical implementation of remedial work in the islands.[6] Thus the importance of the Research Council in the work of the SPC waned dramatically in subsequent years. Presently a small body of officials in the Secretariat, comprising the Program Research and Evaluation Council (the Secretary-General, the three Program Directors, the Administrative Officer, and the Finance Officer), carriers out most of the work previously performed by the Research Council. Although formally still in existence, the Research Council has not met since 1963.

Rising as spectacularly as the Research Council has fallen, the South Pacific Conference has made manifest the determination of the South Pacific peoples to assume responsibility for their own affairs. The Conference is composed of delegates from the thirteen island dependencies, four independent states, and one self-governing territory that fall within the ambit of the SPC.[7] Meetings of the Conference (which were held at triennial intervals until 1967, after which they became annual gatherings taking place immediately prior to Commission sessions) provide representatives from the islands with an opportunity to examine and discuss the work of the SPC and to offer recommendations on future programs. It was expected that these delegates, selected by each territory according to its own constitutional procedures, would represent local opinion rather than simply parroting the metropole's position. After an initial period of awkwardness, this expectation has been fully met; and, as this system has become more institutionalized, the Conference has waxed ever more influential in the direction of SPC policy.

Indeed, in recent years, the importance of the Conference has transcended even the SPC. It has been the premier annual political event in the South Pacific since 1967. Until the formation of the South Pacific Forum in August, 1971, the Conference represented the sole instrument for regional contact at the Governmental level; and even now it is the principal independent outlet for regional communication for the smaller territories. Island delegations to the Conference are commonly led by the head of government or leader of government business. Men of such importance do not attend the Conference merely to allocate the few dollars in the parsimonious budget; they come to discuss, on the floor and in the corridors, the larger concerns of their region. The South Pacific Conference has therefore evolved to become a significant element in the region's diplomatic network.

AMERICA IN NOUMÉA

The institutional configuration of American participation in the SPC centers on the two chief responsibilities that the United States has toward the organization. It must supply men and money: men to serve as delegates to express American opinions at SPC meetings and to fill the personnel requirements of the SPC Secretariat, and money to meet the budgeted expenses of the body's programs.

In the Commission proper, the United States is represented by two Commissioners who, along with any alternate Commissioners, serve as consultants to the Department of State. They are appointed by the President of the United States, but these offices do not require Senate confirmation. The Commissioners, as political appointees of the President, serve at his pleasure. In practice, however, terms are for two-year periods, which may be renewed. American Commissioners receive no salary. Their expenses are paid from a State Department fund for international conferences (which is in no way related to the American contribution to the SPC), but they do not receive any other compensation for their services.

Official American policy is set for the Commissioners before SPC meetings by the State Department in the form of guidance papers and/or direct communication from State Department advisers, who usually accompany the American delegation. The guidance papers outline the American position on the issues that are expected to be raised in the meetings. In the early years of the SPC, the State Department also supplied very detailed instructions to the delegates from American territories to Conference meetings. Although the delegates from the United States dependencies are not similarly instructed today, the Commissioners usually make the information contained in their instructions available to the Conference delegates.

During the 1957 Review Conference, it was suggested that the member governments include qualified local inhabitants of the South Pacific islands as Commissioners in their delegations whenever possible.[8] Few of the metropolitan member governments have, however, seriously attempted to implement this suggestion. Table 8 gives details on the composition of American delegations to the Commission in the past,[9] and it shows that there has been only a moderate shift since 1957 towards using persons with some direct knowledge of the American island dependencies. To date, the United States has only selected two islanders as either a Commissioner or an Alternate Commissioner: Peter Coleman, a part-Samoan from American Samoa, served once as the Alternate Commissioner while he was Governor of American Samoa, and Manuel Guerrero, a former Governor of Guam, served several terms as a Commissioner.

Two features of the American delegations to the Commission not directly pointed up by this table deserve mention since they highlight the prevailing attitude toward the SPC. First, as the table obliquely intimates, the majority of Commissioners and Alternates have no official connection with American policy in the Pacific other than their status as consultants to the State Department. Unlike representatives from other participating powers, particularly Australia and New Zealand, American representatives are neither responsible, themselves, for implementing policies nor are they in a position to bring pressure to bear on those officials who do implement policies.

Second, while over the years the United States has typically sent governmental bureaucrats as advisers with its Commission delegations, these men and women have usually been junior officials in their departments. In the early years, the attitude towards the SPC implied by this approach passed unnoticed, conforming as it did with the general apathy of the other participating governments. Today, however, the situation has changed mainly because of the entry of the island states, which have great respect for the SPC and therefore have chosen to be represented by highly placed governmental officials, often of ministerial rank. Australia, New Zealand, and the United Kingdom have res-

TABLE 8

BACKGROUND OF DELEGATES TO COMMISSION MEETINGS

	1948-1957	1958-1972
Commissioners and Alternates		
Professional and Academic	65.8%	65.4%
State Department	23.7%	3.6%
Interior Department and Islands	10.5%	20.0%
Other	—	11.0%
Advisers		
State Department	81.0%	60.0%
Interior Department and Islands	9.5%	25.5%
Other	9.5%	14.5%

ponded to this expression by the islanders of the Commission's value to them. Since 1970, for example, both the Australasian delegations to the Conference-Commission meetings have been headed by Government Ministers, while in 1971 the British delegation included an Assistant Undersecretary and in 1972 a Parliamentary Undersecretary. The United States has yet to demonstrate unequivocally a similar change in sentiments. A belated step towards correcting this unnecessary embarrassment may have been made when Stanley Carpenter, a Deputy Assistant Secretary for Territorial Affairs in the Department of the Interior, attended the 1972 meeting as an alternate Commissioner. It was not perceived by the islanders, however, as being a significant modification of American policy.

The low rank of the American delegations is a serious problem for the United States in its relationship with the SPC. The other participating states in the regional body, particularly the island states, which are so sensitive to their new role in international affairs, are very aware of the lack of authority and prestige that has characterized the American representation in the SPC. Indeed, at the Twelfth Conference (1972) in Apia, members of both the Western Samoa and Fijian delegations were quite openly outspoken about the political impotence of the Americans; they found the American attitude an affront in view of the very high rank of their own delegations.

Clearly this aspect of American participation in the SPC limits its role in the organization, and it also affects its relations with the region's new states. Outside of Australia and New Zealand, the United States has only one diplomatic mission in the South Pacific, an embassy in Suva headed by a chargé d'affaires. The Conference is thus a point of principal interfacial contact between the United States and the South Pacific. Regardless of State Department intentions, most of the island territories gauge American policy in the Pacific by American policy in the Conference. It is therefore an act of myopic obduracy for the United States to insist, as it does, that the SPC has no political functions. The fact that the islands participate as they do proves otherwise. To pretend that a gathering of the region's leaders does not deserve high level, capable representation is seen locally as a diplomatic blunder.

Little need be said regarding the Research Council and the United States. Originally, the United States was responsible for naming three specialists to the body: one with expertise in health, one in economics, and one in social development. A reduction in the Council's numbers was suggested in 1957, and the result was effected by a rather novel arrangement, which followed a proposal from the Council itself. In addition to the six Secretariat members who would continue as before, it was agreed that only one of the three nominated specialists from each member government would meet annually, thus creating a yearly panel of twelve, half the previous number.[10] By 1963, even this arrangement had collapsed, and the Research Council has become functionally defunct.

For an entirely different reason, there is little to be said at this point about the South Pacific Conference. Delegates to the Conference from the American dependencies are selected by the dependency governments. With the increasingly sophisticated level of politics being demonstrated in the two Pacific territories and Micronesia, little intervention has been required at this level by the American government. Today the Office of Territories (the agency within the Department of the Interior that oversees the American Pacific dependencies) has virtually no administrative interest in the SPC at all. Any work that formerly would have concerned the Office of Territories is now carried out by the island administrations.

With the territorial governments taking over responsibility for more of the routine transactions with the SPC, there has been a shift in the communication pattern of the organization. The original official pattern had been a "V" with Nouméa being at the end of one leg, the territory lying at the end of the other leg, and the metropole situated at the junction of the two legs. The official pattern was not always observed, however, and in 1957 Keesing reported that direct island-SPC contacts were common.[11] Nonetheless, even this partial relaxation was insufficient to relieve the cumbersome burden of the formal "V" pattern. Fully twelve of the forty-six resolutions passed by the 1957 Review Conference dealt with improving the liaison between the organization and the islands. Today the "V" pattern has been re-established in the American territories, but now the base of the "V" is in Nouméa rather than Washington. The direct linkage on SPC matters between the American island territories and Washington has almost wholly disappeared.

On the whole, only a limited number of Americans have served on the staff of the SPC's Secretariat. Dr. Ralph Bedell's term as Secretary-General from 1954 to 1957 has been the only one served by an American. Several Americans have worked as Program Directors, but relatively few have participated in the work of the Secretariat below the level of Program Director. Obern believes four factors have restrained American involvement in the lower ranks: (1) the staff is small (it now numbers about eighty), and consequently the opportunities for advancement are slight; (2) the French culture of New Caledonia is alien to most Americans; (3) the salaries are low by U.S. standards; and (4) the headquarters are located in Nouméa where living costs are high, housing is inadequate, and an aura of isolation prevails.[12]

The United States has been the only member country of the SPC to have a statutory restriction on the amount of money that it could contribute to the SPC.[13] Until late 1972, Congress maintained a ceiling on contributions, despite repeated State Department requests that such a limitation be ended, because, in the view of a subcommittee of the Senate's Committee on Foreign Affairs, "some measure of substantive Congressional control is desirable to afford a review of United States participation in the SPC from time to time as it expands its activities."[14] For nearly a quarter of a century, this ceiling made the SPC's budgetary formula dependent to a certain extent on the good graces of American Congresses, since if the formula was to work the Congress had to appropriate the requisite funds. Thus the United States myopically arrogated to itself a veto on the level of SPC budgets. While the practical effects of this policy were negligible, because the veto remained only potential for the most part, it did adversely affect relations with the other states and territories. This is particularly true of recent years as the SPC has become more islander-dominated.

Originally the ceiling had been set at $20,000, but as the budget of the SPC increased over the years Congress had to raise the ceiling in order to meet its 20 percent assessment. In 1950, the ceiling was raised to $75,000, in 1960 to $100,000, in 1963 to $150,000, in 1965 to $200,000, and in 1970 to $250,000. Due to fluctuations in currency exchange rates in 1971 and 1972, it was necessary to reconsider the ceiling again in 1972. The initial legislation proposed in May supported a rise in the ceiling to $400,000. This was modified in September, however, to eliminate the ceiling while making statutory the 20 percent assessment set by the SPC.

It should be noted that the changes in the monetary ceilings (except for the 1963 modification) reflected real absolute increases in the SPC's budget rather than any change in the United States' assessed percentage rate within the SPC. Despite the expansion of the organization's territorial scope to include Guam and the Trust Territory in 1951, the United States' percentage share of the annual contributions to the SPC was not raised above the original American assessment of 12.5 percent until the Dutch withdrew in 1962. In that year, it was decided that the United States would assume half of the Netherland's 15 percent contribution, and thus the American assessment was increased to the 20 percent figure at which it rests today. The basis for the 20 percent assessment caused a serious dispute in the Senate subcommittee, which was holding hearings on the 1970 ceiling increase. The subcommittee felt that 20 percent was far too high as only about 5.5 percent of the population of SPC members lives in the

American territories. This dispute was responsible for $75,000 being cut from the initial 1970 ceiling increase proposal.[15]

Rather ironically for the United States, just as it repealed the atavistic policy of maintaining a monetary ceiling on contributions, circumstances changed to leave American policy behind the trend in the South Pacific. At the Thirteenth South Pacific Conference (1973), Australia and New Zealand each offered a voluntary contribution of $250,000 to supplement the ordinary budget. Although the move was primarily aimed at France's budgetary blackmail used at the Twelfth Conference, France also made a small voluntary contribution. The United States, however, could not give more than its assessed 20 percent of the ordinary budget. Indeed, rather than receiving credit for eliminating an encumbrance on the budget, the United States had given the impression of establishing a new restriction.

The level of American contributions to the SPC has added significance; despite its very modest proportions, this is an important element in the United States' total foreign aid package to the Pacific. A small education project in Fiji and a number of Peace Corps volunteers are virtually the only other direct aid given to the region.[16] Often American congressmen have mistakenly included expenditures in the American dependencies as part of the government's aid to the South Pacific. Such expenditures, however, represent only the fulfillment of obligations created when the United States undertook political responsibility for these islands. Thus, the amount of aid given by the United States to the Pacific, excluding the American territories, is very small indeed.

THE SPC IN WASHINGTON

South Pacific Commission's relations with the United States are essentially mirror images of American participation in the SPC, since the SPC depends for its communications with America almost exclusively on the same channels of communication that relay information from Washington to Nouméa. The State Department, through the Commissioners and their advisers, is responsible for providing the two-directional function, which represents the United States in Nouméa and the SPC in Washington. Only occasionally does the Secretary-General or Program Director appear in a member country on business. Largely because of the lacuna between the State Department and the Department of the Interior, almost no meaningful information is forwarded to Washington from the American island territories.

Although the State Department handles virtually all of SPC related matters in the United States, there are a small number of other governmental agencies having tangential interests in the SPC: the Office of Territories in the Department of the Interior, for obvious reasons; the Department of Agriculture, because it has been following the rhinoceros beetle project in Western Samoa; and the Peace Corps, because it has some volunteers in the Pacific Islands. As was noted earlier, the

Office of Territories' interest is probably more "tangential" now than in years past.

The State Department Office of Australia, New Zealand, and Pacific Islands Affairs (in the Bureau of Far Eastern Affairs) presently exercises primary responsibility for the SPC. This responsibility was formerly lodged with the Office of Dependent Area Affairs in the Bureau of International Organization Affairs; but during a minor reorganization in 1962 it was decided that, as the organization was purely regional in character, it was better placed in the proper regional bureau. Nonetheless, the Bureau of International Organization Affairs has retained responsibility for shepherding the annual American contribution to the SPC through the Bureau of the Budget.

Until October 1972, the most important representation made by the Department of State in Washington on behalf of the SPC was before the Congress, which had to be approached relatively frequently, since the monetary ceiling was rarely set high enough to last for more than a few years. When the State Department approached Congress to have the ceiling on American contributions to the SPC raised, it had to present testimony on the value of such an increase before subcommittees of the Senate's Committee on Foreign Relations and the House of Representatives' Committee on Foreign Affairs. It was anticipated as this study was being formulated that the reports of these hearings would provide the basis for a formal analysis into the reasons for American involvement in the SPC. After a preliminary examination of the three most lengthy hearings, however, it became evident that the documentation was insufficient to sustain a rigorous analysis. Nonetheless, a count of theme frequencies was undertaken, which, while based on proper content analysis techniques, must be considered somewhat suspect statistically.[17]

Seven principal themes appeared in the three documents examined; they follow in order of frequency: the economic development of the region (12 times), the military value of the area (10), the promotion of the political capabilities of the local population (10), engendering friendship of the islands' peoples towards America (9), the social development of the islanders (9), promotion of their health (6), and the benefits to American territories that occurred from participation (4).

While the frequencies and rankings of the themes may not be significant statistically, the mere presence of some themes is noteworthy. Despite the apolitical, non-military character of the SPC, two of the seven themes relate to the military value of the islands and the diplomatic benefits that may accrue from participation in the organization. Kaplan suggested very early that the military theme would win Congressional support for the SPC because of "the demonstrated strategic importance of the area in World War II and its possible strategic importance in the future."[18] The presence of this theme must be attributed in large part to a perfunctory need to convince Congressmen that the area under consideration may affect the military security of the United States. It is a disquieting feature of the American apathy towards the region that this theme has been pressed in the subcommittees so often without challenge or rebuttal. Equally likely to

raise the eyebrows of a student of American policy in the Pacific is the diplomatic theme since the lackadaisical and low level approach of the United States to
the SPC seems increasingly to have a dysfunctional impact on American relations
with the region. If the State Department is anxious to win advantages from
American participation in the SPC, it must make its participation sizeable enough
to engender the respect and appreciation of the island states, which have assumed
so much influence in recent years over SPC policy.

While most observers have long recognized the value of the SPC as an agency
for promoting political awareness among Pacific islanders, it is interesting that
this view has received some measure of official sanction in Washington. Certainly
the SPC would be as "officially" surprised by this view of its activities as it would
be at being linked to American military security in the South Pacific. Nevertheless, despite rather insincere statements to the contrary by the State Department,
there is evidence to suggest that this impact of the SPC is sincerely acknowledged
by some American officials.[19] Saying that Washington realizes the SPC has had
a political impact in the "South Seas" and that the State Department is even willing
to argue before a Congressional subcommittee that such an impact is a worthwhile
reason for supporting the SPC is not, however, to say that the American government
is prepared to accept the fruits of increased political awareness in the islands, particularly when a sensitive area like Micronesia is involved. That would require a much
more cohesive and coherent policy towards the South Pacific than the United
States has displayed for many years.

It is difficult to understand why—of all the possible motives for supporting
American participation in the SPC—the "benefits for American territories" theme
should rank last. Perhaps there are two plausible explanations. The first arises from
the lacuna (alluded to above) that exists between the Office of Territories and the S
Department. The State Department does not have the same practical, day-to-day
contacts with islanders that are available to the Office of Territories; and yet it
seems unwilling to remedy this deficiency by establishing a reliable liaison with
the Interior branch on South Pacific matters. Thus the State Department may
lack vital sensitivity. Certainly the low frequency of the theme stems from the
fact that the State Department has been more inclined to call upon Defense
Department expertise in appearing before Congressional committees than upon
Interior expertise, despite the apparent anomaly this creates vis-à-vis stated SPC
aims. A second possible explanation for the "benefits" theme may be the recognition by the State Department that many American Congressmen are reluctant to admit that the United States territories could receive any advantage from
outside sources. They apparently hold the opinion that such an admission would
reflect badly on their stewardship.

While the character of official American attitudes towards the SPC represented
by these themes and their frequency may not have been considered a particularly
unacceptable set of values two decades ago, today they are anachronistic and
a discredit to the United States. Such a view of the Pacific region harks back to
the kind of metropolitan paternalism that created the SPC and thus displays
little understanding of the current mood in the area. It cannot be stated conclu-

sively from the evidence in this essay that "official" attitudes towards the SPC have not changed over the years in the United States. Nevertheless, because there has been almost no change over the years in the outward features of American participation in the regional body, there is little reason to believe that Washington's attitudes and perceptions have been altered.

CONCLUDING THOUGHTS

Throughout this analysis, the present has been interspersed with elements of the past to create an explanation of how American involvement has been carried out. In was not the intention of this paper, however, to offer an extensive historical treatment of American-SPC relations. Nonetheless, a few concluding remarks can be made with regard to the changing complexion of American participation in the SPC.

Outwardly the major trend has been the decline in the importance of Washington, as a metropolitan power, in the affairs of the SPC. In part this is attributable to the various internal changes which have taken place within the organization itself. For example, one of the effects of the demise of the Research Council was to limit the opportunities, in numbers at least, for the metropolitan powers such as the United States to involve themselves in SPC matters. Similarly the modification of the organization's pattern of communications has worked to reduce the number of governmental agencies in Washington that come into contact with the SPC and to reduce generally the flow of communications between Nouméa and Washington.

A second element influencing the apparent low profile of the United States in the regional body is the rising stature of the member territories within the organization. These territories have assumed greater responsibility for their own development during the past decade, and concomitantly their rising self-esteem has been reflected in the greater role accorded the island dependencies in the SPC. The Commission's member states have, for the most part, accepted the legitimacy of local involvement and most have even welcomed it. As the South Pacific Conference has gained in prestige, however, the Commission proper has had to share more of its authority and responsibility. Even the Commission itself has begun to change in recent years due to the accession to membership of some island states. This trend is continuing, and it can be expected that in future the Commission will become more representative of local interests, which will thus further reduce the role of metropolitan powers in the SPC.

The changes which have resulted from the trend towards a decreased metropolitan importance for the United States reflect, moreover, circumstances more or less beyond the control of the United States and therefore the apparent modifications in American-SPC relations should not necessarily be seen as a change in the character of American involvement in the organization. Over the years the SPC has grown and matured; it is now more than ever a truly regionally oriented organization. The American approach to the body has not similarly grown, however, and the basic thrust of the American involvement has remained unchanged except in reaction to institutional alterations in the organization. Today, as in 1947, the United States is parsimonious in its contributions to the SPC budget. The State Department sends powerless political appointees as Commissioners, and the American island territories have little influence over the formation of American policy towards the SPC. This unhealthy stagnation has diminished the influence and stature of the United States ih an increasingly independent South Pacific region.

ADDENDUM

Significant developments have taken place in the South Pacific region since mid-1974 which affect some of the information given in the text above. The principal impetus behind the recent changes is the continuing force of decolonization. Papua New Guinea became independent in September 1975; Niue became a self-governing territory earlier in the same year; the Solomons are also self-governing and aspire to independence in 1977; the Marianas have voted to separate from the rest of the TTPI; and Tuvalu (formerly the Ellice Islands) has terminated its relationship with the Gilbert Islands. The process of decolonization has affected the SPC as much as the individual politics within the South Pacific, particularly in strengthening the claim of the indigenous countries to greater control over the regional body.

Largely on the initiative of Australia, a review of the roles of the SPC's various sectors was carried out in Wellington, New Zealand, early in 1974. The upshot was a Memorandum of Understanding signed at the Fourteenth South Pacific Conference on Rarotonga, Cook Islands, in September 1974 which provided for a *de facto* merger of the Commission proper and the Conference. In addition to greatly restricting the despised system of weighted voting, the merger has brought virtually all the powers of the "old" Commission under the control of annual meetings of the Conference. A rump of the Commission has survived as the Committee of Participating Governments that is, a committee of all governments which have acceded to the Canberra Agreement) which still controls the size, but not the allocation, of the budget. The participating governments have also retained the power alone to formally amend the agreement.

Significant though the changes effected through the memorandum are, further modifications are under consideration. A review of the SPC's functions is being undertaken in mid-1976 which may drastically affect the character of the organization's work program in future. Further, a meeting scheduled for Canberra sometime in 1977 will examine the relations between the SPC and other regional bodies. The Australian government has made no secret of its hope that the Canberra meeting will result in a merger of the SPC and the South Pacific Forum, thus "rationalizing" regional organization in the South Pacific.

Throughout all these changes and proposals for change, the United States has played a noticeably passive role. The American posture has been very much in keeping with its attitude toward the SPC since the late 1950s—if anything, the increasing independence of the South Pacific has produced a more conservative, nonparticipatory reaction from the United States. The continuing apathetic outlook of the United States can be explained in part by the lack of diplomatic-military contention over the area and in part by the dominance in the region of two American allies—Australia and New Zealand. The first of these two explanations, however, could be subject to rapid change, particularly in view of the deliberations of the United Nations' Conference on the law of the sea. Should the American government decide to regain lost diplomatic initiatives in the South Pacific, the fact remains that its involvement in the SPC can hardly be expected to serve to its advantage.

NOTES

1. W. D. Forsyth, "France and the S.P.C.," *New Guinea and Australia, The Pacific and South-East Asia* 5 (October-November 1970), 39.

2. Emil J. Sady, "Report on the South Seas Conference," *Department of State Bulletin* 16 (March 16, 1947), 460.

3. During the Thirteenth South Pacific Conference held in September 1973 at Agana, Guam, it was resolved that there be a *de facto* merger of the Conference and the Commission. A meeting of the member Governments convened in February 1974, to consider this and other proposed changes in the Canberra Agreement.

4. *Agreement Establishing the South Pacific Commission,* Art. XXI, para. 66. A copy of the Canberra Agreement can be found in the Appendix to T. R. Smith, *The South Pacific Commission: An Analysis after Twenty-five Years* (Wellington: Price Milburn for the New Zealand Institute of International Affairs, 1972).

5. Australia had five votes, until recently, on the basis of a formula of one vote for each dependency (Nauru, Papua, New Guinea, and Norfolk Island) and one for the metropole. Australia, however, did not give up one vote when Nauru became independent and joined the Commission, and this caused some controversy during the 1970 election for Secretary-General. Subsequently Australia has given up the vote for Nauru, and it will not exercise another vote for Norfolk Island until Norfolk Island takes an active part in the organization. In 1972, Papua New Guinea asked that Australia exercise only one vote for it as it is only one country. This leaves Australia, in practice, with only one vote now that Papua New Guinea is independent.

6. "The South Pacific Commission," *External Affairs Review* (New Zealand) (November 1964), p. 5.

7. The thirteen territories are American Samoa, British Solomon Islands, French Polynesia, Gilbert and Ellice Islands, Guam, New Caledonia, New Hebrides, Niue (with the same status as the Cook Islands since 1974), Papua New Guinea (internally autonomous since December 1973), Pitcarn, Tokelau Islands, Trust Territory of the Pacific Islands, and Wallis and Futuna Islands. The four independent states are Fiji, Nauru, Tonga, and Western Samoa. The Cook Islands sit as the one self-governing territory. Because of the unusual positions of both the Cook Islands

(not a territory or an independent state) and Tonga (never having been either a colony or a metropole), it was decided at the 1971 Conference-Commission meetings to permit both polities to attend Conference meetings as of right through a formal change in the SPC's rules of procedure. Tonga thus far had always attended by special invitation.

8. Norman J. Padelford, "Regional Cooperation in the South Pacific: Twelve Years of the South Pacific Commission," *International Organizations* 13 (Summer 1959), 388.

9. The percentages were obtained simply by aggregating the number of Commissioners, Alternate Commissioners, and Advisers in each category in each period who actually attend SPC meetings and dividing by the total number for each period. The categories are defined as follows: "State" refers to members of the Department of State and the Foreign Service; "Interior and Islands" refers to officials of the Department of the Interior and to individuals, local or expatriate, serving in island administrations (thus this category is intended to convey the idea of persons more or less directly involved in island governance); "Professional and Academic" generally refers to civilians who make their living in either the world of business or academia; and "Other" means not in any of the defined categories.

It should be noted that it was not always easy to decide into which category to place an individual. For instance, Carlton Skinner, a long-time Commissioner, was described as a professional man since he was a businessman when he was selected to represent the United States. Nonetheless, he was once a Governor of Guam and therefore could perhaps have been classed in the category of "Interior and Islands." Similarly, Dr. Douglas Oliver was an official of the State Department when he served as an adviser, and therefore he was counted under "State" even though he is also a noted academic authority on the Pacific region.

10. C. G. R. McKay, "The South Pacific Commission," *New Zealand Journal of Public Administration* 20 (March 1958), 20.

11. Felix M. Keesing, "The South Pacific Commission—The First Ten Years," *Department of State Bulletin* 37 (September 9, 1957), 425.

12. Alfred G. Obern, "Personal Administration in the Caribbean and South Pacific Commissions," *Revue Internationale des Sciences Administratives* 25 (November 3, 1959), 265-69.

13. *The South Pacific Commission, Hearings* before Subcommittee on International Organizations and Movements, House of Representatives, on H.J. Res. 666, 88th Congress, 1st session, 1963 (U.S. Congress, House Committee on Foreign Affairs) p. 3.

14. *U.S. Contributions to the South Pacific Commission,* S. Rept. 361, 89th Congress 1st session, 1965 (U.S. Congress, Senate Committee on Foreign Relations) pp. 4-5.

15. *U.S. Participation in the South Pacific Commission,* S. Rept. 1477, 91st Congress, 2d session, 1970 (U.S. Congress, Senate Committee on Foreign Relations) pp. 4-5.

16. *Parliamentary Debates,* 27th Parliament, 2d session, 3d period, 1971 (Australia, House of Representatives) p. 1655.

17. In counting the themes, the following constraints were used: (1) the statements in support of the SPC had to be positive and assertive (i.e., they should not simply state the purposes of the organization); and (2) they had to

be made by the witnesses before the subcommittees (favorable remarks by the Congressmen were not counted). The three documents used were: (a) House, 88th Congress (1963); (b) *South Pacific Commission, Hearings* before Subcommittee on International Organizations and Movements, House of Representatives, on H.J. Res. 475, 89th Congress, 1st session, 1965 (U.S. Congress, House Committee on Foreign Affairs); (c) *South Pacific Commission, Hearing* before Subcommittee on International Organizations and Movements, House of Representatives, on H.J. Res. 1162, 91st Congress, 2d session, 1970 (U.S. Congress, House Committee on Foreign Affairs).

18. Sheldon Z. Kaplan, "Eightieth Congress, First Session, and the United Nations," *Department of State Bulletin* 17 (November 2, 1947), 849.

19. House, 88th Congress (1963), 44-5.

DONALD D. JOHNSON   **15**

American Impact on the Pacific Islands Since World War II

For the sake of simplicity the American impact on the Pacific islands since 1945 will be discussed under four categories. First in time, and always present in some degree, has been the impact of American strategic plans and policies. Second, we may consider the commercial influence of the United States as supplier of island imports and as a market for their exports. Third, and of growing importance, is the influence of American tourists and the tourist industry. Fourth is the role of the United States in the progress of island peoples toward self-government.

STRATEGIC IMPACT

At the end of World War II, the military power of the United States was dominant in the Pacific, so much so that American planners for the postwar period were inclined to brush aside the views of other nations, even our Pacific allies. What is more, such planning as there was in American hands was primarily devoted to war and immediate postwar problems as perceived from a military viewpoint.

This fact appears clear in the communications between the United States and Australia and New Zealand from at least late 1943, and concern over the unilateral policies of the Americans was an important factor in inducing Foreign Minister Herbert Vere Evatt of Australia to promote the ANZAC Pact of January 1944. At that time, some American newspapers, such as the strongly nationalist *Chicago Tribune,* were suggesting that the funds the United States was pouring into the construction of bases on Pacific island possessions of our allies should entitle the Americans to postwar retention of such bases or even of the islands themselves.[1]

This same theme reappeared in 1945 in the report of a subcommittee on Pacific bases of the House Naval Affairs Committee. Singled out in the Pacific for American retention were Iloilo in the Philippines, Manus in the Admiralty Islands (an Austral ian trust), and Nouméa in French New Caledonia as major bases; Okinawa, Subic Bay, and the Palau group as the site of secondary bases; and Majuro, Kwajalein and Eniwetok in the Marshalls, Truk in the eastern Carolines, and Espiritu Santo in the New Hebrides as "fleet anchorages." Part of the island of Upolu, in Western Samoa, was requested at one point by Washington authorities as a "strategic trust" under the terms of the United Nations charter, with the United States and New Zealand in control.[2]

As late as 1946, discussions with the British, Australians, and New Zealanders were still going on over American requests for retention of control over bases on Canton, Christmas, and Funafuti, with joint rights with the British on Ascension, Espiritu Santo, Guadalcanal-Tulagi, Tarawa, and Viti Levu. Joint rights with Australians were still being sought in Manus and with New Zealand on Upolu.[3]

Rationalization of the American requests rested on two bases. One was the principal role played by the United States in the defeat of the Japanese and the primary use of American funds, personnel, and equipment to construct bases during the war. The second basis related to the future concern of the United Nations with keeping the peace in the Pacific and apparently envisioned Japan as the principal, if not sole, threat to that peace. It was alleged that the United States alone was in a position to carry out the peace-keeping function in the Pacific in the event of major aggression. ANZAC contributions to the Pacific war effort seem to have been consistently underestimated in these calculations, as was the role those nations would play in the Pacific's future.[4]

Through 1944 and 1945, the Australian government countered these American proposals with efforts to create a regional organization for future peace-keeping in the Southwest Pacific. Australia was prepared to concede islands north of the Equator to the unilateral jurisdiction of the United States. Dr. Evatt, Australia's Minister for External Affairs, carried the burden of opposition to the most extreme American demands. In January 1944, with the assent of Prime Minister John Curtin, he took the initiative in calling a joint meeting with New Zealand leaders to pre-pare a joint statement of policy.

Evatt's position was that Australia and New Zealand had a vital interest in the disposition of Pacific islands and wished to be consulted on any treaties or other arrangements for that purpose. The ANZAC agreement, of January 1944, avowed that the wartime construction of bases did not give any power postwar rights to any islands or other territories under Allied sovereignty. Clearly, the last phrase would leave the United States a free hand in Micronesia.[5]

The official American reply was that the war had yet to be won, and thus the time was not ripe to take up territorial questions of this sort. It appeared that Washington was concerned that such discussions might serve as a precedent for the Russians to proceed with their evident desire to arrange East European and Asian territorial questions similarly before a general peace settlement. Evatt had made his proposed settlements contingent upon such a general postwar settlement, however.[6]

There was quite clearly a division in American thinking about the future of the Pacific islands at this point, with military officers concentrating on securing bases adequate to a major presence throughout the Pacific and State Department functionaries more concerned with the danger of such special advance arrangements as precedents for peacemaking. Clearly, the result was one showing highly discrepant attitudes and results, both in the Pacific and in Europe.

The Dutch, French, and Portuguese governments were at first kept quite in the dark about American plans and their possible impact upon Indonesia, the French island possessions, or Timor. President Franklin D. Roosevelt expressed his distaste for returning colonies to French sovereignty, but the Australians felt themselves pledged to such a return, particularly in New Caledonia, where Australian troops had aided the Free French in retaining political and economic control before American bases were established there.

Authorities in Washington were reluctant to press their Pacific island claims with the Australians and New Zealanders without consulting the government of the United Kingdom. The British, moreover, were not in full accord with Evatt's ambitious plan for a Southwest Pacific regional defense organization and a South Seas Commission, lest they represent a weakening of the ties of the Commonwealth. Knowing this, U.S. Secretary of State James Byrnes brought pressure on the British to help frustrate Evatt's designs, including his proposed general conference of powers concerned with the Pacific islands.

By 1946, with wartime pressures removed, some new notes began to appear prominently in the discussions of the Allies concerning Pacific islands. More attention was focused, for example, on the possible usefulness of island bases for purposes of commercial aviation and communications. On this ground, ANZAC and American policies were being formed in an atmosphere of mutual suspicion and jealous regard for the rights of each and its "chosen vehicle" airlines to develop trans-Pacific routes.[7]

Another factor in American planning was the growing evidence that Congress would not countenance the continuing huge expenditures involved in Navy proposals to maintain a whole sweep of island bases. Military advisers to State Department negotiators scaled down both the number and the extent of facilities desired. The elimination of a Japanese military threat and the absence of any other that might make the islands of strategic significance in the near future put an end to Washington's proposals to project American power into the South Pacific, at least as far as bases or island possessions were concerned.

Between 1945 and 1951, millions of tons of material, which could not be used at active military installations in the Pacific or brought back for sale on surplus markets, were simply dumped into the ocean. The deep near Espiritu Santo was the site of one major dump. The shorelines of many islands in Micronesia to this day have the rusting, bulldozed remnants of wartime equipment, American or Japanese, still on view. On many islands, the decaying remnants of buildings or machines were gradually covered by weeds and vines. The scars of that impact remain.

After 1951, when administration of United States-controlled territories in Samoa, Guam, and the Trust Territory of the Pacific Islands was transferred from the Navy Department to the Department of Interior, the military role was further reduced. Additional installations in each area were deactivated, and the surface communications services, which the Navy had provided, were not replaced by Interior. In the Trust Territory, the latter change had profound economic and administrative results.[8]

By the early 1950s, military thinking had ceased to concentrate on Japan as the great potential threat in the Pacific, although amateur and Congressional sources seemed slower to grasp the change. Yet after the Communist victory in China, the outbreak of war in Korea, and the hardening of Cold War lines, it was difficult to project either China or the Soviet Union as a military threat relevant to the islands. Through the 1950s and well into the 1960s, the major role of the Trust Territory, in a strategic sense, appeared to be the negative one of keeping the area out of the hands of any potential foe. The thinking was still defensive and economy-minded, and no great attention to the islands or appropriations for their people were called for in the minds of Congress or of successive administrations.

Then, at least two different forces changed American strategic thinking about the Trust Territory in particular. One was the increasingly sharp criticism of United States policies in Micronesia emanating from the United Nations and spearheaded by the Committee of Twenty-Four. This came at a strategic moment at the start of the Kennedy administration, when a desire for a progressive image in the world combined with a similar desire to at least appear to be doing something more than had been done in the Eisenhower years. Budgets were greatly increased, objectives and programs were reexamined, and, in the process, the strategic significance of the islands to the United States and its Pacific allies was reconsidered.[9]

At the same time, or very nearly so, growing United States involvement in Southeast Asia placed the Trust Territory in a new light, no longer as a protective screen for the eastern Pacific, but now as a base or transit area for the projection of American power into the western Pacific and Asia. Critics of the United States role in Vietnam and of American failures in developing the Trust Territory for the benefit of its people, as urged by the Trusteeship Council and the anti-colonial bloc of the United Nations, have emphasized Vietnam as *the* reason for changes in American policy. In fact, efforts to upgrade Trust Territory administration, for non-military reasons, were already under way before the key Vietnam decisions of the Kennedy years were made.[10]

Through most of the two decades after 1950, there was an astonishing lack of publicly available information on American military-strategic thinking concerning the Pacific islands. This coincided with a period of comparatively low military expenditure there—a period in which the nuclear and missile tests carried out in the Marshall Islands and the activation of Johnston Island installations for storage of "nerve gas" bombs stand out. The activities in the Marshalls caused displacement of population, either through evacuation of target islands, as at Bikini, or by the employment offered at American bases, most notably at Ebeye, adjoining the Kwajalein base.

However diminished the active military role, Pentagon authorities continued to press the Trust Territory administration not to alienate public lands that might have future military significance. This promoted unrest among Micronesians who held traditional claims to the lands in question, antedating even the German period in most cases. The uncertainty and the secrecy surrounding military land claims, moreover, encouraged repeated rumors of planned military takeovers, which in the 1960s became a stock-in-trade of critics of the American civilian administration. The example of the northern Marianas, drawn back under Navy control for a decade after 1952, strengthened the fears of Micronesian leaders.[11]

The central problem of American military policy makers has remained the same. Their nation bears the major responsibility for the defense of the islands, of Australia and the Americas against any threat from Asia. Though changing technology has removed some of the potential importance of Pacific island bases, they would still be useful to aggressors against either Australasia or the Americas. The scattered populations of the islands could not, by themselves, defend their territories against conquest and use by powerful nations from outside. The problem, then, is to keep open the necessary options to use the islands while denying the same freedom, if possible, to potential foes.

In either case the happiness and the good will of the people of the islands are significant factors. That point was recognized during the 1940s in the Navy Department's handbooks for administrators of reconquered territories, and it was given clear expression in Admiral Raymond A. Spruance's "Pacific Charter" of December 12, 1945. The approach, however, at that time was paternalistic and opportunistic.[12]

Clearly an impoverished or disaffected populace would be an obstacle to either efficient administration or military security. Unfortunately, the execution of sound policy protective of both American and island interests was subsequently hampered by maladroit statements of military plans, by secrecy or confusion concerning land claims, and worst of all by condescending, double-standard attitudes toward island peoples.

In the mid-1970s, it is clear that strategic questions cannot be disentangled from those of political status of the islands and the economic bases on which autonomous regimes there can stand. On these matters, consultation with island leaders must be an integral part of Pacific security policy.

ECONOMIC IMPACT

Two generalizations may be offered with regard to American trade and its impact upon the islands, always excepting Hawaii. First, there never was an aggressive, comprehensive government program for the promotion of commerce and investment in island areas, especially in those outside United States jurisdiction. Second, American business itself has not adopted a vigorous program of trade promotion in those areas, in view of the small dimensions of the market. Neither of these statements would deny that the presence of some American products has exerted an appeal and has influenced the consuming habits of Pacific islanders.

Americans were by no means the first Westerners to introduce the desire for the fruits of modern technology. In this regard, Germans and Japanese, in addition to French, British, Australians, and New Zealanders, played a wider and earlier role in most of the islands. But wartime and postwar experiences placed the United States in a prominent position in many islands as an exemplar of contemporary world standards of comfort, convenience, and plenty. Wartime munificence left the jeep, the outboard motor, the quonset hut, galvanized sheets for roofing or walls, and a thousand other artifacts as temporary, and possibly permanent, additions or replacements to the material cultures of island communities.

In the immediate aftermath of the war, leftover equipment, supplies, and structures contributed significantly to island life styles from New Caledonia to Okinawa. Then, as these items wore out or deteriorated beyond the possibility of further use under the influence of a tropical environment, island peoples were thrown back more upon their own depleted resources. In many cases this was a difficult readjustment, with canoes, traditional-style housing, and even coconut trees or farming plots destroyed or neglected under the stress of war.[13]

Then, and this was notably true of the Trust Territory after 1960, a new, higher level of government paternalism brought a larger tide of American money, goods, and equipment to the islands under United States control. Established buying channels, plus discriminatory tariffs and regulations, made sure that this economic impact was almost entirely American until Japanese exports began to make major inroads in the later 1960s in Micronesia.

In the South Pacific, where French, British, Australian, and New Zealand administrators and traders predominated, the American commercial impact was far less important. Canned foods, fabrics, hardware, or appliances were more likely to reach Fiji or Tahiti from Commonwealth nations or from metropolitan France, respectively, than from the United States. Consular reports from the South Pacific islands repeatedly noted the limited opportunities for American manufacturers or investors. Special opportunities arose from time to time, as when Fiji's major road-building program created a temporary market for American heavy equipment. Generally, however, the impact of the West on South Pacific import markets was not notably American.[14]

Where island exports have been concerned, much the same situation has existed. Hawaii, of course, has been bound tightly to mainland markets for its sugar and pineapple. In American Samoa, Guam, and the Trust Territory, preferential laws and administrative favoritism, often unwitting, have encouraged the use of American goods from soft drinks to tractors. Even more, American life styles, as evidenced by motion pictures and visitors or officials in the islands themselves, have encouraged islanders, young and old, to emulate patterns of consumption and behavior alien to their own traditions. In Truk, for example, a highly intelligent and concerned local leader expressed dismay over the desire of his own children to dress like Americans from completely different climates, a status symbol of the moment among their peers. From Yap to American Samoa, similar concerns over the influx of alien goods exist.[15]

Under these circumstances, island leaders (and not only the most hidebound traditionalists) have found the idea of expanded American bases or foreign investment and presence in their lands destructive of what they prized most highly. In this light, a great military base on Babelthuap or a tourist center on Koror could both be seen as threats to Palau's values rather than as protection from conquest or as a desirable boost to the money economy. Americans, whether tourists or soldiers, demonstrated values placed on occupations other than fishing or agriculture—those most available to Micronesians, or Samoans, on their own. And so their young people flocked, as did young people in the Society Islands and the Cooks, to rising urban centers, there to seek "white collar" jobs, while the agricultural infrastructure of the islands was neglected and food imports rose. It cannot be said that this impact was exclusively American, but it was especially noticeable in every island group under American control.

In the non-American islands, from the Gilberts on south, Commonwealth or French controls by both business and government over export distribution have generally kept phosphates, metal ores, copra, or other products outside the range of direct American impact. Even when island products have found eventual markets in the United States, they have commonly flowed through British, Australian, New Zealand, or French hands en route. In Fiji, for example, early in the 1970s the United States was taking about 15 percent of Fiji's exports (mostly sugar) and contributing less than 5 percent of her imports. Even this latter figure was threatened with diminution as the Fiji government was encouraging local production of rice, then the largest single import from America.[16]

TOURISM

Tourism has been discussed in many parts of the Pacific, particularly where agricultural, mineral, or power resources are most limited, as the one major form of economic enterprise readily capable of expansion. The beauty of the islands, the warm climate, friendly inhabitants and their exotic ways have all been cited as lures to the visitor fleeing the less desirable aspects of modern industrial societies. Through the 1960s, as a rule, tourism was thought of largely in terms of Americans.

Hawaii was the first obvious Pacific island target of the American tourist, and the growth of annual visitor figures from 1946 to 1959 was considered remarkable. From about 15,000 visitors in the former year, the total rose to 243,000 in the latter. Then, in the decade and a half following the grant of statehood to Hawaii in 1959, the tourist traffic grew to become the chief source of income, surpassing sugar, pineapple, and eventually even military expenditures by the United States government. In 1972, approximately two and one-quarter million tourists visited the island state, spending more than three quarters of a billion dollars.[17]

Along with the growth of this industry went social and economic changes, which were to serve as a warning to other potential tourist destination areas all over the Pacific. Waikiki, the heart of Hawaii's tourist industry, sprouted multi-story hotels, parking lots, and an atmosphere of commercialism alien to the

Pacific islands. Jobs were created by the thousands in the construction, mainte-nance, and service aspects of the industry, but most of these were among the low-est paying positions, especially those available to island people. Even in outlying areas, the impact of tourism was felt, as in the disruption of family life patterns where women found employment as hotel maids, waitresses, or entertainers.[18]

Pacific islanders visiting Honolulu or Guam saw demonstrations of change warning them of the possible cost of tourism in their own areas, at the same time that they marveled at the wealth it created. When Continental Airlines (Air Micronesia) agreed to build hotels in each of the six districts of the Trust Terri-tory in the 1960s, there was something less than complete enthusiasm among island leaders. In Yap there was, and continues to be, outright resistance.[19]

The growth of tourism in the Trust Territory, therefore, was slower than might have been expected, though fear and opposition were by no means univer-sal. Some Micronesians welcomed and profited from it. An interesting sidelight in the early 1970s has been the eclipse of American tourism, in the western is-lands, by the Japanese. Currency fluctuations, domestic economic uncertainties, and the threat of energy shortages heavily underscored the unstable nature of tourism as a potential economic base for new island economies.

Tahiti also attracted American tourists and hotel industry investors; and by the early 1970s Samoa, Fiji, the Cook Islands, Tonga, and other groups were looking to their tourist potential. In most of these cases, efforts were being made to control the location of destination spots and the impact of tourism employment upon local economies and societies. American Samoa and Tahiti appeared, at first, to be less successful than some of their people hoped in avoiding disruptive change. Advance planning and controls in Tonga, Fiji, and the Cook Islands were designed to mitigate the undesired aspects of tourism while still gaining the economic benefits it could bring.

If the shifts of the world economy that marked the early 1970s represented more than a passing phase, particularly the threat of major energy shortages, the danger of runaway tourist development engulfing island peoples and their cultures seems likely to abate. At the same time, such a trend would illustrate that the tourist trade, after all, is one characterized by highly elastic demand and one with definite economic limits.

POLITICAL SELF-DETERMINATION

Despite nearly two centuries of anti-imperialist rhetoric, following from its own colonial origins, the United States in recent years has hardly been the leader of decolonization in the Pacific. During World War II, President Franklin Roosevelt had expressed interest in the ending of colonial regimes in both Asia and the Pacific, and he had exerted some pressure in that direction. With his passing, however, the control of American policy fell into the hands of men less attuned to the rising forces of nationalism. The independence of the Philippines represented a high water mark in accomplishment perhaps not equalled until the grant of statehood to Hawaii in 1959.

In the meantime, American support for independence movements elsewhere seemed to cool in the chilling atmosphere of the Cold War. Good relations with Britain, France, and the Netherlands became more important than support for the inhabitants of French Polynesia or other aspirants to autonomy. In the Trust Territory, Guam, American Samoa, and even in Hawaii in the late 1940s, the continuance of paternalistic rule under Navy or Interior government-as-usual seemed the rule.

This attitude seemed to contrast with the more active interest in the political future of the islands manifested by New Zealand and Australian leaders. In the ANZAC Pact of 1944, clear concern was expressed for the future welfare and/or self determination of dependent peoples of the Pacific. The South Pacific Commission, which is considered elsewhere in this volume, received its major impetus and support from "Down Under," and the American impact upon or through it has hardly been one of dynamic leadership.[20]

Yet the Truman administration was aware of the incongruity of supporting freedom and self-determination in Eastern Europe and maintaining military rule in its own possessions and the Trust Territory. Plans to change this were set in motion, at the President's order, in 1947. In 1950-1951, Guam, American Samoa, and the Trust Territory were removed from Navy Department jurisdiction and placed in the ill-prepared hands of the Department of the Interior. There was still no American "Colonial Office" with skilled, trained colonial administrators.

Thereafter, United States policy in those islands was limited by small appropriations, in part because of major policy differences between advocates of a "zoo theory" of allowing the islanders to live in their own way as much as possible, and those who felt sincerely that it was America's duty to train and prepare island peoples for participation in the modern world, presumably on an American model. The former appeared to have the upper hand, bolstered by the fact that their policy was cheaper, until about 1960-1961. From that time on pressure from the United Nations, particularly from the newly-enfranchised nations and the Soviet bloc, shifted emphasis to development rather than conservation of traditional ways. Education, medical and public health improvements, economic development, and, most of all, preparation for political autonomy were pushed by successive United Nations visiting missions and by the Trusteeship Council.

Bureaucratic inertia and confused lines of authority continued to make progress toward goals of self-government slow and irregular. Another factor slowing progress was the continued reluctance of the military to release any segment of control which might impair the defenses of the United States or its allies in the event of another threat from Asia. In addition, uncertainties and disagreement among Micronesians, Guamanians, and Samoans themselves over political goals have tended to delay the achievement of self-rule. In spite of these drawbacks, as an example, the acknowledgment of local governments in Micronesian hands, begun during Navy rule, was expanded until a full set of district legislatures was in existence. In 1965, an elected Congress of Micronesia succeeded an advisory council, and over the follow ing years its scope of operations and its budget gradually were increased. By the early 1970s negotiations were being conducted between a Status Commission selected by the Micronesian Congress and representatives of the United States concerning autonomy, with or without special ties; these talks seem likely, despite delays, to reach fruition by the end of the decade.[21]

Both Guam and American Samoa have followed distinctive paths toward increasing self-government under the American flag. But in each of these island dependencies, as in the Trust Territory, the absence of any clear-cut program or goal of political autonomy has left feelings of frustration among local political leaders. The lack of comprehensive planning or thinking about the Pacific, with which the United States began in 1945, has continued despite some excellent proposals dating as far back as the period of Navy rule.

It has thus been easy for critics of American policies in the Pacific to conjure up a plot of deliberate delay designed to retain strategic, political, and economic control in Washington's hands. The halting progress of status negotiations for the Trust Territory, debates over the future of Guam and American Samoa, even the absence of clear and consistent attitudes toward the South Pacific Commission and its agencies, have been cited as evidence of a Machiavellian program of colonialism.[22]

In all honesty, it appears that the Pacific and its peoples simply have not loomed large enough on the horizons of most Americans and their representatives in government to demand serious, concerted policy-making. The Pentagon, the Interior Department, a variety of Congressional committees, and the administrators sent to the islands have frequently found themselves working at cross-purposes, despite similar aims. Even the best of governing officers, such as H. Rex Lee in Samoa, or William Norwood and Edward Johnston in the Trust Territory, have been unable to help the islanders achieve lasting progress, when they were faced with shifting, short-term personnel and a multiplicity of bosses in Washington.

One ray of hope for a future impact better aligned with the interests of all the people of the Pacific may lie in the negative fact that American confusion and indecision may leave room for self-determined action on the part of island leaders. The American impact has not been as powerful as it might have been had there been unity and purpose in the imposition of plans designed to serve Washington bureaus. In the mid-1970s, it appears that success in controlling the American impact may depend more upon the ability of Pacific leaders to develop unity among their peoples than upon unilateral American determinations.

NOTES

1. *Foreign Relations of the United States* (United States, Department of State, 1944), III, 169-75. Johnson (Canberra) to Hull, 1/22/44, makes reference to McCormick's statements and their effect upon External Affairs Minister Evatt.

2. *Study of Pacific Bases* (United States Congress 79:1, House Subcommittee

on Pacific Bases of the Committee on Naval Affairs, House Docs. No. 104). *Foreign Relations,* 1946, V, 3-10, 44.

3. *Foreign Relations,* 1946, V, 1-49.

4. An overall statement of official thinking about the postwar Pacific, including the ANZAC role, may be found in an aide memoir prepared for the State Department on November 6, 1945, in *Foreign Relations, 1945,* VI, 206-11.

5. *Foreign Relations,* 1944, III, 174, Johnson to Hull, 1/22/44.

6. Ibid., Hull to Johnson, 2/1/44; Childs (Wellington) to Hull, 2/8/44.

7. *Foreign Relations,* 1945, VI, 214-5, 222-4.

8. *Report of the Visiting Mission to the Trust Territory of the Pacific Islands, 1950* (United Nations, Trusteeship Council) p. 12; Douglas Oliver, *The Pacific Islands* (Cambridge, Mass., 1967), p. 420.

9. *Report of the Visiting Mission. . . . 1961* (United Nations, Trusteeship Council); United States Congress, 90:1, Appropriations Committee Hearings, February, 1967, 1018-19, testimony of William Norwood.

10. *Annual Report to the United Nations on the Administration of the Trust Territory of the Pacific Islands,* 1955-60, shows the United States administration's view of progress. Critical views appear in the *Official Records, Twenty-sixth Session* (United Nations, Trusteeship Council), 1960, 45-103.

11. E. J. Kahn, Jr., *A Reporter in Micronesia* (New York, 1965), pp. 39-41; *Honolulu Advertiser,* November 1, 1967; Norman Meller, *The Congress of Micronesia: Development of the Legislative Process in the Trust Territory of the Pacific Islands* (Honolulu, 1969), 17, 18, 55; Alex Phillip, "Role of the U.S. Military in Micronesia," *Micronesian Realities: Political and Economic,* ed. Frances McReynolds Smith, ed. (Santa Cruz, California, 1972), pp. 237-43; Interviews with Micronesian leaders and students, Honolulu, 1960-1972.

12. Dorothy E. Richard, *United States Naval Administration of the Trust Territory of the Pacific Islands* (Washington, 1957), I, 18-9, 164-5, 689-709; II, 516-9; III, 6-19.

13. Douglas Oliver, ed., *Planning Micronesia's Future: A Summary of the United States Commercial Company's Economic Survey of Micronesia, 1946* (Honolulu 1971), pp. 11-20, 24, 32; Riley H. Allen, *Journey to the Trust Territory, Uncle Sam's Wards in the Pacific* (Honolulu, 1953), pp. 32-3, 37, 41-2, 56-8.

14. *Foreign Economic Trends and Their Implications for the United States: Fiji* (United States Department of Commerce, Bureau of International Commerce), ET 69-11 (February 14, 1969); ET 70-24 (March 13, 1970); ET 71-024 (March 25, 1971); ET 72-056 (May 11, 1972).

15. Tosiwo Nakayama, interview, Truk, June, 1971; Carl Heine, *Micronesia at the Crossroads: A Reappraisal of the Micronesian Political Dilemma* (Honolulu, 1974), pp. 24-39; Ben R. Finney, *Polynesian Peasants and Proletarians* (Cambridge, Mass., 1973), pp. 78-141.

16. *Foreign Economic Trends . . . .* (United States Department of Commerce) loc. cit.

17. *Hawaii Tourism Impact Plan* (State of Hawaii, Department of Planning and Economic Development [Honolulu, 1972]), I, 7-19; *State of Hawaii Data Book, 1973, A Statistical Abstract* (Honolulu, 1974), pp. 140-8.

18. Frances Cottington, *Socio-psychiatric Effects of Luxury Hotel Growth and Development on a Rural Population* (Honolulu, 1971).

19. Philip W. Quigg, "Coming of Age in Micronesia," *Foreign Affairs* 47 (1969), 500-501; *Honolulu Advertiser,* July 11, 1968.

20. Florence Marie Coffee, "The South Pacific Commission as an Instrument of Australian and New Zealand Administration of Dependent Areas in the Pacific: 1944-1955" (Master's thesis, Duke University, 1957); Theodore Reynolds Smith, *South Pacific Commission: an Analysis after Twenty-five Years* (Wellington, 1972).

21. Meller, op. cit., pp. 384-403; Heine, op. cit., pp. 144-76.

22. Smith, ed., *Micronesian Realities: Political and Economic,* pp. 1-46, 209-15; See also such critical journals as *Micronitor* (Majuro), *The Young Micronesian* (Honolulu), or *Friends of Micronesia Newsletter* (Berkeley, Calif.).

16

Imperial Remnants: Decolonization and Political Change in the British Pacific Islands

It was only with reluctance that Britain assumed formal territorial responsibilities in the Pacific Islands in the nineteenth century. Gradually a Pacific role was accepted until, in the 1960s, a desire to be rid of remote entanglements became a primary feature of British policy.

At the outbreak of World War II, Britain had responsibility for Fiji (a crown colony), the Solomon Islands (a protectorate), the Gilbert and Ellice Islands (protectorates from 1892 that had subsequently been combined with other mid-Pacific possessions to form a crown colony), Tonga (a protected state), the New Hebrides (jointly ruled with France as a condominium), and Pitcairn (a British settlement, home of the descendants of the Bounty mutineers). The Solomon Islands Protectorate, the Gilbert and Ellice Islands Colony, and the New Hebrides came under the jurisdiction of the High Commissioner for the Western Pacific, who was responsible for their administration. This office was conjoint with the Governorship of Fiji until 1952, when a separate High Commissionership was established at Honiara in the Solomons.

Before the war, British dependencies were expected to "live of their own." In the Pacific territories, administration was generally paternal in attitude and indirect in nature, with local affairs being run by chiefs, headmen, or councils under the supervision of expatriate district officers. With limited funds available, services were circumscribed. Education was generally left to Christian missions, and where governments did provide schools, they catered only to the limited numbers destined to fill the lower ranks of the civil service. The Fiji School of Medicine, established in the 1880s, trained islanders for local medical services throughout the region. In the economy, private traders and government taxes provided incentives for production in excess of subsistence needs. Where plantation development was possible in the Solomons and New Hebrides, islanders worked as laborers; Gilbertese and Ellice islanders were employed in the Ocean Island phosphate industry together with indentured Chinese laborers; in Fiji, labor for the sugar industry was provided almost exclusively by Indian immigrants. Only in Fiji was there any significant political advancement, but there the Legislative Council's role was a concession to the numbers of European settlers and a vocal Indian community. The remoteness of Britain's island empire was emphasized when, in the face of the Japanese advance in 1941, British administrative staff were withdrawn from the Gilbert and Ellice Islands and the Solomons, and the allied counterattack was conducted by American troops supported by Australians, New Zealanders, and islanders.[1]

The war had profound consequences for the island societies. The Solomons and Gilberts saw first Japanese and then Allied occupation, while the New Hebrides, the Ellice Islands and Fiji were host to large numbers of troops before and during the Allied thrust to the north. American occupation with its concomitant flood of technology and material items affected islanders' ideas of the wealth and benefits of Western civilization and led in parts of Melanesia to a renewed enthusiasm for cargo cults. Moreover, the egalitarian attitudes of soldiers towards islanders and multiracialism in the American forces were compared with the remote paternalism and racial discrimination practiced by most Europeans in prewar years. These factors, and the Americans' tendency to belittle British rule and to criticize the backwardness of British dependencies, led the islanders to look more critically at their British masters in the subsequent period of reconstruction.

Clearly, the Pacific was a vastly different place after the war, and the 1940s mark the beginning of a period of accelerating change. This change should not be seen only in a Pacific context but also in the light of Britain's changing domestic and international situation: changes that were reflected in revised polices for the Empire. These revised policies are important because they, perhaps even more than developments within the island communities themselves, have determined the nature and pace of postwar developments.

Colonial policy was not a party issue in British politics in the 1940s. Developments in India, conflict over settler or native paramountcy in Kenya, riots in the West Indies, a generally heightened interest in colonial issues, and colonial contributions to the war effort produced a consensus in favor of a new approach. The Colonial Development and Welfare Act of 1940 marked the abandonment of the principle that dependencies should be economically self-sufficient. Then, after the election of a Labor Government, Colonial Secretary Arthur Creech Jones spelled out the new policy: "The central purpose of British colonial policy is simple. It is to guide the colonial territories to responsible self-government within the Commonwealth."[2] The main significance of the full statement was that, for the first time, political development was put ahead of economic and social progress. But the overall emphasis was still on guidance, acceptable social and economic conditions, eventual rather than immediate self-government, and self-government rather than independence.

In the immediate postwar period, Britain was in a difficult financial position and attempted to overcome some of its problems through imperial preference and long-term contracts for food and raw materials with both dominions and dependencies. The late 1940s and early 1950s saw the granting of greater responsibilities to more "advanced" territories. India set the scene for later developments, but the real impetus did not come until Britain had been forced to cope with disorder in the dependent empire. This was also a period in which African nationalist movements emerged and the initiatives were seized increasingly by colonial peoples.[3]

For fifteen years after the war, however, these developments hardly affected the Pacific, which was still regarded as an imperial backwater. Here, educational policies and the limited nature of political involvement, even at the local level, precluded the emergence of educated *élites*. There were movements of local significance in response to colonial rule and the war, but none which could easily become the vehicle for decolonization. Territorial, linguistic, and social fragmentation combined with poor communications to inhibit the growth of any sense of national identity. Where significant resources were absent or exploited by expatriates and a predominantly immigration population, colonial rule had been generally remote and benevolent at least to the extent that it failed to engender any strong anti-colonial sentiment. Despite the readjustments required by the war and its aftermath, islanders were still prepared to accept the constitutional status quo.

From Britain's point of view, there was little need for rapid decolonization. The lack of political awareness was recognized and, more importantly, it was believed that the small remote islands of the Pacific could never be economically self-sufficient in a modern world. The new emphasis, therefore, was on improving and modernizing government services and on the promotion of local government to give village and island communities increased control over their own affairs. Colonial Development and Welfare funds—the only real evidence of a new imperial policy seen in the immediate postwar period—were expended primarily on social welfare projects. At this stage there was little concern with political developments and when, from the 1950s, New Zealand showed a willingness to transfer responsibility to its dependencies, Britain, like Australia, expressed alarm at the precedents being established.

In the mid-1950s, Conservative government took a much stronger line on colonial dissidence. Increasingly, colonial policy became a response to crises with military action becoming necessary in Malaya, Cyprus, and Kenya. There were precedents for colonial territories (as distinct from the settler dominions) becoming independent in India, Ceylon, the Sudan, and the Malayan Federation; but the key to decolonization was the independence of the Gold Coast, as Ghana, in 1957.

The inevitability of similar developments elsewhere was not fully realized until 1959, however, when the Conservative government was returned to office with Harold Macmillan as Prime Minister and Iain Macleod as Colonial Secretary. Macleod saw himself faced with a simple choice between rapid decolonization or bloodshed. Economic viability remained an important consideration, but it was seen as a factor only in the timing of decolonization and in no way removed its inevitability. The essential prerequisite for independence was now political viability construed as a national sentiment and an educated *élite* capable of assuming power. In 1960, Macmillan made his "Wind of Change" speech to a dismayed South African audience and indicated that African national consciousness would have to be given legitimate constitutional expression.[4] Also, Macleod made clear in his concessions to African leaders from Eastern and Central Africa that settler domination would not be perpetuated.

So rapid was the decolonization of Africa and the West Indies that the Colonial Office ceased to exist as a separate entity in 1964. And, in the 1960s, immigration problems at home and the replacement of "British" constitutions in the former dependencies by one-party rule, dictatorships, and military regimes led to a general disillusionment with the Empire. Recognition of Britain's diminished status in a changing world and the desirability of closer ties with Europe had already been evident in the abortive attempt to join the European Economic Community in 1961; it was further emphasized by continuing economic problems in Britain and again reflected in the Common Market negotiations towards the end of the decade. By this time, too, colonial rule was internally unpopular. The composition of the United Nations was changing, and, from 1960 when the resolutions on colonialism were passed, the new nations of the Afro-Asian Bloc brought increasing pressure to bear on the colonial powers.

It was in the 1960s, then, that the island dependencies were brought into line with developments elsewhere; the "Wind of Change," blowing from London rather than from Africa, began to reach the Pacific, and limited concepts of government gave way to new official initiatives. Economic viability was still regarded as only a remote possibility, but now, for the first time, Britain began to accelerate the decolonization of its Pacific dependencies. As it did so, it highlighted the particular local restraints on the transference of political responsibility.

Fiji had long been regarded as Britain's problem area in the South Pacific. In the 1870s Sir Arthur Gordon, Fiji's first Governor, had sought to protect the indigenous Fijians from too rapid an exposure to Western ways by promoting the introduction of indentured Indian laborers for the sugar industry. Under the Fijian Administration, the Fijians were ruled by a hierarchy of chiefs and councils, paid their taxes in produce, and were effectively removed from the mainstream of development. With the end of the indenture system in 1920, the Indians were permitted to remain, and it was they, together with the European settlers and the Colonial Sugar Refining Company (CSR), who dominated the economy.

The 1930s saw the emergence of Indian solidarity and demands for a "better deal" from the colonial government and the CSR. Militant cane farmers' unions were formed in 1937, an almost total Indian boycott of the armed services followed, and the economy was seriously affected by a cane-cutting ban in 1943. The situation was further complicated when the 1946 census confirmed that the Indian population outnumbered the Fijian and thus gave an added edge to Indian demands for political advance under a common electoral role and the removal of restrictions on the sale of Fijian-owned land.

The period from 1946 to 1958 was one of stagnation: Income per head remained static, or possibly declined; there was little capital for land development; the Fijian Administration, despite reform, failed to revitalize Fijian society; aid was concentrated on social services. In the late 1950s, however, advice was sought on economic problems and prospects, but several years elapsed before any change of emphasis became evident.[5]

Apart from procedural changes, the 1937 constitution still applied; the Legislative Council had an official majority and an unofficial membership of fifteen that was divided equally among the three main racial communities. Three Indian and three European members were elected on a restricted male suffrage with the remainder being nominated by the Governor. The Fijians were all appointed on the advice of the Council of Chiefs. This state of affairs had been maintained largely because the British Government had been reluctant to face the fundamental issue of constitutional change in a plural society in which, to further complicate the issue, the indigenous people were now outnumbered by immigrants. The government seemed unwilling to attempt any reconciliation of Fijian demands for special rights and protection, Indian demands for immediate independence and a common roll, and European assertions that, despite their small numbers, their stake in the Colony entitled them to equal representation with Fijians and Indians.

In 1961, when the British Government stated its intention of introducing a "member system" of government as the first step towards self-government, Fijian and European members joined in an opposing alliance, which had been implicit before and, to all intents and purposes, has remained since. In 1963 and 1966, compromise arrangements were reached, which, by the utilization of communal rolls and complex cross-voting procedures, ensured the preeminence of combined Fijian-European interests. This period is crucial to the modern development of Fiji; it not only saw the country firmly committed to self-government but also established the framework within which future struggles would take place.[6]

In the late 1950s and early 1960s, the first steps towards a transfer of responsibility were taken in the British Solomon Islands Protectorate (BSIP), the Gilbert and Ellice Islands Colony (GEIC) and, to a much lesser extent, the New Hebrides. Tonga was the exception. It shared the bleak economic future of the others, but it had special status as a protected state and at no stage had surrendered its sovereignty. The influence of the monarchy was unimpaired. The British Agent and Consul and a few expatriate officials played significant roles, but the initiative in government, together with control over land and the economy, still rested with Queen Salote and the nobles. For most Tongans this meant a life of "affluent subsistence," and there was little questioning of the prevailing political, social, or economic order which unified the Tongan polity and gave to those within it a clearly defined status and sense of identity.

No such identity existed in the Solomons. Within the Protectorate there are six large islands and many smaller ones; there are no less than eighty languages and dialects for 180,000 people. In former times, large political groupings were rare, and authority, whether vested in chiefs or "big-men," was confined to localities. Planters and missionaries succeeded labor recruiters and plantation employment overseas as agents of change. The government gradually eliminated internecine warfare, but it took few other steps to induce change before World War II. Copra became, and has remained, the mainstay of the economy. An Advisory Council met from 1921, but for thirty years its membership was exclusively European. From 1950, five Solomon Islanders—half of its unofficial membership—were nominated to the Council.

Political tension caused by the activities of "Marching Rule," a movement which advocated self-help for economic progress and non-cooperation with mission societies and government, meant that little constitutional progress could be made before the late 1950s. From 1960, the BSIP moved in a steady if unspectacular fashion through the standard phases of "Westminster" constitutional development. Legislative and Executive Councils were established. The former had eleven official and ten unofficial members; all of the unofficial members, six of whom were Solomon Islanders, were nominated by the High Commissioner for the Western Pacific. From 1964, seven of the unofficial members were elected by local government councils, one by direct election for Honiara, and two were nominated. Three years later, the overall size of the Legislative Council was increased with all except one of the unofficial members being returned by direct election. It was at this stage that the Melanesian members adopted a rather more aggressive approach to politics and acted in concerted opposition to the official bench. Despite a continuing lack of political awareness in most constituencies, the British initiative had evoked a positive response from the involved minority and thus opened the way for more rapid constitutional advancement.[7]

Similar initiatives produced rather different results in the GEIC. Here, although there were cultural variations within each group, there were two distinct languages and cultures—one Micronesian and the other Polynesian. The Gilbertese outnumbered the Ellice Islanders by approximately seven to one. The coral islands which make up the Colony could offer little more than an uncertain subsistence existence with the production of a small amount of copra for sale. The most important source of revenue was the phosphate exported from Ocean Island, but as the asset was a wasting one—and the price paid by the British Phosphate Commissioners (controlled by the British, Australian, and New Zealand governments) was well below market value—the administration was both unwilling and unable to expand services.

The sixteen Gilbert and nine Ellice Islands are spread over a distance of more than a thousand miles; other islands which make up the Colony, some of which are uninhabited, are even more remote. Such distance and territorial fragmentation made centralized political councils difficult and expensive to organize, and it was 1963 before an Advisory Council was established. Largely because of the Resident Commissioner's initiative, Britain showed rather more flexibility than had been characteristic. An Executive Council was established at this stage, rather than at the succeeding legislative council phase of development, in an attempt to involve Islanders in policy formation. A legislative council would have required an official majority—an impossibility given the smallness of the administration and the large number of islands, each of which would have expected representation in the legislature.

Under a revised development policy, there was a rapid expansion of administration and services. One consequence was a centralization of services on Tarawa in the Gilberts and an influx of "outer islanders" seeking employment in, and the benefits of, government services. Before the war, educational facilities in the Ellice had matched those in the Gilberts; during hostilities and for some years afterwards, they were substantially better. Thus Ellice Islanders, who also displayed a better adaptive capacity than the Gilbertese, came to occupy a disproportionate number of places in the civil service. This situation, in which Gilbertese and Ellice Islanders were directly competing for the first time, led to some racial disharmony, expressed in the emergence of an anti-Ellice feeling among the Gilbertese élite and a fear of future discrimination and economic deprevation amongst their Ellice equivalents. Dissension was not widespread at this stage, but it was a significant factor when a revised constitution was negotiated in 1966.

Again, the outcome was a unique constitutional experiment. A House of Represntatives was established with seven official and twenty-three unofficial members. The House was consulted on government policies and legislation, but legislative and executive powers were vested in a small Governing Council. Unofficial members of the Governing Council did not hold portfolios. The experiment, which lasted for three years, had little success not so much because of its formal provisions, but because both expatriate and indigenous members had little political experience, few of the Islanders were fluent in English (no satisfactory translation facilities were provided), and there was an almost total lack of political activity and interest outside the House.[8]

In the New Hebrides, such constitutional advance as took place was a mockery of the term. Under the 1914 Protocol, the New Hebrides became an area of joint influence for Britain and France. Then, as now, French economic interests predominated; but Britain was not prepared to withdraw completely in the face of strong representations made by its nationals in the islands, by mission societies, and by Australia and New Zealand. As the New Hebrideans are citizens of neither metropolitan country and other residents have to place themselves under the jurisdiction of one or the other of them, three administrations—British, French, and Joint—have emerged. Customs, revenue, public works, transport, lands, and agricultu were made joint responsibilities, while medical and educational services were left to national administrations. In joint spheres, both have to agree before action can be taken. An Advisory Council was established in 1957 with two official and sixteen unofficial members—four British, four French, and eight New Hebridean, all appointed jointly by the Resident Commissioners.

Although the Condominium has more than enough land for its 90,000 people, more than a third of it has been alienated to European interests—a grievance that has helped to foster political awareness in recent years. In response to this situation, "Nagriamel," a movement which has demanded a return of land to the islanders, was formed in the mid-1960s. There are copra, fishing, and cattle industries in the New Hebrides, but all suffer from a shortage of labor. The islanders preferred to migrate to urban centers and then, from 1968, to New Caledonia for the high wages offered in the nickel mines. Conflicting interpretations of the Protocol and differences in approach between the two metropolitan powers have led to a duplication of services and inhibited development.[9]

The return of a Labor Government in the United Kingdom in 1968 saw renewed pressures for political advance in the dependencies, the creation of the Ministry of Overseas Development, and a revised aid policy. The new ministry took a much more active part in economic planning in the dependencies, and it concentrated its efforts on projects which would produce an economic return. In the Pacific there was considerable investment in agriculture and fisheries. The intentions were clear enough—a reduction of future aid and a maximized exploitation of natural and human resources to provide the economic underpinning for statehood. In recent years, too, federation and self-government with free association have been withdrawn from the list of constitutional alternatives; the period of self-government has been reduced; and the granting of some form of independence, whether or not economic viability has been achieved, has become the primary objective of the United Kingdom Government.

Tonga, the first of Britain's Pacific territories to achieve independence, was the easiest to decolonize. Early in the twentieth century, all external and some internal matters were handled by Britain, but the gradual localization of responsibility had left only foreign affairs and defense to be returned. The initiative for the resumption of independent statehood came from King Taufa'ahau Tupou IV in 1969. He was not simply accepting the realities of a changing Pacific world, but, as had been done so often in the past, he was giving expression to the national pride that is so prominent among the Tongans. The *de facto* status of "dependency" had never been fully accepted by Tongans, and Tonga clearly preferred to lead rather than follow its neighbors to independence. Since independence in June 1970, this sentiment has led to the expansion of the national shipping line and moves to establish an airline.

In the 1960s, increased migration and improved communications lessened Tonga's isolation, assisted in the dissemination of new ideas, and engendered popular support for a reassertion of sovereignty. There was also rapid urbanization on Tongatapu and occasional murmurings of political discontent. Despite some attempts to modernize social services and the economy, some well-educated commoners, and others who were unable to obtain land or employment, began to question the concentration of power in a few hands. The socio-political order was unchanged by independence and the problems of the present—especially those arising from the uneven distribution of power and wealth—were left for the future. Here, where Britain had been guardian rather than master, imperial withdrawal was made easy.[10]

The retreat from Fiji was more difficult. The 1966 elections had seen the return to power of the Alliance Party, which drew its support primarily from Fijians, Europeans, and a few Indians, under the leadership of Ratu Kamisese Mara, a high-ranking chief. In opposition was the National Federation Party led by A.D. Patel, a lawyer who had risen to prominence through the cane farmers' unions and had won support for his politics of intransigence and obstruction in defense of Indian interests. Fiji was committed to self-government, but the initiative for timing now shifted from the United Kingdom to the Alliance Party. The issue was given some urgency after a Federation Party boycott of the Legislative Council in 1968 and race riots had followed the consequent by-elections in which Patel and his followers had increased their majorities. When the parties held informal discussions on the constitution before the official conference, the presence of S. M. Koya, a moderate who had led the Federation Party since Patel's death in 1969, made compromise easier. The Federation Party yielded important ground by agreeing to British arbitration on the common roll issue; in return, the Alliance Party agreed to almost immediate independence. The latter concession was also insisted upon by Britain which would not countenance a prolonged settling-in period between self-government and independence. Britain's stand on this issue is explained by its obvious desire for disengagement and a fear that any delay would undermine the harmonious relationship that seemed to have emerged in 1969-1970.[11]

At the penultimate hour, however, there was a near crisis over aid. During the constitutional conference held in London in mid-1970, the United Kingdom Government announced that future aid would be confined to loans. Both parties reacted strongly to the suggestion and won considerable concessions when they expressed dismay at the implications for development planning and fears that economic uncertainty would breed political instability. Already, the agreement negotiated by Lord Denning on cane prices had brought forth a statement from South Pacific Sugar Mills, Ltd. (SPSM)—successor to, and subsidiary of, the CSR—that it intended to sell its holdings.[12] It appears that, in fact, the SPSM was using the new award as an excuse, at least as much as a reason, for its decision. Later, a government-owned sugar corporation was established—an act of political and economic necessity rather than of economic nationalism.

On October 10, 1970, the 96th anniversary of cession, Fiji became a dominion. The constitution, with its communal and national electoral rolls for the House of Representatives and provisions for appointment to the Senate, recognized existing racial and political divisions and modified the principles of representation that had already been established. Constitutional provisions and legislation that protected Fijian interests were entrenched. The constitution also included provisions intended to make future amendment difficult and thus to ensure the perpetuation of a plural society.

Despite large aid grants in recent years, the United Kingdom will be faced with a continuing financial commitment to its remaining dependencies for some time to come. The GEIC, although economically viable at present, will cease to be so in 1978 or 1979, when the phosphate deposits on Ocean Island, which provide about half of the current revenue, are exhausted. Reserve funds have been accumulated to soften the blow, but it is doubtful whether the return on this investment will be sufficient to meet the shortfall. Aid has been used to finance the investigation of fisheries and mariculture, but future prospects are uncertain.

Constitutional issues are more pressing. In the GEIC, after the experiments of the 1960s, 1970 marked a return to constitutional orthodoxy with the establishment of Legislative and Executive Councils and a "member" system of allocating responsibilities; a "ministerial" system, with finance still a reserved subject, was introduced in 1974.

In the meantime, however, Ellice demands for secession have increased in volume and intensity. In the 1960s, the awareness that had generated such demands had been largely confined to civil servants on Tarawa, but in the 1970s it became widespread in the Ellice Islands themselves. The islanders not only feared future discrimination in employment and in the allocation of resources and services, but the loss of their cultural identity. The United Kingdom Government had previously ignored the issue, but by 1972 some action was imperative.

Still smarting from its Anguillan experience, the United Kingdom agreed to investigate the Ellice Islander's grievances and their assertion that separation was the only solution to racial differences. A special commission recommended that the Ellice Islanders should decide their future by referendum. It is not a precedent that will endear Britain to many countries of the Afro-Asian bloc and some in the Pacific who are or have been faced with secessionist movements. The referendum was observed by the United Nations, the first occasion on which the United Kingdom allowed a UN mission into one of its colonies. Separation was endorsed by 90 percent of Ellice voters and was effected, with both colonies close to self-government, on January 1, 1976.[13]

As the GEIC returned to orthodoxy in 1970, so the BSIP departed from it. In an attempt to find a constitutional arrangement in keeping with indigenous attitudes towards decision-making, the Protectorate adopted a committee system of government with a single Governing Council. The intention was for all members to be involved in policy formation in situations where decisions might be reached by consensus. Although appreciated by some, others found difficulty in the system. Chairmen of committees, for example, found decision-making hampered by the need to consult their members, while the latter objected to what they saw as an attempt by some chairmen to exercise ministerial powers. In 1973, a selected committee recommended a return, once again, to the orthodoxy of a ministerial system as a prelude to self-government and independence.[14]

The Protectorate is heavily grant-aided, but it has considerable potential for development in agriculture, forestry, and fisheries. It will take time however, as development on the required scale is only now being undertaken. A general lack of awareness of central government and its functions is a major obstacle, but it is unlikely to impede progress towards independence. In the short term Britain will be freed from political but not financial responsibilities.

The same may not be true of the New Hebrides which, for Britain, has engendered a sense of impotence and frustration. It is the French who have resisted change throughout the colonial period and who have, despite stirrings of anti-colonialism, insisted on the constitutional status quo. The origins of the French attitude are not to be found in the inherent value of the islands nor, as some would agree, in a desire to irritate the British. Instead this attitude originates from a fear that decolonization here might serve as a precedent for New Caledonia, valuable for its nickel, and French Polynesia, which provides a suitably remote site for nuclear testing. Finally, in 1974, agreement was reached on the transference of limited responsibility to a representative assembly elected on universal suffrage. There is no indication, however that the steps taken will lead to early internal self-government or independence. Thus Britain could be left with a continuing commitment to a colonial absurdity.

Together with a clear intention of shedding its responsibilities in the Pacific, the United Kingdom has exhibited very little interest in territories for which it has not had formal responsibility. It joined with other administering governments in the formation of the South Pacific Commission after the war, but has generally favored a prescribed role for the regional organization. Clearly, too, the willingness of New Zealand and Australia to distribute bilateral aid more widely, especially as British dependencies have approached self-government and independence, has been welcomed. When the South Pacific Forum was formed by the self-governing and independent island nations in 1971, it marked the culmination of a sense of regional awareness that had been growing for several years; but the desire to establish closer links within the Pacific was, for some of the Forum's members, intensified by the knowledge that the United Kingdom was entering the European Economic Community and that it wished to terminate its political and financial role in the Pacific as quickly as possible.

NOTES

I wish to express my appreciation of financial assistance for research and travel received from the Australian National University, the University Grants Committee of New Zealand, The Nuffield Foundation, and Massey University, New Zealand.

An earlier version of this paper appeared in *The Round Table,* No. 259, July 1975. I am grateful to the editor for permission to reprint it here.

1. For general histories of the British Pacific Islands before World War II, see C. Hartley Grattan, *The Southwest Pacific to 1900* (Ann Arbor, 1963) and *The Southwest Pacific Since 1900* (Ann Arbor, 1963); W. P. Morrell, *Britain in the Pacific Islands* (Oxford, 1960); Deryck Scarr, *Fragments of Empire: A History of the Western Pacific High Commission, 1877-1914* (Canberra, 1967); and for a popular, though less reliable, history, Austin Coates, *Western Pacific Islands* (London, 1970).

2. *The Colonial Empire* (Great Britain, Parliamentary Papers, Cmd 7433 [1947-1948]), p. 1.

3. For general coverage of British colonial policy over the period covered by this paper see Colin Cross, *The Fall of the British Empire, 1918-1968* (London 1968); David Goldsworthy, *Colonial Issues in British Politics 1945-1961: From "Colonial Development" to "Wind of Change"* (Oxford, 1971); W. B. Hamilton, Kenneth Robinson, C.D.W. Goodwin (eds.), *A Decade of the Commonwealth, 1955-1964* (Durham, N.C., 1966); Nicholas Mansergh, *The Commonwealth Experience* (London, 1969); Nicholas Mansergh (ed.), *Documents and Speeches on Commonwealth Affairs 1952-1962* (London 1963).

4. Macmillan's speech is reprinted in Mansergh, *Documents and Speeches,* pp. 347-51.

5. Fiji's postwar problems are well discussed in O.H.K. Spate, *The Fijian People: Economic Problems and Prospects* (Fiji Legislative Council Paper No. 13, 1959); Sir Alan Burns, et al., *Report of the Commission of Enquiry into the Natural Resources and Population Trends of the Colony of Fiji, 1959* (Fiji Legislative Council Paper No. 1, 1960).

6. *Fiji Constitutional Conference 1965* (Great Britain, Parliamentary Papers, Cmnd 2783); J. W. Davidson, "Constitutional Changes in Fiji," *The Journal of Pacific History* 1 (1966), 165-8.

7. T. Russell, "The 1970 Constitution for the British Solomon Islands," *The Politics of Melanesia,* ed. Marion W. Ward (Canberra and Port Moresby, 1970), pp. 225-38.

8. Barrie MacDonald, "Constitutional Development in the Gilbert and Ellice Islands Colony," *The Journal of Pacific History* 5 (1970), 139-45.

9. A. G. Kaldoa, "The Political Situation in the New Hebrides," *Politics of Melanesia,* pp. 207-24; A. L. Jackson, "Towards Political Awareness in the New Hebrides," *The Journal of Pacific History* 7 (1972), 155-62.

10. Sione Latukefu, "Tonga after Queen Salote," *The Journal of Pacific History* 2 (1967), 159-62; J. W. Davidson, "The Decolonization of Oceania," *The Journal of Pacific History* 6 (1971), 133-50; for Tonga, see pp. 136-38.

11. *Fiji Constitutional Discussions: Report on Lord Shepherd's Visit to Fiji, January 1970* (Fiji Legislative Council Paper No. 1, 1970); *Report of the Fiji Constitutional Conference, 1970* (Fiji Legislative Council Paper No. 5, 1970); J. M. Anthony, "The 1968 Fiji By-Elections," *The Journal of Pacific History* 4 (1969), 132-35; Davidson, op. cit., pp. 138-41.

12. *The Award of the Rt. Hon. Lord Denning in the Fiji Sugar Cane Contract Dispute 1969* (Supplement to the Fiji Royal Gazette, 1970); *Lord Denning's Award: Statement by South Pacific Sugar Mills Limited* (Suva, 1970).

13. Barrie MacDonald, "Secession in the Defence of Identity: The Making of Tuvalu," *Pacific Viewpoint* 16, No. 1 (May 1975), 26-44.

14. *Report of a Special Select Committee on Constitutional Development* (BSIP, Governing Council Paper No. 89, 1972).

Notes on Contributors

Colin C. Aikman is high commissioner for New Zealand in India. Until recently he served as vice-chancellor of the University of the South Pacific at Fiji. He had previously been legal adviser to the New Zealand Department of External Affairs and professor of constitutional law and dean of the law faculty at Victoria University in Wellington. As constitutional adviser, he was associated with the development of the constitutions of Western Samoa, the Cook Islands, and Niue. He is past president of the New Zealand Institute of International Affairs and a past chairman of Volunteer Service Abroad.

Dirk A. Ballendorf was educated at Pennsylvania State University (B.A.), Howard (M.S.), and Harvard (Ph.D). He has held a number of different positions with the Peace Corps, both in Washington and abroad, since the 1960s. Currently he is the director of planning for higher education in the Commonwealth of Pennsylvania.

Hamlet J. Barry, III, holds degrees from Yale (B.A.) and Columbia University Law School (J.D.). He has held a number of positions and was the directing attorney at the Marshall Islands Office of the Micronesian Legal Services Corporation for over two years. He is now a resources attorney and law and policy analyst for the Western Governors' Regional Energy Policy Office.

C. Hartley Grattan is the dean of Pacific historians. He first became interested in the Southwest Pacific in the late 1920s and is now professor emeritus of history, the University of Texas at Austin, and curator of the Grattan collection of Southwest Pacificana. He holds his degrees (B.A. and an honorary D. Litt.) from Clark University. Among many others, his publications include *The United States and the Southwest Pacific* (Cambridge, Mass., 1961), *The Southwest Pacific to 1900: A Modern History* (Ann Arbor, Mich., 1963), and *The Southwest Pacific Since 1900: A Modern History* (Ann Arbor, Mich., 1963).

Noel Grogan is director of the Center for Pacific Action, a teacher, and a Ph.D. candidate at the University of Hawaii. He is now at work on an analysis of political and economic problems associated with fisheries development in the Central Pacific. From 1968 to 1970, he served as an employment officer and as student services officer on the staff of the High Commissioner of the Trust Territory of the Pacific Islands.

Richard A. Herr was trained as a political scientist at Nebraska (B.A.) and Duke (M.A. and Ph.D.), and most of his academic work has dealt with South Pacific topics. He is a senior tutor in political science at the University of Tasmania.

Daniel T. Hughes holds his B.A. and M.A. degrees from Bellermine College and his Ph.D. from the Catholic University in Washington, D.C. He has taught in the Philippines and has done extensive research there and in Micronesia. At present he is an associate professor of anthropology at Ohio State University. He is the author of *Political Conflict and Harmony on Ponape* (New Haven, 1970) and the co-editor (with Sherwood Lingenfelter) of *Political Development in Micronesia* (Columbus, Ohio, 1974).

Donald D. Johnson is a professor of history at the University of Hawaii. He received his initial training in political science at U.C.L.A. (B.A. and M.A.) and did his graduate work in history at the University of Southern California (Ph.D.). He has in process a book entitled "The United States in the Pacific: Public Policies and Special Interests."

Monika Kehoe has taught at Mills (Brooklyn) and Russell Sage colleges and at Haile Sellassee I (Ethiopia), Montreal, and McGill universities. She is now professor of English at the University of Guam. She has held various government and United Nations posts in Korea, Japan, and Australia and was educated at Mary Manse College (A.B.) and Ohio State University (Ph.D.).

Sherwood G. Lingenfelter, an associate professor of anthropology at the State University of New York (Brockport), was educated at Wheaton College (B.A.) and the University of Pittsburgh (Ph.D.). He is the co-editor of *World Culture Series* (Englewood Cliffs, N.J., 1974) and (with Daniel Hughes) of *Political Development in Micronesia* (Columbus, Ohio, 1974), and the author of *Political Leadership and Culture Change on Yap* (Honolulu, 1975).

Barrie MacDonald has been a lecturer in history at Massey University in New Zealand since completing his doctorate at the Australian National University. His dissertation dealt with the history and politics of the Gilbert and Ellice Islands, and he is at present researching the decolonization of Oceania.

W. Donald McTaggart is an associate professor of geography and a member of the

Center for Asian Studies at Arizona State University. He was educated at the University of St. Andrews in Scotland (B.A. and M.A.) and the Australian National University (Ph.D.). He has taught at the Universities of Malaysia, Strasbourg, and Cincinnati; and he is the author of a number of articles about Malaysia, New Caledonia, and Indonesia.

Ralph R. Premdas received his Ph.D. from the University of Illinois and has taught both in the United States and in South America. At present he is a senior lecturer in the department of political and administrative studies at the University of Papua New Guinea.

W. T. Roy is professor of politics at the University of Waikato in New Zealand. He was educated in India at La Mariniere Military College (the St. Xavier's of Kipling's *Kim*) and the universities of Lucknow and Aukland. After serving with the Gurka Rifles in Burma during World War II, he was district officer in India until independence. An active writer, lecturer, and member of the New Zealand Institute of International Affairs, Professor Roy is currently working on a book dealing with India's Commonwealth relations since 1947.

Lazarus E. Salii was educated as a political scientist at the University of Hawaii. He has also been a graduate fellow at the Institute of International Studies at the University of California at Berkeley. After serving in the Palau District Legislature, the Council of Micronesia, and the House of Representatives of the First Congress of Micronesia (1965), he was elected to the Senate of the Congress in 1968. He has been chairman of the House Ways and Means Committee and a Special Advisor to the United States Delegation to the United Nations Trusteeship Council. At present he is chairman of the Congressional Committee on the Future Status of Micronesia (since 1967) and vice-president of the Senate.

Howard Seay is a retired U.S. Navy Commander. From 1967 to 1970, he was the director of the Peace Corps in the Truk District of Micronesia; subsequently he served as a consultant on Micronesian affairs for the Peace Corps. He now teaches at Monterey State College in California.

Duane Stormont is a graduate student of geography at Arizona State University. He is particularly interested in the economic development and urbanization of East and Southeast Asia and the Pacific.

William E. Tagupa was educated at the University of Hawaii (B.A. and M.A.) before serving in the U.S. Army in Vietnam. He is now working concurrently on terminal degrees in socio-cultural history and law at the University of Hawaii.

John Kearsley Thomson studied economics at Strathclyde University in Scotland (B.A. and M.A.) and has worked for several years as an economist for the South

Pacific Bureau for Economic Co-operation in Suva. Currently he is doing graduate work at Oxford University.

Felise Va'a was educated in Western Samoa and New Zealand, at Canterbury and Massey Universities. Since being initially employed as a public relations officer by the Western Samoan government, he has held various positions as a journalist, correspondent, and editor with the *Pacific Star, Samoa News, Samoa Times,* the *Pacific Islands Monthly,* and the *Samoa Sun.*

Index

ABOUT THE EDITOR

F. P. King took degrees in English at the Universities of Denver and Northern Colorado (M.A.) before going on to study history in the United Kingdom at Keele (M.A.) and Cambridge (Ph.D). He has served as a planning consultant to the Office of the Governor of Guam, as an adviser to the Palau legislature's Select Committee on Development, as a member of the Economic Task Force for the Study of Political Status (established by the Guam legislature), and as an instructor in history at the University of Guam. He is currently on the staff of the English Language Center of the University of Denver. He is the author of *The New Internationalism: Allied Policy and the European Peace, 1939-1945* (Newton Abbot, England, and Hamden, Conn. 1973).